Distinctions Between Believers versus Disbelievers

By Gregory Heary

This book seeks to make clear the differences between the 2 distinct groups of believers and disbelievers. Verily these 2 groups and their various sub-categories (divisible by degrees of piety) constitute the only just way to divide and judge mankind and jinnkind. By learning of each of the 2 main group's distinguishing features, one is better able to choose which group they belong to. May we all be guided to the best of the two parties. The difference in life quality between the two groups is great in this world and even greater in the next. This book contains a listing of the successful attributes followed by a listing of the damnable attributes. May we be of the blessed and not the cursed, by utilizing the knowledge to know the difference. Every creature's faith increases with good deeds and decreases with bad deeds and there is no better deed than faith while there is no deed worse than major disbelief which nullifies any and all "good" deeds. Whereas minor disbelief can remove one from having the label of a "believer" while still remaining a Muslim eligible for eventual eternal paradise. Every believer is a Muslim but not every Muslim is a "believer" though they have elements of belief; while every non-Muslim is a disbeliever. The term believer and Muslim are not necessarily identical or synonymous though some Muslims may say/think otherwise because the terms are sometimes used interchangeably. When I refer to a believer in this book I am referring to a Mumin rather than a Muslim, of which Mumin is a higher level of Muslim and there exists even a higher level called

Muhsin which is the sincere believer. Scholastically believers go to paradise without punishment, while Muslims who don't reach the level of believer may or may not be punished before eventual paradise and disbelievers who do not reach the status of Muslim will be punished eternally in hell far from paradise.

We judge people based on what is apparent not on what is hidden, those who outwardly express Islam we don't declare as disbelievers even if internally unbeknownst to us they may be munafiqs/hypocrites hiding disbelief. While those who outwardly commit disbelief or ally with disbelievers we judge their external speech and actions accordingly. Without hesitation we declare all unislamic statements or deeds to be unislamic and condemn them, the only hesitation is in how to label those guilty of saying/doing unislamic/anti-islamic things claiming they are Muslims or Islamic. Maybe they are just sinful. Maybe they are an innovator. Maybe they are an apostate. Maybe they are just ignorant. Yet we always condemn the statements/deeds as kufr if they are kufr, bida if bida, and sinful if sinful. We sincerely try to peacefully correct the individual/group in private but sometimes public corrections or condemnations are needed so the public is not misinformed and led astray. This is because levels of faith and disbelief fluctuate, the speech one hears/speaks/writes and the deeds one learns about or does effects the levels of belief/faith one has and the levels of disbelief within the heart, mind and soul determining one's status as a believer or disbeliever. Belief/Disbelief levels are not static they can change every second. Below is a graphic example of a Muslim that combined pieces of faith + pieces of minor disbelief.

One important factor that extremists forget is that there is major disbelief and minor disbelief as well as major hypocrisy and minor hypocrisy. All those black pieces of kufr/shirk in the image above are various types of "minor disbelief". 1 piece of major disbelief puts one above the limit and can make one a disbeliever, unless there are special conditions such as ignorance that render one's piece of major disbelief to be minor disbelief. Yet ignorance does not apply to every type of major disbelief, for instance thinking God doesn't exist or is a parent, a child or an animal or plural is inexcusable. As is thinking non-Muslims are not disbelievers because the shahada is not valid if one doesn't believe all non-Muslims are disbelievers, except for the insane the insane is regarded as unaccountable while insane but treated for what they were upon/did before they became insane. The previous page has a Muslim chart of belief/disbelief, the non-Muslims cannot have enough pieces of Iman or Tawheed to ever qualify as a believer let alone Muslim. While a Muslim needs a certain level to be Muslim, their level of belief/guidance can increase beyond that minimum just as the guidance instructions for traveling on the road can. For example directions provide guidance, a map provides better guidance, a GPS provides more guidance and the one who has certain detailed knowledge is a guide for others and themselves. One other important caveat to note is if one believes or does enough pieces of minor disbelief it can cross the line and amount to major disbelief. (Its implied in the chart but I wanted to clarify.) Again the chart on the previous page teaches multiple concepts and principles and generally the disbelief one can be guilty of while still being a Muslim is a small level of "minor disbelief", not major. While both minor and major pieces of belief are needed to be a Muslim. Take care to specifically note that not everything that is called a statement or action of disbelief or hypocrisy in Islam constitutes theological disbelief in Islam. For example to steal, backbite or fornicate is sinful and forbidden. If one does such sins that implies they think it is lawful else they wouldn't do it "if they were a believer", so for that moment of sin they technically disbelieve in the law of God and can't be considered a "true believer" since a believer is one who believes in and submits to Allah's law while the active sinner or linguistically labeled disbeliever circumvents it. This is what Muhammad pbuh taught in that the one who steals is not a believer while stealing, yet when cutting off the hand of thieves who stole more than a quarter of a dinar's value Muhammad pbuh didn't execute them for apostasy because their action of theft was minor disbelief meaning they weren't a believer in action but in their heart they still could have been Muslim. Likewise if one dies committing such a sin of minor disbelief, it doesn't mean they are going to hell forever for being a "disbeliever" while committing the deed, it's a bad indication but they could possibly go to paradise still; or eventually. The same could apply to any sin, if we do something we know is wrong then technically we are implying we believe it to be right or else we wouldn't do it. Technically every type of sin is ignorance and a type of disbelief, for if we believed in the reality of hell/paradise we wouldn't sin and and if we believed in God's religion we wouldn't do what it prohibits. However that's just linguistic, not literal in that any sin = disbelief, it's just a linguistic technicality. Minor sins don't make one a disbeliever by default, nor do major sins make one a disbeliever by default. The Khawarij believe this but it is wrong, however under certain conditions sins could make one a disbeliever for instance to say or believe the prophets taught people to steal when the opposite has been proven to you can amount to disbelief making one a disbeliever because you are legalizing what Allah forbade or forbidding what Allah allowed or speaking about God without knowledge. Or some sins like performing magic can make one a disbeliever. This is a very complex matter though so it can lead to confusion if dwelled on too much or in too much detail. I'm just saying that sins that are linguistically described as "disbelief" may not make one a "disbeliever" spiritually. To sin is not to disbelieve but some sins amount to disbelief since every act/speech/belief of disbelief is a type of sin. So what about leaders who rule by other than Shariah? A leader is not just a political leader but the leader of a household too such as a husband, wife, father, mother, or a group of friends or even you acting as a leader over yourself. For a leader to sin or not do the 100% perfect islamic thing is to technically "*not rule by the law of Allah*" which is labeled as disbelief in the Quran. But <u>the act</u> itself, of sinning/not ruling by Allah's law, is minor disbelief and those who commit minor disbelief are not necessarily out of the fold of Islam. Regarding not ruling by Allah's laws it depends on the belief of the ruler too and their abilities. Similarly there is minor hypocrisy and major hypocrisy, of which only major hypocrisy equals disbelief and minor hypocrisy is sinful. However with that said do know that for a leader to believe that ruling by other than Shariah (God's law) is okay can be major disbelief, but to simply do the act of ruling by other than Shariah by itself is only "minor disbelief" which is sinful but not a type of disbelief that amounts to disbelief in Islam persay. Basically a ruler could rule by other than Shariah and just be sinful, but they can't think that it's okay or permissible to rule by other than Shariah or they'd be disbelievers. However simply witnessing someone in any authority position sin or rule by other than the law of God, is something where the average individual doesn't know what the leader's belief about that is unless they share their belief. For instance a Muslim ruler might not rule by Shariah but he might wish he could and know that by not doing so he is sinful like Najashi did, thus he would still be Muslim but a sinful one. Yet if a Muslim ruler did not rule by Shariah and believed/said stuff like his laws are better than or equal to God's Islamic Shariah and he doesn't need to rule by Shariah then that would be clear disbelief. Most Muslim leaders don't dare express their beliefs about Shariah though because of political reasons since if they say they believe it they have to implement it and if they say they don't then they'd be denounced as disbelievers. So if Muslim rulers are silent on it, or give the standard pro-Shariah lipservice then Muslims give them the benefit of the doubt. Although since non-Muslims openly say things like Democracy is better than Shariah or that their man-made Constitution or laws are better than what Muhammad pbuh brought, they are clear disbelievers; a few may claim to be Muslims but the only way they could be is if they were extremely ignorant about Islam and were never informed about Islam in a way they understood. Other things constitute major disbelief, and can involve things one believes, says or does. The deviant Murjia think disbelief can only happen in the heart or only via intentions and not through speech or deeds, but they are wrong; sometimes something one says or does can constitute major disbelief even if the heart/mind intends to still be a believer. You don't have to intend to disbelieve to be a disbeliever. Below is a graphic guide to takfir (declaring someone to be a disbeliever).

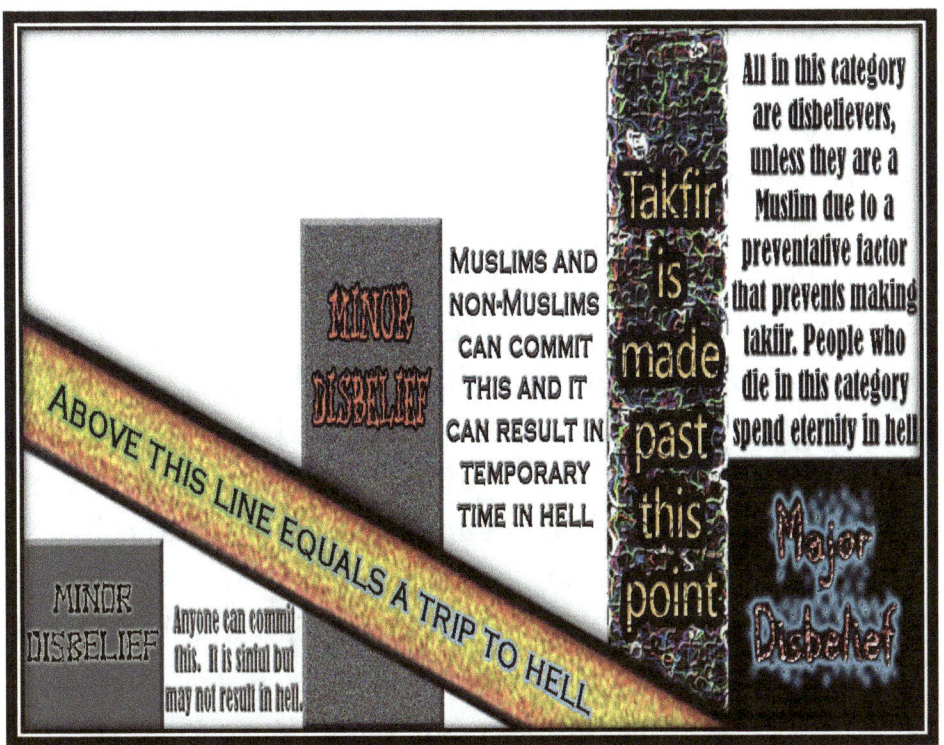

Note there is a minor disbelief that doesn't result in a trip to hell and a type of minor disbelief that results in temporary time in hell, if not repented from before it is too late to repent. Know that one can technically commit major disbelief while still being a Muslim due to the presence of a preventative factor, such as compulsion, insanity, ignorance or misunderstandings due to language or something. Even a mistake in interpretation can prevent takfir (declaring one to be a disbeliever). However fear for a loss of wealth, friends, family or reputation is NOT a preventative factor to ally with disbelief or disbelievers by promoting disbelief. Believers never theologically ally with disbelievers and must never voluntarily preach their religions or doctrines whether that's in the name of the non-Muslims or their faiths, or if it's done in the name of Islam, Allah or Muslims. Just by someone saying they are preaching "true Islam" doesn't mean a thing. Ignorant Muslims with good sincere intentions teaching unislamic doctrines to people constitute major disbelief, but just because one does an act of disbelief it doesn't automatically expel one from belief. A foolish preacher trying to teach Islam to people is not a good deed just because they tried, they either teach Islam or they don't. If they are ignorant teaching unislamic doctrines their preaching is sinful even if it improves the perception people have of Islam/Muslims or causes conversions. Such preaching is actually forbidden for Muslims to do, despite whatever benefits it may have, and it does have some benefits, so know that preaching unislamic doctrines is a type of major disbelief. There remain conditions that prevent takfir so a Muslim cannot label any who preach unislamic doctrines as disbelievers, you can label them as wrong and sinful but to label them disbeliever is a very serious thing which is very risky to do; and most shouldn't because just saying they are wrong and unislamic can suffice when the goal is to guide them and those they preach to. The only times a crime, like preaching words/doctrines of disbelief, is "permitted" is if all 4 conditions of compulsion are met, if they aren't met the person guilty of doing such things which constitute major disbelief is either ignorant, insane or miscommunication/misunderstandings occurred, or they are a disbeliever. But again it is very risky to label one claiming to be a Muslim a disbeliever, because whenever labeling someone a disbeliever either the one labeled is a disbeliever or the labeler is for wrongfully labeling. Though unknown to many, wrongly labelling a disbeliever itself does not necessarily expel one from islam either, it would mean the label of disbelief would apply to that person due to their mistaken labelling but there may be preventative factors that prevent labeling a mistaken Muslim takfiri(labeler) as a disbeliever. It could be minor disbelief or major disbelief or if major there may be excusable reasons for the mistaken labelling. But just because the prophet said the label of kafir will apply to one of the two when takfir of a Muslim occurs it doesn't automatically mean if one mistakenly labels, especially due to anger or a valid mistake, that you are defacto disbeliever just because you incorrectly label a Muslim person a disbeliever. This is a popular problem where some label takfiris as disbelievers thereby falling into the very error they themselves are condemning causing a domino effect. Or worse instead of educating them their first solution is to boycott, imprison or fight them with the stigma and isolation causing the ignorant Muslim takfiri to become even more misguided, extreme and dangerous. Someone can be kafir by action of kufr, in this case mistaken takfir, without necessarily being a major disbeliever or non-Muslim, just as those who don't rule by the law of Allah are linguistically kafirs though not necessarily major non-Muslim disbelievers by virtue of such speech or action though it is kufr/disbelief. There is such a thing as a linguistically labeled kafir who is not a non-Muslim disbeliever though kafir is a label usually used for non-Muslims. Similarly the sahabah fought though the prophet said fighting a believer is kufr and fighting a Muslim is kufr, still no sahabi made takfir of another sahabi even though they knew fighting each other was an act of kufr because the Quran says when <u>two groups of believers fight</u> to reconcile between them or unitedly fight the one that transgresses thereby indicating that the kufr of fighting a believer or Muslim is not a defacto expulsion from islam. Or else the Quranic verse would not label both parties of fighters as believers. The level of kufr, intentions and circumstances factor in when determining one to be believer, Muslim or disbeliever. The great sahabi Ali taught us regarding the fighting that occurred amongst the sahabah that one is to pray for forgiveness for the slain (which is forbidden to do for kuffar) and not to distribute their belongings as war spoils and to hope the slain of both parties will eventually enter paradise, though they fought each other and such fighting is an act of kufr. Whereas these things were not done with those who were fought for not paying the zakat because that level of kufr was greater than the level of kufr of fighting a believer or Muslim. Yet the prophet stated when 2 Muslims fight intending to kill each other both the killer and the killed will be in hell (due to the killed intending to kill a Muslim). This is due to intentions which the sahabah did not have when they fought, they fought intending to wound/neutralize not to kill a Muslim though some did indeed die due to the fighting. Also that prophetic hadith doesn't state the Muslim who killed or intended such will be in hell forever, just that they will enter it. Thus there is still hope for eventual salvation for such despite the gravity of the sin depending on the circumstance of course. Likewise there is the report of Usama bin Zaid regarding his mistake in killing a former disbeliever on the battlefield after they said the shahada, Usama was reprimanded by the prophet for this but not labeled a kafir. Likewise Khalid bin Walid mistakenly killed Muslims from Banu Jadhimah when they didn't know how to properly inform him of their faith, the prophet absolved himself of this mistake but didn't brand Khalid a disbeliever or doom him to eternal hell. So circumstances must always be factored in when branding someone a disbeliever, even regarding something as grievous and seemingly apparent as physically fighting or killing a believer. You really have to know what you are talking/writing about and some even say only a scholar is capable of making takfir of a self-proclaimed Muslim or else it is automatically sinful even if you do it correctly because such takfir is a legal verdict that involves the loss of their rights. Allah knows best. One should limit discussion of the sahabah's political disputes but it's important to know the lessons to be learned from those disputes lest people fall into unjust mislabeling of their opponents today. Any act of kufr diminishes one's faith but it is either a minor kufr or a major kufr based on knowledge, intentions and circumstances. So there are minor kafirs and major kafirs just as there is minor kufr and shirk and major kufr and shirk. A label can be linguistically applied without the ruling of the label being enforced. To be safe never commit major disbelief or minor disbelief. If you are ever in a situation where you could possibly be guilty of disbelief whether major or minor that means you made some mistakes in your knowledge, beliefs, speech or actions along the way. Its best to rectify all our errors, repent sincerely and learn so as to avoid repeating them.

The fundamental problem today with some "Muslims" is that they have theologically allied with non-Muslims and/or physically allied with them and claim their messages and actions are Islamic. So they are literally preaching and practicing a different religion than Islam but they are publicly claiming to be Muslims preaching Islam. Such people are failing the test of life to submit to the Creator of the Universe and obey his prophets. It is our job to try to help them pass the test of life because for us to pass our test then God tells us to try to help them pass theirs. The tricky part is they don't think they need help and might not help us to help them but hinder us from helping them. Since most of the time they are tragically ignorant in my experience, especially about the 4 conditions to justify compulsion, it is usually better or more useful to avoid takfir and instead teach them their doctrines are unislamic, forbid/oppose them and try to teach them Islam. By us helping them to pass their test of life, despite the difficulty of teaching them the right answers, this becomes a Jihad. Especially when Satan is simultaneously trying to help them fail. Just don't expect them to thank you for teaching them they are seriously wrong regarding religious beliefs. We don't help them for them, but for the sake of God. There are even "Muslims" whom I know that are proven to be insincere hypocrites with deviant beliefs trying to destroy Islam from the inside, even if they don't realize it, yet the prophets had to preach to people like this too. Why? Primarily because ignorant ones follow them, particularly if they are in authority or have popularity so to just treat them for what they are may end up causing their ignorant followers to follow them to hell. So as the prophet Muhammad pbuh dealt with hypocrites politely even though he knew 100% they were hypocrites, sometimes Muslims also must restrain themselves from treating hypocrites as harshly as they deserve to be treated because of the damage it could cause should their followers be forced to pick sides and side with them instead of the party of God. Also nobody knows whether a deviant anti-islamic ignorant hypocrite will ever sincerely repent. Sure they may be ignorant arrogant innovators and the way of the salaf is to denounce and shun them when the Muslims are in authority, but when the hypocrites/innovators are in charge or popular, as happens to be the case in most places today, polite treatment as if they were Muslims can sometimes be the correct medicine that cures their companions or themselves. However I only said sometimes, one should overlook deviance, hypocrisy, bida or kufr with kindness; sometimes it would be wrong, sinful and unislamic to do so. It's very complicated as there are many variables based on all individuals and all circumstances and potential outcomes and the specific errors it concerns. Is teaching them the truth the prophetic way hard? Most definitely it's very hard. But slaves don't have a choice in who/how they teach the message their Creator has created them to preach. You may feel/think "someone has to guide them, but not me". Well if you see that "someone" must do X then you see that need because God wanted you to see that need and destined you to see that need and gave you the opportunity to fulfill that purpose to do good deeds which God loves so you can get a great reward. Don't ever look at something hard and good that needs to be done and think "someone else should do that", take it as an opportunity for you to do that and please God. Now if that means you have to do a lot of studying to get qualified to fulfill that need then do it, because preaching to deviant innovators is extremely dangerous since they can corrupt one to the core without perceiving the effects of their influence, but instead of fleeing the theological battlefields it may be that God wants you to train/study and equip yourself to be the one to win those theological wars. I'm not saying to be reckless with preaching to anyone and everyone, but if you aren't preaching to them then they are preaching to you. Thus when surrounded by devils one either seeks protection from God or preaches/fights back and sometimes seeking safety by avoiding the conflict with the ignorant can be the more dangerous choice. I don't just get exposed to their deviance and politely ignore their errors, I either correct them privately (sometimes publicly if needed or private advice consistently goes unheeded and they continue to misguide people) or flee from them as the Quran 4:140 says to do when Islam is disparaged/distorted and how there is no sin for not forbidding evil as long as you don't remain and witness it. However the infection of ignorance among our species will not cure itself, the medicine of Islam must be administered the prophetic way to many people in many places. Fitnah (tribulation/dissension) is not when people are disunited or fighting each other, it is when evil is done and nobody refutes it, forbids it and prevents it. If forbidding evil divides a community between truth and falsehood, thereby protecting some from falsehood then that is wisdom. Having people united upon error is a great evil, and unity can not exist between people of truth and those of falsehood. To be united with disbelievers is to be disunited with Allah. Human unity is NOT the most important thing people need. Prophetic guidance is, and the prophetic guidance can never be compromised for the sake of "unity". The prophets did not come to unite the world they came to bring proof from God that divided the people between good and evil. World unity and world peace was never preached by God's prophets, because to achieve that the truth would need to be compromised. So while Muslim unity is important, having Muslims follow prophetic Islam is more important than unity. Both the Muslim and non-Muslim world needs to know the prophetic faith and practice it correctly with sincerity. If you see a need for X (like the one just mentioned) then ask God to fulfill that need and if you can't/don't/won't fulfill that need then make sure you do what God wants and what the prophets would've done. You can't stop every evil or correct every idiot, but you can do something and that's all God wants from you, do what you can when you can and strive to improve to do more. Sometimes prophets left the ignorant on the road to hell, but that was not their number 1 response/choice. Some prophets even died without getting a single follower despite all their preaching and others died with only 1 follower. The ones I find most heroic is not the prophets who died with nobody believing in them, they were prophets. Those that amaze and inspire me are the non-prophets who were the 1 person to believe in their prophet and then their prophet died making them the only believer on earth with the job of preaching the prophetic religion all by themselves without any special prophetic abilities or miracles or revelations. There were such people who did that, all by themselves because they loved God. They were regular humans just like us, the only difference is they just didn't make the excuses that we make for ourselves. Now what I'm advising on preaching to misguided innovators can be dangerous for those Muslims without extensive knowledge but it must be done and globally there is a need for Muslims who are qualified to do this task. The Muslims who know the truth must refute those who preach falsehood, Muslims can no longer let the ignorant mislead the masses because of fear in refuting/forbidding or lack of courage. The truth must triumph and those on the side of the truth will always be more bold and confident than those upon falsehood UNLESS those upon the truth are committing sins. Avoiding sins can give one courage. For those who do sins then they definitely have to stand up for the truth fearlessly in order to compensate for sinning fearlessly. It's crazy how people with knowledge will sometimes be more afraid to say what is right/true in the face of public/popular error/evil than they will be to commit sins. If you can sin without fear then you can do good deeds without fear. True cowards don't do any sins because they fear God. So if you ever do sins then you are not a coward but very courageous in a evil sense, but God wants you to be courageous in a good sense to do the good deeds despite difficulty. Instead of fearing the consequences of fighting evil/error fear the consequences of disappointing God by not doing so and missing out on rewards. In this era ignorance, innovation and deviant beliefs are so widespread that if you don't get the knowledge you will go astray. You can't afford to not learn Islam in depth in this era. People will either learn or burn. The thing is you won't know whether you are qualified to stay amongst ignorant/deviant/hypocritical people unless you have knowledge. It's like how they say in the modern military, during war the only ones who are safe are the elite soldiers. So if you aren't one of those elite theological soldiers then you are in danger of being misled by Satan. As a disclaimer though if you think you are qualified or an "elite theological soldier" then you probably aren't and Satan is trying to get you into a battle you'll end up losing. Although the same also applies to those who think they aren't qualified to forbid/refute, just because you think you aren't qualified doesn't mean that's humble cautious underestimation, you might really just be plain unqualified. So it's tricky to determine what you can and cannot do since Satan always tries to make you jump into danger and frighten you from jumping into victory against him. A good rule I take is that getting more knowledge always helps and delaying the reformation of others can sometimes be safer than trying too soon. However every attempt at enjoining good/forbidding evil is different and requires different rulings as to who, when and how it is to be done in every instance. Sometimes it is a communal obligation to do/say the right thing and stop the evil/error and other times it is an individual obligation and other times some individuals are unqualified to do it and other times may require unqualified individuals to try despite them being the unideal candidates for the job. The point is there are 5 types of options when individuals are confronted with evil/error, 3 of which are good options, 1 is sinful in the vast majority of cases except in rare instances and 1 is always sinful and usually a type of minor or major disbelief. The 5 options are as follows, 1. If you witness an evil/error you forbid/prevent it via your hand/force. (This is ideal but not always possible, practical, wise or the best option.) 2. If you witness an evil/error you forbid/prevent it by using your tongue or communication abilities. (This is more common, and frequently more practical, wise or best.) 3. If you witness an evil/error then based on 4:140 of the Quran you hate it in your heart but instead of using force or communication to forbid/prevent it , instead of denouncing it they simply leave the place of sin (preferably with social dignity if possible, although the one who flees sin is always honorable with God) so they are no longer witness to it. (This type of forbidding is sometimes socially difficult but very effective since the forbidding via the movement of the feet and lack of presence imply and convey a sense of denouncing that typically provides less risk of social backlash.) Basically if you can't forbid something then just walk away so you are away from the evil. 4. You hate it in your heart but do nothing at all to stop the evil/error either by the hand or tongue nor do you flee the scene of the crime (evil/deviance/sin). In most cases this is sinful and amounts to conveying implicit acceptance of and silent promotion of the evil. Very rarely does one have a valid excuse to do this instead of options #1-3, but Satan always makes us think we should. 5. People witness evil/error and join in, praise, enjoy or promote it. (This is nearly always sinful except in cases of military espionage and sometimes doing this can be minor or major disbelief.) Of these 5 possible options for every scenario one must have knowledge of the nature of the evil, as well as how to choose the best option of 1-3 (rarely ever 4) and how to best enjoin good/forbid evil after deciding which type of 1-3 steps to take. Every scenario and circumstance is different and frequently little time is afforded to one before they must make a decision. Hence one must prepare for such situations in advance by gaining the knowledge of what is right/wrong and how to correctly enjoin good/forbid evil in the most effective prophetic manner in every possible scenario. Much of it though is based on trial and error where unfortunately you end up upsetting a lot of people before experience teaches you how to wisely and most effectively enjoin good and forbid evil as an individual. Scholars are the ones who disseminate that type of knowledge. Sure some Muslims might do it once in awhile but in the long run if evil is to be stopped the masses must learn how to stop it in every situation, because Scholars cannot be everywhere or do everything, average people (the masses) are the only ones who can truly eradicate the evil of the world. However the masses must be taught just as the prophets taught us. Fundamentally the prophets came to teach people to teach others and adhere to what the prophets taught them. To practice and to preach was the message and mission the prophets gave us, ideally both are achieved but even if neither are both must be attempted. This is not just the job of Muslim Scholars but every Muslim, the

Scholars are just supposed to be doing a better job of it on a larger scale making a bigger impact thus getting more reward. Muslims need sincere scholars, they can't expect others to fill that need and live the easy life. Not being a scholar doesn't excuse a Muslim from the basic responsibility of the prophetic mission given to every Muslim to "learn, practice and preach". It's not even about changing the world or people, if improvements happen that's good but God expects this regardless of whether the changes happen or not. We do this because God tells us to and as slaves we obey God and he makes the changes, God just wants to see if we will try no matter what and if so we get rewarded if not then we are sinful. For example Lot pbuh condemned Sodomy, but did he change the people? No, nobody but his daughters listened to him and changed. But because he did his duty as God told him then when the evildoers were destroyed he was saved from the punishment which the others received. Had he not done his duty he would have been responsible for their crimes for not having tried to reform them. We only preach to be free from blame for failing to do so and so that God doesn't punish us in the afterlife for not doing so. The positive worldly results, if any, of our attempts to improve humanity with the prophetic faith are not a reason to preach. A preacher must only preach to please God, but with that said that doesn't mean you can use "not caring about people and doing it for God's sake only" as an excuse to act in emotionally unwise or insensitive manners. There is saying and doing the prophetic thing for the right reasons as you see/feel fit and there is saying/doing it for the prophetic reasons in the truly prophetic way as God truly sees/feels is best. Doing something for God's sake does not give one a license to be unprophetically unwise, unrefined, or emotionally irresponsible. Basically don't make your battles against evil bigger or harder than they need to be. If we lack knowledge or emotional control then Satan can defeat us on the battlefield even if we have the right reasons and do all the right things. For instance there is a big difference between you "telling it the way it is" and you "telling it the way it is the way you feel like telling it". The 2nd method can feel and seem so right, but it's not 100% what God wants and that's why it can sometimes lead to results that please Satan. Never let your battles against evil or for God's sake be personal, always make them prophetic with prophetic emotions as well as prophetic control over your emotions and actions. Don't let Satan influence even a little bit how you do something to please God. Sometimes one can think it's a pure deed done for God's sake but Satan could've had some influence over the deed and thus due to that tiny influence it is technically in some respect partially in that part at least for the sake of Satan though it may be something that is apparently against Satan and his designs. Hence Sincerity, Knowledge and Patience are crucial to success. If the Muslims don't take the initiative to be as knowledgeable as they can then that knowledge will vanish and the devil will dominate in this war like never before. In this era of the eternal theological war, learning/implementing as much as you can of the prophetic religion is an act of warfare and the one who does it is comparable to a mujahid. Muslims don't need more gunslingers (numbers don't win military wars) instead we need sincere Islamic scholars to revive the prophetic religion and purify our ranks. Moses pbuh didn't lead a people who had sincere Islamic scholars and that's why they didn't achieve worldly victory over their enemies and needed miraculous divine intervention just to be kept alive. Heroes only rise when the society is spiritually heroic, even when Jesus pbuh returns he will be returning to join heroes not ignorant hypocritical sinners. Becoming a theological hero is the duty of every Muslim citizen and scholars are needed to train the Muslim nation to be heroic. Maybe you can't be an elite Muslim scholar but you could try, and God will greatly reward the effort. If you don't who will? Ad-Darami reported Muhammad pbuh said what means: *"Whoever dies seeking knowledge to revive Islam, will be in paradise and nothing would be between him and the prophets except 1 degree."* A slave of God doesn't let another slave do their job and get the extra credit from their master, slaves compete with each other to be the best out of all the rest. Don't just be one of God's many sincere slaves, be the very best slave God ever had. Never think that you can just take the easy road to paradise and let someone else take the hard road. The road to paradise is hard and those people who choose to avoid the hard way and opt for the easy way are the same types who go astray and end up in the hellfire for eternity. You can't even count the numbers of those who thought they'd take the "easy way to paradise" and took the road which Satan paved. The easy way to paradise is not the prophetic way, it's Satan's first salespitch. Man's first mistake was taking Satan as a friend and guide to eternal paradise. Don't make that mistake too. Work in life as true winners do to avoid the loss of the losers, as the prophets taught us to do according to the creed and method of our salaf (pious believing predecessors). May you live and die as a believer. For the "death of a believer" should be our #1 lifetime goal. And though I may have digressed in this introduction it is important to know how to believe and act upon acquiring knowledge of the distinctions between believers versus disbelievers, so as not to fall into any of the various extremes. For the believer is the furthest from extremism though disbelievers and fools label them as such. Likewise actions such as acquiring knowledge are based on intentions so keep in mind your goal constantly. Again and always the goal is to achieve the death of a believer and avoid meeting our death as a disbeliever. Every believer is tasked with conveying the religion of the prophets even if it be one verse, and they should convey what they know accurately with wisdom. So believe, act and inform others for the sake of God only. A trait of disbelievers is they don't seek knowledge of the true religion, nor act upon it, nor teach it to others. Thus when reading this book or any other seek to believe in the good of it, act upon it and patiently teach it to all others. For failing to teach means failing to act and failing to act is a failure to truly believe and there is a vast difference between knowing and believing. Knowers get no reward but their knowledge counts against them and those who don't know are punished. So you will either know and act correctly, know and act incorrectly or you won't know at all and only the first of the 3 are successful. Lastly our goal is the death of a believer. So now that you know, act upon that goal, learn and teach the means to that goal to all others, as the prophets taught us; or else I fear for you.

Distinctions of the Believers

Quran 2:2-5

ذَٰلِكَ ٱلْكِتَٰبُ لَا رَيْبَ ۛ فِيهِ ۛ هُدًى لِّلْمُتَّقِينَ (٢) ٱلَّذِينَ يُؤْمِنُونَ بِٱلْغَيْبِ وَيُقِيمُونَ ٱلصَّلَوٰةَ وَمِمَّا رَزَقْنَٰهُمْ يُنفِقُونَ (٣) وَٱلَّذِينَ يُؤْمِنُونَ بِمَآ أُنزِلَ إِلَيْكَ وَمَآ أُنزِلَ مِن قَبْلِكَ وَبِٱلْءَاخِرَةِ هُمْ يُوقِنُونَ (٤) أُو۟لَٰٓئِكَ عَلَىٰ هُدًى مِّن رَّبِّهِمْ ۖ وَأُو۟لَٰٓئِكَ هُمُ ٱلْمُفْلِحُونَ (٥)

This is the Book (the Qur'ân), whereof there is no doubt, a guidance to those who are Al-Muttaqûn [the pious and righteous persons who fear Allâh much (abstain from all kinds of sins and evil deeds which He has forbidden) and love Allâh much (perform all kinds of good deeds which He has ordained)]. (2) Who believe in the Ghaib[unseen] and perform As-Salât (Iqâmat-as-Salât), and spend out of what we have provided for them [i.e. give Zakât, spend on themselves, their parents, their children, their wives, etc., and also give charity to the poor and also in Allâh's Cause - Jihâd]. (3) And who believe in (the Qurân and the Sunnah) which has been sent down (revealed) to you (Muhammad) and in that which we sent down before [the Taurât (Torah) and the Injeel, etc.] and they believe with certainty in the Hereafter. (Resurrection, recompense of their good and bad deeds, Paradise and Hell,) (4) They are on (true) guidance from their Lord, and they are the successful. (5)

Quran 2:25-26

وَبَشِّرِ ٱلَّذِينَ ءَامَنُوا۟ وَعَمِلُوا۟ ٱلصَّٰلِحَٰتِ أَنَّ لَهُمْ جَنَّٰتٍ تَجْرِى مِن تَحْتِهَا ٱلْأَنْهَٰرُ ۖ كُلَّمَا رُزِقُوا۟ مِنْهَا مِن ثَمَرَةٍ رِّزْقًا ۙ قَالُوا۟ هَٰذَا ٱلَّذِى رُزِقْنَا مِن قَبْلُ ۖ وَأُتُوا۟ بِهِۦ مُتَشَٰبِهًا ۖ وَلَهُمْ فِيهَآ أَزْوَٰجٌ مُّطَهَّرَةٌ ۖ وَهُمْ فِيهَا خَٰلِدُونَ (٢٥) إِنَّ ٱللَّهَ لَا يَسْتَحْىِۦٓ أَن يَضْرِبَ مَثَلًا مَّا بَعُوضَةً فَمَا فَوْقَهَا ۚ فَأَمَّا ٱلَّذِينَ ءَامَنُوا۟ فَيَعْلَمُونَ أَنَّهُ ٱلْحَقُّ مِن رَّبِّهِمْ ۖ وَأَمَّا ٱلَّذِينَ كَفَرُوا۟ فَيَقُولُونَ مَاذَآ أَرَادَ ٱللَّهُ بِهَٰذَا مَثَلًا ۘ يُضِلُّ بِهِۦ كَثِيرًا وَيَهْدِى بِهِۦ كَثِيرًا ۚ وَمَا يُضِلُّ بِهِۦٓ إِلَّا ٱلْفَٰسِقِينَ (٢٦)

And give glad tidings to those who believe and do righteous good deeds, that for them will be Gardens under which rivers flow (Paradise). Every time they will be provided with a fruit therefrom, they will say: "This is what we were provided with before," and they will be given things in resemblance (i.e. in the same form but different in taste) and they shall have therein Azwâjun Mutahharatun (purified mates or wives), and they will abide therein forever. (25) Verily, Allâh is not ashamed to set forth a parable even of a mosquito or so much more when it is bigger (or less when it is smaller) than it. And as for those who believe, they know that it is the Truth from their Lord, but as for those who disbelieve, they say: "What did Allâh intend by this parable?" By it He misleads many, and many He guides thereby. And He misleads thereby only those who are Al-Fâsiqûn (the rebellious, disobedient to Allâh). (26)

Quran 2:82

وَٱلَّذِينَ ءَامَنُوا۟ وَعَمِلُوا۟ ٱلصَّٰلِحَٰتِ أُو۟لَٰٓئِكَ أَصْحَٰبُ ٱلْجَنَّةِ ۖ هُمْ فِيهَا خَٰلِدُونَ

And those who believe (in the Oneness of Allâh - Islâmic Monotheism) and do righteous good deeds, they are dwellers of Paradise, they will dwell therein forever. (82)

Quran 2:104-105

يَٰٓأَيُّهَا ٱلَّذِينَ ءَامَنُواْ لَا تَقُولُواْ رَٰعِنَا وَقُولُواْ ٱنظُرْنَا وَٱسْمَعُواْ ۗ وَلِلْكَٰفِرِينَ عَذَابٌ أَلِيمٌ (١٠٤) مَّا يَوَدُّ ٱلَّذِينَ كَفَرُواْ مِنْ أَهْلِ ٱلْكِتَٰبِ وَلَا ٱلْمُشْرِكِينَ أَن يُنَزَّلَ عَلَيْكُم مِّنْ خَيْرٍ مِّن رَّبِّكُمْ ۗ وَٱللَّهُ يَخْتَصُّ بِرَحْمَتِهِۦ مَن يَشَآءُ ۚ وَٱللَّهُ ذُو ٱلْفَضْلِ ٱلْعَظِيمِ (١٠٥)

O you who believe! Say not (to the Messenger) Râ'ina but say Unzurna (make us understand) and hear. And for the disbelievers there is a painful torment. (104) Neither those who disbelieve among the people of the Scripture (Jews and Christians) nor Al-Mushrikûn (the idolaters, polytheists, disbelievers in the Oneness of Allâh, pagans, etc.) like that there should be sent down unto you any good from your Lord. But Allâh chooses for His Mercy whom He wills. And Allâh is the Owner of Great Bounty. (105)

Quran 2:109

وَدَّ كَثِيرٌ مِّنْ أَهْلِ ٱلْكِتَٰبِ لَوْ يَرُدُّونَكُم مِّنۢ بَعْدِ إِيمَٰنِكُمْ كُفَّارًا حَسَدًا مِّنْ عِندِ أَنفُسِهِم مِّنۢ بَعْدِ مَا تَبَيَّنَ لَهُمُ ٱلْحَقُّ ۖ فَٱعْفُواْ وَٱصْفَحُواْ حَتَّىٰ يَأْتِىَ ٱللَّهُ بِأَمْرِهِۦٓ ۗ إِنَّ ٱللَّهَ عَلَىٰ كُلِّ شَىْءٍ قَدِيرٌ

Many of the people of the Scripture (Jews and Christians) wish that they could turn you away as disbelievers after you have believed, out of envy from their ownselves, even after the truth (that Muhammad is Allâh's

Messenger) has become manifest unto them. But forgive and overlook, till Allâh brings His Command. Verily, Allâh is Able to do all things. (109)

Quran 2:121

ٱلَّذِينَ ءَاتَيْنَٰهُمُ ٱلْكِتَٰبَ يَتْلُونَهُۥ حَقَّ تِلَاوَتِهِۦٓ أُو۟لَٰٓئِكَ يُؤْمِنُونَ بِهِۦ وَمَن يَكْفُرْ بِهِۦ فَأُو۟لَٰٓئِكَ هُمُ ٱلْخَٰسِرُونَ

Those (who embraced Islâm from Banî Israel) to whom We gave the Book [the Taurât (Torah)] [or those (Muhammad's companions) to whom We have given the Book (the Qur'ân)] recite it (i.e. obey its orders and follow its teachings) as it should be recited (i.e. followed), they are the ones that believe therein. And whoso disbelieves in it (the Qur'ân), those are they who are the losers.

Quran 2:153-157

يَٰٓأَيُّهَا ٱلَّذِينَ ءَامَنُوا۟ ٱسْتَعِينُوا۟ بِٱلصَّبْرِ وَٱلصَّلَوٰةِ إِنَّ ٱللَّهَ مَعَ ٱلصَّٰبِرِينَ (١٥٣) وَلَا تَقُولُوا۟ لِمَن يُقْتَلُ فِى سَبِيلِ ٱللَّهِ أَمْوَٰتٌۢ بَلْ أَحْيَآءٌ وَلَٰكِن لَّا تَشْعُرُونَ (١٥٤) وَلَنَبْلُوَنَّكُم بِشَىْءٍ مِّنَ ٱلْخَوْفِ وَٱلْجُوعِ وَنَقْصٍ مِّنَ ٱلْأَمْوَٰلِ وَٱلْأَنفُسِ وَٱلثَّمَرَٰتِ وَبَشِّرِ ٱلصَّٰبِرِينَ (١٥٥) ٱلَّذِينَ إِذَآ أَصَٰبَتْهُم مُّصِيبَةٌ قَالُوٓا۟ إِنَّا لِلَّهِ وَإِنَّآ إِلَيْهِ رَٰجِعُونَ (١٥٦) أُو۟لَٰٓئِكَ عَلَيْهِمْ صَلَوَٰتٌ مِّن رَّبِّهِمْ وَرَحْمَةٌ وَأُو۟لَٰٓئِكَ هُمُ ٱلْمُهْتَدُونَ (١٥٧)

O you who believe! Seek help in patience and As-Salât (the prayer). Truly! Allâh is with As-Sâbirun (the patient.) (153) And say not of those who are killed in the Way of Allâh, "They are dead." Nay, they are living, but you perceive (it) not. (154) And certainly, We shall test you with something of fear, hunger, loss of wealth, lives and fruits, but give glad tidings to As-Sâbirun (the patient) (155) Who, when afflicted with calamity, say: "Truly! To Allâh we belong and truly, to Him we shall return." (156) They are those on whom are the Salawât (i.e. who are blessed and will be forgiven) from their Lord, and (they are those who) receive His Mercy, and it is they who are the guided-ones. (157)

Quran 2:172

يَـٰٓأَيُّهَا ٱلَّذِينَ ءَامَنُوا۟ كُلُوا۟ مِن طَيِّبَـٰتِ مَا رَزَقْنَـٰكُمْ وَٱشْكُرُوا۟ لِلَّهِ إِن كُنتُمْ إِيَّاهُ تَعْبُدُونَ

O you who believe (in the Oneness of Allâh - Islâmic Monotheism)! Eat of the lawful things that We have provided you with, and be grateful to Allâh, if it is indeed He Whom you worship. (172)

Quran 2:178

يَـٰٓأَيُّهَا ٱلَّذِينَ ءَامَنُوا۟ كُتِبَ عَلَيْكُمُ ٱلْقِصَاصُ فِى ٱلْقَتْلَى ٱلْحُرُّ بِٱلْحُرِّ وَٱلْعَبْدُ بِٱلْعَبْدِ وَٱلْأُنثَىٰ بِٱلْأُنثَىٰ فَمَنْ عُفِىَ لَهُۥ مِنْ أَخِيهِ شَىْءٌ فَٱتِّبَاعٌۢ بِٱلْمَعْرُوفِ وَأَدَآءٌ إِلَيْهِ بِإِحْسَـٰنٍ ذَٰلِكَ تَخْفِيفٌ مِّن رَّبِّكُمْ وَرَحْمَةٌ فَمَنِ ٱعْتَدَىٰ بَعْدَ ذَٰلِكَ فَلَهُۥ عَذَابٌ أَلِيمٌ

O you who believe! Al-Qisâs (the Law of Equality in punishment) is prescribed for you in case of murder: the free for the free, the slave for the slave, and the female for the female. But if the killer is forgiven by the brother (or the relatives, etc.) of the killed against blood money then adhering to it with fairness and payment of the blood money, to the heir should be made in fairness. This is an alleviation and a mercy from your Lord. So after this whoever transgresses the limits (i.e. kills the killer after taking the blood money), he shall have a painful torment. (178)

Quran 2:183

يَـٰٓأَيُّهَا ٱلَّذِينَ ءَامَنُوا۟ كُتِبَ عَلَيْكُمُ ٱلصِّيَامُ كَمَا كُتِبَ عَلَى ٱلَّذِينَ مِن قَبْلِكُمْ لَعَلَّكُمْ تَتَّقُونَ

O you who believe! Observing As-Saum (the fasting) is prescribed for you as it was prescribed for those before you, that you may become Al-Muttaqûn (the pious). (183)

Quran 2:208

يَـٰٓأَيُّهَا ٱلَّذِينَ ءَامَنُوا۟ ٱدْخُلُوا۟ فِى ٱلسِّلْمِ كَآفَّةً وَلَا تَتَّبِعُوا۟ خُطُوَٰتِ ٱلشَّيْطَـٰنِ إِنَّهُۥ لَكُمْ عَدُوٌّ مُّبِينٌ

O you who believe! Enter perfectly in Islâm (by obeying all the rules and regulations of the Islâmic religion) and follow not the footsteps of Shaitân (Satan). Verily! He is to you a plain enemy. (208)

Quran 2:213

كَانَ ٱلنَّاسُ أُمَّةً وَٰحِدَةً فَبَعَثَ ٱللَّهُ ٱلنَّبِيِّـۧنَ مُبَشِّرِينَ وَمُنذِرِينَ وَأَنزَلَ مَعَهُمُ ٱلْكِتَـٰبَ بِٱلْحَقِّ لِيَحْكُمَ بَيْنَ ٱلنَّاسِ فِيمَا ٱخْتَلَفُوا۟ فِيهِ وَمَا ٱخْتَلَفَ فِيهِ إِلَّا ٱلَّذِينَ أُوتُوهُ مِنۢ بَعْدِ مَا جَآءَتْهُمُ ٱلْبَيِّنَـٰتُ بَغْيًۢا بَيْنَهُمْ فَهَدَى ٱللَّهُ ٱلَّذِينَ ءَامَنُوا۟ لِمَا ٱخْتَلَفُوا۟ فِيهِ مِنَ ٱلْحَقِّ بِإِذْنِهِۦ وَٱللَّهُ يَهْدِى مَن يَشَآءُ إِلَىٰ صِرَٰطٍ مُّسْتَقِيمٍ

Mankind were one community and Allâh sent Prophets with glad tidings and warnings, and with them He sent the Scripture in truth to judge between people in matters wherein they differed. And only those to whom (the Scripture) was given differed concerning it after clear proofs had come unto them through hatred, one to another. Then Allâh by His Leave guided those who believed to the truth of that wherein they differed. And Allâh guides whom He wills to a Straight Path. (213)

Quran 2:218

إِنَّ ٱلَّذِينَ ءَامَنُواْ وَٱلَّذِينَ هَاجَرُواْ وَجَٰهَدُواْ فِى سَبِيلِ ٱللَّهِ أُوْلَٰٓئِكَ يَرْجُونَ رَحْمَتَ ٱللَّهِ ۚ وَٱللَّهُ غَفُورٌ رَّحِيمٌ

Verily, those who have believed, and those who have emigrated (for Allâh's Religion) and have striven hard in the Way of Allâh, all these hope for Allâh's Mercy. And Allâh is Oft-Forgiving, Most-Merciful. (218)

Quran 2:221

وَلَا تَنكِحُواْ ٱلْمُشْرِكَٰتِ حَتَّىٰ يُؤْمِنَّ ۚ وَلَأَمَةٌ مُّؤْمِنَةٌ خَيْرٌ مِّن مُّشْرِكَةٍ وَلَوْ أَعْجَبَتْكُمْ ۗ وَلَا تُنكِحُواْ ٱلْمُشْرِكِينَ حَتَّىٰ يُؤْمِنُواْ ۚ وَلَعَبْدٌ مُّؤْمِنٌ خَيْرٌ مِّن مُّشْرِكٍ وَلَوْ أَعْجَبَكُمْ ۗ أُوْلَٰٓئِكَ يَدْعُونَ إِلَى ٱلنَّارِ ۖ وَٱللَّهُ يَدْعُوٓاْ إِلَى ٱلْجَنَّةِ وَٱلْمَغْفِرَةِ بِإِذْنِهِۦ ۖ وَيُبَيِّنُ ءَايَٰتِهِۦ لِلنَّاسِ لَعَلَّهُمْ يَتَذَكَّرُونَ

And do not marry Al-Mushrikât (idolatresses, etc.) till they believe (worship Allâh Alone). And indeed a slave woman who believes is better than a (free) Mushrikah (idolatress), even though she pleases you. And give not (your daughters) in marriage to Al-Mushrikûn till they believe (in Allâh Alone) and verily, a believing slave is better than a (free) Mushrik (idolater), even though he pleases you. Those (Al-Mushrikûn) invite you to the Fire, but Allâh invites (you) to Paradise and Forgiveness by His Leave, and makes His Ayât (proofs, evidences, verses, lessons, signs, revelations, etc.) clear to mankind that they may remember. (221)

Quran 2:256-257

لَآ إِكۡرَاهَ فِى ٱلدِّينِ‌ۖ قَد تَّبَيَّنَ ٱلرُّشۡدُ مِنَ ٱلۡغَىِّ‌ۚ فَمَن يَكۡفُرۡ بِٱلطَّـٰغُوتِ وَيُؤۡمِنۢ بِٱللَّهِ فَقَدِ ٱسۡتَمۡسَكَ بِٱلۡعُرۡوَةِ ٱلۡوُثۡقَىٰ لَا ٱنفِصَامَ لَهَا‌ۗ وَٱللَّهُ سَمِيعٌ عَلِيمٌ (٢٥٦) ٱللَّهُ وَلِىُّ ٱلَّذِينَ ءَامَنُواْ يُخۡرِجُهُم مِّنَ ٱلظُّلُمَـٰتِ إِلَى ٱلنُّورِ‌ۖ وَٱلَّذِينَ كَفَرُوٓاْ أَوۡلِيَآؤُهُمُ ٱلطَّـٰغُوتُ يُخۡرِجُونَهُم مِّنَ ٱلنُّورِ إِلَى ٱلظُّلُمَـٰتِ‌ۗ أُوْلَـٰٓئِكَ أَصۡحَـٰبُ ٱلنَّارِ‌ۖ هُمۡ فِيهَا خَـٰلِدُونَ (٢٥٧)

There is no compulsion in religion. Verily, the Right Path has become distinct from the wrong path. Whoever disbelieves in Tâghût [false deities and false leaders] and believes in Allâh, then he has grasped the most trustworthy handhold that will never break. And Allâh is All-Hearer, All-Knower. (256) Allâh is the Walî (Protector or Guardian) of those who believe. He brings them out from darkness into light. But as for those who disbelieve, their Auliyâ (supporters and helpers) are Tâghût [false deities and false leaders], they bring them out from light into darkness. Those are the dwellers of the Fire, and they will abide therein forever. (257)

Quran 2:264-265

يَـٰٓأَيُّهَا ٱلَّذِينَ ءَامَنُواْ لَا تُبْطِلُواْ صَدَقَـٰتِكُم بِٱلْمَنِّ وَٱلْأَذَىٰ كَٱلَّذِى يُنفِقُ مَالَهُۥ رِئَآءَ ٱلنَّاسِ وَلَا يُؤْمِنُ بِٱللَّهِ وَٱلْيَوْمِ ٱلْـَٔاخِرِۖ فَمَثَلُهُۥ كَمَثَلِ صَفْوَانٍ عَلَيْهِ تُرَابٌ فَأَصَابَهُۥ وَابِلٌ فَتَرَكَهُۥ صَلْدًا ۖ لَّا يَقْدِرُونَ عَلَىٰ شَىْءٍ مِّمَّا كَسَبُواْ ۗ وَٱللَّهُ لَا يَهْدِى ٱلْقَوْمَ ٱلْكَـٰفِرِينَ (٢٦٤) وَمَثَلُ ٱلَّذِينَ يُنفِقُونَ أَمْوَٰلَهُمُ ٱبْتِغَآءَ مَرْضَاتِ ٱللَّهِ وَتَثْبِيتًا مِّنْ أَنفُسِهِمْ كَمَثَلِ جَنَّةٍۭ بِرَبْوَةٍ أَصَابَهَا وَابِلٌ فَـَٔاتَتْ أُكُلَهَا ضِعْفَيْنِ فَإِن لَّمْ يُصِبْهَا وَابِلٌ فَطَلٌّ ۗ وَٱللَّهُ بِمَا تَعْمَلُونَ بَصِيرٌ (٢٦٥)

O you who believe! Do not render in vain your Sadaqah (charity) by reminders of your generosity or by injury, like him who spends his wealth to be seen of men, and he does not believe in Allâh, nor in the Last Day. His likeness is the likeness of a smooth rock on which is a little dust; on it falls heavy rain which leaves it bare. They are not able to do anything with what they have earned. And Allâh does not guide the disbelieving people. (264) And the likeness of those who spend their wealth seeking Allâh's Pleasure while they in their ownselves are sure and certain that Allâh will reward them (for their spending in His Cause), is the likeness of a garden on a height; heavy rain falls on it and it doubles its yield of harvest. And if it does not receive heavy rain, light rain suffices it. And Allâh is All-Seer of (knows well) what you do. (265)

Quran 2:267

يَـٰٓأَيُّهَا ٱلَّذِينَ ءَامَنُوٓاْ أَنفِقُواْ مِن طَيِّبَـٰتِ مَا كَسَبْتُمْ وَمِمَّآ أَخْرَجْنَا لَكُم مِّنَ ٱلْأَرْضِۖ وَلَا تَيَمَّمُواْ ٱلْخَبِيثَ مِنْهُ تُنفِقُونَ وَلَسْتُم بِـَٔاخِذِيهِ إِلَّآ أَن تُغْمِضُواْ فِيهِۚ وَٱعْلَمُوٓاْ أَنَّ ٱللَّهَ غَنِىٌّ حَمِيدٌ

O you who believe! Spend of the good things which you have (legally) earned, and of that which We have produced from the earth for you, and do not aim at that which is bad to spend from it, (though) you would not accept it save if you close your eyes and tolerate therein. And know that Allâh is Rich (Free of all wants), and Worthy of all praise. (267)

Quran 2:277-279

إِنَّ ٱلَّذِينَ ءَامَنُواْ وَعَمِلُواْ ٱلصَّٰلِحَٰتِ وَأَقَامُواْ ٱلصَّلَوٰةَ وَءَاتَوُاْ ٱلزَّكَوٰةَ لَهُمْ أَجْرُهُمْ عِندَ رَبِّهِمْ وَلَا خَوْفٌ عَلَيْهِمْ وَلَا هُمْ يَحْزَنُونَ (٢٧٧) يَٰٓأَيُّهَا ٱلَّذِينَ ءَامَنُواْ ٱتَّقُواْ ٱللَّهَ وَذَرُواْ مَا بَقِىَ مِنَ ٱلرِّبَوٰٓاْ إِن كُنتُم مُّؤْمِنِينَ (٢٧٨) فَإِن لَّمْ تَفْعَلُواْ فَأْذَنُواْ بِحَرْبٍ مِّنَ ٱللَّهِ وَرَسُولِهِۦ ۖ وَإِن تُبْتُمْ فَلَكُمْ رُءُوسُ أَمْوَٰلِكُمْ لَا تَظْلِمُونَ وَلَا تُظْلَمُونَ (٢٧٩)

Truly those who believe, and do deeds of righteousness, and perform As-Salât (Iqâmat-as-Salât), and give Zakât, they will have their reward with their Lord. On them shall be no fear, nor shall they grieve. (277) O you who believe! Be afraid of Allâh and give up what remains (due to you) from Ribâ (usury) (from now onward), if you are (really) believers. (278) And if you do not do it, then take a notice of war from Allâh and His Messenger but if you repent, you shall have your capital sums. Deal not unjustly (by asking more than your capital sums), and you shall not be dealt with unjustly (by receiving less than your capital sums). (279)

Quran 2:285

ءَامَنَ ٱلرَّسُولُ بِمَآ أُنزِلَ إِلَيْهِ مِن رَّبِّهِۦ وَٱلْمُؤْمِنُونَ ۚ كُلٌّ ءَامَنَ بِٱللَّهِ وَمَلَـٰٓئِكَتِهِۦ وَكُتُبِهِۦ وَرُسُلِهِۦ لَا نُفَرِّقُ بَيْنَ أَحَدٍ مِّن رُّسُلِهِۦ ۚ وَقَالُوا۟ سَمِعْنَا وَأَطَعْنَا ۖ غُفْرَانَكَ رَبَّنَا وَإِلَيْكَ ٱلْمَصِيرُ

The Messenger (Muhammad) believes in what has been sent down to him from his Lord, and (so do) the believers. Each one believes in Allâh, His Angels, His Books, and His Messengers. (They say), "We make no distinction between one another of His Messengers" and they say, "We hear, and we obey. (We seek) Your Forgiveness, our Lord, and to You is the return (of all)." (285)

Quran 3:28

لَّا يَتَّخِذِ ٱلْمُؤْمِنُونَ ٱلْكَـٰفِرِينَ أَوْلِيَآءَ مِن دُونِ ٱلْمُؤْمِنِينَ ۖ وَمَن يَفْعَلْ ذَٰلِكَ فَلَيْسَ مِنَ ٱللَّهِ فِى شَىْءٍ إِلَّآ أَن تَتَّقُوا۟ مِنْهُمْ تُقَىٰةً ۗ وَيُحَذِّرُكُمُ ٱللَّهُ نَفْسَهُۥ ۗ وَإِلَى ٱللَّهِ ٱلْمَصِيرُ

Let not the believers take the disbelievers as Auliyâ (supporters, helpers) instead of the believers, and whoever does that will never be helped by Allâh in any way, except if you indeed fear a danger from them. And Allâh warns you against Himself, and to Allâh is the final return. (28)

Quran 3:100-105

يَـٰٓأَيُّهَا ٱلَّذِينَ ءَامَنُوٓا۟ إِن تُطِيعُوا۟ فَرِيقًا مِّنَ ٱلَّذِينَ أُوتُوا۟ ٱلْكِتَـٰبَ يَرُدُّوكُم بَعْدَ إِيمَـٰنِكُمْ كَـٰفِرِينَ (١٠٠) وَكَيْفَ تَكْفُرُونَ وَأَنتُمْ تُتْلَىٰ عَلَيْكُمْ ءَايَـٰتُ ٱللَّهِ وَفِيكُمْ رَسُولُهُۥ ۗ وَمَن يَعْتَصِم بِٱللَّهِ فَقَدْ هُدِىَ إِلَىٰ صِرَٰطٍ مُّسْتَقِيمٍ (١٠١) يَـٰٓأَيُّهَا ٱلَّذِينَ ءَامَنُوا۟ ٱتَّقُوا۟ ٱللَّهَ حَقَّ تُقَاتِهِۦ وَلَا تَمُوتُنَّ إِلَّا وَأَنتُم مُّسْلِمُونَ (١٠٢) وَٱعْتَصِمُوا۟ بِحَبْلِ ٱللَّهِ جَمِيعًا وَلَا تَفَرَّقُوا۟ ۚ وَٱذْكُرُوا۟ نِعْمَتَ

اللَّهِ عَلَيْكُمْ إِذْ كُنتُمْ أَعْدَاءً فَأَلَّفَ بَيْنَ قُلُوبِكُمْ فَأَصْبَحْتُم بِنِعْمَتِهِ إِخْوَٰنًا وَكُنتُمْ عَلَىٰ شَفَا حُفْرَةٍ مِّنَ ٱلنَّارِ فَأَنقَذَكُم مِّنْهَا ۗ كَذَٰلِكَ يُبَيِّنُ ٱللَّهُ لَكُمْ ءَايَٰتِهِ لَعَلَّكُمْ تَهْتَدُونَ (١٠٣) وَلْتَكُن مِّنكُمْ أُمَّةٌ يَدْعُونَ إِلَى ٱلْخَيْرِ وَيَأْمُرُونَ بِٱلْمَعْرُوفِ وَيَنْهَوْنَ عَنِ ٱلْمُنكَرِ ۚ وَأُوْلَٰٓئِكَ هُمُ ٱلْمُفْلِحُونَ (١٠٤) وَلَا تَكُونُوا۟ كَٱلَّذِينَ تَفَرَّقُوا۟ وَٱخْتَلَفُوا۟ مِنۢ بَعْدِ مَا جَآءَهُمُ ٱلْبَيِّنَٰتُ ۚ وَأُوْلَٰٓئِكَ لَهُمْ عَذَابٌ عَظِيمٌ (١٠٥)

O you who believe! If you obey a group of those who were given the Scripture (Jews and Christians), they would (indeed) render you disbelievers after you have believed! (100) And how would you disbelieve, while unto you are recited the Verses of Allâh, and among you is His Messenger (Muhammad)? And whoever holds firmly to Allâh, (i.e. follows Islâm — Allâh's Religion, and obeys all that Allâh has ordered, practically), then he is indeed guided to a Right Path. (101) O you who believe! Fear Allâh (by doing all that He has ordered and by abstaining from all that He has forbidden) as He should be feared. [Obey Him, be thankful to Him, and remember Him always], and die not except in a state of Islâm [as Muslims (with complete submission to Allâh)]. (102) And hold fast, all of you together, to the Rope of Allâh (i.e. this Qur'ân), and be not divided among yourselves, and remember Allâh's Favour on you, for you were enemies one to another but He joined your hearts together, so that, by His Grace, you became brethren (in Islâmic Faith), and you were on the brink of a pit of Fire, and He saved you from it. Thus Allâh makes His Ayât (proofs, evidences, verses, lessons, signs, revelations, etc.,) clear to you, that you may be guided. (103) Let there arise out of you a group of people inviting to all that is good (Islâm), enjoining Al-Ma'rûf (i.e. Islâmic Monotheism and all that Islâm orders one to do) and forbidding Al-Munkar (polytheism and disbelief and all that Islâm has forbidden). And it is they who are the successful. (104) And be not as those who divided and differed among themselves after the clear proofs had come to them. It is they for whom there is an awful torment. (105)

Quran 3:118-120

يَٰٓأَيُّهَا ٱلَّذِينَ ءَامَنُوا۟ لَا تَتَّخِذُوا۟ بِطَانَةً مِّن دُونِكُمْ لَا يَأْلُونَكُمْ خَبَالًا وَدُّوا۟ مَا عَنِتُّمْ قَدْ بَدَتِ ٱلْبَغْضَآءُ مِنْ أَفْوَٰهِهِمْ وَمَا تُخْفِى صُدُورُهُمْ أَكْبَرُ قَدْ بَيَّنَّا لَكُمُ ٱلْءَايَٰتِ إِن كُنتُمْ تَعْقِلُونَ (١١٨) هَٰٓأَنتُمْ أُو۟لَآءِ تُحِبُّونَهُمْ وَلَا يُحِبُّونَكُمْ وَتُؤْمِنُونَ بِٱلْكِتَٰبِ كُلِّهِۦ وَإِذَا لَقُوكُمْ قَالُوٓا۟ ءَامَنَّا وَإِذَا خَلَوْا۟ عَضُّوا۟ عَلَيْكُمُ ٱلْأَنَامِلَ مِنَ ٱلْغَيْظِ قُلْ مُوتُوا۟ بِغَيْظِكُمْ إِنَّ ٱللَّهَ عَلِيمٌۢ بِذَاتِ ٱلصُّدُورِ (١١٩) إِن تَمْسَسْكُمْ حَسَنَةٌ تَسُؤْهُمْ وَإِن تُصِبْكُمْ سَيِّئَةٌ يَفْرَحُوا۟ بِهَا وَإِن تَصْبِرُوا۟ وَتَتَّقُوا۟ لَا يَضُرُّكُمْ كَيْدُهُمْ شَيْـًٔا إِنَّ ٱللَّهَ بِمَا يَعْمَلُونَ مُحِيطٌ (١٢٠)

O you who believe! Take not as (your) Bitânah (advisors, consultants, protectors, helpers, friends) those outside your religion (pagans, Jews, Christians, and hypocrites) since they will not fail to do their best to corrupt you. They desire to harm you severely. Hatred has already appeared from their mouths, but what their breasts conceal is far worse. Indeed We have made plain to you the Ayât (proofs, evidences, verses) if you understand. (118) Lo! You are the ones who love them but they love you not, and you believe in all the Scriptures [i.e. you believe in the Taurât (Torah) and the Injeel, while they disbelieve in your Book, the Qur'ân]. And when they meet you, they say, "We believe". But when they are alone, they bite the tips of their fingers at you in rage. Say: "Perish in your rage. Certainly, Allâh knows what is in the breasts (all the secrets)." (119) If a good befalls you, it grieves them, but if some evil overtakes you, they rejoice at it. But if you remain patient and become Al-Muttaqûn (the pious), not the least harm will their cunning do to you. Surely, Allâh surrounds all that they do. (120)

Quran 3:130-136

يَـٰٓأَيُّهَا ٱلَّذِينَ ءَامَنُوا۟ لَا تَأْكُلُوا۟ ٱلرِّبَوٰٓا۟ أَضْعَـٰفًا مُّضَـٰعَفَةً ۖ وَٱتَّقُوا۟ ٱللَّهَ لَعَلَّكُمْ تُفْلِحُونَ (١٣٠) وَٱتَّقُوا۟ ٱلنَّارَ ٱلَّتِىٓ أُعِدَّتْ لِلْكَـٰفِرِينَ (١٣١) وَأَطِيعُوا۟ ٱللَّهَ وَٱلرَّسُولَ لَعَلَّكُمْ تُرْحَمُونَ (١٣٢) ۞ وَسَارِعُوٓا۟ إِلَىٰ مَغْفِرَةٍ مِّن رَّبِّكُمْ وَجَنَّةٍ عَرْضُهَا ٱلسَّمَـٰوَٰتُ وَٱلْأَرْضُ أُعِدَّتْ لِلْمُتَّقِينَ (١٣٣) ٱلَّذِينَ يُنفِقُونَ فِى ٱلسَّرَّآءِ وَٱلضَّرَّآءِ وَٱلْكَـٰظِمِينَ ٱلْغَيْظَ وَٱلْعَافِينَ عَنِ ٱلنَّاسِ ۗ وَٱللَّهُ يُحِبُّ ٱلْمُحْسِنِينَ (١٣٤) وَٱلَّذِينَ إِذَا فَعَلُوا۟ فَـٰحِشَةً أَوْ ظَلَمُوٓا۟ أَنفُسَهُمْ ذَكَرُوا۟ ٱللَّهَ فَٱسْتَغْفَرُوا۟ لِذُنُوبِهِمْ وَمَن يَغْفِرُ ٱلذُّنُوبَ إِلَّا ٱللَّهُ وَلَمْ يُصِرُّوا۟ عَلَىٰ مَا فَعَلُوا۟ وَهُمْ يَعْلَمُونَ (١٣٥)

O you who believe! Eat not Ribâ (usury) doubled and multiplied, but fear Allâh that you may be successful. (130) And fear the Fire, which is prepared for the disbelievers. (131) And obey Allâh and the Messenger (Muhammad) that you may obtain mercy. (132) And march forth in the way (which leads to) forgiveness from your Lord, and for Paradise as wide as are the heavens and the earth, prepared for Al-Muttaqûn (the pious).

(133) Those who spend [in Allâh's Cause] in prosperity and in adversity, who repress anger, and who pardon men; verily, Allâh loves Al-Muhsinûn (the good - doers). (134) And those who, when they have committed Fahishah (illegal sexual intercourse) or wronged themselves with evil, remember Allâh and ask forgiveness for their sins; - and none can forgive sins but Allâh - And do not persist in what (wrong) they have done, while they know. (135)

Quran 3:139

وَلَا تَهِنُواْ وَلَا تَحْزَنُواْ وَأَنتُمُ ٱلْأَعْلَوْنَ إِن كُنتُم مُّؤْمِنِينَ

So do not become weak (against your enemy), nor be sad, and you will be superior (in victory) if you are indeed (true) believers. (139)

Quran 3:146-147

وَكَأَيِّن مِّن نَّبِيٍّ قَٰتَلَ مَعَهُۥ رِبِّيُّونَ كَثِيرٌ فَمَا وَهَنُواْ لِمَآ أَصَابَهُمْ فِى سَبِيلِ ٱللَّهِ وَمَا ضَعُفُواْ وَمَا ٱسْتَكَانُواْ وَٱللَّهُ يُحِبُّ ٱلصَّٰبِرِينَ (١٤٦) وَمَا كَانَ قَوْلَهُمْ إِلَّآ أَن قَالُواْ رَبَّنَا ٱغْفِرْ لَنَا ذُنُوبَنَا وَإِسْرَافَنَا فِىٓ أَمْرِنَا وَثَبِّتْ أَقْدَامَنَا وَٱنصُرْنَا عَلَى ٱلْقَوْمِ ٱلْكَٰفِرِينَ (١٤٧)

And many a Prophet fought (in Allâh's Cause) and along with him (fought) large bands of religious learned men. But they never lost heart for that which did befall them in Allâh's Way, nor did they weaken nor degrade themselves. And Allâh loves As-Sâbirun (the patient). (146) And they said nothing but: "Our Lord! Forgive us our sins and our transgressions (in keeping our duties to

You), establish our feet firmly, and give us victory over the disbelieving folk." (147)

Quran 3:149

$$\text{يَٰٓأَيُّهَا ٱلَّذِينَ ءَامَنُوٓا۟ إِن تُطِيعُوا۟ ٱلَّذِينَ كَفَرُوا۟ يَرُدُّوكُمْ عَلَىٰٓ أَعْقَـٰبِكُمْ فَتَنقَلِبُوا۟ خَـٰسِرِينَ}$$

O you who believe! If you obey those who disbelieve, they will send you back on your heels, and you will turn back (from Faith) as losers. (149)

Quran 3:156

$$\text{يَـٰٓأَيُّهَا ٱلَّذِينَ ءَامَنُوا۟ لَا تَكُونُوا۟ كَٱلَّذِينَ كَفَرُوا۟ وَقَالُوا۟ لِإِخْوَٰنِهِمْ إِذَا ضَرَبُوا۟ فِى ٱلْأَرْضِ أَوْ كَانُوا۟ غُزًّى لَّوْ كَانُوا۟ عِندَنَا مَا مَاتُوا۟ وَمَا قُتِلُوا۟ لِيَجْعَلَ ٱللَّهُ ذَٰلِكَ حَسْرَةً فِى قُلُوبِهِمْ ۗ وَٱللَّهُ يُحْىِۦ وَيُمِيتُ ۗ وَٱللَّهُ بِمَا تَعْمَلُونَ بَصِيرٌ}$$

O you who believe! Be not like those who disbelieve (hypocrites) and who say to their brethren when they travel through the earth or go out to fight: "If they had stayed with us, they would not have died or been killed," so that Allâh may make it a cause of regret in their hearts. It is Allâh that gives life and causes death. And Allâh is All¬Seer of what you do. (156)

Quran 3:160

$$\text{إِن يَنصُرْكُمُ ٱللَّهُ فَلَا غَالِبَ لَكُمْ ۖ وَإِن يَخْذُلْكُمْ فَمَن ذَا ٱلَّذِى يَنصُرُكُم مِّنۢ بَعْدِهِۦ ۗ وَعَلَى ٱللَّهِ فَلْيَتَوَكَّلِ ٱلْمُؤْمِنُونَ}$$

If Allâh helps you, none can overcome you; and if He forsakes you, who is there after Him that can help you? And in Allâh (Alone) let believers put their trust. (160)

Quran 3:175-176

إِنَّمَا ذَٰلِكُمُ ٱلشَّيْطَٰنُ يُخَوِّفُ أَوْلِيَآءَهُۥ فَلَا تَخَافُوهُمْ وَخَافُونِ إِن كُنتُم مُّؤْمِنِينَ (١٧٥) وَلَا يَحْزُنكَ ٱلَّذِينَ يُسَٰرِعُونَ فِى ٱلْكُفْرِ إِنَّهُمْ لَن يَضُرُّوا۟ ٱللَّهَ شَيْـًٔا يُرِيدُ ٱللَّهُ أَلَّا يَجْعَلَ لَهُمْ حَظًّا فِى ٱلْءَاخِرَةِ وَلَهُمْ عَذَابٌ عَظِيمٌ (١٧٦)

It is only Shaitân (Satan) that suggests to you the fear of his Auliyâ' [supporters and friends (polytheists, disbelievers in the Oneness of Allâh and in His Messenger)], so fear them not, but fear Me, if you are (true) believers. (175) And let not those grieve you who rush with haste to disbelieve; verily, not the least harm will they do to Allâh. It is Allâh's Will to give them no portion in the Hereafter. For them there is a great torment. (176)

Quran 3:179

مَّا كَانَ ٱللَّهُ لِيَذَرَ ٱلْمُؤْمِنِينَ عَلَىٰ مَآ أَنتُمْ عَلَيْهِ حَتَّىٰ يَمِيزَ ٱلْخَبِيثَ مِنَ ٱلطَّيِّبِ وَمَا كَانَ ٱللَّهُ لِيُطْلِعَكُمْ عَلَى ٱلْغَيْبِ وَلَٰكِنَّ ٱللَّهَ يَجْتَبِى مِن رُّسُلِهِۦ مَن يَشَآءُ فَـَٔامِنُوا۟ بِٱللَّهِ وَرُسُلِهِۦ وَإِن تُؤْمِنُوا۟ وَتَتَّقُوا۟ فَلَكُمْ أَجْرٌ عَظِيمٌ

Allâh will not leave the believers in the state in which you are now, until He distinguishes the wicked from the good. Nor will Allâh disclose to you the secrets of the Ghaib (unseen), but Allâh chooses of His Messengers whom He wills. So believe in Allâh and His Messengers.

And if you believe and fear Allâh, then for you there is a great reward. (179)

Quran 3:199-200

وَإِنَّ مِنْ أَهْلِ ٱلْكِتَٰبِ لَمَن يُؤْمِنُ بِٱللَّهِ وَمَآ أُنزِلَ إِلَيْكُمْ وَمَآ أُنزِلَ إِلَيْهِمْ خَٰشِعِينَ لِلَّهِ لَا يَشْتَرُونَ بِـَٔايَٰتِ ٱللَّهِ ثَمَنًا قَلِيلًا ۗ أُو۟لَٰٓئِكَ لَهُمْ أَجْرُهُمْ عِندَ رَبِّهِمْ ۗ إِنَّ ٱللَّهَ سَرِيعُ ٱلْحِسَابِ (١٩٩) يَٰٓأَيُّهَا ٱلَّذِينَ ءَامَنُوا۟ ٱصْبِرُوا۟ وَصَابِرُوا۟ وَرَابِطُوا۟ وَٱتَّقُوا۟ ٱللَّهَ لَعَلَّكُمْ تُفْلِحُونَ (٢٠٠)

And there are, certainly, among the people of the Scripture (Jews and Christians), those who believe in Allâh and in that which has been revealed to you, and in that which has been revealed to them, humbling themselves before Allâh. They do not sell the Verses of Allâh for a little price, for them is a reward with their Lord. Surely, Allâh is Swift in account. (199) O you who believe! Endure and be more patient (than your enemy), and guard your territory by stationing army units permanently at the places from where the enemy can attack you, and fear Allâh, so that you may be successful. (200)

Quran 4:19-21

يَٰٓأَيُّهَا ٱلَّذِينَ ءَامَنُوا۟ لَا يَحِلُّ لَكُمْ أَن تَرِثُوا۟ ٱلنِّسَآءَ كَرْهًا ۖ وَلَا تَعْضُلُوهُنَّ لِتَذْهَبُوا۟ بِبَعْضِ مَآ ءَاتَيْتُمُوهُنَّ إِلَّآ أَن يَأْتِينَ بِفَٰحِشَةٍ مُّبَيِّنَةٍ ۚ وَعَاشِرُوهُنَّ بِٱلْمَعْرُوفِ ۚ فَإِن كَرِهْتُمُوهُنَّ فَعَسَىٰٓ أَن تَكْرَهُوا۟ شَيْـًٔا وَيَجْعَلَ ٱللَّهُ فِيهِ خَيْرًا كَثِيرًا (١٩) وَإِنْ أَرَدتُّمُ ٱسْتِبْدَالَ زَوْجٍ مَّكَانَ زَوْجٍ وَءَاتَيْتُمْ إِحْدَىٰهُنَّ قِنطَارًا فَلَا تَأْخُذُوا۟ مِنْهُ شَيْـًٔا ۚ أَتَأْخُذُونَهُۥ بُهْتَٰنًا وَإِثْمًا مُّبِينًا (٢٠) وَكَيْفَ

تَأْخُذُونَهُ وَقَدْ أَفْضَىٰ بَعْضُكُمْ إِلَىٰ بَعْضٍ وَأَخَذْنَ مِنكُم مِّيثَٰقًا غَلِيظًا (٢١)

O you who believe! You are forbidden to inherit women against their will, and you should not treat them with harshness, that you may take away part of the Mahr[dowry] you have given them, unless they commit open illegal sexual intercourse. And live with them honorably. If you dislike them, it may be that you dislike a thing and Allâh brings through it a great deal of good. (19) But if you intend to replace a wife by another and you have given one of them a Qintar (of gold i.e. a great amount as Mahr), take not the least bit of it back; would you take it wrongfully without a right and (with) a manifest sin? (20) And how could you take it (back) while you have gone in unto each other, and they have taken from you a firm and strong covenant? (21)

Quran 4:29-32

يَٰٓأَيُّهَا ٱلَّذِينَ ءَامَنُوا۟ لَا تَأْكُلُوٓا۟ أَمْوَٰلَكُم بَيْنَكُم بِٱلْبَٰطِلِ إِلَّآ أَن تَكُونَ تِجَٰرَةً عَن تَرَاضٍ مِّنكُمْ ۚ وَلَا تَقْتُلُوٓا۟ أَنفُسَكُمْ ۚ إِنَّ ٱللَّهَ كَانَ بِكُمْ رَحِيمًا (٢٩) وَمَن يَفْعَلْ ذَٰلِكَ عُدْوَٰنًا وَظُلْمًا فَسَوْفَ نُصْلِيهِ نَارًا ۚ وَكَانَ ذَٰلِكَ عَلَى ٱللَّهِ يَسِيرًا (٣٠) إِن تَجْتَنِبُوا۟ كَبَآئِرَ مَا تُنْهَوْنَ عَنْهُ نُكَفِّرْ عَنكُمْ سَيِّـَٔاتِكُمْ وَنُدْخِلْكُم مُّدْخَلًا كَرِيمًا (٣١) وَلَا تَتَمَنَّوْا۟ مَا فَضَّلَ ٱللَّهُ بِهِۦ بَعْضَكُمْ عَلَىٰ بَعْضٍ ۚ لِّلرِّجَالِ نَصِيبٌ مِّمَّا ٱكْتَسَبُوا۟ ۖ وَلِلنِّسَآءِ نَصِيبٌ مِّمَّا ٱكْتَسَبْنَ ۚ وَسْـَٔلُوا۟ ٱللَّهَ مِن فَضْلِهِۦٓ ۗ إِنَّ ٱللَّهَ كَانَ بِكُلِّ شَىْءٍ عَلِيمًا (٣٢)

O you who believe! Eat not up your property among yourselves unjustly except it be a trade amongst you, by mutual consent. And do not kill yourselves (nor kill one another). Surely, Allâh is Most Merciful to you. (29) And whoever commits that through aggression and injustice, We shall cast him into the Fire, and that is easy for Allâh. (30) If you avoid the great sins which you are forbidden to do, We shall expiate from you your (small) sins, and admit you to a Noble Entrance (i.e. Paradise). (31) And wish not for the things in which Allâh has made some of you to excel others. For men there is reward for what they have earned, (and likewise) for women there is reward for what they have earned, and ask Allâh of His Bounty. Surely, Allâh is Ever All¬Knower of everything. (32)

Quran 4:43

يَٰٓأَيُّهَا ٱلَّذِينَ ءَامَنُوا۟ لَا تَقْرَبُوا۟ ٱلصَّلَوٰةَ وَأَنتُمْ سُكَٰرَىٰ حَتَّىٰ تَعْلَمُوا۟ مَا تَقُولُونَ وَلَا جُنُبًا إِلَّا عَابِرِى سَبِيلٍ حَتَّىٰ تَغْتَسِلُوا۟ۚ وَإِن كُنتُم مَّرْضَىٰٓ أَوْ عَلَىٰ سَفَرٍ أَوْ جَآءَ أَحَدٌ مِّنكُم مِّنَ ٱلْغَآئِطِ أَوْ لَٰمَسْتُمُ ٱلنِّسَآءَ فَلَمْ تَجِدُوا۟ مَآءً فَتَيَمَّمُوا۟ صَعِيدًا طَيِّبًا فَٱمْسَحُوا۟ بِوُجُوهِكُمْ وَأَيْدِيكُمْۗ إِنَّ ٱللَّهَ كَانَ عَفُوًّا غَفُورًا

O you who believe! Approach not As¬Salât (the prayer) when you are in a drunken state until you know (the meaning) of what you utter, nor when you are in a state of Janâba, (i.e. in a state of sexual impurity and have not yet taken a bath) except when travelling on the road (without enough water, or just passing through a mosque), till you wash your whole body. And if you are ill, or on a journey, or one of you comes after answering the call of nature, or you have been in contact with women (by sexual relations) and you find no water, perform Tayammum with clean earth and rub therewith your faces and hands (Tayammum). Truly, Allâh is Ever Oft¬Pardoning, Oft¬Forgiving. (43)

Quran 4:57-59

وَٱلَّذِينَ ءَامَنُواْ وَعَمِلُواْ ٱلصَّٰلِحَٰتِ سَنُدْخِلُهُمْ جَنَّٰتٍ تَجْرِى مِن تَحْتِهَا ٱلْأَنْهَٰرُ خَٰلِدِينَ فِيهَآ أَبَدًا لَّهُمْ فِيهَآ أَزْوَٰجٌ مُّطَهَّرَةٌ وَنُدْخِلُهُمْ ظِلًّا ظَلِيلًا (٥٧) إِنَّ ٱللَّهَ يَأْمُرُكُمْ أَن تُؤَدُّواْ ٱلْأَمَٰنَٰتِ إِلَىٰٓ أَهْلِهَا وَإِذَا حَكَمْتُم بَيْنَ ٱلنَّاسِ أَن تَحْكُمُواْ بِٱلْعَدْلِ إِنَّ ٱللَّهَ نِعِمَّا يَعِظُكُم بِهِۦٓ إِنَّ ٱللَّهَ كَانَ سَمِيعًۢا بَصِيرًا (٥٨) يَٰٓأَيُّهَا ٱلَّذِينَ ءَامَنُوٓاْ أَطِيعُواْ ٱللَّهَ وَأَطِيعُواْ ٱلرَّسُولَ وَأُوْلِى ٱلْأَمْرِ مِنكُمْ فَإِن تَنَٰزَعْتُمْ فِى شَىْءٍ فَرُدُّوهُ إِلَى ٱللَّهِ وَٱلرَّسُولِ إِن كُنتُمْ تُؤْمِنُونَ بِٱللَّهِ وَٱلْيَوْمِ ٱلْءَاخِرِ ذَٰلِكَ خَيْرٌ وَأَحْسَنُ تَأْوِيلًا (٥٩)

But those who believe (in the Oneness of Allâh - Islâmic Monotheism) and do deeds of righteousness, We shall admit them to Gardens under which rivers flow (Paradise), abiding therein forever. Therein they shall have Azwâjun Mutahharatun [purified mates or wives] and We shall admit them to shades wide and ever deepening (Paradise). (57) Verily! Allâh commands that you should render back the trusts to those, to whom they are due; and that when you judge between men, you judge with justice. Verily, how excellent is the teaching which He (Allâh) gives you! Truly, Allâh is Ever All¬Hearer, All¬Seer. (58) O you who believe! Obey Allâh and obey the Messenger (Muhammad), and those of you (Muslims) who are in authority. (And) if you differ in anything amongst yourselves, refer it to Allâh and His Messenger, if you believe in Allâh and in the Last Day.

That is better and more suitable for final determination. (59)

Quran 4:71

$$\text{يَٰٓأَيُّهَا ٱلَّذِينَ ءَامَنُواْ خُذُواْ حِذْرَكُمْ فَٱنفِرُواْ ثُبَاتٍ أَوِ ٱنفِرُواْ جَمِيعًا}$$

O you who believe! Take your precautions, and either go forth (on an expedition) in parties, or go forth all together. (71)

Quran 4:74-76

فَلْيُقَٰتِلْ فِى سَبِيلِ ٱللَّهِ ٱلَّذِينَ يَشْرُونَ ٱلْحَيَوٰةَ ٱلدُّنْيَا بِٱلْءَاخِرَةِ وَمَن يُقَٰتِلْ فِى سَبِيلِ ٱللَّهِ فَيُقْتَلْ أَوْ يَغْلِبْ فَسَوْفَ نُؤْتِيهِ أَجْرًا عَظِيمًا (٧٤) وَمَا لَكُمْ لَا تُقَٰتِلُونَ فِى سَبِيلِ ٱللَّهِ وَٱلْمُسْتَضْعَفِينَ مِنَ ٱلرِّجَالِ وَٱلنِّسَآءِ وَٱلْوِلْدَٰنِ ٱلَّذِينَ يَقُولُونَ رَبَّنَآ أَخْرِجْنَا مِنْ هَٰذِهِ ٱلْقَرْيَةِ ٱلظَّالِمِ أَهْلُهَا وَٱجْعَل لَّنَا مِن لَّدُنكَ وَلِيًّا وَٱجْعَل لَّنَا مِن لَّدُنكَ نَصِيرًا (٧٥) ٱلَّذِينَ ءَامَنُواْ يُقَٰتِلُونَ فِى سَبِيلِ ٱللَّهِ وَٱلَّذِينَ كَفَرُواْ يُقَٰتِلُونَ فِى سَبِيلِ ٱلطَّٰغُوتِ فَقَٰتِلُوٓاْ أَوْلِيَآءَ ٱلشَّيْطَٰنِ إِنَّ كَيْدَ ٱلشَّيْطَٰنِ كَانَ ضَعِيفًا (٧٦)

Let those (believers) who sell the life of this world for the Hereafter fight in the Cause of Allâh, and whoso fights in the Cause of Allâh, and is killed or gets victory, We shall bestow on him a great reward. (74) And what is wrong with you that you fight not in the Cause of Allâh, and for those weak, ill¬treated and oppressed among men, women, and children, whose cry is: "Our Lord! Rescue us from this town whose people are oppressors; and raise for us from You one who will protect, and raise for us from You one who will help." (75) Those who believe, fight in the Cause of Allâh, and those who disbelieve, fight in the cause of Tâghût (Satan,). So fight you against the friends of Shaitân (Satan); Ever feeble indeed is the plot of Shaitân (Satan). (76)

Quran 4:92-96

وَمَا كَانَ لِمُؤْمِنٍ أَن يَقْتُلَ مُؤْمِنًا إِلَّا خَطَـًٔا ۚ وَمَن قَتَلَ مُؤْمِنًا خَطَـًٔا فَتَحْرِيرُ رَقَبَةٍ مُّؤْمِنَةٍ وَدِيَةٌ مُّسَلَّمَةٌ إِلَىٰٓ أَهْلِهِۦٓ إِلَّآ أَن يَصَّدَّقُوا۟ ۚ فَإِن كَانَ مِن قَوْمٍ عَدُوٍّ لَّكُمْ وَهُوَ مُؤْمِنٌ فَتَحْرِيرُ رَقَبَةٍ مُّؤْمِنَةٍ ۖ وَإِن كَانَ مِن قَوْمٍۭ بَيْنَكُمْ وَبَيْنَهُم مِّيثَـٰقٌ فَدِيَةٌ مُّسَلَّمَةٌ إِلَىٰٓ أَهْلِهِۦ وَتَحْرِيرُ رَقَبَةٍ مُّؤْمِنَةٍ ۖ فَمَن لَّمْ يَجِدْ فَصِيَامُ شَهْرَيْنِ مُتَتَابِعَيْنِ تَوْبَةً مِّنَ ٱللَّهِ ۗ وَكَانَ ٱللَّهُ عَلِيمًا حَكِيمًا (٩٢) وَمَن يَقْتُلْ مُؤْمِنًا مُّتَعَمِّدًا فَجَزَآؤُهُۥ جَهَنَّمُ خَـٰلِدًا فِيهَا وَغَضِبَ ٱللَّهُ عَلَيْهِ وَلَعَنَهُۥ وَأَعَدَّ لَهُۥ عَذَابًا عَظِيمًا (٩٣) يَـٰٓأَيُّهَا ٱلَّذِينَ ءَامَنُوٓا۟ إِذَا ضَرَبْتُمْ فِى سَبِيلِ ٱللَّهِ فَتَبَيَّنُوا۟ وَلَا تَقُولُوا۟ لِمَنْ أَلْقَىٰٓ إِلَيْكُمُ ٱلسَّلَـٰمَ لَسْتَ مُؤْمِنًا تَبْتَغُونَ عَرَضَ ٱلْحَيَوٰةِ ٱلدُّنْيَا فَعِندَ ٱللَّهِ مَغَانِمُ كَثِيرَةٌ ۚ كَذَٰلِكَ كُنتُم مِّن قَبْلُ فَمَنَّ ٱللَّهُ عَلَيْكُمْ فَتَبَيَّنُوٓا۟ ۚ إِنَّ ٱللَّهَ كَانَ بِمَا تَعْمَلُونَ خَبِيرًا (٩٤) لَّا يَسْتَوِى ٱلْقَـٰعِدُونَ مِنَ ٱلْمُؤْمِنِينَ غَيْرُ أُو۟لِى ٱلضَّرَرِ وَٱلْمُجَـٰهِدُونَ فِى سَبِيلِ ٱللَّهِ بِأَمْوَٰلِهِمْ وَأَنفُسِهِمْ ۚ فَضَّلَ ٱللَّهُ ٱلْمُجَـٰهِدِينَ بِأَمْوَٰلِهِمْ وَأَنفُسِهِمْ عَلَى ٱلْقَـٰعِدِينَ دَرَجَةً ۚ وَكُلًّا وَعَدَ ٱللَّهُ ٱلْحُسْنَىٰ ۚ وَفَضَّلَ ٱللَّهُ ٱلْمُجَـٰهِدِينَ عَلَى ٱلْقَـٰعِدِينَ أَجْرًا عَظِيمًا (٩٥) دَرَجَـٰتٍ مِّنْهُ وَمَغْفِرَةً وَرَحْمَةً ۚ وَكَانَ ٱللَّهُ غَفُورًا رَّحِيمًا (٩٦)

It is not for a believer to kill a believer except (that it be) by mistake, and whosoever kills a believer by mistake, (it is ordained that) he must set free a believing slave and a compensation (blood money, i.e Diya) be given to the deceased's family, unless they remit it. If the deceased belonged to a people at war with you and he was a believer; the freeing of a believing slave (is prescribed), and if he belonged to a people with whom you have a treaty of mutual alliance, compensation (blood money -

Diya) must be paid to his family, and a believing slave must be freed. And whoso finds this (the penance of freeing a slave) beyond his means, he must fast for two consecutive months in order to seek repentance from Allâh. And Allâh is Ever All¬Knowing, All¬Wise. (92) And whoever kills a believer intentionally, his recompense is Hell to abide therein, and the Wrath and the Curse of Allâh are upon him, and a great punishment is prepared for him. (93) O you who believe! When you go (to fight) in the Cause of Allâh, verify (the truth), and say not to anyone who greets you (by embracing Islâm): "You are not a believer"; seeking the perishable goods of the worldly life. There are much more profits and booties with Allâh. Even as he is now, so were you yourselves before till Allâh conferred on you His Favours (i.e. guided you to Islâm), therefore, be cautious in discrimination. Allâh is Ever Well¬Aware of what you do. (94) Not equal are those of the believers who sit (at home), except those who are disabled (by injury or are blind or lame), and those who strive hard and fight in the Cause of Allâh with their wealth and their lives. Allâh has preferred in grades those who strive hard and fight with their wealth and their lives above those who sit (at home). Unto each, Allâh has promised good (Paradise), but Allâh has preferred those who strive hard and fight, above those who sit (at home) by a huge reward; (95) Degrees of (higher) grades from Him, and Forgiveness and Mercy. And Allâh is Ever Oft¬Forgiving, Most Merciful. (96)

Quran 4:122-124

وَٱلَّذِينَ ءَامَنُواْ وَعَمِلُواْ ٱلصَّٰلِحَٰتِ سَنُدۡخِلُهُمۡ جَنَّٰتٍ تَجۡرِى مِن تَحۡتِهَا ٱلۡأَنۡهَٰرُ خَٰلِدِينَ فِيهَآ أَبَدًاۖ وَعۡدَ ٱللَّهِ حَقًّاۚ وَمَنۡ أَصۡدَقُ مِنَ ٱللَّهِ قِيلًا (١٢٢) لَّيۡسَ بِأَمَانِيِّكُمۡ وَلَآ أَمَانِىِّ أَهۡلِ ٱلۡكِتَٰبِۗ مَن يَعۡمَلۡ سُوٓءًا يُجۡزَ بِهِۦ وَلَا يَجِدۡ لَهُۥ مِن دُونِ ٱللَّهِ وَلِيًّا وَلَا نَصِيرًا (١٢٣) وَمَن يَعۡمَلۡ مِنَ ٱلصَّٰلِحَٰتِ مِن ذَكَرٍ أَوۡ أُنثَىٰ وَهُوَ مُؤۡمِنٌ فَأُوْلَٰٓئِكَ يَدۡخُلُونَ ٱلۡجَنَّةَ وَلَا يُظۡلَمُونَ نَقِيرًا (١٢٤)

But those who believe and do deeds of righteousness, We shall admit them to the Gardens under which rivers flow (i.e. in Paradise) to dwell therein forever. Allâh's Promise is the Truth, and whose words can be truer than those of Allâh? (122) It will not be in accordance with your desires (Muslims), nor those of the people of the Scripture (Jews and Christians), whosoever works evil, will have the recompense thereof, and he will not find any protector or helper besides Allâh. (123) And whoever does righteous good deeds, male or female, and is a (true) believer [in the Oneness of Allâh], such will enter Paradise and not the least injustice, even to the size of a speck on the back of a date-stone, will be done to them. (124)

Quran 4:135-136

۞ يَٰٓأَيُّهَا ٱلَّذِينَ ءَامَنُواْ كُونُواْ قَوَّٰمِينَ بِٱلۡقِسۡطِ شُهَدَآءَ لِلَّهِ وَلَوۡ عَلَىٰٓ أَنفُسِكُمۡ أَوِ ٱلۡوَٰلِدَيۡنِ وَٱلۡأَقۡرَبِينَۚ إِن يَكُنۡ غَنِيًّا أَوۡ فَقِيرًا فَٱللَّهُ أَوۡلَىٰ بِهِمَاۖ فَلَا تَتَّبِعُواْ ٱلۡهَوَىٰٓ أَن تَعۡدِلُواْۚ وَإِن تَلۡوُۥٓاْ أَوۡ تُعۡرِضُواْ فَإِنَّ ٱللَّهَ كَانَ بِمَا تَعۡمَلُونَ خَبِيرًا (١٣٥) يَٰٓأَيُّهَا ٱلَّذِينَ ءَامَنُوٓاْ ءَامِنُواْ بِٱللَّهِ وَرَسُولِهِۦ وَٱلۡكِتَٰبِ ٱلَّذِى نَزَّلَ عَلَىٰ رَسُولِهِۦ وَٱلۡكِتَٰبِ ٱلَّذِىٓ أَنزَلَ مِن قَبۡلُۚ وَمَن يَكۡفُرۡ بِٱللَّهِ وَمَلَٰٓئِكَتِهِۦ وَكُتُبِهِۦ وَرُسُلِهِۦ وَٱلۡيَوۡمِ ٱلۡأَخِرِ فَقَدۡ ضَلَّ ضَلَٰلَۢا بَعِيدًا (١٣٦)

O you who believe! Stand out firmly for justice, as witnesses to Allâh, even though it be against yourselves, or your parents, or your kin, be he rich or poor, Allâh is a Better Protector to both (than you). So follow not the lusts (of your hearts), lest you avoid justice, and if you distort your witness or refuse to give it, verily, Allâh is Ever Well-Acquainted with what you do. (135) O you who believe! Believe in Allâh, and His Messenger (Muhammad), and the Book (the Qur'ân) which He has sent down to His Messenger, and the Scripture which He sent down to those before (him), and whosoever disbelieves in Allâh, His Angels, His Books, His Messengers, and the Last Day, then indeed he has strayed far away (136)

Quran 4:144-147

يَٰٓأَيُّهَا ٱلَّذِينَ ءَامَنُوا۟ لَا تَتَّخِذُوا۟ ٱلْكَٰفِرِينَ أَوْلِيَآءَ مِن دُونِ ٱلْمُؤْمِنِينَ ۚ أَتُرِيدُونَ أَن تَجْعَلُوا۟ لِلَّهِ عَلَيْكُمْ سُلْطَٰنًا مُّبِينًا (١٤٤) إِنَّ ٱلْمُنَٰفِقِينَ فِى ٱلدَّرْكِ ٱلْأَسْفَلِ مِنَ ٱلنَّارِ وَلَن تَجِدَ لَهُمْ نَصِيرًا (١٤٥) إِلَّا ٱلَّذِينَ تَابُوا۟ وَأَصْلَحُوا۟ وَٱعْتَصَمُوا۟ بِٱللَّهِ وَأَخْلَصُوا۟ دِينَهُمْ لِلَّهِ فَأُو۟لَٰٓئِكَ مَعَ ٱلْمُؤْمِنِينَ ۖ وَسَوْفَ يُؤْتِ ٱللَّهُ ٱلْمُؤْمِنِينَ أَجْرًا عَظِيمًا (١٤٦) مَّا يَفْعَلُ ٱللَّهُ بِعَذَابِكُمْ إِن شَكَرْتُمْ وَءَامَنتُمْ ۚ وَكَانَ ٱللَّهُ شَاكِرًا عَلِيمًا (١٤٧)

O you who believe! Take not for Auliyâ' (protectors or helpers or friends) disbelievers instead of believers. Do you wish to offer Allâh a manifest proof against yourselves? (144) Verily, the hyprocrites will be in the lowest depths (grade) of the Fire; no helper will you find for them. (145) Except those who repent (from hypocrisy), do righteous good deeds, hold fast to Allâh, and purify their religion for Allâh (by worshipping none but Allâh, and do good for Allâh's sake only, not to show off), then they will be with the believers. And Allâh will grant the believers a great reward. (146) Why should Allâh punish you if you have thanked (Him) and have believed in Him. And Allâh is Ever All¬Appreciative (of good), All¬Knowing. (147)

Quran 4:152

وَٱلَّذِينَ ءَامَنُواْ بِٱللَّهِ وَرُسُلِهِۦ وَلَمْ يُفَرِّقُواْ بَيْنَ أَحَدٍ مِّنْهُمْ أُوْلَٰٓئِكَ سَوْفَ يُؤْتِيهِمْ أُجُورَهُمْ وَكَانَ ٱللَّهُ غَفُورًا رَّحِيمًا

And those who believe in Allâh and His Messengers and make no distinction between any of them (Messengers), We shall give them their rewards, and Allâh is Ever Oft¬Forgiving, Most Merciful. (152)

Quran 4:162

لَّٰكِنِ ٱلرَّٰسِخُونَ فِى ٱلْعِلْمِ مِنْهُمْ وَٱلْمُؤْمِنُونَ يُؤْمِنُونَ بِمَآ أُنزِلَ إِلَيْكَ وَمَآ أُنزِلَ مِن قَبْلِكَ وَٱلْمُقِيمِينَ ٱلصَّلَوٰةَ وَٱلْمُؤْتُونَ ٱلزَّكَوٰةَ وَٱلْمُؤْمِنُونَ بِٱللَّهِ وَٱلْيَوْمِ ٱلْءَاخِرِ أُوْلَٰٓئِكَ سَنُؤْتِيهِمْ أَجْرًا عَظِيمًا

But those among them who are well-grounded in knowledge, and the believers, believe in what has been sent down to you (Muhammad) and what was sent down before you, and those who perform As-Salât (Iqâmat-as-Salât), and give Zakât and believe in Allâh and in the Last Day, it is they to whom We shall give a great reward. (162)

Quran 4:173-175

فَأَمَّا ٱلَّذِينَ ءَامَنُوا۟ وَعَمِلُوا۟ ٱلصَّٰلِحَٰتِ فَيُوَفِّيهِمْ أُجُورَهُمْ وَيَزِيدُهُم مِّن فَضْلِهِۦ ۖ وَأَمَّا ٱلَّذِينَ ٱسْتَنكَفُوا۟ وَٱسْتَكْبَرُوا۟ فَيُعَذِّبُهُمْ عَذَابًا أَلِيمًا وَلَا يَجِدُونَ لَهُم مِّن دُونِ ٱللَّهِ وَلِيًّا وَلَا نَصِيرًا (١٧٣) يَٰٓأَيُّهَا ٱلنَّاسُ قَدْ جَآءَكُم بُرْهَٰنٌ مِّن رَّبِّكُمْ وَأَنزَلْنَآ إِلَيْكُمْ نُورًا مُّبِينًا (١٧٤) فَأَمَّا ٱلَّذِينَ ءَامَنُوا۟ بِٱللَّهِ وَٱعْتَصَمُوا۟ بِهِۦ فَسَيُدْخِلُهُمْ فِى رَحْمَةٍ مِّنْهُ وَفَضْلٍ وَيَهْدِيهِمْ إِلَيْهِ صِرَٰطًا مُّسْتَقِيمًا (١٧٥)

So, as for those who believed (in the Oneness of Allâh - Islâmic Monotheism) and did deeds of righteousness, He will give their (due) rewards, and more out of His Bounty. But as for those who refused His worship and were proud, He will punish them with a painful torment. And they will not find for themselves besides Allâh any protector or helper. (173) O mankind! Verily, there has come to you a convincing proof (Prophet Muhammad) from your Lord, and We sent down to you a manifest light (this Qur'ân). (174) So, as for those who believed in Allâh and held fast to Him, He will admit them to His Mercy and Grace (i.e. Paradise), and guide them to Himself by a Straight Path. (175)

Quran 5:1-5

يَٰٓأَيُّهَا ٱلَّذِينَ ءَامَنُوٓا۟ أَوْفُوا۟ بِٱلْعُقُودِ ۚ أُحِلَّتْ لَكُم بَهِيمَةُ ٱلْأَنْعَٰمِ إِلَّا مَا يُتْلَىٰ عَلَيْكُمْ غَيْرَ مُحِلِّى ٱلصَّيْدِ وَأَنتُمْ حُرُمٌ ۗ إِنَّ ٱللَّهَ يَحْكُمُ مَا يُرِيدُ (١) يَٰٓأَيُّهَا ٱلَّذِينَ ءَامَنُوا۟ لَا تُحِلُّوا۟ شَعَٰٓئِرَ ٱللَّهِ وَلَا ٱلشَّهْرَ ٱلْحَرَامَ وَلَا ٱلْهَدْىَ وَلَا ٱلْقَلَٰٓئِدَ وَلَآ ءَآمِّينَ ٱلْبَيْتَ ٱلْحَرَامَ يَبْتَغُونَ فَضْلًا مِّن رَّبِّهِمْ وَرِضْوَٰنًا ۚ وَإِذَا حَلَلْتُمْ فَٱصْطَادُوا۟ ۚ وَلَا يَجْرِمَنَّكُمْ شَنَـَٔانُ قَوْمٍ أَن صَدُّوكُمْ عَنِ ٱلْمَسْجِدِ ٱلْحَرَامِ أَن تَعْتَدُوا۟ ۘ وَتَعَاوَنُوا۟ عَلَى ٱلْبِرِّ وَٱلتَّقْوَىٰ ۖ وَلَا تَعَاوَنُوا۟ عَلَى ٱلْإِثْمِ وَٱلْعُدْوَٰنِ ۚ وَٱتَّقُوا۟ ٱللَّهَ ۖ إِنَّ ٱللَّهَ شَدِيدُ ٱلْعِقَابِ (٢) حُرِّمَتْ عَلَيْكُمُ ٱلْمَيْتَةُ وَٱلدَّمُ وَلَحْمُ ٱلْخِنزِيرِ وَمَآ أُهِلَّ لِغَيْرِ ٱللَّهِ بِهِۦ وَٱلْمُنْخَنِقَةُ وَٱلْمَوْقُوذَةُ وَٱلْمُتَرَدِّيَةُ وَٱلنَّطِيحَةُ وَمَآ أَكَلَ ٱلسَّبُعُ إِلَّا مَا ذَكَّيْتُمْ وَمَا

ذُبِحَ عَلَى ٱلنُّصُبِ وَأَن تَسْتَقْسِمُوا۟ بِٱلْأَزْلَٰمِ ذَٰلِكُمْ فِسْقٌ ٱلْيَوْمَ يَئِسَ ٱلَّذِينَ كَفَرُوا۟ مِن دِينِكُمْ فَلَا تَخْشَوْهُمْ وَٱخْشَوْنِ ٱلْيَوْمَ أَكْمَلْتُ لَكُمْ دِينَكُمْ وَأَتْمَمْتُ عَلَيْكُمْ نِعْمَتِى وَرَضِيتُ لَكُمُ ٱلْإِسْلَٰمَ دِينًا فَمَنِ ٱضْطُرَّ فِى مَخْمَصَةٍ غَيْرَ مُتَجَانِفٍ لِّإِثْمٍ فَإِنَّ ٱللَّهَ غَفُورٌ رَّحِيمٌ (٣)

O you who believe! Fulfill (your) obligations. Lawful to you (for food) are all the beasts of cattle except that which will be announced to you (herein), game (also) being unlawful when you assume Ihrâm for Hajj or 'Umrah (pilgrimage). Verily, Allâh commands that which He wills. (1) O you who believe! Violate not the sanctity of the Symbols of Allâh, nor of the Sacred Month, nor of the animals brought for sacrifice, nor the garlanded people or animals, and others nor the people coming to the Sacred House (Makkah), seeking the bounty and good pleasure of their Lord. But when you finish the Ihrâm (of Hajj or 'Umrah), you may hunt, and let not the hatred of some people in (once) stopping you from Al-Masjid-Al-Harâm (at Makkah) lead you to transgression (and hostility on your part). Help you one another in Al-Birr and At-Taqwa (virtue, righteousness and piety); but do not help one another in sin and transgression. And fear Allâh. Verily, Allâh is Severe in punishment. (2) Forbidden to you (for food) are: Al-Maitah (the dead animals - cattle - beast not slaughtered), blood, the flesh of swine, and that on which Allâh's Name has not been mentioned while slaughtering, (that which has been slaughtered as a sacrifice for others than Allâh, or has been slaughtered for idols) and that which has been killed by strangling, or by a violent blow, or by a headlong fall, or by the goring of horns - and that which has been (partly) eaten by a wild animal - unless you are able to slaughter it (before its death) - and that which is sacrificed (slaughtered) on An-Nusub (stone-altars). (Forbidden) also is to use arrows seeking luck or decision; (all) that is Fisqun (disobedience of Allâh and sin). This day, those who disbelieved have given up all hope of your religion; so fear them not, but fear Me. This day, I have perfected your religion for you, completed My Favour upon you, and have chosen for you Islâm as your religion. But as for him who is forced by severe hunger, with no inclination to sin (such can eat these above mentioned meats), then surely, Allâh is Oft-Forgiving, Most Merciful. (3)

Quran 5:6-11

يَٰٓأَيُّهَا ٱلَّذِينَ ءَامَنُوٓاْ إِذَا قُمْتُمْ إِلَى ٱلصَّلَوٰةِ فَٱغْسِلُواْ وُجُوهَكُمْ وَأَيْدِيَكُمْ إِلَى ٱلْمَرَافِقِ وَٱمْسَحُواْ بِرُءُوسِكُمْ وَأَرْجُلَكُمْ إِلَى ٱلْكَعْبَيْنِۚ وَإِن كُنتُمْ جُنُبًا فَٱطَّهَّرُواْۚ وَإِن كُنتُم مَّرْضَىٰٓ أَوْ عَلَىٰ سَفَرٍ أَوْ جَآءَ أَحَدٌ مِّنكُم مِّنَ ٱلْغَآئِطِ أَوْ لَٰمَسْتُمُ ٱلنِّسَآءَ فَلَمْ تَجِدُواْ مَآءً فَتَيَمَّمُواْ صَعِيدًا طَيِّبًا فَٱمْسَحُواْ بِوُجُوهِكُمْ وَأَيْدِيكُم مِّنْهُۚ مَا يُرِيدُ ٱللَّهُ لِيَجْعَلَ عَلَيْكُم مِّنْ حَرَجٍ وَلَٰكِن يُرِيدُ لِيُطَهِّرَكُمْ وَلِيُتِمَّ نِعْمَتَهُۥ عَلَيْكُمْ لَعَلَّكُمْ تَشْكُرُونَ (٦) وَٱذْكُرُواْ نِعْمَةَ ٱللَّهِ عَلَيْكُمْ وَمِيثَٰقَهُ ٱلَّذِى وَاثَقَكُم بِهِۦٓ إِذْ قُلْتُمْ سَمِعْنَا وَأَطَعْنَاۖ وَٱتَّقُواْ ٱللَّهَۚ إِنَّ ٱللَّهَ عَلِيمٌۢ بِذَاتِ ٱلصُّدُورِ (٧) يَٰٓأَيُّهَا ٱلَّذِينَ ءَامَنُواْ كُونُواْ قَوَّٰمِينَ لِلَّهِ شُهَدَآءَ بِٱلْقِسْطِۖ وَلَا يَجْرِمَنَّكُمْ شَنَـَٔانُ قَوْمٍ عَلَىٰٓ أَلَّا تَعْدِلُواْۚ ٱعْدِلُواْ هُوَ أَقْرَبُ لِلتَّقْوَىٰۖ وَٱتَّقُواْ ٱللَّهَۚ إِنَّ ٱللَّهَ خَبِيرٌۢ بِمَا تَعْمَلُونَ (٨) وَعَدَ ٱللَّهُ ٱلَّذِينَ ءَامَنُواْ وَعَمِلُواْ ٱلصَّٰلِحَٰتِۙ لَهُم مَّغْفِرَةٌ وَأَجْرٌ عَظِيمٌ (٩) وَٱلَّذِينَ كَفَرُواْ وَكَذَّبُواْ بِـَٔايَٰتِنَآ أُوْلَٰٓئِكَ أَصْحَٰبُ ٱلْجَحِيمِ (١٠) يَٰٓأَيُّهَا ٱلَّذِينَ ءَامَنُواْ ٱذْكُرُواْ نِعْمَتَ ٱللَّهِ عَلَيْكُمْ إِذْ هَمَّ قَوْمٌ

أَن يَبْسُطُوٓاْ إِلَيْكُمْ أَيْدِيَهُمْ فَكَفَّ أَيْدِيَهُمْ عَنكُمْۖ وَٱتَّقُواْ ٱللَّهَۚ وَعَلَى ٱللَّهِ فَلْيَتَوَكَّلِ ٱلْمُؤْمِنُونَ ﴿١١﴾

O you who believe! When you intend to offer As-Salât (the prayer), wash your faces and your hands (forearms) up to the elbows, rub (by passing wet hands over) your heads, and (wash) your feet up to ankles. If you are in a state of Janâba (i.e. after a sexual discharge), purify yourself (bathe your whole body). But if you are ill or on a journey or any of you comes after answering the call of nature, or you have been in contact with women (i.e. sexual intercourse) and you find no water, then perform Tayammum with clean earth and rub therewith your faces and hands. Allâh does not want to place you in difficulty, but He wants to purify you, and to complete His Favour to you that you may be thankful (6) And remember Allâh's Favour to you and His Covenant with which He bound you when you said: "We hear and we obey." And fear Allâh. Verily, Allâh is All-Knower of that which is in (secrets of your) breasts. (7) O you who believe! Stand out firmly for Allâh as just witnesses and let not the enmity and hatred of others make you avoid justice. Be just: that is nearer to piety, and fear Allâh. Verily, Allâh is Well-Acquainted with what you do. (8) Allâh has promised those who believe (in the Oneness of Allâh - Islâmic Monotheism) and do deeds of righteousness, that for them there is forgiveness and a great reward (i.e. Paradise) (9) And those who disbelieve and deny our Ayât (proofs, evidences, verses, lessons, signs, revelations, etc.) are those who will be the dwellers of the Hell-fire. (10) O you who believe! Remember the Favour of Allâh unto you when some people desired (made a plan) to stretch out their hands against you, but (Allâh) held back their hands from you. So fear Allâh. And in Allâh let the believers put their trust. (11)

Quran 5:35

يَـٰٓأَيُّهَا ٱلَّذِينَ ءَامَنُواْ ٱتَّقُواْ ٱللَّهَ وَٱبْتَغُوٓاْ إِلَيْهِ ٱلْوَسِيلَةَ وَجَـٰهِدُواْ فِى سَبِيلِهِۦ لَعَلَّكُمْ تُفْلِحُونَ

O you who believe! Do your duty to Allâh and fear Him. Seek the means of approach to Him, and strive hard in His Cause (as much as you can). So that you may be successful. (35)

Quran 5:51-59

۞ يَـٰٓأَيُّهَا ٱلَّذِينَ ءَامَنُواْ لَا تَتَّخِذُواْ ٱلْيَهُودَ وَٱلنَّصَـٰرَىٰٓ أَوْلِيَآءَ بَعْضُهُمْ أَوْلِيَآءُ بَعْضٍ وَمَن يَتَوَلَّهُم مِّنكُمْ فَإِنَّهُۥ مِنْهُمْ إِنَّ ٱللَّهَ لَا يَهْدِى ٱلْقَوْمَ ٱلظَّـٰلِمِينَ (٥١) فَتَرَى ٱلَّذِينَ فِى قُلُوبِهِم مَّرَضٌ يُسَـٰرِعُونَ فِيهِمْ يَقُولُونَ نَخْشَىٰٓ أَن تُصِيبَنَا دَآئِرَةٌ فَعَسَى ٱللَّهُ أَن يَأْتِىَ بِٱلْفَتْحِ أَوْ أَمْرٍ مِّنْ عِندِهِۦ فَيُصْبِحُواْ عَلَىٰ مَآ أَسَرُّواْ فِىٓ أَنفُسِهِمْ نَـٰدِمِينَ (٥٢) وَيَقُولُ ٱلَّذِينَ ءَامَنُوٓاْ أَهَـٰٓؤُلَآءِ ٱلَّذِينَ أَقْسَمُواْ بِٱللَّهِ جَهْدَ أَيْمَـٰنِهِمْ إِنَّهُمْ لَمَعَكُمْ حَبِطَتْ أَعْمَـٰلُهُمْ فَأَصْبَحُواْ خَـٰسِرِينَ (٥٣) يَـٰٓأَيُّهَا ٱلَّذِينَ ءَامَنُواْ مَن يَرْتَدَّ مِنكُمْ عَن دِينِهِۦ فَسَوْفَ يَأْتِى ٱللَّهُ بِقَوْمٍ يُحِبُّهُمْ وَيُحِبُّونَهُۥٓ أَذِلَّةٍ عَلَى ٱلْمُؤْمِنِينَ أَعِزَّةٍ عَلَى ٱلْكَـٰفِرِينَ يُجَـٰهِدُونَ فِى سَبِيلِ ٱللَّهِ وَلَا يَخَافُونَ لَوْمَةَ لَآئِمٍ ذَٰلِكَ فَضْلُ ٱللَّهِ يُؤْتِيهِ مَن يَشَآءُ وَٱللَّهُ وَٰسِعٌ عَلِيمٌ (٥٤) إِنَّمَا وَلِيُّكُمُ ٱللَّهُ وَرَسُولُهُۥ وَٱلَّذِينَ ءَامَنُواْ ٱلَّذِينَ يُقِيمُونَ ٱلصَّلَوٰةَ وَيُؤْتُونَ ٱلزَّكَوٰةَ وَهُمْ رَٰكِعُونَ (٥٥) وَمَن يَتَوَلَّ ٱللَّهَ وَرَسُولَهُۥ وَٱلَّذِينَ ءَامَنُواْ فَإِنَّ حِزْبَ ٱللَّهِ هُمُ ٱلْغَـٰلِبُونَ (٥٦) يَـٰٓأَيُّهَا ٱلَّذِينَ ءَامَنُواْ لَا تَتَّخِذُواْ ٱلَّذِينَ ٱتَّخَذُواْ دِينَكُمْ هُزُوًا وَلَعِبًا مِّنَ ٱلَّذِينَ أُوتُواْ ٱلْكِتَـٰبَ مِن قَبْلِكُمْ وَٱلْكُفَّارَ

أَوْلِيَآءَۘ وَٱتَّقُواْ ٱللَّهَ إِن كُنتُم مُّؤْمِنِينَ (٥٧) وَإِذَا نَادَيْتُمْ إِلَى ٱلصَّلَوٰةِ ٱتَّخَذُوهَا هُزُوًا وَلَعِبًاۚ ذَٰلِكَ بِأَنَّهُمْ قَوْمٌ لَّا يَعْقِلُونَ (٥٨) قُلْ يَٰٓأَهْلَ ٱلْكِتَٰبِ هَلْ تَنقِمُونَ مِنَّآ إِلَّآ أَنْ ءَامَنَّا بِٱللَّهِ وَمَآ أُنزِلَ إِلَيْنَا وَمَآ أُنزِلَ مِن قَبْلُ وَأَنَّ أَكْثَرَكُمْ فَٰسِقُونَ (٥٩)

O you who believe! Take not the Jews and the Christians as Auliyâ' (friends, protectors, helpers), they are but Auliyâ' of each other. And if any amongst you takes them (as Auliyâ'), then surely he is one of them. Verily, Allâh guides not those people who are the Zâlimûn (polytheists and wrong-doers and unjust). (51) And you see those in whose hearts there is a disease (of hypocrisy), they hurry to their friendship, saying: "We fear lest some misfortune of a disaster may befall us." Perhaps Allâh may bring a victory or a decision according to His Will. Then they will become regretful for what they have been keeping as a secret in themselves. (52) And those who believe will say: "Are these the men (hypocrites) who swore their strongest oaths by Allâh that they were with you (Muslims)?" All that they did has been in vain (because of their hypocrisy), and they have become the losers. (53) O you who believe! Whoever from among you turns back from his religion (Islâm), Allâh will bring a people whom He will love and they will love Him; humble towards the believers, stern towards the disbelievers, fighting in the Way of Allâh, and never fear of the blame of the blamers. That is the Grace of Allâh which He bestows on whom He wills. And Allâh is All-Sufficient for His creatures' needs, All-Knower. (54) Verily, your Walî (Protector or Helper) is none other than Allâh, His Messenger, and the believers, - those who perform As-Salât (Iqâmat-as-Salât), and give Zakât, and they are Rakiun (those who bow down or submit themselves with obedience to Allâh in prayer). (55) And whosoever takes Allâh, His Messenger, and those who have believed, as Protectors, then the party of Allâh will be the victorious. (56) O you who believe! Take not as Auliyâ' (protectors and helpers) those who take your religion as a mockery and fun from among those who received the Scripture (Jews and Christians) before you, nor from among the disbelievers; and fear Allâh if you indeed are true believers. (57) And when you proclaim the call for As-Salât [call for the prayer (Adhân)], they take it (but) as a mockery and fun; that is because they are a people who understand not. (58) Say: "O people of the Scripture (Jews and Christians)! Do you criticize us for no other reason than that we believe in Allâh, and in (the revelation) which has been sent down to us and in that which has been sent down before (us), and that most of you are Fâsiqûn [rebellious and disobedient (to Allâh)]?" (59)

Quran 5:87-95

يَـٰٓأَيُّهَا ٱلَّذِينَ ءَامَنُوا۟ لَا تُحَرِّمُوا۟ طَيِّبَـٰتِ مَآ أَحَلَّ ٱللَّهُ لَكُمْ وَلَا تَعْتَدُوٓا۟ إِنَّ ٱللَّهَ لَا يُحِبُّ ٱلْمُعْتَدِينَ (٨٧) وَكُلُوا۟ مِمَّا رَزَقَكُمُ ٱللَّهُ حَلَـٰلًا طَيِّبًا وَٱتَّقُوا۟ ٱللَّهَ ٱلَّذِىٓ أَنتُم بِهِۦ مُؤْمِنُونَ (٨٨) لَا يُؤَاخِذُكُمُ ٱللَّهُ بِٱللَّغْوِ فِىٓ أَيْمَـٰنِكُمْ وَلَـٰكِن يُؤَاخِذُكُم بِمَا عَقَّدتُّمُ ٱلْأَيْمَـٰنَ فَكَفَّـٰرَتُهُۥٓ إِطْعَامُ عَشَرَةِ مَسَـٰكِينَ مِنْ أَوْسَطِ مَا تُطْعِمُونَ أَهْلِيكُمْ أَوْ كِسْوَتُهُمْ أَوْ تَحْرِيرُ رَقَبَةٍ فَمَن لَّمْ يَجِدْ فَصِيَامُ ثَلَـٰثَةِ أَيَّامٍ ذَٰلِكَ كَفَّـٰرَةُ أَيْمَـٰنِكُمْ إِذَا حَلَفْتُمْ وَٱحْفَظُوٓا۟ أَيْمَـٰنَكُمْ كَذَٰلِكَ يُبَيِّنُ ٱللَّهُ لَكُمْ ءَايَـٰتِهِۦ لَعَلَّكُمْ

تَشْكُرُونَ (٨٩) يَـٰٓأَيُّهَا ٱلَّذِينَ ءَامَنُوٓاْ إِنَّمَا ٱلْخَمْرُ وَٱلْمَيْسِرُ وَٱلْأَنصَابُ وَٱلْأَزْلَـٰمُ رِجْسٌ مِّنْ عَمَلِ ٱلشَّيْطَـٰنِ فَٱجْتَنِبُوهُ لَعَلَّكُمْ تُفْلِحُونَ (٩٠) إِنَّمَا يُرِيدُ ٱلشَّيْطَـٰنُ أَن يُوقِعَ بَيْنَكُمُ ٱلْعَدَٰوَةَ وَٱلْبَغْضَآءَ فِى ٱلْخَمْرِ وَٱلْمَيْسِرِ وَيَصُدَّكُمْ عَن ذِكْرِ ٱللَّهِ وَعَنِ ٱلصَّلَوٰةِ فَهَلْ أَنتُم مُّنتَهُونَ (٩١) وَأَطِيعُواْ ٱللَّهَ وَأَطِيعُواْ ٱلرَّسُولَ وَٱحْذَرُواْ فَإِن تَوَلَّيْتُمْ فَٱعْلَمُوٓاْ أَنَّمَا عَلَىٰ رَسُولِنَا ٱلْبَلَـٰغُ ٱلْمُبِينُ (٩٢) لَيْسَ عَلَى ٱلَّذِينَ ءَامَنُواْ وَعَمِلُواْ ٱلصَّـٰلِحَـٰتِ جُنَاحٌ فِيمَا طَعِمُوٓاْ إِذَا مَا ٱتَّقَواْ وَّءَامَنُواْ وَعَمِلُواْ ٱلصَّـٰلِحَـٰتِ ثُمَّ ٱتَّقَواْ وَّءَامَنُواْ ثُمَّ ٱتَّقَواْ وَّأَحْسَنُواْ وَٱللَّهُ يُحِبُّ ٱلْمُحْسِنِينَ (٩٣) يَـٰٓأَيُّهَا ٱلَّذِينَ ءَامَنُواْ لَيَبْلُوَنَّكُمُ ٱللَّهُ بِشَىْءٍ مِّنَ ٱلصَّيْدِ تَنَالُهُۥٓ أَيْدِيكُمْ وَرِمَاحُكُمْ لِيَعْلَمَ ٱللَّهُ مَن يَخَافُهُۥ بِٱلْغَيْبِ فَمَنِ ٱعْتَدَىٰ بَعْدَ ذَٰلِكَ فَلَهُۥ عَذَابٌ أَلِيمٌ (٩٤) يَـٰٓأَيُّهَا ٱلَّذِينَ ءَامَنُواْ لَا تَقْتُلُواْ ٱلصَّيْدَ وَأَنتُمْ حُرُمٌ وَمَن قَتَلَهُۥ مِنكُم مُّتَعَمِّدًا فَجَزَآءٌ مِّثْلُ مَا قَتَلَ مِنَ ٱلنَّعَمِ يَحْكُمُ بِهِۦ ذَوَا عَدْلٍ مِّنكُمْ هَدْيًۢا بَـٰلِغَ ٱلْكَعْبَةِ أَوْ كَفَّـٰرَةٌ طَعَامُ مَسَـٰكِينَ أَوْ عَدْلُ ذَٰلِكَ صِيَامًا لِّيَذُوقَ وَبَالَ أَمْرِهِۦ عَفَا ٱللَّهُ عَمَّا سَلَفَ وَمَنْ عَادَ فَيَنتَقِمُ ٱللَّهُ مِنْهُ وَٱللَّهُ عَزِيزٌ ذُو ٱنتِقَامٍ (٩٥)

O you who believe! Make not unlawful the Tayyibât (all that is good as regards foods, things, deeds, beliefs, persons) which Allâh has made lawful to you, and transgress not. Verily, Allâh does not like the transgressors. (87) And eat of the things which Allâh has provided for you, lawful and good, and fear Allâh in Whom you believe. (88) Allâh will not punish you for what is unintentional in your oaths, but He will punish you for your deliberate oaths; for its expiation feed ten Masâkîn (poor persons), on a scale of the average of that with which you feed your own families, or clothe them or manumit a slave. But whosoever cannot afford (that), then he should fast for three days. That is the expiation for the oaths when you have sworn. And protect your oaths (i.e. do not swear much). Thus Allâh make clear to you His Ayât (proofs, evidence, verses, lessons, signs, revelations, etc.) that you may be grateful. (89) O you who believe! Intoxicants, gambling, and Al-Ansâb, and Al¬Azlâm (arrows for seeking luck or decision) are an abomination of Shaitân's (Satan) handiwork. So avoid (strictly all) that (abomination) in order that you may be successful. (90) Shaitân (Satan) wants only to excite enmity and hatred between you with intoxicants (alcoholic drinks) and gambling, and hinder you from the remembrance of Allâh and from As-Salât (the prayer). So, will you not then abstain? (91) And obey Allâh and the Messenger (Muhammad), and beware (of even coming near to drinking or gambling or Al-Ansâb, or Al-Azlâm, etc.) and fear Allâh. Then if you turn away, you should know that it is Our Messenger's duty to convey (the Message) in the clearest way. (92) Those who believe and do righteous good deeds, there is no sin on them for what they ate (in the past), if they fear Allâh (by keeping away from His forbidden things), and believe and do righteous good deeds, and again fear Allâh and believe, and once again fear Allâh and do good deeds with Ihsân (perfection). And Allâh loves the good-doers. (93) O you who believe! Allâh will certainly make a trial of you with something in (the matter of) the game that is well within reach of your hands and your lances, that Allâh may test who fears Him unseen. Then whoever transgresses thereafter, for him there is a painful torment (94) O you who believe! Kill not game while you are in a state of

Ihrâm for Hajj or 'Umrah (pilgrimage), and whosoever of you kills it intentionally, the penalty is an offering, brought to the Ka'bah, of an eatable animal equivalent to the one he killed, as adjudged by two just men among you; or, for expiation, he should feed Masâkin (poor persons), or its equivalent in Saum (fasting), that he may taste the heaviness (punishment) of his deed. Allâh has forgiven what is past, but whosoever commits it again, Allâh will take retribution from him. And Allâh is All¬Mighty, All-Able of Retribution (95)

Quran 5:101-102

يَـٰٓأَيُّهَا ٱلَّذِينَ ءَامَنُواْ لَا تَسْـَٔلُواْ عَنْ أَشْيَآءَ إِن تُبْدَ لَكُمْ تَسُؤْكُمْ وَإِن تَسْـَٔلُواْ عَنْهَا حِينَ يُنَزَّلُ ٱلْقُرْءَانُ تُبْدَ لَكُمْ عَفَا ٱللَّهُ عَنْهَاۗ وَٱللَّهُ غَفُورٌ حَلِيمٌ (١٠١) قَدْ سَأَلَهَا قَوْمٌ مِّن قَبْلِكُمْ ثُمَّ أَصْبَحُواْ بِهَا كَـٰفِرِينَ (١٠٢)

O you who believe! Ask not about things which, if made plain to you, may cause you trouble. But if you ask about them while the Qur'ân is being revealed, they will be made plain to you. Allâh has forgiven that, and Allâh is Oft¬Forgiving, Most Forbearing. (101) Before you, a community asked such questions, then on that account they became disbelievers. (102)

Quran 5:105-108

يَـٰٓأَيُّهَا ٱلَّذِينَ ءَامَنُواْ عَلَيْكُمْ أَنفُسَكُمْۖ لَا يَضُرُّكُم مَّن ضَلَّ إِذَا ٱهْتَدَيْتُمْۚ إِلَى ٱللَّهِ مَرْجِعُكُمْ جَمِيعًا فَيُنَبِّئُكُم بِمَا كُنتُمْ تَعْمَلُونَ (١٠٥) يَـٰٓأَيُّهَا ٱلَّذِينَ ءَامَنُواْ شَهَـٰدَةُ بَيْنِكُمْ إِذَا حَضَرَ أَحَدَكُمُ ٱلْمَوْتُ حِينَ ٱلْوَصِيَّةِ ٱثْنَانِ ذَوَا عَدْلٍ مِّنكُمْ أَوْ ءَاخَرَانِ مِنْ غَيْرِكُمْ إِنْ أَنتُمْ ضَرَبْتُمْ فِى ٱلْأَرْضِ فَأَصَـٰبَتْكُم مُّصِيبَةُ ٱلْمَوْتِۚ تَحْبِسُونَهُمَا مِنۢ بَعْدِ ٱلصَّلَوٰةِ فَيُقْسِمَانِ بِٱللَّهِ إِنِ ٱرْتَبْتُمْ لَا نَشْتَرِى بِهِۦ ثَمَنًا

وَلَوْ كَانَ ذَا قُرْبَىٰ وَلَا نَكْتُمُ شَهَٰدَةَ ٱللَّهِ إِنَّآ إِذًا لَّمِنَ ٱلْـَٔاثِمِينَ (١٠٦) فَإِنْ عُثِرَ عَلَىٰٓ أَنَّهُمَا ٱسْتَحَقَّآ إِثْمًا فَـَٔاخَرَانِ يَقُومَانِ مَقَامَهُمَا مِنَ ٱلَّذِينَ ٱسْتَحَقَّ عَلَيْهِمُ ٱلْأَوْلَيَٰنِ فَيُقْسِمَانِ بِٱللَّهِ لَشَهَٰدَتُنَآ أَحَقُّ مِن شَهَٰدَتِهِمَا وَمَا ٱعْتَدَيْنَآ إِنَّآ إِذًا لَّمِنَ ٱلظَّٰلِمِينَ (١٠٧) ذَٰلِكَ أَدْنَىٰٓ أَن يَأْتُوا۟ بِٱلشَّهَٰدَةِ عَلَىٰ وَجْهِهَآ أَوْ يَخَافُوٓا۟ أَن تُرَدَّ أَيْمَٰنٌ بَعْدَ أَيْمَٰنِهِمْ وَٱتَّقُوا۟ ٱللَّهَ وَٱسْمَعُوا۟ وَٱللَّهُ لَا يَهْدِى ٱلْقَوْمَ ٱلْفَٰسِقِينَ (١٠٨)

O you who believe! Take care of your ownselves, If you follow the (right) guidance (and enjoin what is right Islâmic Monotheism and all that Islâm orders one to do) and forbid what is wrong (polytheism, disbelief and all that Islâm has forbidden) no hurt can come to you from those who are in error. The return of you all is to Allâh, then He will inform you about (all) that which you used to do. (105) O you who believe! When death approaches any of you, and you make a bequest, (then take) the testimony of two just men of your own folk or two others from outside, While you are travelling through the land and death befalls you. Detain them both after As-Salât (the prayer), (then) if you are in doubt (about their truthfulness), let them both swear by Allâh (saying): "We wish not for any worldly gain in this, even though he (the beneficiary) be our near relative. We shall not hide Testimony of Allâh, for then indeed we should be of the sinful." (106) If then it gets known that these two had been guilty of sin, let two others stand forth in their places, nearest in kin from among those who claim a lawful right. Let them swear by Allâh (saying): "We affirm that our testimony is truer than that of both of them, and that we have not trespassed (the truth), for then indeed we should be of the wrong-doers." (107) That should make it closer (to the fact) that their testimony would be in its true shape (and thus accepted), or else they would fear that (other) oaths would be admitted after their oaths. And fear Allâh and listen (with obedience to Him). And Allâh guides not the people who are Al-Fâsiqûn (the rebellious and disobedient). (108)

Quran 6:54

وَإِذَا جَآءَكَ ٱلَّذِينَ يُؤْمِنُونَ بِـَٔايَٰتِنَا فَقُلْ سَلَٰمٌ عَلَيْكُمْ ۖ كَتَبَ رَبُّكُمْ عَلَىٰ نَفْسِهِ ٱلرَّحْمَةَ ۖ أَنَّهُۥ مَنْ عَمِلَ مِنكُمْ سُوٓءًۢا بِجَهَٰلَةٍ ثُمَّ تَابَ مِنۢ بَعْدِهِۦ وَأَصْلَحَ فَأَنَّهُۥ غَفُورٌ رَّحِيمٌ

When those who believe in Our Ayât (proofs, evidences, verses, lessons, signs, revelations, etc.) come to you, say: "Salâmun 'Alaikum" (peace be on you); your Lord has written (prescribed) Mercy for Himself, so that, if any of you does evil in ignorance, and thereafter repents and does righteous good deeds (by obeying Allâh), then surely, He is Oft-Forgiving, Most Merciful. (54)

Quran 6:92

وَهَٰذَا كِتَٰبٌ أَنزَلْنَٰهُ مُبَارَكٌ مُّصَدِّقُ ٱلَّذِى بَيْنَ يَدَيْهِ وَلِتُنذِرَ أُمَّ ٱلْقُرَىٰ وَمَنْ حَوْلَهَا ۚ وَٱلَّذِينَ يُؤْمِنُونَ بِٱلْـَٔاخِرَةِ يُؤْمِنُونَ بِهِۦ ۖ وَهُمْ عَلَىٰ صَلَاتِهِمْ يُحَافِظُونَ

And this (the Qur'ân) is a blessed Book which We have sent down, confirming (the revelations) which came before it, so that you may warn the Mother of Towns (i.e.

Makkah) and all those around it. Those who believe in the Hereafter believe in it (the Qur'ân), and they are constant in guarding their Salât (prayers). (92)

Quran 6:99

وَهُوَ ٱلَّذِىٓ أَنزَلَ مِنَ ٱلسَّمَآءِ مَآءً فَأَخْرَجْنَا بِهِۦ نَبَاتَ كُلِّ شَىْءٍ فَأَخْرَجْنَا مِنْهُ خَضِرًا نُّخْرِجُ مِنْهُ حَبًّا مُّتَرَاكِبًا وَمِنَ ٱلنَّخْلِ مِن طَلْعِهَا قِنْوَانٌ دَانِيَةٌ وَجَنَّـٰتٍ مِّنْ أَعْنَابٍ وَٱلزَّيْتُونَ وَٱلرُّمَّانَ مُشْتَبِهًا وَغَيْرَ مُتَشَـٰبِهٍ ٱنظُرُوٓاْ إِلَىٰ ثَمَرِهِۦٓ إِذَآ أَثْمَرَ وَيَنْعِهِۦٓ إِنَّ فِى ذَٰلِكُمْ لَأَيَـٰتٍ لِّقَوْمٍ يُؤْمِنُونَ

It is He Who sends down water (rain) from the sky, and with it We bring forth vegetation of all kinds, and out of it We bring forth green stalks, from which We bring forth thick clustered grain. And out of the date-palm and its spathe come forth clusters of dates hanging low and near, and gardens of grapes, olives and pomegranates, each similar (in kind) yet different (in variety and taste). Look at their fruits when they begin to bear, and the ripeness thereof. Verily! In these things there are signs for people who believe. (99)

Quran 6:125

وَلَا تَأْكُلُواْ مِمَّا لَمْ يُذْكَرِ ٱسْمُ ٱللَّهِ عَلَيْهِ وَإِنَّهُۥ لَفِسْقٌ وَإِنَّ ٱلشَّيَـٰطِينَ لَيُوحُونَ إِلَىٰٓ أَوْلِيَآئِهِمْ لِيُجَـٰدِلُوكُمْ وَإِنْ أَطَعْتُمُوهُمْ إِنَّكُمْ لَمُشْرِكُونَ (١٢١) أَوَمَن كَانَ مَيْتًا فَأَحْيَيْنَـٰهُ وَجَعَلْنَا لَهُۥ نُورًا يَمْشِى بِهِۦ فِى ٱلنَّاسِ كَمَن مَّثَلُهُۥ فِى ٱلظُّلُمَـٰتِ لَيْسَ بِخَارِجٍ مِّنْهَا كَذَٰلِكَ زُيِّنَ لِلْكَـٰفِرِينَ مَا كَانُواْ يَعْمَلُونَ (١٢٢) وَكَذَٰلِكَ جَعَلْنَا فِى كُلِّ قَرْيَةٍ أَكَـٰبِرَ مُجْرِمِيهَا لِيَمْكُرُواْ فِيهَا وَمَا يَمْكُرُونَ إِلَّا بِأَنفُسِهِمْ وَمَا يَشْعُرُونَ (١٢٣) وَإِذَا جَآءَتْهُمْ ءَايَةٌ قَالُواْ لَن نُّؤْمِنَ حَتَّىٰ نُؤْتَىٰ مِثْلَ مَآ أُوتِىَ رُسُلُ ٱللَّهِ ٱللَّهُ أَعْلَمُ حَيْثُ يَجْعَلُ رِسَالَتَهُۥ

سَيُصِيبُ ٱلَّذِينَ أَجْرَمُوا۟ صَغَارٌ عِندَ ٱللَّهِ وَعَذَابٌ شَدِيدٌۢ بِمَا كَانُوا۟ يَمْكُرُونَ (١٢٤) فَمَن يُرِدِ ٱللَّهُ أَن يَهْدِيَهُۥ يَشْرَحْ صَدْرَهُۥ لِلْإِسْلَٰمِ ۖ وَمَن يُرِدْ أَن يُضِلَّهُۥ يَجْعَلْ صَدْرَهُۥ ضَيِّقًا حَرَجًا كَأَنَّمَا يَصَّعَّدُ فِى ٱلسَّمَآءِ ۚ كَذَٰلِكَ يَجْعَلُ ٱللَّهُ ٱلرِّجْسَ عَلَى ٱلَّذِينَ لَا يُؤْمِنُونَ (١٢٥)

Eat not (O believers) of that (meat) on which Allâh's Name has not been pronounced (at the time of the slaughtering of the animal), for sure it is Fisq (a sin and disobedience of Allâh). And certainly, the Shayâtin (devils) do inspire their friends (from mankind) to dispute with you, and if you obey them [by making Al¬Maitah (a dead animal) legal by eating it], then you would indeed be Mushrikûn (polytheists) [because they (devils and their friends) made lawful to you to eat that which Allâh has made unlawful to eat and you obeyed them by considering it lawful to eat, and by doing so you worshipped them, and to worship others besides Allâh is polytheism]. (121) Is he who was dead (without Faith by ignorance and disbelief) and We gave him life (by knowledge and Faith) and set for him a light (of Belief) whereby he can walk amongst men — like him who is in the darkness (of disbelief, polytheism and hypocrisy) from which he can never come out? Thus it is made fair¬seeming to the disbelievers that which they used to do. (122) And thus We have set up in every town great ones of its wicked people to plot therein. But they plot not except against their ownselves, and they perceive (it) not. (123) And when there comes to them a sign (from Allâh) they say: "We shall not believe until we receive the like of that which the Messengers of Allâh had received." Allâh knows best with whom to place His Message. Humiliation and disgrace from Allâh and a severe torment will overtake the criminals (polytheists, sinners) for that which they used to plot. (124) And whomsoever Allâh wills to guide, He opens his breast to Islâm, and whomsoever He wills to send astray, He makes his breast closed and constricted, as if he is climbing up to the sky. Thus Allâh puts the wrath on those who believe not. (125)

Quran 7:2

كِتَٰبٌ أُنزِلَ إِلَيْكَ فَلَا يَكُن فِى صَدْرِكَ حَرَجٌ مِّنْهُ لِتُنذِرَ بِهِۦ وَذِكْرَىٰ لِلْمُؤْمِنِينَ

(This is the) Book (the Qur'ân) sent down unto you (O Muhammad), so let not your breast be narrow therefrom, that you warn thereby, and a reminder unto the believers. (2)

Quran 7:42-44

وَٱلَّذِينَ ءَامَنُواْ وَعَمِلُواْ ٱلصَّٰلِحَٰتِ لَا نُكَلِّفُ نَفْسًا إِلَّا وُسْعَهَآ أُوْلَٰٓئِكَ أَصْحَٰبُ ٱلْجَنَّةِ هُمْ فِيهَا خَٰلِدُونَ (٤٢) وَنَزَعْنَا مَا فِى صُدُورِهِم مِّنْ غِلٍّ تَجْرِى مِن تَحْتِهِمُ ٱلْأَنْهَٰرُ وَقَالُواْ ٱلْحَمْدُ لِلَّهِ ٱلَّذِى هَدَىٰنَا لِهَٰذَا وَمَا كُنَّا لِنَهْتَدِىَ لَوْلَآ أَنْ هَدَىٰنَا ٱللَّهُ لَقَدْ جَآءَتْ رُسُلُ رَبِّنَا بِٱلْحَقِّ وَنُودُوٓاْ أَن تِلْكُمُ ٱلْجَنَّةُ أُورِثْتُمُوهَا بِمَا كُنتُمْ تَعْمَلُونَ (٤٣) وَنَادَىٰٓ أَصْحَٰبُ ٱلْجَنَّةِ أَصْحَٰبَ ٱلنَّارِ أَن قَدْ وَجَدْنَا مَا وَعَدَنَا رَبُّنَا حَقًّا فَهَلْ وَجَدتُّم مَّا وَعَدَ رَبُّكُمْ حَقًّا قَالُواْ نَعَمْ فَأَذَّنَ مُؤَذِّنٌۢ بَيْنَهُمْ أَن لَّعْنَةُ ٱللَّهِ عَلَى ٱلظَّٰلِمِينَ (٤٤)

But those who believed (in the Oneness of Allâh - Islâmic Monotheism), and worked righteousness - We tax not any person beyond his scope, — such are the dwellers of Paradise. They will abide therein. (42) And We shall remove from their breasts any (mutual) hatred or sense of injury (which they had, if at all, in the life of this world); rivers flowing under them, and they will say: "All the praises and thanks be to Allâh, Who has guided us to this, and never could we have found guidance, were it not that Allâh had guided us! Indeed, the Messengers of our Lord did come with the truth." And it will be cried out to them: "This is the Paradise which you have inherited for what you used to do." (43) And the dwellers of Paradise will call out to the dwellers of the Fire (saying): "We have indeed found true what our Lord had promised us; have you also found true, what your Lord promised (warnings)?" They shall say: "Yes." Then a crier will proclaim between them: "The Curse of Allâh is on the Zâlimûn (polytheists and wrong-doers)," (44)

Quran 8:2-4

إِنَّمَا ٱلْمُؤْمِنُونَ ٱلَّذِينَ إِذَا ذُكِرَ ٱللَّهُ وَجِلَتْ قُلُوبُهُمْ وَإِذَا تُلِيَتْ عَلَيْهِمْ ءَايَٰتُهُۥ زَادَتْهُمْ إِيمَٰنًا وَعَلَىٰ رَبِّهِمْ يَتَوَكَّلُونَ (٢) ٱلَّذِينَ يُقِيمُونَ ٱلصَّلَوٰةَ وَمِمَّا رَزَقْنَٰهُمْ يُنفِقُونَ (٣) أُو۟لَٰٓئِكَ هُمُ ٱلْمُؤْمِنُونَ حَقًّا ۚ لَّهُمْ دَرَجَٰتٌ عِندَ رَبِّهِمْ وَمَغْفِرَةٌ وَرِزْقٌ كَرِيمٌ (٤)

The believers are only those who, when Allâh is mentioned, feel a fear in their hearts and when His Verses (this Qur'ân) are recited unto them, they (i.e. the Verses) increase their Faith; and they put their trust in their Lord (Alone); (2) Who perform As-Salât (Iqâmat-as-Salât) and spend out of that We have provided them. (3) It is they who are the believers in truth. For them are grades of dignity with their Lord, and Forgiveness and a generous provision (Paradise). (4)

Quran 8:15-16

يَـٰٓأَيُّهَا ٱلَّذِينَ ءَامَنُوٓاْ إِذَا لَقِيتُمُ ٱلَّذِينَ كَفَرُواْ زَحْفًا فَلَا تُوَلُّوهُمُ ٱلْأَدْبَارَ (١٥) وَمَن يُوَلِّهِمْ يَوْمَئِذٍ دُبُرَهُۥٓ إِلَّا مُتَحَرِّفًا لِّقِتَالٍ أَوْ مُتَحَيِّزًا إِلَىٰ فِئَةٍ فَقَدْ بَآءَ بِغَضَبٍ مِّنَ ٱللَّهِ وَمَأْوَىٰهُ جَهَنَّمُ وَبِئْسَ ٱلْمَصِيرُ (١٦)

O you who believe! When you meet those who disbelieve, in a battle-field, never turn your backs to them. (15) And whoever turns his back to them on such a day - unless it be a stratagem of war, or to retreat to a troop (of his own), - he indeed has drawn upon himself wrath from Allâh. And his abode is Hell, and worst indeed is that destination! (16)

Quran 8:20-29

يَـٰٓأَيُّهَا ٱلَّذِينَ ءَامَنُوٓاْ أَطِيعُواْ ٱللَّهَ وَرَسُولَهُۥ وَلَا تَوَلَّوْاْ عَنْهُ وَأَنتُمْ تَسْمَعُونَ (٢٠) وَلَا تَكُونُواْ كَٱلَّذِينَ قَالُواْ سَمِعْنَا وَهُمْ لَا يَسْمَعُونَ (٢١) ۞ إِنَّ شَرَّ ٱلدَّوَآبِّ عِندَ ٱللَّهِ ٱلصُّمُّ ٱلْبُكْمُ ٱلَّذِينَ لَا يَعْقِلُونَ (٢٢) وَلَوْ عَلِمَ ٱللَّهُ فِيهِمْ خَيْرًا لَّأَسْمَعَهُمْ وَلَوْ أَسْمَعَهُمْ لَتَوَلَّواْ وَّهُم مُّعْرِضُونَ (٢٣) يَـٰٓأَيُّهَا ٱلَّذِينَ ءَامَنُواْ ٱسْتَجِيبُواْ لِلَّهِ وَلِلرَّسُولِ إِذَا دَعَاكُمْ لِمَا يُحْيِيكُمْ وَٱعْلَمُوٓاْ أَنَّ ٱللَّهَ يَحُولُ بَيْنَ ٱلْمَرْءِ وَقَلْبِهِۦ وَأَنَّهُۥٓ إِلَيْهِ تُحْشَرُونَ (٢٤) وَٱتَّقُواْ فِتْنَةً لَّا تُصِيبَنَّ ٱلَّذِينَ ظَلَمُواْ مِنكُمْ خَآصَّةً وَٱعْلَمُوٓاْ أَنَّ ٱللَّهَ شَدِيدُ ٱلْعِقَابِ (٢٥) وَٱذْكُرُوٓاْ إِذْ أَنتُمْ قَلِيلٌ مُّسْتَضْعَفُونَ فِى ٱلْأَرْضِ تَخَافُونَ أَن يَتَخَطَّفَكُمُ ٱلنَّاسُ فَـَٔاوَىٰكُمْ وَأَيَّدَكُم بِنَصْرِهِۦ وَرَزَقَكُم مِّنَ ٱلطَّيِّبَاتِ لَعَلَّكُمْ تَشْكُرُونَ (٢٦) يَـٰٓأَيُّهَا ٱلَّذِينَ ءَامَنُواْ لَا تَخُونُواْ ٱللَّهَ وَٱلرَّسُولَ وَتَخُونُوٓاْ أَمَـٰنَـٰتِكُمْ وَأَنتُمْ تَعْلَمُونَ (٢٧) وَٱعْلَمُوٓاْ

أَنَّمَآ أَمْوَٰلُكُمْ وَأَوْلَٰدُكُمْ فِتْنَةٌ وَأَنَّ ٱللَّهَ عِندَهُۥٓ أَجْرٌ عَظِيمٌ (٢٨) يَٰٓأَيُّهَا ٱلَّذِينَ ءَامَنُوٓا۟ إِن تَتَّقُوا۟ ٱللَّهَ يَجْعَل لَّكُمْ فُرْقَانًا وَيُكَفِّرْ عَنكُمْ سَيِّـَٔاتِكُمْ وَيَغْفِرْ لَكُمْ ۗ وَٱللَّهُ ذُو ٱلْفَضْلِ ٱلْعَظِيمِ (٢٩)

O you who believe! Obey Allâh and His Messenger, and turn not away from him (i.e. Messenger Muhammad) while you are hearing. (20) And be not like those who say: "We have heard," but they hear not. (21) Verily! The worst of (moving) living creatures with Allâh are the deaf and the dumb, who understand not (i.e. the disbelievers) (22) Had Allâh known of any good in them, He would indeed have made them listen; and even if He had made them listen, they would but have turned away with aversion (to the truth). (23) O you who believe! Answer Allâh (by obeying Him) and (His) Messenger when he calls you to that which will give you life, and know that Allâh comes in between a person and his heart (i.e. He prevents an evil person to decide anything). And verily to Him you shall (all) be gathered. (24) And fear the Fitnah (affliction and trial) which affects not in particular (only) those of you who do wrong (but it may afflict all the good and the bad people), and know that Allâh is Severe in punishment. (25) And remember when you were few and were reckoned weak in the land, and were afraid that men might kidnap you, but He provided a safe place for you, strengthened you with His Help, and provided you with good things so that you might be grateful. (26) O you who believe! Betray not Allâh and His Messenger, nor betray knowingly your Amânât (things entrusted to you, and all the duties which Allâh has ordained for you). (27) And know that your possessions and your children are but a trial and that surely with Allâh is a mighty reward. (28) O you who believe! If you obey and fear Allâh, He will grant you Furqân [(a criterion to judge between right and wrong), or (Makhraj, i.e. a way for you to get out from every difficulty)], and will expiate for you your sins, and forgive you; and Allâh is the Owner of the Great Bounty. (29)

Quran 8:45-47

يَٰٓأَيُّهَا ٱلَّذِينَ ءَامَنُوٓاْ إِذَا لَقِيتُمْ فِئَةً فَٱثْبُتُواْ وَٱذْكُرُواْ ٱللَّهَ كَثِيرًا لَّعَلَّكُمْ تُفْلِحُونَ (٤٥) وَأَطِيعُواْ ٱللَّهَ وَرَسُولَهُۥ وَلَا تَنَٰزَعُواْ فَتَفْشَلُواْ وَتَذْهَبَ رِيحُكُمْ ۖ وَٱصْبِرُوٓاْ إِنَّ ٱللَّهَ مَعَ ٱلصَّٰبِرِينَ (٤٦) وَلَا تَكُونُواْ كَٱلَّذِينَ خَرَجُواْ مِن دِيَٰرِهِم بَطَرًا وَرِئَآءَ ٱلنَّاسِ وَيَصُدُّونَ عَن سَبِيلِ ٱللَّهِ ۚ وَٱللَّهُ بِمَا يَعْمَلُونَ مُحِيطٌ (٤٧)

O you who believe! When you meet (an enemy) force, take a firm stand against them and remember the Name of Allâh much (both with tongue and mind), so that you may be successful. (45) And obey Allâh and His Messenger, and do not dispute (with one another) lest you lose courage and your strength departs, and be patient. Surely, Allâh is with those who are As-Sâbirûn (the patient). (46) And be not like those who come out of their homes boastfully and to be seen of men, and hinder (men) from the Path of Allâh. and Allâh is Muhîtun (encircling and thoroughly comprehending) all that they do. (47)

Quran 8:72-75

إِنَّ ٱلَّذِينَ ءَامَنُواْ وَهَاجَرُواْ وَجَٰهَدُواْ بِأَمْوَٰلِهِمْ وَأَنفُسِهِمْ فِى سَبِيلِ ٱللَّهِ وَٱلَّذِينَ ءَاوَواْ وَّنَصَرُواْ أُوْلَٰٓئِكَ بَعْضُهُمْ أَوْلِيَآءُ بَعْضٍۢ ۚ وَٱلَّذِينَ ءَامَنُواْ وَلَمْ يُهَاجِرُواْ مَا لَكُم مِّن وَلَٰيَتِهِم مِّن شَىْءٍ حَتَّىٰ يُهَاجِرُواْ ۚ وَإِنِ ٱسْتَنصَرُوكُمْ فِى ٱلدِّينِ فَعَلَيْكُمُ ٱلنَّصْرُ إِلَّا عَلَىٰ قَوْمٍۭ بَيْنَكُمْ وَبَيْنَهُم مِّيثَٰقٌۭ ۗ وَٱللَّهُ بِمَا تَعْمَلُونَ بَصِيرٌۭ (٧٢) وَٱلَّذِينَ كَفَرُواْ بَعْضُهُمْ أَوْلِيَآءُ بَعْضٍ ۚ إِلَّا تَفْعَلُوهُ تَكُن فِتْنَةٌۭ فِى ٱلْأَرْضِ وَفَسَادٌۭ كَبِيرٌۭ (٧٣) وَٱلَّذِينَ ءَامَنُواْ وَهَاجَرُواْ وَجَٰهَدُواْ فِى سَبِيلِ ٱللَّهِ وَٱلَّذِينَ ءَاوَواْ وَّنَصَرُواْ أُوْلَٰٓئِكَ هُمُ ٱلْمُؤْمِنُونَ حَقًّۭا ۚ لَّهُم مَّغْفِرَةٌۭ وَرِزْقٌۭ كَرِيمٌۭ (٧٤) وَٱلَّذِينَ ءَامَنُواْ مِنۢ بَعْدُ وَهَاجَرُواْ وَجَٰهَدُواْ مَعَكُمْ فَأُوْلَٰٓئِكَ مِنكُمْ ۚ وَأُوْلُواْ ٱلْأَرْحَامِ بَعْضُهُمْ أَوْلَىٰ بِبَعْضٍۢ فِى كِتَٰبِ ٱللَّهِ ۗ إِنَّ ٱللَّهَ بِكُلِّ شَىْءٍ عَلِيمٌۢ (٧٥)

Verily, those who believed, and emigrated and strove hard and fought with their property and their lives in the Cause of Allâh as well as those who gave (them) asylum and help, - these are (all) allies to one another. And as to those who believed but did not emigrate, you owe no duty of protection to them until they emigrate, but if they seek your help in religion, it is your duty to help them except against a people with whom you have a treaty of mutual alliance, and Allâh is the All-Seer of what you do. (72) And those who disbelieve are allies of one another, (and) if you (Muslims of the whole world collectively) do not do so [i.e. become allies, as one united block under one Khalifah (a chief Muslim ruler for the whole Muslim world) to make victorious Allâh's religion of Islâmic Monotheism], there will be Fitnah (wars, battles, polytheism) and oppression on the earth, and a great mischief and corruption (appearance of polytheism). (73) And those who believed, and emigrated and strove hard in the Cause of Allâh (Al-Jihâd), as well as those who gave (them) asylum and aid; - these are the believers in truth, for them is forgiveness and Rizqun Karîm (a generous provision i.e. Paradise). (74) And those who believed afterwards, and emigrated and strove hard along with you, (in the Cause of Allâh) they are of you. But kindred by blood are nearer to one another (regarding inheritance) in the decree ordained by Allâh. Verily, Allâh is the All-Knower of everything. (75)

Quran 9:18-20

إِنَّمَا يَعْمُرُ مَسَٰجِدَ ٱللَّهِ مَنْ ءَامَنَ بِٱللَّهِ وَٱلْيَوْمِ ٱلْءَاخِرِ وَأَقَامَ ٱلصَّلَوٰةَ وَءَاتَى ٱلزَّكَوٰةَ وَلَمْ يَخْشَ إِلَّا ٱللَّهَ فَعَسَىٰٓ أُوْلَٰٓئِكَ أَن يَكُونُوا۟ مِنَ ٱلْمُهْتَدِينَ (١٨) ۞ أَجَعَلْتُمْ سِقَايَةَ ٱلْحَآجِّ وَعِمَارَةَ ٱلْمَسْجِدِ ٱلْحَرَامِ كَمَنْ ءَامَنَ بِٱللَّهِ وَٱلْيَوْمِ ٱلْءَاخِرِ وَجَٰهَدَ فِى سَبِيلِ ٱللَّهِ لَا يَسْتَوُۥنَ عِندَ ٱللَّهِ وَٱللَّهُ لَا يَهْدِى ٱلْقَوْمَ ٱلظَّٰلِمِينَ (١٩) ٱلَّذِينَ ءَامَنُوا۟ وَهَاجَرُوا۟ وَجَٰهَدُوا۟ فِى سَبِيلِ ٱللَّهِ بِأَمْوَٰلِهِمْ وَأَنفُسِهِمْ أَعْظَمُ دَرَجَةً عِندَ ٱللَّهِ وَأُوْلَٰٓئِكَ هُمُ ٱلْفَآئِزُونَ (٢٠)

The Mosques of Allâh shall be maintained only by those who believe in Allâh and the Last Day; perform As-Salât (Iqâmat-as-Salât), and give Zakât and fear none but Allâh. It is they who are on true guidance. (18) Do you consider the providing of drinking water to the pilgrims and the maintenance of Al-Masjid-al-Harâm (at Makkah) as equal to the worth of those who believe in Allâh and the Last Day, and strive hard and fight in the Cause of Allâh? They are not equal before Allâh. And Allâh guides not those people who are the Zâlimûn (polytheists and wrong-doers). (19) Those who believed (in the Oneness of Allâh - Islâmic Monotheism) and emigrated and strove hard and fought in Allâh's Cause with their wealth and their lives are far higher in degree with Allâh. They are the successful. (20)

Quran 9:23-24

يَٰٓأَيُّهَا ٱلَّذِينَ ءَامَنُوا۟ لَا تَتَّخِذُوٓا۟ ءَابَآءَكُمْ وَإِخْوَٰنَكُمْ أَوْلِيَآءَ إِنِ ٱسْتَحَبُّوا۟ ٱلْكُفْرَ عَلَى ٱلْإِيمَٰنِ وَمَن يَتَوَلَّهُم مِّنكُمْ فَأُو۟لَٰٓئِكَ هُمُ ٱلظَّٰلِمُونَ (٢٣) قُلْ إِن كَانَ ءَابَآؤُكُمْ وَأَبْنَآؤُكُمْ وَإِخْوَٰنُكُمْ وَأَزْوَٰجُكُمْ وَعَشِيرَتُكُمْ وَأَمْوَٰلٌ ٱقْتَرَفْتُمُوهَا وَتِجَٰرَةٌ تَخْشَوْنَ كَسَادَهَا وَمَسَٰكِنُ تَرْضَوْنَهَآ أَحَبَّ إِلَيْكُم مِّنَ ٱللَّهِ وَرَسُولِهِۦ وَجِهَادٍ فِى سَبِيلِهِۦ فَتَرَبَّصُوا۟ حَتَّىٰ يَأْتِىَ ٱللَّهُ بِأَمْرِهِۦ وَٱللَّهُ لَا يَهْدِى ٱلْقَوْمَ ٱلْفَٰسِقِينَ (٢٤)

O you who believe! Take not for Auliyâ' (supporters and helpers) your fathers and your brothers if they prefer disbelief to Belief. And whoever of you does so, then he is one of the Zâlimûn (wrong-doers). (23) Say: If your fathers, your sons, your brothers, your wives, your kindred, the wealth that you have gained, the commerce in which you fear a decline, and the dwellings in which you delight are dearer to you than Allâh and His Messenger, and striving hard and fighting in His Cause, then wait until Allâh brings about His Decision (torment). And Allâh guides not the people who are Al-Fâsiqûn (the rebellious, disobedient to Allâh) (24)

Quran 9:28-34

يَـٰٓأَيُّهَا ٱلَّذِينَ ءَامَنُوٓا۟ إِنَّمَا ٱلْمُشْرِكُونَ نَجَسٌ فَلَا يَقْرَبُوا۟ ٱلْمَسْجِدَ ٱلْحَرَامَ بَعْدَ عَامِهِمْ هَـٰذَا ۚ وَإِنْ خِفْتُمْ عَيْلَةً فَسَوْفَ يُغْنِيكُمُ ٱللَّهُ مِن فَضْلِهِۦٓ إِن شَآءَ ۚ إِنَّ ٱللَّهَ عَلِيمٌ حَكِيمٌ (٢٨) قَـٰتِلُوا۟ ٱلَّذِينَ لَا يُؤْمِنُونَ بِٱللَّهِ وَلَا بِٱلْيَوْمِ ٱلْـَٔاخِرِ وَلَا يُحَرِّمُونَ مَا حَرَّمَ ٱللَّهُ وَرَسُولُهُۥ وَلَا يَدِينُونَ دِينَ ٱلْحَقِّ مِنَ ٱلَّذِينَ أُوتُوا۟ ٱلْكِتَـٰبَ حَتَّىٰ يُعْطُوا۟ ٱلْجِزْيَةَ عَن يَدٍ وَهُمْ صَـٰغِرُونَ (٢٩) وَقَالَتِ ٱلْيَهُودُ عُزَيْرٌ ٱبْنُ ٱللَّهِ وَقَالَتِ ٱلنَّصَـٰرَى ٱلْمَسِيحُ ٱبْنُ ٱللَّهِ ۖ ذَٰلِكَ قَوْلُهُم بِأَفْوَٰهِهِمْ ۖ يُضَـٰهِـُٔونَ قَوْلَ ٱلَّذِينَ كَفَرُوا۟ مِن قَبْلُ ۚ قَـٰتَلَهُمُ ٱللَّهُ ۚ أَنَّىٰ يُؤْفَكُونَ (٣٠) ٱتَّخَذُوٓا۟ أَحْبَارَهُمْ وَرُهْبَـٰنَهُمْ أَرْبَابًا مِّن دُونِ ٱللَّهِ وَٱلْمَسِيحَ ٱبْنَ مَرْيَمَ وَمَآ أُمِرُوٓا۟ إِلَّا لِيَعْبُدُوٓا۟ إِلَـٰهًا وَٰحِدًا ۖ لَّآ إِلَـٰهَ إِلَّا هُوَ ۚ سُبْحَـٰنَهُۥ عَمَّا يُشْرِكُونَ (٣١) يُرِيدُونَ أَن يُطْفِـُٔوا۟ نُورَ ٱللَّهِ بِأَفْوَٰهِهِمْ وَيَأْبَى ٱللَّهُ إِلَّآ أَن يُتِمَّ نُورَهُۥ وَلَوْ كَرِهَ ٱلْكَـٰفِرُونَ (٣٢) هُوَ ٱلَّذِىٓ أَرْسَلَ رَسُولَهُۥ بِٱلْهُدَىٰ وَدِينِ ٱلْحَقِّ لِيُظْهِرَهُۥ عَلَى ٱلدِّينِ كُلِّهِۦ وَلَوْ كَرِهَ ٱلْمُشْرِكُونَ (٣٣) ۞ يَـٰٓأَيُّهَا ٱلَّذِينَ ءَامَنُوٓا۟ إِنَّ كَثِيرًا مِّنَ ٱلْأَحْبَارِ وَٱلرُّهْبَانِ لَيَأْكُلُونَ أَمْوَٰلَ ٱلنَّاسِ بِٱلْبَـٰطِلِ وَيَصُدُّونَ عَن سَبِيلِ ٱللَّهِ ۗ وَٱلَّذِينَ يَكْنِزُونَ ٱلذَّهَبَ وَٱلْفِضَّةَ وَلَا يُنفِقُونَهَا فِى سَبِيلِ ٱللَّهِ فَبَشِّرْهُم بِعَذَابٍ أَلِيمٍ (٣٤)

O you who believe! Verily, the Mushrikûn (polytheists, pagans, idolaters, disbelievers in the Oneness of Allâh, and in the Message of Muhammad) are Najasun (impure). So let them not come near Al-Masjid-al-Harâm (at Makkah) after this year, and if you fear poverty, Allâh will enrich you if He wills, out of His Bounty. Surely, Allâh is All-Knowing, All-Wise. (28) Fight against those who (1) believe not in Allâh, (2) nor in the Last Day, (3) nor forbid that which has been forbidden by Allâh and His Messenger (Muhammad) (4) and those who acknowledge not the religion of truth (i.e. Islâm) among the people of the Scripture (Jews and Christians), until they pay the Jizyah with willing submission, and feel themselves subdued. (29) And the Jews say: 'Uzair (Ezra) is the son of Allâh, and the Christians say: Messiah is the son of Allâh. That is their saying with their mouths, resembling the saying of the those who disbelieved aforetime. Allâh's Curse be on them, how they are deluded away from the truth! (30) They (Jews and Christians) took their rabbis and their monks to be their lords besides Allâh (by obeying them in things which they made lawful or unlawful according to their own desires without being ordered by Allâh), and (they also took as their Lord) Messiah, son of Maryam (Mary), while they (Jews and Christians) were commanded [in the Taurât (Torah) and the Injeel) to worship none but One Ilâh (God - Allâh) Lâ ilâha illa Huwa (none has the right to be worshipped but He). Praise and glory is to Him, (far above is He) from having the partners they associate (with Him)." (31) They (the disbelievers, the Jews and the Christians) want to extinguish Allâh's Light (with which Muhammad has been sent - Islâmic Monotheism) with their mouths, but Allâh will not allow except that His Light should be perfected even though the Kâfirûn (disbelievers) hate (it). (32) It is He Who has sent His Messenger (Muhammad) with guidance and the religion of truth (Islâm), to make it superior over all religions even though the Mushrikûn (polytheists, pagans, idolaters, disbelievers in the Oneness of Allâh) hate (it). (33) O you who believe! Verily, there are many of the (Jewish) rabbis and the (Christian) monks who devour the wealth of mankind in falsehood, and hinder (them) from the Way of Allâh (i.e. Allâh's religion of Islâmic Monotheism). And those who hoard up gold and silver [Al-Kanz: the money, the Zakât of which has not been paid], and spend them not in the Way of Allâh, -announce unto them a painful torment. (34)

Quran 9:38-41

يَٰٓأَيُّهَا ٱلَّذِينَ ءَامَنُواْ مَا لَكُمْ إِذَا قِيلَ لَكُمُ ٱنفِرُواْ فِى سَبِيلِ ٱللَّهِ ٱثَّاقَلْتُمْ إِلَى ٱلْأَرْضِۚ أَرَضِيتُم بِٱلْحَيَوٰةِ ٱلدُّنْيَا مِنَ ٱلْءَاخِرَةِۚ فَمَا مَتَٰعُ ٱلْحَيَوٰةِ ٱلدُّنْيَا فِى ٱلْءَاخِرَةِ إِلَّا قَلِيلٌ (٣٨) إِلَّا تَنفِرُواْ يُعَذِّبْكُمْ عَذَابًا أَلِيمًا وَيَسْتَبْدِلْ قَوْمًا غَيْرَكُمْ وَلَا تَضُرُّوهُ شَيْئًاۗ وَٱللَّهُ عَلَىٰ كُلِّ شَىْءٍ قَدِيرٌ (٣٩) إِلَّا تَنصُرُوهُ فَقَدْ نَصَرَهُ ٱللَّهُ إِذْ أَخْرَجَهُ ٱلَّذِينَ كَفَرُواْ ثَانِىَ ٱثْنَيْنِ إِذْ هُمَا فِى ٱلْغَارِ إِذْ يَقُولُ لِصَٰحِبِهِۦ لَا تَحْزَنْ إِنَّ ٱللَّهَ مَعَنَاۖ فَأَنزَلَ ٱللَّهُ سَكِينَتَهُۥ عَلَيْهِ وَأَيَّدَهُۥ بِجُنُودٍ لَّمْ تَرَوْهَا وَجَعَلَ كَلِمَةَ ٱلَّذِينَ كَفَرُواْ ٱلسُّفْلَىٰۗ وَكَلِمَةُ ٱللَّهِ هِىَ ٱلْعُلْيَاۗ وَٱللَّهُ عَزِيزٌ حَكِيمٌ (٤٠) ٱنفِرُواْ خِفَافًا وَثِقَالًا وَجَٰهِدُواْ بِأَمْوَٰلِكُمْ وَأَنفُسِكُمْ فِى سَبِيلِ ٱللَّهِۚ ذَٰلِكُمْ خَيْرٌ لَّكُمْ إِن كُنتُمْ تَعْلَمُونَ (٤١)

O you who believe! What is the matter with you, that when you are asked to march forth in the Cause of Allâh (i.e. Jihâd) you cling heavily to the earth? Are you pleased with the life of this world rather than the Hereafter? But little is the enjoyment of the life of this world as compared to the Hereafter. (38) If you march not forth, He will punish you with a painful torment and will replace you by another people, and you cannot harm Him at all, and Allâh is Able to do all things (39) If you help him (Muhammad) not (it does not matter), for Allâh did indeed help him when the disbelievers drove him out, the second of two, when they (Muhammad and Abu Bakr) were in the cave, and he said to his companion (Abu Bakr): "Be not sad (or afraid), surely Allâh is with us." Then Allâh sent down His Sakînah (calmness, tranquillity, peace) upon him, and strengthened him with forces (angels) which you saw not, and made the word of those who disbelieved the lowermost, while the Word of Allâh that became the uppermost, and Allâh is All-Mighty, All-Wise. (40) March forth, whether you are light (being healthy, young and wealthy) or heavy (being ill, old and poor), strive hard with your wealth and your lives in the Cause of Allâh. This is better for you, if you but knew. (41)

Quran 9:44

لَا يَسْتَـْٔذِنُكَ ٱلَّذِينَ يُؤْمِنُونَ بِٱللَّهِ وَٱلْيَوْمِ ٱلْأَخِرِ أَن يُجَـٰهِدُواْ بِأَمْوَٰلِهِمْ وَأَنفُسِهِمْۗ وَٱللَّهُ عَلِيمٌۢ بِٱلْمُتَّقِينَ

Those who believe in Allâh and the Last Day would not ask your leave to be exempted from fighting with their properties and their lives, and Allâh is the All-Knower of Al-Muttaqûn (the pious) (44)

Quran 9:51

قُل لَّن يُصِيبَنَآ إِلَّا مَا كَتَبَ ٱللَّهُ لَنَا هُوَ مَوْلَىٰنَاۚ وَعَلَى ٱللَّهِ فَلْيَتَوَكَّلِ ٱلْمُؤْمِنُونَ

Say: "Nothing shall ever happen to us except what Allâh has ordained for us. He is our Maulâ (Lord, Helper and

Protector)." And in Allâh let the believers put their trust. (51)

Quran 9:71-72

وَٱلْمُؤْمِنُونَ وَٱلْمُؤْمِنَٰتُ بَعْضُهُمْ أَوْلِيَآءُ بَعْضٍ ۚ يَأْمُرُونَ بِٱلْمَعْرُوفِ وَيَنْهَوْنَ عَنِ ٱلْمُنكَرِ وَيُقِيمُونَ ٱلصَّلَوٰةَ وَيُؤْتُونَ ٱلزَّكَوٰةَ وَيُطِيعُونَ ٱللَّهَ وَرَسُولَهُ ۚ أُو۟لَٰٓئِكَ سَيَرْحَمُهُمُ ٱللَّهُ ۗ إِنَّ ٱللَّهَ عَزِيزٌ حَكِيمٌ (٧١) وَعَدَ ٱللَّهُ ٱلْمُؤْمِنِينَ وَٱلْمُؤْمِنَٰتِ جَنَّٰتٍ تَجْرِى مِن تَحْتِهَا ٱلْأَنْهَٰرُ خَٰلِدِينَ فِيهَا وَمَسَٰكِنَ طَيِّبَةً فِى جَنَّٰتِ عَدْنٍ ۚ وَرِضْوَٰنٌ مِّنَ ٱللَّهِ أَكْبَرُ ۚ ذَٰلِكَ هُوَ ٱلْفَوْزُ ٱلْعَظِيمُ (٧٢)

The believers, men and women, are Auliyâ' (helpers, supporters, friends, protectors) of one another; they enjoin (on the people) Al-Ma'rûf (i.e. Islâmic Monotheism and all that Islâm orders one to do), and forbid (people) from Al-Munkar (i.e. polytheism and disbelief of all kinds, and all that Islâm has forbidden); they perform As-Salât (Iqâmat-as-Salât), and give the Zakât, and obey Allâh and His Messenger. Allâh will have His Mercy on them. Surely Allâh is All-Mighty, All-Wise. (71) Allâh has promised the believers -men and women, - Gardens under which rivers flow to dwell therein forever, and beautiful mansions in Gardens of 'Adn (Eden Paradise). But the greatest bliss is the Good Pleasure of Allâh. That is the supreme success. (72)

Quran 9:111-113

إِنَّ ٱللَّهَ ٱشْتَرَىٰ مِنَ ٱلْمُؤْمِنِينَ أَنفُسَهُمْ وَأَمْوَٰلَهُم بِأَنَّ لَهُمُ ٱلْجَنَّةَ ۚ يُقَٰتِلُونَ فِى سَبِيلِ ٱللَّهِ فَيَقْتُلُونَ وَيُقْتَلُونَ ۖ وَعْدًا عَلَيْهِ حَقًّا فِى ٱلتَّوْرَىٰةِ وَٱلْإِنجِيلِ وَٱلْقُرْءَانِ ۚ وَمَنْ أَوْفَىٰ بِعَهْدِهِۦ مِنَ ٱللَّهِ ۚ فَٱسْتَبْشِرُوا۟ بِبَيْعِكُمُ ٱلَّذِى بَايَعْتُم بِهِۦ ۚ

وَذَٰلِكَ هُوَ ٱلْفَوْزُ ٱلْعَظِيمُ (١١١) ٱلتَّٰٓئِبُونَ ٱلْعَٰبِدُونَ ٱلْحَٰمِدُونَ ٱلسَّٰٓئِحُونَ ٱلرَّٰكِعُونَ ٱلسَّٰجِدُونَ ٱلْءَامِرُونَ بِٱلْمَعْرُوفِ وَٱلنَّاهُونَ عَنِ ٱلْمُنكَرِ وَٱلْحَٰفِظُونَ لِحُدُودِ ٱللَّهِ وَبَشِّرِ ٱلْمُؤْمِنِينَ (١١٢) مَا كَانَ لِلنَّبِيِّ وَٱلَّذِينَ ءَامَنُوٓا۟ أَن يَسْتَغْفِرُوا۟ لِلْمُشْرِكِينَ وَلَوْ كَانُوٓا۟ أُو۟لِى قُرْبَىٰ مِنۢ بَعْدِ مَا تَبَيَّنَ لَهُمْ أَنَّهُمْ أَصْحَٰبُ ٱلْجَحِيمِ (١١٣)

Verily, Allâh has purchased of the believers their lives and their properties for (the price) that theirs shall be the Paradise. They fight in Allâh's Cause, so they kill (others) and are killed. It is a promise in truth which is binding on Him in the Taurât (Torah) and the Injeel and the Qur'ân. And who is truer to his covenant than Allâh? Then rejoice in the bargain which you have concluded. That is the supreme success. (111) (The believers whose lives Allâh has purchased are) those who turn to Allâh in repentance (from polytheism and hypocrisy, etc.), who worship (Him), who praise (Him), who fast (or go out in Allâhs Cause), who bow down (in prayer), who prostrate themselves (in prayer), who enjoin (on people) Al-Marûf (i.e. Islâmic Monotheism and all what Islâm has ordained) and forbid (people) from Al-Munkar (i.e. disbelief, polytheism of all kinds and all that Islâm has forbidden), and who observe the limits set by Allâh (do all that Allâh has ordained and abstain from all kinds of sins and evil deeds which Allâh has forbidden). And give glad tidings to the believers. (112) It is not (proper) for the Prophet and those who believe to ask Allâh's Forgiveness for the Mushrikûn (polytheists, idolaters, pagans, disbelievers in the Oneness of Allâh) even though they be of kin, after it has become clear to them that they are the dwellers of the Fire (because they died in a state of disbelief). (113)

Quran 9:119

يَـٰٓأَيُّهَا ٱلَّذِينَ ءَامَنُوا۟ ٱتَّقُوا۟ ٱللَّهَ وَكُونُوا۟ مَعَ ٱلصَّـٰدِقِينَ

O you who believe! Be afraid of Allâh, and be with those who are true (in words and deeds). (119)

Quran 9:122-128

۞ وَمَا كَانَ ٱلْمُؤْمِنُونَ لِيَنفِرُوا۟ كَآفَّةً ۚ فَلَوْلَا نَفَرَ مِن كُلِّ فِرْقَةٍ مِّنْهُمْ طَآئِفَةٌ لِّيَتَفَقَّهُوا۟ فِى ٱلدِّينِ وَلِيُنذِرُوا۟ قَوْمَهُمْ إِذَا رَجَعُوٓا۟ إِلَيْهِمْ لَعَلَّهُمْ يَحْذَرُونَ (١٢٢) يَـٰٓأَيُّهَا ٱلَّذِينَ ءَامَنُوا۟ قَـٰتِلُوا۟ ٱلَّذِينَ يَلُونَكُم مِّنَ ٱلْكُفَّارِ وَلْيَجِدُوا۟ فِيكُمْ غِلْظَةً ۚ وَٱعْلَمُوٓا۟ أَنَّ ٱللَّهَ مَعَ ٱلْمُتَّقِينَ (١٢٣) وَإِذَا مَآ أُنزِلَتْ سُورَةٌ فَمِنْهُم مَّن يَقُولُ أَيُّكُمْ زَادَتْهُ هَـٰذِهِۦٓ إِيمَـٰنًا ۚ فَأَمَّا ٱلَّذِينَ ءَامَنُوا۟ فَزَادَتْهُمْ إِيمَـٰنًا وَهُمْ يَسْتَبْشِرُونَ (١٢٤) وَأَمَّا ٱلَّذِينَ فِى قُلُوبِهِم مَّرَضٌ فَزَادَتْهُمْ رِجْسًا إِلَىٰ رِجْسِهِمْ وَمَاتُوا۟ وَهُمْ كَـٰفِرُونَ (١٢٥) أَوَلَا يَرَوْنَ أَنَّهُمْ يُفْتَنُونَ فِى كُلِّ عَامٍ مَّرَّةً أَوْ مَرَّتَيْنِ ثُمَّ لَا يَتُوبُونَ وَلَا هُمْ يَذَّكَّرُونَ (١٢٦) وَإِذَا مَآ أُنزِلَتْ سُورَةٌ نَّظَرَ بَعْضُهُمْ إِلَىٰ بَعْضٍ هَلْ يَرَىٰكُم مِّنْ أَحَدٍ ثُمَّ ٱنصَرَفُوا۟ ۚ صَرَفَ ٱللَّهُ قُلُوبَهُم بِأَنَّهُمْ قَوْمٌ لَّا يَفْقَهُونَ (١٢٧) لَقَدْ جَآءَكُمْ رَسُولٌ مِّنْ أَنفُسِكُمْ عَزِيزٌ عَلَيْهِ مَا عَنِتُّمْ حَرِيصٌ عَلَيْكُم بِٱلْمُؤْمِنِينَ رَءُوفٌ رَّحِيمٌ (١٢٨)

And it is not (proper) for the believers to go out to fight (Jihâd) all together. Of every troop of them, a party only should go forth, that they (who are left behind) may get instructions in (Islâmic) religion, and that they may warn their people when they return to them, so that they may beware (of evil). (122) O you who believe! Fight those of the disbelievers who are close to you, and let them find harshness in you, and know that Allâh is with those who are the Al-Muttaqûn (the pious). (123) And whenever there comes down a Sûrah (chapter from the Qur'ân), some of them (hypocrites) say: "Which of you has had his Faith increased by it?" As for those who believe, it has increased their Faith, and they rejoice. (124) But as for those in whose hearts is a disease (of doubt, disbelief and hypocrisy), it will add suspicion and doubt to their suspicion, disbelief and doubt, and they die while they are disbelievers. (125) See they not that they are put in trial once or twice every year (with different kinds of calamities, disease, famine)? Yet, they turn not in repentance, nor do they learn a lesson (from it). (126) And whenever there comes down a Sûrah (chapter from the Qur'ân), they look at one another (saying): "Does anyone see you?" Then they turn away. Allâh has turned their hearts (from the light) because they are a people that understand not. (127) Verily, there has come unto you a Messenger (Muhammad) from amongst yourselves (i.e. whom you know well). It grieves him that you should receive any injury or difficulty. He (Muhammad) is anxious over you (to be rightly guided, to repent to Allâh, and beg Him to pardon and forgive your sins, in order that you may enter Paradise and be saved from the punishment of the Hell-fire), for the believers (he is) full of pity, kind, and merciful. (128)

Quran 10:2

$$\text{أَكَانَ لِلنَّاسِ عَجَبًا أَنْ أَوْحَيْنَا إِلَىٰ رَجُلٍ مِّنْهُمْ أَنْ أَنذِرِ ٱلنَّاسَ وَبَشِّرِ ٱلَّذِينَ ءَامَنُوا أَنَّ لَهُمْ قَدَمَ صِدْقٍ عِندَ رَبِّهِمْ ۗ قَالَ ٱلْكَافِرُونَ إِنَّ هَٰذَا لَسَاحِرٌ مُّبِينٌ}$$

Is it wonder for mankind that We have sent Our Revelation to a man from among themselves (i.e. Prophet Muhammad) (saying): "Warn mankind (of the coming torment in Hell), and give good news to those who believe (in the Oneness of Allâh and in His Prophet) that they shall have with their Lord the rewards of their good deeds?" (But) the disbelievers say: "This is indeed an evident sorcerer (i.e. Prophet Muhammad and the Qur'ân)! (2)

Quran 10:9

$$\text{إِنَّ ٱلَّذِينَ ءَامَنُوا وَعَمِلُوا ٱلصَّالِحَاتِ يَهْدِيهِمْ رَبُّهُم بِإِيمَانِهِمْ ۖ تَجْرِي مِن تَحْتِهِمُ ٱلْأَنْهَارُ فِي جَنَّاتِ ٱلنَّعِيمِ}$$

Verily, those who believe and do deeds of righteousness, their Lord will guide them through their Faith; under them will flow rivers in the Gardens of Delight (Paradise). (9)

Quran 10:57

$$\text{يَٰٓأَيُّهَا ٱلنَّاسُ قَدْ جَآءَتْكُم مَّوْعِظَةٌ مِّن رَّبِّكُمْ وَشِفَآءٌ لِّمَا فِي ٱلصُّدُورِ وَهُدًى وَرَحْمَةٌ لِّلْمُؤْمِنِينَ}$$

O mankind! There has come to you a good advice from your Lord (i.e. the Qur'an, enjoining all that is good and forbidding all that is evil), and a healing for that (disease of ignorance, doubt, hypocrisy and differences,) Which is in your breasts, - a guidance and a mercy (explaining lawful and unlawful things) for the believers. (57)

Quran 10:62-64

أَلَا إِنَّ أَوْلِيَاءَ ٱللَّهِ لَا خَوْفٌ عَلَيْهِمْ وَلَا هُمْ يَحْزَنُونَ (٦٢) ٱلَّذِينَ ءَامَنُوا۟ وَكَانُوا۟ يَتَّقُونَ (٦٣) لَهُمُ ٱلْبُشْرَىٰ فِى ٱلْحَيَوٰةِ ٱلدُّنْيَا وَفِى ٱلْءَاخِرَةِ لَا تَبْدِيلَ لِكَلِمَٰتِ ٱللَّهِ ذَٰلِكَ هُوَ ٱلْفَوْزُ ٱلْعَظِيمُ (٦٤)

No doubt! Verily, the Auliyâ' of Allâh [i.e. those who believe in the Oneness of Allâh and fear Allâh much (abstain from all kinds of sins and evil deeds which he has forbidden), and love Allâh much (perform all kinds of good deeds which He has ordained)], no fear shall come upon them nor shall they grieve, - (62) Those who believed (in the Oneness of Allâh - Islâmic Monotheism), and used to fear Allâh much (by abstaining from evil deeds and sins and by doing righteous deeds) (63) For them are glad tidings, in the life of the present world (i.e. through a righteous dream seen by the person himself or shown to others), and in the Hereafter. No change can there be in the Words of Allâh, this is indeed the supreme success. (64)

Quran 11:23-24

إِنَّ ٱلَّذِينَ ءَامَنُوا۟ وَعَمِلُوا۟ ٱلصَّٰلِحَٰتِ وَأَخْبَتُوٓا۟ إِلَىٰ رَبِّهِمْ أُو۟لَٰٓئِكَ أَصْحَٰبُ ٱلْجَنَّةِ هُمْ فِيهَا خَٰلِدُونَ (٢٣) ۞ مَثَلُ ٱلْفَرِيقَيْنِ كَٱلْأَعْمَىٰ وَٱلْأَصَمِّ وَٱلْبَصِيرِ وَٱلسَّمِيعِ هَلْ يَسْتَوِيَانِ مَثَلًا أَفَلَا تَذَكَّرُونَ (٢٤)

Verily, those who believe (in the Oneness of Allâh - Islâmic Monotheism) and do righteous good deeds, and humble themselves (in repentance and obedience) before their Lord, - they will be dwellers of Paradise to dwell therein forever. (23) The likeness of the two parties is as the blind and the deaf and the seer and the hearer. Are they equal when compared? Will you not then take heed? (24)

Quran 12:111

لَقَدْ كَانَ فِى قَصَصِهِمْ عِبْرَةٌ لِّأُوْلِى ٱلْأَلْبَٰبِ ۗ مَا كَانَ حَدِيثًا يُفْتَرَىٰ وَلَٰكِن تَصْدِيقَ ٱلَّذِى بَيْنَ يَدَيْهِ وَتَفْصِيلَ كُلِّ شَىْءٍ وَهُدًى وَرَحْمَةً لِّقَوْمٍ يُؤْمِنُونَ

Indeed in their stories, there is a lesson for men of understanding. It (the Quran) is not a forged statement but a confirmation of Allâhs existing Books which were before it [the Taurât (Torah), the Injeel and other Scriptures of Allâh] and a detailed explanation of everything and a guide and a Mercy for the people who believe. (111)

Quran 13:28-29

ٱلَّذِينَ ءَامَنُواْ وَتَطْمَئِنُّ قُلُوبُهُم بِذِكْرِ ٱللَّهِ أَلَا بِذِكْرِ ٱللَّهِ تَطْمَئِنُّ ٱلْقُلُوبُ (٢٨) ٱلَّذِينَ ءَامَنُواْ وَعَمِلُواْ ٱلصَّٰلِحَٰتِ طُوبَىٰ لَهُمْ وَحُسْنُ مَـَٔابٍ

Those who believed (in the Oneness of Allâh - Islâmic Monotheism), and whose hearts find rest in the remembrance of Allâh, Verily, in the remembrance of Allâh do hearts find rest (28) Those who believed (in the Oneness of Allâh - Islâmic Monotheism), and work righteousness, Tûbâ (all kinds of happiness or name of a tree in Paradise) is for them and a beautiful place of (final) return. (29)

Quran 16:98-100

فَإِذَا قَرَأْتَ ٱلْقُرْءَانَ فَٱسْتَعِذْ بِٱللَّهِ مِنَ ٱلشَّيْطَٰنِ ٱلرَّجِيمِ (٩٨) إِنَّهُۥ لَيْسَ لَهُۥ سُلْطَٰنٌ عَلَى ٱلَّذِينَ ءَامَنُوا۟ وَعَلَىٰ رَبِّهِمْ يَتَوَكَّلُونَ (٩٩) إِنَّمَا سُلْطَٰنُهُۥ عَلَى ٱلَّذِينَ يَتَوَلَّوْنَهُۥ وَٱلَّذِينَ هُم بِهِۦ مُشْرِكُونَ (١٠٠)

So when you want to recite the Qur'ân, seek refuge with Allâh from Shaitân (Satan), the outcast (the cursed one). (98) Verily! He has no power over those who believe and put their trust only in their Lord (Allâh). (99) His power is only over those who obey and follow him (Satan), and those who join partners with Him (Allâh) [i.e. those who are Mushrikûn - polytheists] (100)

Quran 17:9

إِنَّ هَٰذَا ٱلْقُرْءَانَ يَهْدِى لِلَّتِى هِىَ أَقْوَمُ وَيُبَشِّرُ ٱلْمُؤْمِنِينَ ٱلَّذِينَ يَعْمَلُونَ ٱلصَّٰلِحَٰتِ أَنَّ لَهُمْ أَجْرًا كَبِيرًا

Verily, this Qur'ân guides to that which is most just and right and gives glad tidings to the believers who work deeds of righteousness, that they shall have a great reward. (9)

Quran 18:1-6

ٱلْحَمْدُ لِلَّهِ ٱلَّذِىٓ أَنزَلَ عَلَىٰ عَبْدِهِ ٱلْكِتَٰبَ وَلَمْ يَجْعَل لَّهُۥ عِوَجَا (١) قَيِّمًا لِّيُنذِرَ بَأْسًا شَدِيدًا مِّن لَّدُنْهُ وَيُبَشِّرَ ٱلْمُؤْمِنِينَ ٱلَّذِينَ يَعْمَلُونَ ٱلصَّٰلِحَٰتِ أَنَّ لَهُمْ أَجْرًا حَسَنًا (٢) مَّٰكِثِينَ فِيهِ أَبَدًا (٣) وَيُنذِرَ ٱلَّذِينَ قَالُوا۟ ٱتَّخَذَ ٱللَّهُ وَلَدًا

مَّا لَهُم بِهِۦ مِنْ عِلْمٍ وَلَا لِأَبَآئِهِمْ ۚ كَبُرَتْ كَلِمَةً تَخْرُجُ مِنْ أَفْوَٰهِهِمْ ۚ إِن يَقُولُونَ إِلَّا كَذِبًا (٥) فَلَعَلَّكَ بَٰخِعٌ نَّفْسَكَ عَلَىٰٓ ءَاثَٰرِهِمْ إِن لَّمْ يُؤْمِنُوا۟ بِهَٰذَا ٱلْحَدِيثِ أَسَفًا (٦)

All the praises and thanks are to Allâh, Who has sent down to His slave the Book (the Qur'ân), and has not placed therein any crookedness. (1) (He has made it) Straight to give warning (to the disbelievers) of a severe punishment from Him, and to give glad tidings to the believers (in the Oneness of Allâh Islâmic Monotheism), who do righteous - deeds, that they shall have a fair reward (Paradise). (2) They shall abide therein forever. (3) And to warn those (Jews, Christians, and pagans) who say, "Allâh has begotten a son (or offspring or children)." (4) No knowledge have they of such a thing, nor had their fathers. Mighty is the word that comes out of their mouths (i.e. He begot sons and daughters). They utter nothing but a lie. (5) Perhaps, you, would kill yourself in grief, over their footsteps (for their turning away from you), because they believe not in this narration (the Qur'ân). (6)

Quran 18:30

إِنَّ ٱلَّذِينَ ءَامَنُوا۟ وَعَمِلُوا۟ ٱلصَّٰلِحَٰتِ إِنَّا لَا نُضِيعُ أَجْرَ مَنْ أَحْسَنَ عَمَلًا

Verily As for those who believed and did righteous deeds, certainly We shall not make to be lost the reward of anyone who does his (righteous) deeds in the most perfect manner. (30)

Quran 18:107

إِنَّ ٱلَّذِينَ ءَامَنُواْ وَعَمِلُواْ ٱلصَّٰلِحَٰتِ كَانَتْ لَهُمْ جَنَّٰتُ ٱلْفِرْدَوْسِ نُزُلاً

"Verily! those who believe (in the Oneness of Allâh - Islâmic Monotheism) and do righteous deeds, shall have the Gardens of Al-Firdaus (the Paradise) for their entertainment. (107)

Quran 20:82

وَإِنِّى لَغَفَّارٌ لِّمَن تَابَ وَءَامَنَ وَعَمِلَ صَٰلِحًا ثُمَّ ٱهْتَدَىٰ

And verily, I am indeed forgiving to him who repents, believes (in My Oneness, and associates none in worship with Me) and does righteous good deeds, and then remains constant in doing them, (till his death). (82)

Quran 20:112

وَمَن يَعْمَلْ مِنَ ٱلصَّٰلِحَٰتِ وَهُوَ مُؤْمِنٌ فَلَا يَخَافُ ظُلْمًا وَلَا هَضْمًا

And he who works deeds of righteousness, while he is a believer (in Islâmic Monotheism) then he will have no fear of injustice, nor of any curtailment (of his reward). (112)

Quran 21:94

فَمَن يَعْمَلْ مِنَ ٱلصَّٰلِحَٰتِ وَهُوَ مُؤْمِنٌ فَلَا كُفْرَانَ لِسَعْيِهِۦ وَإِنَّا لَهُۥ كَٰتِبُونَ

So whoever does righteous good deeds while he is a believer (in the Oneness of Allâh, Islâmic Monotheism), his efforts will not be rejected. Verily! We record it for him (in his Book of deeds). (94)

Quran 22:14

إِنَّ ٱللَّهَ يُدْخِلُ ٱلَّذِينَ ءَامَنُوا۟ وَعَمِلُوا۟ ٱلصَّٰلِحَٰتِ جَنَّٰتٍ تَجْرِى مِن تَحْتِهَا ٱلْأَنْهَٰرُ ۚ إِنَّ ٱللَّهَ يَفْعَلُ مَا يُرِيدُ

Truly, Allâh will admit those who believe (in Islâmic Monotheism) and do righteous good deeds (according to the Qur'ân and the Sunnah) to Gardens underneath which rivers flow (in Paradise). Verily, Allâh does what He wills. (14)

Quran 22:23-24

إِنَّ ٱللَّهَ يُدْخِلُ ٱلَّذِينَ ءَامَنُوا۟ وَعَمِلُوا۟ ٱلصَّٰلِحَٰتِ جَنَّٰتٍ تَجْرِى مِن تَحْتِهَا ٱلْأَنْهَٰرُ يُحَلَّوْنَ فِيهَا مِنْ أَسَاوِرَ مِن ذَهَبٍ وَلُؤْلُؤًا ۖ وَلِبَاسُهُمْ فِيهَا حَرِيرٌ (٢٣) وَهُدُوٓا۟ إِلَى ٱلطَّيِّبِ مِنَ ٱلْقَوْلِ وَهُدُوٓا۟ إِلَىٰ صِرَٰطِ ٱلْحَمِيدِ (٢٤)

Truly, Allâh will admit those who believe (in the Oneness of Allâh - Islâmic Monotheism) and do righteous good deeds, to Gardens underneath which rivers flow (in Paradise), wherein they will be adorned with bracelets of gold and pearls and their garments therein will be of silk. (23) And they are guided (in this world) unto goodly speech (i.e. Lâ ilâha ill-allâh, Alhamdu lillâh, recitation of the Qur'ân, etc.) and they are guided to the Path of Him (i.e. Allâh's religion of Islâmic Monotheism), Who is Worthy of all praises. (24)

Quran 22:38

$$\text{إِنَّ ٱللَّهَ يُدَٰفِعُ عَنِ ٱلَّذِينَ ءَامَنُوٓاْ ۗ إِنَّ ٱللَّهَ لَا يُحِبُّ كُلَّ خَوَّانٍ كَفُورٍ}$$

Truly, Allâh defends those who believe. Verily! Allâh likes not any treacherous ingrate to Allâh [those who disobey Allâh but obey Shaitân (Satan)]. (38)

Quran 22:50

$$\text{فَٱلَّذِينَ ءَامَنُواْ وَعَمِلُواْ ٱلصَّٰلِحَٰتِ لَهُم مَّغْفِرَةٌ وَرِزْقٌ كَرِيمٌ}$$

So those who believe (in the Oneness of Allâh - Islâmic Monotheism) and do righteous good deeds, for them is forgiveness and Rizqûn Karîm (generous provision, i.e. Paradise). (50)

Quran 22:54

$$\text{وَلِيَعْلَمَ ٱلَّذِينَ أُوتُواْ ٱلْعِلْمَ أَنَّهُ ٱلْحَقُّ مِن رَّبِّكَ فَيُؤْمِنُواْ بِهِۦ فَتُخْبِتَ لَهُۥ قُلُوبُهُمْ ۗ وَإِنَّ ٱللَّهَ لَهَادِ ٱلَّذِينَ ءَامَنُوٓاْ إِلَىٰ صِرَٰطٍ مُّسْتَقِيمٍ}$$

And that those who have been given knowledge may know that it (this Qur'ân) is the truth from your Lord, so that they may believe therein, and their hearts may submit to it with humility. And verily, Allâh is the Guide of those who believe, to the Straight Path. (54)

Quran 22:77-78

$$\text{يَٰٓأَيُّهَا ٱلَّذِينَ ءَامَنُواْ ٱرْكَعُواْ وَٱسْجُدُواْ وَٱعْبُدُواْ رَبَّكُمْ وَٱفْعَلُواْ ٱلْخَيْرَ لَعَلَّكُمْ تُفْلِحُونَ ۩ (٧٧) وَجَٰهِدُواْ فِي ٱللَّهِ حَقَّ جِهَادِهِۦ ۚ هُوَ ٱجْتَبَىٰكُمْ وَمَا جَعَلَ عَلَيْكُمْ فِي ٱلدِّينِ مِنْ حَرَجٍ ۚ مِّلَّةَ أَبِيكُمْ إِبْرَٰهِيمَ ۚ هُوَ سَمَّىٰكُمُ ٱلْمُسْلِمِينَ مِن قَبْلُ وَفِي هَٰذَا لِيَكُونَ ٱلرَّسُولُ شَهِيدًا عَلَيْكُمْ وَتَكُونُواْ شُهَدَآءَ عَلَى ٱلنَّاسِ}$$

فَأَقِيمُوا۟ ٱلصَّلَوٰةَ وَءَاتُوا۟ ٱلزَّكَوٰةَ وَٱعْتَصِمُوا۟ بِٱللَّهِ هُوَ مَوْلَىٰكُمْ ۖ فَنِعْمَ ٱلْمَوْلَىٰ وَنِعْمَ ٱلنَّصِيرُ (٧٨)

O you who have believed! Bow down, and prostrate yourselves, and worship your Lord and do good that you may be successful. (77) And strive hard in Allâh's Cause as you ought to strive (with sincerity and with all your efforts that His Name should be superior). He has chosen you (to convey His Message of Islâmic Monotheism to mankind by inviting them to His religion, of Islâm), and has not laid upon you in religion any hardship, it is the religion of your father Ibrahim (Abraham) (Islâmic Monotheism). It is He (Allâh) Who has named you Muslims both before and in this (the Qur'ân), that the Messenger (Muhammad) may be a witness over you and you be witness over mankind! So perform As¬Salât (Iqamat-as-Salât), give Zakât and hold fast to Allâh [i.e. have confidence in Allâh, and depend upon Him in all your affairs] He is your Maula (Patron, Lord), what an Excellent Maula (Patron, Lord) and what an Excellent Helper! (78)

Quran 23:1-11

قَدْ أَفْلَحَ ٱلْمُؤْمِنُونَ (١) ٱلَّذِينَ هُمْ فِى صَلَاتِهِمْ خَٰشِعُونَ (٢) وَٱلَّذِينَ هُمْ عَنِ ٱللَّغْوِ مُعْرِضُونَ (٣) وَٱلَّذِينَ هُمْ لِلزَّكَوٰةِ فَٰعِلُونَ (٤) وَٱلَّذِينَ هُمْ لِفُرُوجِهِمْ حَٰفِظُونَ (٥) إِلَّا عَلَىٰٓ أَزْوَٰجِهِمْ أَوْ مَا مَلَكَتْ أَيْمَٰنُهُمْ فَإِنَّهُمْ غَيْرُ مَلُومِينَ (٦) فَمَنِ ٱبْتَغَىٰ وَرَآءَ ذَٰلِكَ فَأُو۟لَٰٓئِكَ هُمُ ٱلْعَادُونَ (٧) وَٱلَّذِينَ هُمْ لِأَمَٰنَٰتِهِمْ وَعَهْدِهِمْ رَٰعُونَ (٨) وَٱلَّذِينَ هُمْ عَلَىٰ صَلَوَٰتِهِمْ يُحَافِظُونَ (٩) أُو۟لَٰٓئِكَ هُمُ ٱلْوَٰرِثُونَ (١٠) ٱلَّذِينَ يَرِثُونَ ٱلْفِرْدَوْسَ هُمْ فِيهَا خَٰلِدُونَ (١١)

Successful indeed are the believers. (1) Those who offer their Salât (prayers) with all solemnity and full submissiveness. (2) And those who turn away from Al-Laghw (dirty, false, evil vain talk, falsehood, and all that Allâh has forbidden). (3) And those who pay the Zakât. (4) And those who guard their chastity (i.e. private parts, from illegal sexual acts). (5) Except from their wives or (slaves) that their right hands possess, - for then, they are free from blame; (6) But whoever seeks beyond that, then those are the transgressors; (7) Those who are faithfully true to their Amanât (all the duties which Allâh has ordained, honesty, moral responsibility and trusts) and to their covenants; (8) And those who strictly guard their (five compulsory congregational) Salawât (prayers) (at their fixed stated hours). (9) These are indeed the inheritors. (10) Who shall inherit the Firdaus (Paradise). They shall dwell therein forever. (11)

Quran 23:57-61

إِنَّ ٱلَّذِينَ هُم مِّنْ خَشْيَةِ رَبِّهِم مُّشْفِقُونَ (٥٧) وَٱلَّذِينَ هُم بِـَٔايَـٰتِ رَبِّهِمْ يُؤْمِنُونَ (٥٨) وَٱلَّذِينَ هُم بِرَبِّهِمْ لَا يُشْرِكُونَ (٥٩) وَٱلَّذِينَ يُؤْتُونَ مَآ ءَاتَوا۟ وَّقُلُوبُهُمْ وَجِلَةٌ أَنَّهُمْ إِلَىٰ رَبِّهِمْ رَٰجِعُونَ (٦٠) أُو۟لَـٰٓئِكَ يُسَـٰرِعُونَ فِى ٱلْخَيْرَٰتِ وَهُمْ لَهَا سَـٰبِقُونَ (٦١)

Verily! those who live in awe for fear of their Lord; (57) And those who believe in the Ayât (proofs, evidences, verses, lessons, signs, revelations, etc.) of their Lord, (58) And those who join not anyone (in worship) as partners with their Lord; (59) And those who give that (their charity) which they give (and also do other good deeds) with their hearts full of fear (whether their alms and charities, have been accepted or not), because they are sure to return to their Lord (for reckoning). (60) It is these who hasten in the good deeds, and they are foremost in them [e.g. offering the compulsory Salât (prayers) in their (early) stated, fixed times and so on]. (61)

Quran 24:2-3

ٱلزَّانِيَةُ وَٱلزَّانِى فَٱجْلِدُواْ كُلَّ وَٰحِدٍ مِّنْهُمَا مِاْئَةَ جَلْدَةٍ وَلَا تَأْخُذْكُم بِهِمَا رَأْفَةٌ فِى دِينِ ٱللَّهِ إِن كُنتُمْ تُؤْمِنُونَ بِٱللَّهِ وَٱلْيَوْمِ ٱلْأَخِرِ وَلْيَشْهَدْ عَذَابَهُمَا طَآئِفَةٌ مِّنَ ٱلْمُؤْمِنِينَ (٢) ٱلزَّانِى لَا يَنكِحُ إِلَّا زَانِيَةً أَوْ مُشْرِكَةً وَٱلزَّانِيَةُ لَا يَنكِحُهَآ إِلَّا زَانٍ أَوْ مُشْرِكٌ وَحُرِّمَ ذَٰلِكَ عَلَى ٱلْمُؤْمِنِينَ (٣)

The woman and the man guilty of illegal sexual intercourse, flog each of them with a hundred stripes. Let not pity withhold you in their case, in a punishment prescribed by Allâh, if you believe in Allâh and the Last Day. And let a party of the believers witness their punishment. (This punishment is for unmarried persons guilty of the above crime but if married persons commit it, the punishment is to stone them to death, according to Allâh's Law) (2) The adulterer marries not but an adulteress or a Mushrikah and the adulteress none marries her except an adulterer or a Muskrik [and that means that the man who agrees to marry (have a sexual relation with) a Mushrikah (female polytheist, pagan or idolatress) or a prostitute, then surely he is either an adulterer, or a Mushrik (polytheist, pagan or idolater)

And the woman who agrees to marry (have a sexual relation with) a Mushrik (polytheist, pagan or idolater) or an adulterer, then she is either a prostitute or a Mushrikah (female polytheist, pagan, or idolatress)]. Such a thing is forbidden to the believers (of Islâmic Monotheism). (3)

Quran 24:12-17

لَّوْلَآ إِذْ سَمِعْتُمُوهُ ظَنَّ ٱلْمُؤْمِنُونَ وَٱلْمُؤْمِنَٰتُ بِأَنفُسِهِمْ خَيْرًا وَقَالُوا۟ هَٰذَآ إِفْكٌ مُّبِينٌ (١٢) لَّوْلَا جَآءُو عَلَيْهِ بِأَرْبَعَةِ شُهَدَآءَ ۚ فَإِذْ لَمْ يَأْتُوا۟ بِٱلشُّهَدَآءِ فَأُو۟لَٰٓئِكَ عِندَ ٱللَّهِ هُمُ ٱلْكَٰذِبُونَ (١٣) وَلَوْلَا فَضْلُ ٱللَّهِ عَلَيْكُمْ وَرَحْمَتُهُۥ فِى ٱلدُّنْيَا وَٱلْءَاخِرَةِ لَمَسَّكُمْ فِى مَآ أَفَضْتُمْ فِيهِ عَذَابٌ عَظِيمٌ (١٤) إِذْ تَلَقَّوْنَهُۥ بِأَلْسِنَتِكُمْ وَتَقُولُونَ بِأَفْوَاهِكُم مَّا لَيْسَ لَكُم بِهِۦ عِلْمٌ وَتَحْسَبُونَهُۥ هَيِّنًا وَهُوَ عِندَ ٱللَّهِ عَظِيمٌ (١٥) وَلَوْلَآ إِذْ سَمِعْتُمُوهُ قُلْتُم مَّا يَكُونُ لَنَآ أَن نَّتَكَلَّمَ بِهَٰذَا سُبْحَٰنَكَ هَٰذَا بُهْتَٰنٌ عَظِيمٌ (١٦) يَعِظُكُمُ ٱللَّهُ أَن تَعُودُوا۟ لِمِثْلِهِۦٓ أَبَدًا إِن كُنتُم مُّؤْمِنِينَ (١٧)

Why then, did not the believers, men and women, when you heard it (the slander) think good of their own people and say: "This (charge) is an obvious lie?" (12) Why did they not produce four witnesses? Since they (the slanderers) have not produced witnesses! Then with Allâh they are the liars. (13) Had it not been for the Grace of Allâh and His Mercy unto you in this world and in the Hereafter, a great torment would have touched you for that whereof you had spoken. (14) When you were propagating it with your tongues, and uttering with your mouths that whereof you had no knowledge, you counted it a little thing, while with Allâh it was very great. (15) And why did you not, when you heard it, say "It is not right for us to speak of this. Glory is to You (O Allâh) this is a great lie." (16) Allâh forbids you from it and warns you not to repeat the like of it forever, if you are believers. (17)

Quran 24:21-22

﴿يَٰٓأَيُّهَا ٱلَّذِينَ ءَامَنُوا۟ لَا تَتَّبِعُوا۟ خُطُوَٰتِ ٱلشَّيْطَٰنِ وَمَن يَتَّبِعْ خُطُوَٰتِ ٱلشَّيْطَٰنِ فَإِنَّهُۥ يَأْمُرُ بِٱلْفَحْشَآءِ وَٱلْمُنكَرِ وَلَوْلَا فَضْلُ ٱللَّهِ عَلَيْكُمْ وَرَحْمَتُهُۥ مَا زَكَىٰ مِنكُم مِّنْ أَحَدٍ أَبَدًا وَلَٰكِنَّ ٱللَّهَ يُزَكِّى مَن يَشَآءُ وَٱللَّهُ سَمِيعٌ عَلِيمٌ (٢١) وَلَا يَأْتَلِ أُو۟لُوا۟ ٱلْفَضْلِ مِنكُمْ وَٱلسَّعَةِ أَن يُؤْتُوٓا۟ أُو۟لِى ٱلْقُرْبَىٰ وَٱلْمَسَٰكِينَ وَٱلْمُهَٰجِرِينَ فِى سَبِيلِ ٱللَّهِ وَلْيَعْفُوا۟ وَلْيَصْفَحُوٓا۟ أَلَا تُحِبُّونَ أَن يَغْفِرَ ٱللَّهُ لَكُمْ وَٱللَّهُ غَفُورٌ رَّحِيمٌ (٢٢)﴾

O you who believe! Follow not the footsteps of Shaitân (Satan). And whosoever follows the footsteps of Shaitân (Satan), then, verily he commands Al-Fahshâ' [i.e. to commit indecency (illegal sexual intercourse)], and Al-Munkar [disbelief and polytheism (i.e. to do evil and wicked deeds; and to speak or to do what is forbidden in Islâm)]. And had it not been for the Grace of Allâh and His Mercy on you, not one of you would ever have been pure from sins. But Allâh purifies (guides to Islâm) whom He wills, and Allâh is All-Hearer, All-Knower. (21) And let not those among you who are blessed with graces and wealth swear not to give (any sort of help) to their kinsmen, Al-Masâkîn (the poor), and those who left their homes for Allâh's Cause. Let them pardon and forgive.

Do you not love that Allâh should forgive you? And Allâh is Oft-Forgiving, Most Merciful. (22)

Quran 24:27-33

يَـٰٓأَيُّهَا ٱلَّذِينَ ءَامَنُوا۟ لَا تَدْخُلُوا۟ بُيُوتًا غَيْرَ بُيُوتِكُمْ حَتَّىٰ تَسْتَأْنِسُوا۟ وَتُسَلِّمُوا۟ عَلَىٰٓ أَهْلِهَا ۚ ذَٰلِكُمْ خَيْرٌ لَّكُمْ لَعَلَّكُمْ تَذَكَّرُونَ (٢٧) فَإِن لَّمْ تَجِدُوا۟ فِيهَآ أَحَدًا فَلَا تَدْخُلُوهَا حَتَّىٰ يُؤْذَنَ لَكُمْ ۖ وَإِن قِيلَ لَكُمُ ٱرْجِعُوا۟ فَٱرْجِعُوا۟ ۖ هُوَ أَزْكَىٰ لَكُمْ ۚ وَٱللَّهُ بِمَا تَعْمَلُونَ عَلِيمٌ (٢٨) لَّيْسَ عَلَيْكُمْ جُنَاحٌ أَن تَدْخُلُوا۟ بُيُوتًا غَيْرَ مَسْكُونَةٍ فِيهَا مَتَـٰعٌ لَّكُمْ ۚ وَٱللَّهُ يَعْلَمُ مَا تُبْدُونَ وَمَا تَكْتُمُونَ (٢٩) قُل لِّلْمُؤْمِنِينَ يَغُضُّوا۟ مِنْ أَبْصَـٰرِهِمْ وَيَحْفَظُوا۟ فُرُوجَهُمْ ۚ ذَٰلِكَ أَزْكَىٰ لَهُمْ ۗ إِنَّ ٱللَّهَ خَبِيرٌۢ بِمَا يَصْنَعُونَ (٣٠) وَقُل لِّلْمُؤْمِنَـٰتِ يَغْضُضْنَ مِنْ أَبْصَـٰرِهِنَّ وَيَحْفَظْنَ فُرُوجَهُنَّ وَلَا يُبْدِينَ زِينَتَهُنَّ إِلَّا مَا ظَهَرَ مِنْهَا ۖ وَلْيَضْرِبْنَ بِخُمُرِهِنَّ عَلَىٰ جُيُوبِهِنَّ ۖ وَلَا يُبْدِينَ زِينَتَهُنَّ إِلَّا لِبُعُولَتِهِنَّ أَوْ ءَابَآئِهِنَّ أَوْ ءَابَآءِ بُعُولَتِهِنَّ أَوْ أَبْنَآئِهِنَّ أَوْ أَبْنَآءِ بُعُولَتِهِنَّ أَوْ إِخْوَٰنِهِنَّ أَوْ بَنِىٓ إِخْوَٰنِهِنَّ أَوْ بَنِىٓ أَخَوَٰتِهِنَّ أَوْ نِسَآئِهِنَّ أَوْ مَا مَلَكَتْ أَيْمَـٰنُهُنَّ أَوِ ٱلتَّـٰبِعِينَ غَيْرِ أُو۟لِى ٱلْإِرْبَةِ مِنَ ٱلرِّجَالِ أَوِ ٱلطِّفْلِ ٱلَّذِينَ لَمْ يَظْهَرُوا۟ عَلَىٰ عَوْرَٰتِ ٱلنِّسَآءِ ۖ وَلَا يَضْرِبْنَ بِأَرْجُلِهِنَّ لِيُعْلَمَ مَا يُخْفِينَ مِن زِينَتِهِنَّ ۚ وَتُوبُوٓا۟ إِلَى ٱللَّهِ جَمِيعًا أَيُّهَ ٱلْمُؤْمِنُونَ لَعَلَّكُمْ تُفْلِحُونَ (٣١) وَأَنكِحُوا۟ ٱلْأَيَـٰمَىٰ مِنكُمْ وَٱلصَّـٰلِحِينَ مِنْ عِبَادِكُمْ وَإِمَآئِكُمْ ۚ إِن يَكُونُوا۟ فُقَرَآءَ يُغْنِهِمُ ٱللَّهُ مِن فَضْلِهِ ۗ وَٱللَّهُ وَٰسِعٌ عَلِيمٌ (٣٢) وَلْيَسْتَعْفِفِ ٱلَّذِينَ لَا يَجِدُونَ نِكَاحًا حَتَّىٰ يُغْنِيَهُمُ ٱللَّهُ مِن فَضْلِهِ ۗ وَٱلَّذِينَ يَبْتَغُونَ ٱلْكِتَـٰبَ مِمَّا مَلَكَتْ أَيْمَـٰنُكُمْ فَكَاتِبُوهُمْ إِنْ عَلِمْتُمْ فِيهِمْ خَيْرًا ۖ وَءَاتُوهُم مِّن مَّالِ ٱللَّهِ ٱلَّذِىٓ ءَاتَىٰكُمْ ۚ وَلَا تُكْرِهُوا۟ فَتَيَـٰتِكُمْ عَلَى ٱلْبِغَآءِ إِنْ أَرَدْنَ تَحَصُّنًا لِّتَبْتَغُوا۟ عَرَضَ ٱلْحَيَوٰةِ ٱلدُّنْيَا ۚ وَمَن يُكْرِههُّنَّ فَإِنَّ ٱللَّهَ مِنۢ بَعْدِ إِكْرَٰهِهِنَّ غَفُورٌ رَّحِيمٌ (٣٣)

O you who believe! Enter not houses other than your own, until you have asked permission and greeted those in them, that is better for you, in order that you may remember. (27) And if you find no one therein, still, enter not until permission has been given. And if you are asked to go back, go back, for it is purer for you, and Allâh is All-Knower of what you do. (28) There is no sin on you that you enter (without taking permission) houses uninhabited (i.e. not possessed by anybody), (when) you have any interest in them. And Allâh has knowledge of what you reveal and what you conceal. (29) Tell the believing men to lower their gaze (from looking at forbidden things), and protect their private parts (from illegal sexual acts). That is purer for them. Verily, Allâh is All-Aware of what they do. (30) And tell the believing women to lower their gaze (from looking at forbidden things), and protect their private parts (from illegal sexual acts) and not to show off their adornment except only that which is apparent (like both eyes for necessity to see the way or outer dress like veil, gloves, head-cover, apron, etc.), and to draw their veils all over Juyubihinna (i.e. their bodies, faces, necks and bosoms,) and not to reveal their adornment except to their husbands, or their fathers, or their husband's fathers, or their sons, or their husband's sons, or their brothers or their brother's sons, or their sister's sons, or their (Muslim) women (i.e. their sisters in Islâm), or the (female) slaves whom their right hands possess, or old male servants who lack vigour, or small children who have no sense of the feminine sex. And let them not stamp their feet so as to reveal what they hide of their adornment. And all of you beg Allâh to forgive you all, O believers, that you may be successful (31) And marry those among you who are single (i.e. a man who has no wife and the woman who has no husband) and (also marry) the Sâlihûn (pious, fit and capable ones) of your (male) slaves and maid-servants (female slaves). If they be poor, Allâh will enrich them out of His Bounty. And Allâh is All-Sufficent for His creatures' needs, All-Knowing (about the state of the people). (32) And let those who find not the financial means for marriage keep themselves chaste, until Allâh enriches them of His Bounty. And such of your slaves as seek a writing (of emancipation), give them such writing, if you find that there is good and honesty in them. And give them something (yourselves) out of the wealth of Allâh which He has bestowed upon you. And force not your maids to prostitution, if they desire chastity, in order that you may make a gain in the (perishable) goods of this worldly life. But if anyone compels them (to prostitution), then after such compulsion, Allâh is Oft-Forgiving, Most Merciful. (33)

Quran 24:51-52

إِنَّمَا كَانَ قَوْلَ ٱلْمُؤْمِنِينَ إِذَا دُعُوٓا۟ إِلَى ٱللَّهِ وَرَسُولِهِۦ لِيَحْكُمَ بَيْنَهُمْ أَن يَقُولُوا۟ سَمِعْنَا وَأَطَعْنَا ۚ وَأُو۟لَٰٓئِكَ هُمُ ٱلْمُفْلِحُونَ (٥١) وَمَن يُطِعِ ٱللَّهَ وَرَسُولَهُۥ وَيَخْشَ ٱللَّهَ وَيَتَّقْهِ فَأُو۟لَٰٓئِكَ هُمُ ٱلْفَآئِزُونَ (٥٢)

The only saying of the faithful believers, when they are called to Allâh (His Words, the Qur'ân) and His Messenger, to judge between them, is that they say: "We hear and we obey." And such are the successful (who will live forever in Paradise). (51) And whosoever obeys Allâh and His Messenger, fears Allâh, and keeps his duty (to Him), such are the successful. (52)

Quran 24:55-59

وَعَدَ ٱللَّهُ ٱلَّذِينَ ءَامَنُوا۟ مِنكُمْ وَعَمِلُوا۟ ٱلصَّٰلِحَٰتِ لَيَسْتَخْلِفَنَّهُمْ فِى ٱلْأَرْضِ كَمَا ٱسْتَخْلَفَ ٱلَّذِينَ مِن قَبْلِهِمْ وَلَيُمَكِّنَنَّ لَهُمْ دِينَهُمُ ٱلَّذِى ٱرْتَضَىٰ لَهُمْ وَلَيُبَدِّلَنَّهُم مِّنۢ بَعْدِ خَوْفِهِمْ أَمْنًا يَعْبُدُونَنِى لَا يُشْرِكُونَ بِى شَيْـًٔا وَمَن كَفَرَ بَعْدَ ذَٰلِكَ فَأُو۟لَٰٓئِكَ هُمُ ٱلْفَٰسِقُونَ (٥٥) وَأَقِيمُوا۟ ٱلصَّلَوٰةَ وَءَاتُوا۟ ٱلزَّكَوٰةَ وَأَطِيعُوا۟ ٱلرَّسُولَ لَعَلَّكُمْ تُرْحَمُونَ (٥٦) لَا تَحْسَبَنَّ ٱلَّذِينَ كَفَرُوا۟ مُعْجِزِينَ فِى ٱلْأَرْضِ وَمَأْوَىٰهُمُ ٱلنَّارُ وَلَبِئْسَ ٱلْمَصِيرُ (٥٧) يَٰٓأَيُّهَا ٱلَّذِينَ ءَامَنُوا۟ لِيَسْتَـْٔذِنكُمُ ٱلَّذِينَ مَلَكَتْ أَيْمَٰنُكُمْ وَٱلَّذِينَ لَمْ يَبْلُغُوا۟ ٱلْحُلُمَ مِنكُمْ ثَلَٰثَ مَرَّٰتٍ مِّن قَبْلِ صَلَوٰةِ ٱلْفَجْرِ وَحِينَ تَضَعُونَ ثِيَابَكُم مِّنَ ٱلظَّهِيرَةِ وَمِنۢ بَعْدِ صَلَوٰةِ ٱلْعِشَآءِ ثَلَٰثُ عَوْرَٰتٍ لَّكُمْ لَيْسَ عَلَيْكُمْ وَلَا عَلَيْهِمْ جُنَاحٌۢ بَعْدَهُنَّ طَوَّٰفُونَ عَلَيْكُم بَعْضُكُمْ عَلَىٰ بَعْضٍ كَذَٰلِكَ يُبَيِّنُ ٱللَّهُ لَكُمُ ٱلْءَايَٰتِ وَٱللَّهُ عَلِيمٌ حَكِيمٌ (٥٨) وَإِذَا بَلَغَ ٱلْأَطْفَٰلُ مِنكُمُ ٱلْحُلُمَ فَلْيَسْتَـْٔذِنُوا۟ كَمَا ٱسْتَـْٔذَنَ ٱلَّذِينَ مِن قَبْلِهِمْ كَذَٰلِكَ يُبَيِّنُ ٱللَّهُ لَكُمْ ءَايَٰتِهِۦ وَٱللَّهُ عَلِيمٌ حَكِيمٌ (٥٩)

Allâh has promised those among you who believe, and do righteous good deeds, that He will certainly grant them succession to (the present rulers) in the land, as He granted it to those before them, and that He will grant them the authority to practice their religion, which He has chosen for them (i.e. Islâm). And He will surely give them in exchange a safe security after their fear (provided) they (believers) worship Me and do not associate anything (in worship) with Me. But whoever disbelieves after this, they are the Fâsiqûn (rebellious, disobedient to Allâh). (55) And perform As¬Salât (Iqâmat¬as¬Salât), and give Zakât and obey the Messenger (Muhammad) that you may receive mercy (from Allâh). (56) Consider not that the disbelievers can escape in the land. Their abode shall be the Fire,- and worst indeed is that destination. (57) O you who believe! Let your slaves and slave-girls, and those among you who have not come to the age of puberty ask your permission (before they come to your presence) on three occasions; before Fajr (morning) Salât (prayer), and while you put off your clothes for the noonday (rest), and after the 'Ishâ' (late-night) Salât (prayer). (These) three times are of privacy for you, other than these times there is no sin on you or on them to move about, attending to each other. Thus Allâh makes clear the Ayât (the Verses of this Qur'ân, showing proofs for the legal aspects of permission for visits) to you. And Allâh is All-Knowing, All-Wise. (58) And when the children among you come to puberty, then let them (also) ask for permission, as those senior to them (in age). Thus Allâh makes clear His Ayât (Commandments and legal obligations) for you. And Allâh is All-Knowing, All-Wise. (59)

Quran 24:62-63

إِنَّمَا ٱلْمُؤْمِنُونَ ٱلَّذِينَ ءَامَنُوا۟ بِٱللَّهِ وَرَسُولِهِۦ وَإِذَا كَانُوا۟ مَعَهُۥ عَلَىٰٓ أَمْرٍ جَامِعٍ لَّمْ يَذْهَبُوا۟ حَتَّىٰ يَسْتَـْٔذِنُوهُ إِنَّ ٱلَّذِينَ يَسْتَـْٔذِنُونَكَ أُو۟لَـٰٓئِكَ ٱلَّذِينَ يُؤْمِنُونَ بِٱللَّهِ وَرَسُولِهِۦ فَإِذَا ٱسْتَـْٔذَنُوكَ لِبَعْضِ شَأْنِهِمْ فَأْذَن لِّمَن شِئْتَ مِنْهُمْ وَٱسْتَغْفِرْ لَهُمُ ٱللَّهَ إِنَّ ٱللَّهَ غَفُورٌ رَّحِيمٌ (٦٢) لَّا تَجْعَلُوا۟ دُعَآءَ ٱلرَّسُولِ بَيْنَكُمْ كَدُعَآءِ بَعْضِكُم بَعْضًا قَدْ يَعْلَمُ ٱللَّهُ ٱلَّذِينَ يَتَسَلَّلُونَ مِنكُمْ لِوَاذًا فَلْيَحْذَرِ ٱلَّذِينَ يُخَالِفُونَ عَنْ أَمْرِهِۦٓ أَن تُصِيبَهُمْ فِتْنَةٌ أَوْ يُصِيبَهُمْ عَذَابٌ أَلِيمٌ (٦٣)

The true believers are only those, who believe in (the Oneness of) Allâh and His Messenger (Muhammad), and when they are with him on some common matter, they go not away until they have asked his permission. Verily! those who ask your permission, those are they who (really) believe in Allâh and His Messenger. So if they ask your permission for some affairs of theirs, give permission to whom you will of them, and ask Allâh for their forgiveness. Truly, Allâh is Oft-Forgiving, Most Merciful. (62) Make not the calling of the Messenger (Muhammad) among you as your calling one of another. Allâh knows those of you who slip away under shelter (of some excuse without taking the permission to leave, from the Messenger). And let those who oppose the Messenger's (Muhammad) commandment (i.e. his Sunnah — legal ways, orders, acts of worship, statements) (among the sects) beware, lest some Fitnah (disbelief, trials, afflictions, earthquakes, killing, overpowered by a tyrant) should befall them or a painful torment be inflicted on them. (63)

Quran 27:1-3

طسٓ تِلْكَ ءَايَٰتُ ٱلْقُرْءَانِ وَكِتَابٍ مُّبِينٍ (١) هُدًى وَبُشْرَىٰ لِلْمُؤْمِنِينَ (٢) ٱلَّذِينَ يُقِيمُونَ ٱلصَّلَوٰةَ وَيُؤْتُونَ ٱلزَّكَوٰةَ وَهُم بِٱلْءَاخِرَةِ هُمْ يُوقِنُونَ (٣)

Tâ-Sîn. These are the Verses of the Qur'ân, and (it is) a Book (that makes things) clear; (1) A guide (to the Right Path); and glad tidings for the believers [who believe in the Oneness of Allâh (i.e. Islâmic Monotheism)]. (2) Those who perform As-Salât (Iqâmat-as-Salât) and give Zakât and they believe with certainty in the Hereafter (resurrection, recompense of their good and bad deeds, Paradise and Hell). (3)

Quran 27:76-77

إِنَّ هَٰذَا ٱلْقُرْءَانَ يَقُصُّ عَلَىٰ بَنِىٓ إِسْرَٰٓءِيلَ أَكْثَرَ ٱلَّذِى هُمْ فِيهِ يَخْتَلِفُونَ (٧٦) وَإِنَّهُۥ لَهُدًى وَرَحْمَةٌ لِّلْمُؤْمِنِينَ (٧٧)

Verily, this Qur'ân narrates to the Children of Israel most of that in which they differ. (76) And truly, it (this Qur'ân) is a guide and a mercy for the believers. (77)

Quran 27:81

وَمَآ أَنتَ بِهَٰدِى ٱلْعُمْىِ عَن ضَلَٰلَتِهِمْ ۖ إِن تُسْمِعُ إِلَّا مَن يُؤْمِنُ بِـَٔايَٰتِنَا فَهُم مُّسْلِمُونَ

Nor can you lead the blind out of their error, you can only make to hear those who believe in Our Ayât (proofs, evidences, verses, lessons, signs, revelations, etc.), and who have submitted (themselves to Allâh in Islâm as Muslims) (81)

Quran 28:47

وَلَوْلَآ أَن تُصِيبَهُم مُّصِيبَةٌۢ بِمَا قَدَّمَتْ أَيْدِيهِمْ فَيَقُولُوا۟ رَبَّنَا لَوْلَآ أَرْسَلْتَ إِلَيْنَا رَسُولًا فَنَتَّبِعَ ءَايَٰتِكَ وَنَكُونَ مِنَ ٱلْمُؤْمِنِينَ

And if (We had) not (sent you to the people of Makkah) - in case a calamity should seize them for (the deeds) that their hands have sent forth, they would have said: "Our Lord! Why did You not send us a Messenger? We would then have followed Your Ayât (Verses of the Qur'ân) and would have been among the believers." (47)

Quran 28:52-55

ٱلَّذِينَ ءَاتَيْنَـٰهُمُ ٱلْكِتَـٰبَ مِن قَبْلِهِۦ هُم بِهِۦ يُؤْمِنُونَ (٥٢) وَإِذَا يُتْلَىٰ عَلَيْهِمْ قَالُوٓاْ ءَامَنَّا بِهِۦٓ إِنَّهُ ٱلْحَقُّ مِن رَّبِّنَآ إِنَّا كُنَّا مِن قَبْلِهِۦ مُسْلِمِينَ (٥٣) أُوْلَـٰٓئِكَ يُؤْتَوْنَ أَجْرَهُم مَّرَّتَيْنِ بِمَا صَبَرُواْ وَيَدْرَءُونَ بِٱلْحَسَنَةِ ٱلسَّيِّئَةَ وَمِمَّا رَزَقْنَـٰهُمْ يُنفِقُونَ (٥٤) وَإِذَا سَمِعُواْ ٱللَّغْوَ أَعْرَضُواْ عَنْهُ وَقَالُواْ لَنَآ أَعْمَـٰلُنَا وَلَكُمْ أَعْمَـٰلُكُمْ سَلَـٰمٌ عَلَيْكُمْ لَا نَبْتَغِى ٱلْجَـٰهِلِينَ (٥٥)

Those to whom We gave the Scripture [i.e. the Taurât (Torah) and the Injeel] before it, - they believe in it (the Qur'ân). (52) And when it is recited to them, they say: "We believe in it. Verily, it is the truth from our Lord. Indeed even before it we have been from those who submit themselves to Allâh in Islâm as Muslims (like 'Abdullâh bin Salâm and Salmân Al-Farisî). (53) These will be given their reward twice over, because they are patient, and repel evil with good, and spend (in charity) out of what We have provided them. (54) And when they hear Al¬Laghw (dirty, false, evil vain talk), they withdraw from it and say: "To us our deeds, and to you your deeds. Peace be to you. We seek not (the way of) the ignorant." (55)

Quran 29:7

وَٱلَّذِينَ ءَامَنُواْ وَعَمِلُواْ ٱلصَّـٰلِحَـٰتِ لَنُكَفِّرَنَّ عَنْهُمْ سَيِّـَٔاتِهِمْ وَلَنَجْزِيَنَّهُمْ أَحْسَنَ ٱلَّذِى كَانُواْ يَعْمَلُونَ

Those who believe [in the Oneness of Allâh (Monotheism) and in Messenger Muhammad, and do not give up their faith because of the harm they receive from the polytheists], and do righteous good deeds, surely, We shall expiate from them their evil deeds and shall reward them according to the best of that which they used to do. (7)

Quran 29:9

وَٱلَّذِينَ ءَامَنُوا۟ وَعَمِلُوا۟ ٱلصَّٰلِحَٰتِ لَنُدْخِلَنَّهُمْ فِى ٱلصَّٰلِحِينَ

And for those who believe (in the Oneness of Allâh and other articles of Faith) and do righteous good deeds, surely, We shall make them enter with (in the enterance of) the righteous (in Paradise). (9)

Quran 29:44

خَلَقَ ٱللَّهُ ٱلسَّمَٰوَٰتِ وَٱلْأَرْضَ بِٱلْحَقِّ إِنَّ فِى ذَٰلِكَ لَءَايَةً لِّلْمُؤْمِنِينَ

"Allâh (Alone) created the heavens and the earth with truth (and none shared Him in their creation)." Verily! Therein is surely a sign for those who believe. (44)

Quran 29:51

أَوَلَمْ يَكْفِهِمْ أَنَّآ أَنزَلْنَا عَلَيْكَ ٱلْكِتَٰبَ يُتْلَىٰ عَلَيْهِمْ إِنَّ فِى ذَٰلِكَ لَرَحْمَةً وَذِكْرَىٰ لِقَوْمٍ يُؤْمِنُونَ

Is it not sufficient for them that We have sent down to you the Book (the Qur'ân) which is recited to them? Verily, herein is mercy and a reminder (or an admonition) for a people who believe. (51)

Quran 29:56-59

يَـٰعِبَادِىَ ٱلَّذِينَ ءَامَنُوٓا۟ إِنَّ أَرْضِى وَٰسِعَةٌ فَإِيَّـٰىَ فَٱعْبُدُونِ (٥٦) كُلُّ نَفْسٍ ذَآئِقَةُ ٱلْمَوْتِ ۖ ثُمَّ إِلَيْنَا تُرْجَعُونَ (٥٧) وَٱلَّذِينَ ءَامَنُوا۟ وَعَمِلُوا۟ ٱلصَّـٰلِحَـٰتِ لَنُبَوِّئَنَّهُم مِّنَ ٱلْجَنَّةِ غُرَفًا تَجْرِى مِن تَحْتِهَا ٱلْأَنْهَـٰرُ خَـٰلِدِينَ فِيهَا ۚ نِعْمَ أَجْرُ ٱلْعَـٰمِلِينَ (٥٨) ٱلَّذِينَ صَبَرُوا۟ وَعَلَىٰ رَبِّهِمْ يَتَوَكَّلُونَ (٥٩)

O My slaves who believe! Certainly, spacious is My earth. Therefore worship Me (Alone)." (56) Everyone shall taste the death. Then unto Us you shall be returned. (57) And those who believe (in the Oneness of Allâh Islâmic Monotheism) and do righteous good deeds, to them We shall surely give lofty dwellings in Paradise, underneath which rivers flow, to live therein forever. Excellent is the reward of the workers. (58) Those who are patient, and put their trust (only) in their Lord (Allâh). (59)

Quran 30:15

فَأَمَّا ٱلَّذِينَ ءَامَنُوا۟ وَعَمِلُوا۟ ٱلصَّـٰلِحَـٰتِ فَهُمْ فِى رَوْضَةٍ يُحْبَرُونَ

Then as for those who believed (in the Oneness of Allâh - Islâmic Monotheism) and did righteous good deeds, such shall be honoured and made to enjoy luxurious life (forever) in a Garden of Delight (Paradise). (15)

Quran 30:37-38

أَوَلَمْ يَرَوْا۟ أَنَّ ٱللَّهَ يَبْسُطُ ٱلرِّزْقَ لِمَن يَشَآءُ وَيَقْدِرُ ۚ إِنَّ فِى ذَٰلِكَ لَءَايَـٰتٍ لِّقَوْمٍ يُؤْمِنُونَ (٣٧) فَـَٔاتِ ذَا ٱلْقُرْبَىٰ حَقَّهُۥ وَٱلْمِسْكِينَ وَٱبْنَ ٱلسَّبِيلِ ۚ ذَٰلِكَ خَيْرٌ لِّلَّذِينَ يُرِيدُونَ وَجْهَ ٱللَّهِ ۖ وَأُو۟لَـٰٓئِكَ هُمُ ٱلْمُفْلِحُونَ (٣٨)

Do they not see that Allâh enlarges the provision for whom He wills and straitens (it for whom He wills). Verily, in that are indeed signs for a people who believe. (37) So give to the kindred his due, and to Al¬Miskîn (the poor) and to the wayfarer; That is best for those who seek Allâh's Countenance, and it is they who will be successful. (38)

Quran 30:53

وَمَآ أَنتَ بِهَٰدِ ٱلْعُمْىِ عَن ضَلَٰلَتِهِمْ ۖ إِن تُسْمِعُ إِلَّا مَن يُؤْمِنُ بِـَٔايَٰتِنَا فَهُم مُّسْلِمُونَ

And you cannot guide the blind from their straying; you can make to hear only those who believe in Our Ayât (proofs, evidences, verses, lessons, signs, revelations, etc.), and have submitted to Allâh in Islâm (as Muslims). (53)

Quran 31:8

إِنَّ ٱلَّذِينَ ءَامَنُوا۟ وَعَمِلُوا۟ ٱلصَّٰلِحَٰتِ لَهُمْ جَنَّٰتُ ٱلنَّعِيمِ

Verily, those who believe (in Islâmic Monotheism) and do righteous good deeds, for them are Gardens of Delight (Paradise). (8)

Quran 32:18-19

أَفَمَن كَانَ مُؤْمِنًا كَمَن كَانَ فَاسِقًا ۚ لَّا يَسْتَوُۥنَ (١٨) أَمَّا ٱلَّذِينَ ءَامَنُوا۟ وَعَمِلُوا۟ ٱلصَّٰلِحَٰتِ فَلَهُمْ جَنَّٰتُ ٱلْمَأْوَىٰ نُزُلًۢا بِمَا كَانُوا۟ يَعْمَلُونَ (١٩)

Is then he who is a believer like him who is Fâsiq (disbeliever and disobedient to Allâh)? Not equal are they (18) As for those who believe and do righteous good deeds, for them are Gardens (Paradise) as an entertainment, for what they used to do (19)

Quran 33:6

ٱلنَّبِىُّ أَوْلَىٰ بِٱلْمُؤْمِنِينَ مِنْ أَنفُسِهِمْ ۖ وَأَزْوَٰجُهُۥٓ أُمَّهَٰتُهُمْ ۗ وَأُو۟لُوا۟ ٱلْأَرْحَامِ بَعْضُهُمْ أَوْلَىٰ بِبَعْضٍ فِى كِتَٰبِ ٱللَّهِ مِنَ ٱلْمُؤْمِنِينَ وَٱلْمُهَٰجِرِينَ إِلَّآ أَن تَفْعَلُوٓا۟ إِلَىٰٓ أَوْلِيَآئِكُم مَّعْرُوفًا ۚ كَانَ ذَٰلِكَ فِى ٱلْكِتَٰبِ مَسْطُورًا

The Prophet is closer to the believers than their ownselves, and his wives are their (believers') mothers (as regards respect and marriage). And blood relations among each other have closer personal ties in the Decree of Allâh (regarding inheritance) than (the brotherhood of) the believers and the Muhajirûn (emigrants from Makkah), except that you do kindness to those brothers (when the Prophet joined them in brotherhood ties). This has been written in the (Book of Divine) Decrees (Al¬Lauh Al¬Mahfûz)." (6)

Quran 33:9

يَٰٓأَيُّهَا ٱلَّذِينَ ءَامَنُوا۟ ٱذْكُرُوا۟ نِعْمَةَ ٱللَّهِ عَلَيْكُمْ إِذْ جَآءَتْكُمْ جُنُودٌ فَأَرْسَلْنَا عَلَيْهِمْ رِيحًا وَجُنُودًا لَّمْ تَرَوْهَا ۚ وَكَانَ ٱللَّهُ بِمَا تَعْمَلُونَ بَصِيرًا

O you who believe! Remember Allâh's Favour to you, when there came against you hosts, and We sent against them a wind and forces that you saw not. And Allâh is Ever All¬Seer of what you do. (9)

Quran 33:23

$$\text{مِنَ ٱلْمُؤْمِنِينَ رِجَالٌ صَدَقُوا۟ مَا عَـٰهَدُوا۟ ٱللَّهَ عَلَيْهِ ۖ فَمِنْهُم مَّن قَضَىٰ نَحْبَهُۥ وَمِنْهُم مَّن يَنتَظِرُ ۖ وَمَا بَدَّلُوا۟ تَبْدِيلًا}$$

Among the believers are men who have been true to their covenant with Allâh [i.e. they have gone out for Jihâd (holy fighting), and showed not their backs to the disbelievers], of them some have fulfilled their obligations (i.e. have been martyred), and some of them are still waiting, but they have never changed [i.e. they never proved treacherous to their covenant which they concluded with Allâh] in the least (23)

Quran 35:36

$$\text{إِنَّ ٱلْمُسْلِمِينَ وَٱلْمُسْلِمَـٰتِ وَٱلْمُؤْمِنِينَ وَٱلْمُؤْمِنَـٰتِ وَٱلْقَـٰنِتِينَ وَٱلْقَـٰنِتَـٰتِ وَٱلصَّـٰدِقِينَ وَٱلصَّـٰدِقَـٰتِ وَٱلصَّـٰبِرِينَ وَٱلصَّـٰبِرَٰتِ وَٱلْخَـٰشِعِينَ وَٱلْخَـٰشِعَـٰتِ وَٱلْمُتَصَدِّقِينَ وَٱلْمُتَصَدِّقَـٰتِ وَٱلصَّـٰٓئِمِينَ وَٱلصَّـٰٓئِمَـٰتِ وَٱلْحَـٰفِظِينَ فُرُوجَهُمْ وَٱلْحَـٰفِظَـٰتِ وَٱلذَّٰكِرِينَ ٱللَّهَ كَثِيرًا وَٱلذَّٰكِرَٰتِ أَعَدَّ ٱللَّهُ لَهُم مَّغْفِرَةً وَأَجْرًا عَظِيمًا (٣٥) وَمَا كَانَ لِمُؤْمِنٍ وَلَا مُؤْمِنَةٍ إِذَا قَضَى ٱللَّهُ وَرَسُولُهُۥٓ أَمْرًا أَن يَكُونَ لَهُمُ ٱلْخِيَرَةُ مِنْ أَمْرِهِمْ ۗ وَمَن يَعْصِ ٱللَّهَ وَرَسُولَهُۥ فَقَدْ ضَلَّ ضَلَـٰلًا مُّبِينًا (٣٦)}$$

Verily, the Muslims (those who submit to Allâh in Islâm) men and women, the believers men and women (who believe in Islâmic Monotheism), the men and the women who are obedient (to Allâh), the men and women who are truthful (in their speech and deeds), the men and the women who are patient (in performing all the duties which Allâh has ordered and in abstaining from all that Allâh has forbidden), the men and the women who are humble (before their Lord Allâh), the men and the women who give Sadaqât (i.e. Zakât, and alms), the men and the women who observe Saum (fast) (the obligatory fasting during the month of Ramadân, and the optional Nawâfil fasting), the men and the women who guard their chastity (from illegal sexual acts) and the men and the women who remember Allâh much with their hearts and tongues. Allâh has prepared for them forgiveness and a great reward (i.e. Paradise). (35) It is not for a believer, man or woman, when Allâh and His Messenger have decreed a matter that they should have any option in their decision. And whoever disobeys Allâh and His Messenger, he has indeed strayed in to a plain error. (36)

Quran 33:41-49

يَٰٓأَيُّهَا ٱلَّذِينَ ءَامَنُواْ ٱذْكُرُواْ ٱللَّهَ ذِكْرًا كَثِيرًا (٤١) وَسَبِّحُوهُ بُكْرَةً وَأَصِيلاً (٤٢) هُوَ ٱلَّذِى يُصَلِّى عَلَيْكُمْ وَمَلَٰٓئِكَتُهُۥ لِيُخْرِجَكُم مِّنَ ٱلظُّلُمَٰتِ إِلَى ٱلنُّورِ ۚ وَكَانَ بِٱلْمُؤْمِنِينَ رَحِيمًا (٤٣) تَحِيَّتُهُمْ يَوْمَ يَلْقَوْنَهُۥ سَلَٰمٌ ۚ وَأَعَدَّ لَهُمْ أَجْرًا كَرِيمًا (٤٤) يَٰٓأَيُّهَا ٱلنَّبِىُّ إِنَّآ أَرْسَلْنَٰكَ شَٰهِدًا وَمُبَشِّرًا وَنَذِيرًا (٤٥) وَدَاعِيًا إِلَى ٱللَّهِ بِإِذْنِهِۦ وَسِرَاجًا مُّنِيرًا (٤٦) وَبَشِّرِ ٱلْمُؤْمِنِينَ بِأَنَّ لَهُم مِّنَ ٱللَّهِ فَضْلاً كَبِيرًا (٤٧) وَلَا تُطِعِ ٱلْكَٰفِرِينَ وَٱلْمُنَٰفِقِينَ وَدَعْ أَذَىٰهُمْ وَتَوَكَّلْ عَلَى ٱللَّهِ ۚ وَكَفَىٰ بِٱللَّهِ وَكِيلاً (٤٨) يَٰٓأَيُّهَا ٱلَّذِينَ ءَامَنُوٓاْ إِذَا نَكَحْتُمُ ٱلْمُؤْمِنَٰتِ ثُمَّ طَلَّقْتُمُوهُنَّ مِن قَبْلِ أَن تَمَسُّوهُنَّ فَمَا لَكُمْ عَلَيْهِنَّ مِنْ عِدَّةٍ تَعْتَدُّونَهَآ ۖ فَمَتِّعُوهُنَّ وَسَرِّحُوهُنَّ سَرَاحًا جَمِيلاً (٤٩)

O you who believe! Remember Allâh with much remembrance. (41) And glorify His Praises morning and afternoon [the early morning (Fajr) and 'Asr prayers]. (42) He it is Who sends Salât (His blessings) on you, and His angels too (ask Allâh to bless and forgive you), that He may bring you out from darkness into light. And He is Ever Most Merciful to the believers. (43) Their greeting on the Day they shall meet Him will be "Salâm: Peace (i.e. the angels will say to them: Salâmu 'Alaikum)!" And He has prepared for them a generous reward (i.e. Paradise). (44) O Prophet (Muhammad)! Verily, We have sent you as witness, and a bearer of glad tidings, and a warner, (45) And as one who invites to Allâh [Islâmic Monotheism, i.e. to worship none but Allâh (Alone)] by His Leave, and as a lamp spreading light (through your instructions from the Qur'ân and the Sunnah the legal ways of the Prophet). (46) And announce to the believers (in the Oneness of Allâh and in His Messenger Muhammad) the glad tidings, that they will have from Allâh a Great Bounty. (47) And obey not the disbelievers and the hypocrites, and harm them not (in revenge for their harming you till you are ordered). And put your trust in Allâh, and Sufficient is Allâh as a Wakîl (Trustee, or Disposer of affairs). (48) O you who believe! When you marry believing women, and then divorce them before you have sexual intercourse with them, no 'Iddah [divorce prescribed period] have you to count in respect of them. So give them a present, and set them free (i.e. divorce), in a handsome manner. (49)

Quran 33:53

يَـٰٓأَيُّهَا ٱلَّذِينَ ءَامَنُوا۟ لَا تَدْخُلُوا۟ بُيُوتَ ٱلنَّبِىِّ إِلَّآ أَن يُؤْذَنَ لَكُمْ إِلَىٰ طَعَامٍ غَيْرَ نَـٰظِرِينَ إِنَىٰهُ وَلَـٰكِنْ إِذَا دُعِيتُمْ فَٱدْخُلُوا۟ فَإِذَا طَعِمْتُمْ فَٱنتَشِرُوا۟ وَلَا مُسْتَـْٔنِسِينَ لِحَدِيثٍ إِنَّ ذَٰلِكُمْ كَانَ يُؤْذِى ٱلنَّبِىَّ فَيَسْتَحْىِۦ مِنكُمْ وَٱللَّهُ

$$\text{لَا يَسْتَحْيِ مِنَ ٱلْحَقِّ وَإِذَا سَأَلْتُمُوهُنَّ مَتَـٰعًا فَسْـَٔلُوهُنَّ مِن وَرَآءِ حِجَابٍ ۚ}$$
$$\text{ذَٰلِكُمْ أَطْهَرُ لِقُلُوبِكُمْ وَقُلُوبِهِنَّ ۚ وَمَا كَانَ لَكُمْ أَن تُؤْذُوا۟ رَسُولَ ٱللَّهِ}$$
$$\text{وَلَآ أَن تَنكِحُوٓا۟ أَزْوَٰجَهُۥ مِنۢ بَعْدِهِۦٓ أَبَدًا ۚ إِنَّ ذَٰلِكُمْ كَانَ عِندَ ٱللَّهِ عَظِيمًا}$$

O you who believe! Enter not the Prophet's houses, unless permission is given to you for a meal, (and then) not (so early as) to wait for its preparation. But when you are invited, enter, and when you have taken your meal, disperse, without sitting for a talk. Verily, such (behaviour) annoys the Prophet, and he is shy of (asking) you (to go), but Allâh is not shy of (telling you) the truth. And when you ask (his wives) for anything you want, ask them from behind a screen, that is purer for your hearts and for their hearts. And it is not (right) for you that you should annoy Allâh's Messenger, nor that you should ever marry his wives after him (his death). Verily! With Allâh that shall be an enormity (53)

Quran 33:56

$$\text{إِنَّ ٱللَّهَ وَمَلَـٰٓئِكَتَهُۥ يُصَلُّونَ عَلَى ٱلنَّبِىِّ ۚ يَـٰٓأَيُّهَا ٱلَّذِينَ ءَامَنُوا۟ صَلُّوا۟ عَلَيْهِ وَسَلِّمُوا۟ تَسْلِيمًا}$$

Allâh sends His Salât (Graces, Honours, Blessings, Mercy) on the Prophet (Muhammad) and also His angels (ask Allâh to bless and forgive him). O you who believe! Send your Salât on (ask Allâh to bless) him (Muhammad), and (you should) greet (salute) him with the Islâmic way of greeting (salutation i.e. As¬Salâmu 'Alaikum). (56)

Quran 33:69-73

يَـٰٓأَيُّهَا ٱلَّذِينَ ءَامَنُواْ لَا تَكُونُواْ كَٱلَّذِينَ ءَاذَوْاْ مُوسَىٰ فَبَرَّأَهُ ٱللَّهُ مِمَّا قَالُواْ وَكَانَ عِندَ ٱللَّهِ وَجِيهًا (٦٩) يَـٰٓأَيُّهَا ٱلَّذِينَ ءَامَنُواْ ٱتَّقُواْ ٱللَّهَ وَقُولُواْ قَوْلاً سَدِيدًا (٧٠) يُصْلِحْ لَكُمْ أَعْمَـٰلَكُمْ وَيَغْفِرْ لَكُمْ ذُنُوبَكُمْ وَمَن يُطِعِ ٱللَّهَ وَرَسُولَهُ فَقَدْ فَازَ فَوْزًا عَظِيمًا (٧١) إِنَّا عَرَضْنَا ٱلْأَمَانَةَ عَلَى ٱلسَّمَـٰوَٰتِ وَٱلْأَرْضِ وَٱلْجِبَالِ فَأَبَيْنَ أَن يَحْمِلْنَهَا وَأَشْفَقْنَ مِنْهَا وَحَمَلَهَا ٱلْإِنسَـٰنُ إِنَّهُ كَانَ ظَلُومًا جَهُولاً (٧٢) لِيُعَذِّبَ ٱللَّهُ ٱلْمُنَـٰفِقِينَ وَٱلْمُنَـٰفِقَـٰتِ وَٱلْمُشْرِكِينَ وَٱلْمُشْرِكَـٰتِ وَيَتُوبَ ٱللَّهُ عَلَى ٱلْمُؤْمِنِينَ وَٱلْمُؤْمِنَـٰتِ وَكَانَ ٱللَّهُ غَفُورًا رَّحِيمًا (٧٣)

O you who believe! Be not like those who annoyed Mûsa (Moses), but Allâh cleared him of that which they alleged, and he was honourable before Allâh (69) O you who believe! Keep your duty to Allâh and fear Him, and speak (always) the truth. (70) He will direct you to do righteous good deeds and will forgive you your sins. And whosoever obeys Allâh and His Messenger he has indeed achieved a great achievement (i.e. he will be saved from the Hell-fire and will be admitted to Paradise). (71) Truly, We did offer Al¬Amânah (the trust or moral responsibility or honesty and all the duties which Allâh has ordained) to the heavens and the earth, and the mountains, but they declined to bear it and were afraid of it (i.e. afraid of Allâh's Torment). But man bore it. Verily, he was unjust (to himself) and ignorant (of its results). (72) So that Allâh will punish the hypocrites, men and women, and the men and women who are Al¬Mushrikûn (polytheists, idolaters, pagans, disbelievers in the Oneness of Allâh, and His Messenger Muhammad). And Allâh will pardon (accept the repentance of) the true believers of the Islâmic Monotheism, men and women. And Allâh is Ever Oft-Forgiving, Most Merciful. (73)

Quran 34:4

لِّيَجْزِىَ ٱلَّذِينَ ءَامَنُواْ وَعَمِلُواْ ٱلصَّٰلِحَٰتِ أُوْلَٰٓئِكَ لَهُم مَّغْفِرَةٌ وَرِزْقٌ كَرِيمٌ

That He may recompense those who believe (in the Oneness of Allâh Islâmic Monotheism) and do righteous good deeds. Those, theirs is forgiveness and Rizq Karîm (generous provision, i.e. Paradise). (4)

Quran 34:37

وَمَآ أَمْوَٰلُكُمْ وَلَآ أَوْلَٰدُكُم بِٱلَّتِى تُقَرِّبُكُمْ عِندَنَا زُلْفَىٰٓ إِلَّا مَنْ ءَامَنَ وَعَمِلَ صَٰلِحًا فَأُوْلَٰٓئِكَ لَهُمْ جَزَآءُ ٱلضِّعْفِ بِمَا عَمِلُواْ وَهُمْ فِى ٱلْغُرُفَٰتِ ءَامِنُونَ

And it is not your wealth, nor your children that bring you nearer to Us (i.e. pleases Allâh), but only he who believes (in the Islâmic Monotheism), and does righteous deeds (will please us); as for such, there will be twofold reward for what they did, and they will reside in the high dwellings (Paradise) in peace and security. (37)

Quran 35:7

ٱلَّذِينَ كَفَرُواْ لَهُمْ عَذَابٌ شَدِيدٌ وَٱلَّذِينَ ءَامَنُواْ وَعَمِلُواْ ٱلصَّٰلِحَٰتِ لَهُم مَّغْفِرَةٌ وَأَجْرٌ كَبِيرٌ

Those who disbelieve, theirs will be a severe torment; and those who believe (in the Oneness of Allâh Islâmic

Monotheism) and do righteous good deeds, theirs will be forgiveness and a great reward (i.e. Paradise). (7)

Quran 37:51-61

قَالَ قَآئِلٌ مِّنْهُمْ إِنِّى كَانَ لِى قَرِينٌ (٥١) يَقُولُ أَءِنَّكَ لَمِنَ ٱلْمُصَدِّقِينَ (٥٢) أَءِذَا مِتْنَا وَكُنَّا تُرَابًا وَعِظَـٰمًا أَءِنَّا لَمَدِينُونَ (٥٣) قَالَ هَلْ أَنتُم مُّطَّلِعُونَ (٥٤) فَٱطَّلَعَ فَرَءَاهُ فِى سَوَآءِ ٱلْجَحِيمِ (٥٥) قَالَ تَٱللَّهِ إِن كِدتَّ لَتُرْدِينِ (٥٦) وَلَوْلَا نِعْمَةُ رَبِّى لَكُنتُ مِنَ ٱلْمُحْضَرِينَ (٥٧) أَفَمَا نَحْنُ بِمَيِّتِينَ (٥٨) إِلَّا مَوْتَتَنَا ٱلْأُولَىٰ وَمَا نَحْنُ بِمُعَذَّبِينَ (٥٩) إِنَّ هَـٰذَا لَهُوَ ٱلْفَوْزُ ٱلْعَظِيمُ (٦٠) لِمِثْلِ هَـٰذَا فَلْيَعْمَلِ ٱلْعَـٰمِلُونَ (٦١)

A speaker of them will say: "Verily, I had a companion (in the world), (51) Who used to say: "Are you among those who believe (in resurrection after death). (52) "(That) when we die and become dust and bones, shall we indeed (be raised up) to receive reward or punishment (according to our deeds)?" (53) (The speaker) said: "Will you look down?" (54) So he looked down and saw him in the midst of the Fire. (55) He said: "By Allâh! You have nearly ruined me. (56) "Had it not been for the Grace of my Lord, I would certainly have been among those brought forth (to Hell)." (57) (The dwellers of Paradise will say): "Are we then not to die (any more)? (58) "Except our first death, and we shall not be punished?" (59) Truly, this is the supreme success! (60) For the like of this let the workers work. (61)

Quran 38:28

$$\text{أَمْ نَجْعَلُ ٱلَّذِينَ ءَامَنُوا۟ وَعَمِلُوا۟ ٱلصَّٰلِحَٰتِ كَٱلْمُفْسِدِينَ فِى ٱلْأَرْضِ أَمْ نَجْعَلُ ٱلْمُتَّقِينَ كَٱلْفُجَّارِ}$$

Shall We treat those who believe (in the Oneness of Allâh — Islâmic Monotheism) and do righteous good deeds, as Mufsidûn (those who associate partners in worship with Allâh and commit crimes) on earth? Or shall We treat the Muttaqûn (pious), as the Fujjâr (criminals, disbelievers, the wicked)? (28)

Quran 39:9-10

$$\text{أَمَّنْ هُوَ قَٰنِتٌ ءَانَآءَ ٱلَّيْلِ سَاجِدًا وَقَآئِمًا يَحْذَرُ ٱلْءَاخِرَةَ وَيَرْجُوا۟ رَحْمَةَ رَبِّهِۦ ۗ قُلْ هَلْ يَسْتَوِى ٱلَّذِينَ يَعْلَمُونَ وَٱلَّذِينَ لَا يَعْلَمُونَ ۗ إِنَّمَا يَتَذَكَّرُ أُو۟لُوا۟ ٱلْأَلْبَٰبِ (٩) قُلْ يَٰعِبَادِ ٱلَّذِينَ ءَامَنُوا۟ ٱتَّقُوا۟ رَبَّكُمْ ۚ لِلَّذِينَ أَحْسَنُوا۟ فِى هَٰذِهِ ٱلدُّنْيَا حَسَنَةٌ ۗ وَأَرْضُ ٱللَّهِ وَٰسِعَةٌ ۗ إِنَّمَا يُوَفَّى ٱلصَّٰبِرُونَ أَجْرَهُم بِغَيْرِ حِسَابٍ (١٠)}$$

Is one who is obedient to Allâh, prostrating himself or standing (in prayer) during the hours of the night, fearing the Hereafter and hoping for the Mercy of his Lord (like one who disbelieves)? Say: "Are those who know equal to those who know not?" It is only men of understanding who will remember (i.e. get a lesson from Allâh's Signs and Verses). (9) Say: "O My slaves who believe (in the Oneness of Allâh Islâmic — Monotheism), be afraid of your Lord (Allâh) and keep your duty to Him. Good is (the reward) for those who do good in this world, and Allâh's earth is spacious (so if you cannot worship Allâh at a place, then go to another)! Only those who are patient shall receive their reward in full, without reckoning." (10)

Quran 39:52-55

أَوَلَمْ يَعْلَمُوٓا۟ أَنَّ ٱللَّهَ يَبْسُطُ ٱلرِّزْقَ لِمَن يَشَآءُ وَيَقْدِرُ ۚ إِنَّ فِى ذَٰلِكَ لَءَايَٰتٍ لِّقَوْمٍ يُؤْمِنُونَ (٥٢) قُلْ يَٰعِبَادِىَ ٱلَّذِينَ أَسْرَفُوا۟ عَلَىٰٓ أَنفُسِهِمْ لَا تَقْنَطُوا۟ مِن رَّحْمَةِ ٱللَّهِ ۚ إِنَّ ٱللَّهَ يَغْفِرُ ٱلذُّنُوبَ جَمِيعًا ۚ إِنَّهُۥ هُوَ ٱلْغَفُورُ ٱلرَّحِيمُ (٥٣) وَأَنِيبُوٓا۟ إِلَىٰ رَبِّكُمْ وَأَسْلِمُوا۟ لَهُۥ مِن قَبْلِ أَن يَأْتِيَكُمُ ٱلْعَذَابُ ثُمَّ لَا تُنصَرُونَ (٥٤) وَٱتَّبِعُوٓا۟ أَحْسَنَ مَآ أُنزِلَ إِلَيْكُم مِّن رَّبِّكُم مِّن قَبْلِ أَن يَأْتِيَكُمُ ٱلْعَذَابُ بَغْتَةً وَأَنتُمْ لَا تَشْعُرُونَ (٥٥)

Do they not know that Allâh enlarges the provision for whom He wills, and straitens it (for whom He wills). Verily, in this are signs for the folk who believe! (52) Say: "O 'Ibâdî (My slaves) who have transgressed against themselves (by committing evil deeds and sins)! Despair not of the Mercy of Allâh, verily Allâh forgives all sins. Truly, He is Oft-Forgiving, Most Merciful (53) "And turn in repentance and in obedience with true Faith (Islâmic Monotheism) to your Lord and submit to Him, (in Islâm), before the torment comes upon you, (and) then you will not be helped. (54) "And follow the best of that which is sent down to you from your Lord (i.e. this Qur'ân, do what it orders you to do and keep away from what it forbids), before the torment comes on you suddenly while you perceive not!" (55)

Quran 40:7-9

ٱلَّذِينَ يَحْمِلُونَ ٱلْعَرْشَ وَمَنْ حَوْلَهُۥ يُسَبِّحُونَ بِحَمْدِ رَبِّهِمْ وَيُؤْمِنُونَ بِهِۦ وَيَسْتَغْفِرُونَ لِلَّذِينَ ءَامَنُوا۟ رَبَّنَا وَسِعْتَ كُلَّ شَىْءٍ رَّحْمَةً وَعِلْمًا فَٱغْفِرْ لِلَّذِينَ تَابُوا۟ وَٱتَّبَعُوا۟ سَبِيلَكَ وَقِهِمْ عَذَابَ ٱلْجَحِيمِ (٧) رَبَّنَا وَأَدْخِلْهُمْ جَنَّٰتِ عَدْنٍ ٱلَّتِى وَعَدتَّهُمْ وَمَن صَلَحَ مِنْ ءَابَآئِهِمْ وَأَزْوَٰجِهِمْ وَذُرِّيَّٰتِهِمْ ۚ إِنَّكَ أَنتَ

$$\text{ٱلْعَزِيزُ ٱلْحَكِيمُ (٨) وَقِهِمُ ٱلسَّيِّئَاتِ وَمَن تَقِ ٱلسَّيِّئَاتِ يَوْمَئِذٍ فَقَدْ رَحِمْتَهُ وَذَٰلِكَ هُوَ ٱلْفَوْزُ ٱلْعَظِيمُ (٩)}$$

Those (angels) who bear the Throne (of Allâh) and those around it glorify the praises of their Lord, and believe in Him, and ask forgiveness for those who believe (in the Oneness of Allâh) (saying): "Our Lord! You comprehend all things in mercy and knowledge, so forgive those who repent and follow Your Way, and save them from the torment of the blazing Fire! (7) "Our Lord! And make them enter the 'Adn (Eden) Paradise (everlasting Gardens) which you have promised them, — and to the righteous among their fathers, their wives, and their offspring! Verily, You are the All-Mighty, the All-Wise. (8) "And save them from the sins, and whomsoever You save from the sins (i.e. pardon him) that Day, him verily, You have taken into mercy." And that is the supreme success. (9)

Quran 40:35

$$\text{ٱلَّذِينَ يُجَٰدِلُونَ فِىٓ ءَايَٰتِ ٱللَّهِ بِغَيْرِ سُلْطَٰنٍ أَتَىٰهُمْ كَبُرَ مَقْتًا عِندَ ٱللَّهِ وَعِندَ ٱلَّذِينَ ءَامَنُوا۟ كَذَٰلِكَ يَطْبَعُ ٱللَّهُ عَلَىٰ كُلِّ قَلْبِ مُتَكَبِّرٍ جَبَّارٍ}$$

Those who dispute about the Ayât (proofs, evidences, verses, lessons, signs, revelations, etc.) of Allâh, without any authority that has come to them, it is greatly hateful and disgusting to Allâh and to those who believe. Thus does Allâh seal up the heart of every arrogant, tyrant. (So they cannot guide themselves to the Right Path). (35)

Quran 40:58

وَمَا يَسْتَوِى ٱلْأَعْمَىٰ وَٱلْبَصِيرُ وَٱلَّذِينَ ءَامَنُواْ وَعَمِلُواْ ٱلصَّٰلِحَٰتِ وَلَا ٱلْمُسِىٓءُ ۚ قَلِيلًا مَّا تَتَذَكَّرُونَ

And not equal are the blind and those who see, nor are (equal) those who believe (in the Oneness of Allâh — Islâmic Monotheism), and do righteous good deeds, and those who do evil. Little do you remember! (58)

Quran 41:8

إِنَّ ٱلَّذِينَ ءَامَنُواْ وَعَمِلُواْ ٱلصَّٰلِحَٰتِ لَهُمْ أَجْرٌ غَيْرُ مَمْنُونٍ

Truly, those who believe (in the Oneness of Allâh and in His Messenger Muhammad — Islâmic Monotheism) and do righteous good deeds, for them will be an endless reward that will never stop (i.e. Paradise). (8)

Quran 41:18

وَنَجَّيْنَا ٱلَّذِينَ ءَامَنُواْ وَكَانُواْ يَتَّقُونَ

And We saved those who believed and used to fear Allâh, keep their duty to Him and avoid evil. (18)

Quran 41:44

وَلَوْ جَعَلْنَٰهُ قُرْءَانًا أَعْجَمِيًّا لَّقَالُواْ لَوْلَا فُصِّلَتْ ءَايَٰتُهُۥٓ ۖ ءَا۬عْجَمِىٌّ وَعَرَبِىٌّ ۗ قُلْ هُوَ لِلَّذِينَ ءَامَنُواْ هُدًى وَشِفَآءٌ ۖ وَٱلَّذِينَ لَا يُؤْمِنُونَ فِىٓ ءَاذَانِهِمْ وَقْرٌ وَهُوَ عَلَيْهِمْ عَمًى ۚ أُوْلَٰٓئِكَ يُنَادَوْنَ مِن مَّكَانٍ بَعِيدٍ

And if We had sent this as a Qur'ân in a foreign language (other than Arabic), they would have said: "Why are not its Verses explained in detail (in our language)? What! (A

Book) not in Arabic and (the Messenger) an Arab?" Say: "It is for those who believe, a guide and a healing. And as for those who disbelieve, there is heaviness (deafness) in their ears, and it (the Qur'ân) is blindness for them. They are those who are called from a place far away (so they neither listen nor understand). (44)

Quran 42:22-23

تَرَى ٱلظَّٰلِمِينَ مُشْفِقِينَ مِمَّا كَسَبُواْ وَهُوَ وَاقِعٌۢ بِهِمْۗ وَٱلَّذِينَ ءَامَنُواْ وَعَمِلُواْ ٱلصَّٰلِحَٰتِ فِى رَوْضَاتِ ٱلْجَنَّاتِۖ لَهُم مَّا يَشَآءُونَ عِندَ رَبِّهِمْۚ ذَٰلِكَ هُوَ ٱلْفَضْلُ ٱلْكَبِيرُ (٢٢) ذَٰلِكَ ٱلَّذِى يُبَشِّرُ ٱللَّهُ عِبَادَهُ ٱلَّذِينَ ءَامَنُواْ وَعَمِلُواْ ٱلصَّٰلِحَٰتِۗ قُل لَّآ أَسْـَٔلُكُمْ عَلَيْهِ أَجْرًا إِلَّا ٱلْمَوَدَّةَ فِى ٱلْقُرْبَىٰۗ وَمَن يَقْتَرِفْ حَسَنَةً نَّزِدْ لَهُۥ فِيهَا حُسْنًاۚ إِنَّ ٱللَّهَ غَفُورٌ شَكُورٌ (٢٣)

You will see (on the Day of Resurrection), the Zâlimûn (polytheists and wrong-doers) fearful of that which they have earned, and it (Allâhs Torment) will surely befall them, But those who believe (in the Oneness of Allâh Islâmic Monotheism) and do righteous deeds (will be) in the flowering meadows of the Gardens (Paradise), having what they wish from their Lord. That is the supreme Grace, (Paradise). (22) That is (the Paradise) whereof Allâh gives glad tidings to His slaves who believe (in the Oneness of Allâh — Islâmic Monotheism) and do righteous good deeds. Say: "No reward do I ask of you for this except to be kind to me for my kinship with you." And whoever earns a good righteous deed, We shall give him an increase of good in respect thereof. Verily, Allâh is

Oft-Forgiving, Most Ready to appreciate (the deeds of those who are obedient to Him). (23)

Quran 43:68-72

يَـٰعِبَادِ لَا خَوْفٌ عَلَيْكُمُ ٱلْيَوْمَ وَلَآ أَنتُمْ تَحْزَنُونَ (٦٨) ٱلَّذِينَ ءَامَنُوا بِـَٔايَـٰتِنَا وَكَانُوا مُسْلِمِينَ (٦٩) ٱدْخُلُوا ٱلْجَنَّةَ أَنتُمْ وَأَزْوَٰجُكُمْ تُحْبَرُونَ (٧٠) يُطَافُ عَلَيْهِم بِصِحَافٍ مِّن ذَهَبٍ وَأَكْوَابٍ ۖ وَفِيهَا مَا تَشْتَهِيهِ ٱلْأَنفُسُ وَتَلَذُّ ٱلْأَعْيُنُ ۖ وَأَنتُمْ فِيهَا خَـٰلِدُونَ (٧١) وَتِلْكَ ٱلْجَنَّةُ ٱلَّتِىٓ أُورِثْتُمُوهَا بِمَا كُنتُمْ تَعْمَلُونَ (٧٢)

It will be said to the true believers of Islâmic Monotheism): My worshippers! No fear shall be on you this Day, nor shall you grieve, (68) (You) who believed in Our Ayât (proofs, verses, lessons, signs, revelations, etc.) and were Muslims (i.e. who submit totally to Allâh's Will, and believe in the Oneness of Allâh - Islâmic Monotheism) (69) Enter Paradise, you and your wives, in happiness. (70) Trays of gold and cups will be passed round them, (there will be) therein all that the inner-selves could desire, and all that the eyes could delight in, and you will abide therein forever. (71) This is the Paradise which you have been made to inherit because of your deeds which you used to do (in the life of the world). (72)

Quran 45:3-4

إِنَّ فِى ٱلسَّمَـٰوَٰتِ وَٱلْأَرْضِ لَـَٔايَـٰتٍ لِّلْمُؤْمِنِينَ (٣) وَفِى خَلْقِكُمْ وَمَا يَبُثُّ مِن دَآبَّةٍ ءَايَـٰتٌ لِّقَوْمٍ يُوقِنُونَ (٤)

Verily, in the heavens and the earth are signs for the believers. (3) And in your creation, and what He scattered (through the earth) of moving (living) creatures are signs for people who have Faith with certainty. (4)

Quran 45:14

قُل لِّلَّذِينَ ءَامَنُوا۟ يَغْفِرُوا۟ لِلَّذِينَ لَا يَرْجُونَ أَيَّامَ ٱللَّهِ لِيَجْزِىَ قَوْمًا بِمَا كَانُوا۟ يَكْسِبُونَ

Say to the believers to forgive those who (harm them and) hope not for the Days of Allâh (i.e. His Recompense), that He may recompense people according to what they have earned (i.e. to punish these disbelievers, who harm the believers). (14)

Quran 45:20-21

هَٰذَا بَصَٰٓئِرُ لِلنَّاسِ وَهُدًى وَرَحْمَةٌ لِّقَوْمٍ يُوقِنُونَ (٢٠) أَمْ حَسِبَ ٱلَّذِينَ ٱجْتَرَحُوا۟ ٱلسَّيِّـَٔاتِ أَن نَّجْعَلَهُمْ كَٱلَّذِينَ ءَامَنُوا۟ وَعَمِلُوا۟ ٱلصَّٰلِحَٰتِ سَوَآءً مَّحْيَاهُمْ وَمَمَاتُهُمْ ۚ سَآءَ مَا يَحْكُمُونَ (٢١)

This (Qur'ân) is a clear insight and evidence for mankind, and a guidance and a mercy for people who have Faith with certainty. (20) Or do those who earn evil deeds think that We shall hold them equal with those who believe (in the Oneness of Allâh — Islâmic Monotheism) and do righteous good deeds, in their present life and after their death? Worst is the judgement that they make. (21)

Quran 45:30

فَأَمَّا ٱلَّذِينَ ءَامَنُوا۟ وَعَمِلُوا۟ ٱلصَّٰلِحَٰتِ فَيُدْخِلُهُمْ رَبُّهُمْ فِى رَحْمَتِهِۦ ۚ ذَٰلِكَ هُوَ ٱلْفَوْزُ ٱلْمُبِينُ

Then, as for those who believed (in the Oneness of Allâh — Islâmic Monotheism) and did righteous good deeds, their Lord will admit them to His Mercy. That will be the evident success. (30)

Quran 47:2

وَٱلَّذِينَ ءَامَنُوا۟ وَعَمِلُوا۟ ٱلصَّٰلِحَٰتِ وَءَامَنُوا۟ بِمَا نُزِّلَ عَلَىٰ مُحَمَّدٍ وَهُوَ ٱلْحَقُّ مِن رَّبِّهِمْ ۙ كَفَّرَ عَنْهُمْ سَيِّـَٔاتِهِمْ وَأَصْلَحَ بَالَهُمْ

But those who believe and do righteous good deeds, and believe in that which is sent down to Muhammad — for it is the truth from their Lord, He will expiate from them their sins, and will make good their state. (2)

Quran 47:7

يَٰٓأَيُّهَا ٱلَّذِينَ ءَامَنُوٓا۟ إِن تَنصُرُوا۟ ٱللَّهَ يَنصُرْكُمْ وَيُثَبِّتْ أَقْدَامَكُمْ

O you who believe! If you help (in the cause of) Allâh, He will help you, and make your foothold firm. (7)

Quran 47:11-12

ذَٰلِكَ بِأَنَّ ٱللَّهَ مَوْلَى ٱلَّذِينَ ءَامَنُوا۟ وَأَنَّ ٱلْكَٰفِرِينَ لَا مَوْلَىٰ لَهُمْ (١١) إِنَّ ٱللَّهَ يُدْخِلُ ٱلَّذِينَ ءَامَنُوا۟ وَعَمِلُوا۟ ٱلصَّٰلِحَٰتِ جَنَّٰتٍ تَجْرِى مِن تَحْتِهَا ٱلْأَنْهَٰرُ ۖ وَٱلَّذِينَ كَفَرُوا۟ يَتَمَتَّعُونَ وَيَأْكُلُونَ كَمَا تَأْكُلُ ٱلْأَنْعَٰمُ وَٱلنَّارُ مَثْوًى لَّهُمْ (١٢)

That is because Allâh is the Maula (Lord, Master, Helper, Protector, etc.) of those who believe, and the disbelievers have no Maula (lord, master, helper, protector). (11)

Certainly! Allâh will admit those who believe (in the Oneness of Allâh Islâmic Monotheism) and do righteous good deeds, to Gardens under which rivers flow (Paradise), while those who disbelieve enjoy themselves and eat as cattle eat, and the Fire will be their abode. (12)

Quran 47:20-21

وَيَقُولُ ٱلَّذِينَ ءَامَنُوا۟ لَوْلَا نُزِّلَتْ سُورَةٌ ۖ فَإِذَآ أُنزِلَتْ سُورَةٌ مُّحْكَمَةٌ وَذُكِرَ فِيهَا ٱلْقِتَالُ ۙ رَأَيْتَ ٱلَّذِينَ فِى قُلُوبِهِم مَّرَضٌ يَنظُرُونَ إِلَيْكَ نَظَرَ ٱلْمَغْشِىِّ عَلَيْهِ مِنَ ٱلْمَوْتِ ۖ فَأَوْلَىٰ لَهُمْ (٢٠) طَاعَةٌ وَقَوْلٌ مَّعْرُوفٌ ۚ فَإِذَا عَزَمَ ٱلْأَمْرُ فَلَوْ صَدَقُوا۟ ٱللَّهَ لَكَانَ خَيْرًا لَّهُمْ (٢١)

Those who believe say: "Why is not a Sûrah (chapter of the Qur'ân) sent down (for us)? But when a decisive Sûrah (explaining and ordering things) is sent down, and fighting (Jihâd — holy fighting in Allâh's Cause) is mentioned (i.e. ordained) therein, you will see those in whose hearts is a disease (of hypocrisy) looking at you with a look of one fainting to death. But it was better for them (hypocrites, to listen to Allâh and to obey Him). (20) Obedience (to Allâh) and good words (were better for them). And when the matter (preparation for Jihâd) is resolved on, then if they had been true to Allâh, it would have been better for them. (21)

Quran 47:36-38

إِنَّمَا ٱلْحَيَوٰةُ ٱلدُّنْيَا لَعِبٌ وَلَهْوٌ ۚ وَإِن تُؤْمِنُوا۟ وَتَتَّقُوا۟ يُؤْتِكُمْ أُجُورَكُمْ وَلَا يَسْـَٔلْكُمْ أَمْوَٰلَكُمْ (٣٦) إِن يَسْـَٔلْكُمُوهَا فَيُحْفِكُمْ تَبْخَلُوا۟ وَيُخْرِجْ أَضْغَٰنَكُمْ (٣٧) هَٰٓأَنتُمْ هَٰٓؤُلَآءِ تُدْعَوْنَ لِتُنفِقُوا۟ فِى سَبِيلِ ٱللَّهِ فَمِنكُم مَّن يَبْخَلُ ۖ وَمَن

$$\text{يَبْخَلْ فَإِنَّمَا يَبْخَلُ عَن نَّفْسِهِۦ ۚ وَٱللَّهُ ٱلْغَنِىُّ وَأَنتُمُ ٱلْفُقَرَآءُ ۚ وَإِن تَتَوَلَّوْا۟ يَسْتَبْدِلْ قَوْمًا غَيْرَكُمْ ثُمَّ لَا يَكُونُوٓا۟ أَمْثَٰلَكُم (٣٨)}$$

The life of this world is but play and pastime, but if you believe (in the Oneness of Allâh — Islâmic Monotheism), and fear Allâh, and avoid evil, He will grant you your wages, and will not ask you your wealth. (36) If He were to ask you of it, and press you, you would covetously withhold, and He will bring out all your (secret) ill-wills. (37) Behold! You are those who are called to spend in the Cause of Allâh, yet among you are some who are niggardly. And whoever is niggardly, it is only at the expense of his ownself. But Allâh is Rich (Free of all needs), and you (mankind) are poor. And if you turn away (from Islâm and the obedience to Allâh), He will exchange you for some other people, and they will not be your likes. (38)

Quran 48:4-5

$$\text{هُوَ ٱلَّذِىٓ أَنزَلَ ٱلسَّكِينَةَ فِى قُلُوبِ ٱلْمُؤْمِنِينَ لِيَزْدَادُوٓا۟ إِيمَٰنًا مَّعَ إِيمَٰنِهِمْ ۗ وَلِلَّهِ جُنُودُ ٱلسَّمَٰوَٰتِ وَٱلْأَرْضِ ۚ وَكَانَ ٱللَّهُ عَلِيمًا حَكِيمًا (٤) لِّيُدْخِلَ ٱلْمُؤْمِنِينَ وَٱلْمُؤْمِنَٰتِ جَنَّٰتٍ تَجْرِى مِن تَحْتِهَا ٱلْأَنْهَٰرُ خَٰلِدِينَ فِيهَا وَيُكَفِّرَ عَنْهُمْ سَيِّـَٔاتِهِمْ ۚ وَكَانَ ذَٰلِكَ عِندَ ٱللَّهِ فَوْزًا عَظِيمًا (٥)}$$

He it is Who sent down As-Sakinah (calmness and tranquillity) into the hearts of the believers, that they may grow more in Faith along with their (present) Faith. And to Allâh belong the hosts of the heavens and the earth, and Allâh is Ever All-Knower, All-Wise. (4) That He may admit the believing men and the believing women to

Gardens under which rivers flow (i.e. Paradise), to abide therein forever, and He may expiate from them their sins, and that is with Allâh, a supreme success, (5)

Quran 48:18

لَقَدْ رَضِىَ ٱللَّهُ عَنِ ٱلْمُؤْمِنِينَ إِذْ يُبَايِعُونَكَ تَحْتَ ٱلشَّجَرَةِ فَعَلِمَ مَا فِى قُلُوبِهِمْ فَأَنزَلَ ٱلسَّكِينَةَ عَلَيْهِمْ وَأَثَـٰبَهُمْ فَتْحًا قَرِيبًا

Indeed, Allâh was pleased with the believers when they gave the Bai'âh (pledge) to you (O Muhammad) under the tree, He knew what was in their hearts, and He sent down As-Sakinah (calmness and tranquillity) upon them, and He rewarded them with a near victory, (18)

Quran 48:29

مُّحَمَّدٌ رَّسُولُ ٱللَّهِ وَٱلَّذِينَ مَعَهُۥٓ أَشِدَّآءُ عَلَى ٱلْكُفَّارِ رُحَمَآءُ بَيْنَهُمْ تَرَىٰهُمْ رُكَّعًا سُجَّدًا يَبْتَغُونَ فَضْلًا مِّنَ ٱللَّهِ وَرِضْوَٰنًا ۖ سِيمَاهُمْ فِى وُجُوهِهِم مِّنْ أَثَرِ ٱلسُّجُودِ ۚ ذَٰلِكَ مَثَلُهُمْ فِى ٱلتَّوْرَىٰةِ ۚ وَمَثَلُهُمْ فِى ٱلْإِنجِيلِ كَزَرْعٍ أَخْرَجَ شَطْـَٔهُۥ فَـَٔازَرَهُۥ فَٱسْتَغْلَظَ فَٱسْتَوَىٰ عَلَىٰ سُوقِهِۦ يُعْجِبُ ٱلزُّرَّاعَ لِيَغِيظَ بِهِمُ ٱلْكُفَّارَ ۗ وَعَدَ ٱللَّهُ ٱلَّذِينَ ءَامَنُوا۟ وَعَمِلُوا۟ ٱلصَّـٰلِحَـٰتِ مِنْهُم مَّغْفِرَةً وَأَجْرًا عَظِيمًۢا

Muhammad is the Messenger of Allâh, And those who are with him are severe against disbelievers, and merciful among themselves. You see them bowing and falling down prostrate (in prayer), seeking Bounty from Allâh and (His) Good Pleasure. The mark of them (i.e. of their Faith) is on their faces (foreheads) from the traces of prostration (during prayers). This is their description in the Taurât (Torah). But their description in the Injeel is like a (sown) seed which sends forth its shoot, then makes it strong, and becomes thick, and it stands straight on its stem, delighting the sowers that He may enrage the disbelievers with them. Allâh has promised those among them who believe and do righteous good deeds, forgiveness and a mighty reward (i.e. Paradise). (29)

Quran 49:1-6

يَـٰٓأَيُّهَا ٱلَّذِينَ ءَامَنُوا۟ لَا تُقَدِّمُوا۟ بَيْنَ يَدَىِ ٱللَّهِ وَرَسُولِهِۦ ۖ وَٱتَّقُوا۟ ٱللَّهَ ۚ إِنَّ ٱللَّهَ سَمِيعٌ عَلِيمٌ (١) يَـٰٓأَيُّهَا ٱلَّذِينَ ءَامَنُوا۟ لَا تَرْفَعُوٓا۟ أَصْوَٰتَكُمْ فَوْقَ صَوْتِ ٱلنَّبِىِّ وَلَا تَجْهَرُوا۟ لَهُۥ بِٱلْقَوْلِ كَجَهْرِ بَعْضِكُمْ لِبَعْضٍ أَن تَحْبَطَ أَعْمَـٰلُكُمْ وَأَنتُمْ لَا تَشْعُرُونَ (٢) إِنَّ ٱلَّذِينَ يَغُضُّونَ أَصْوَٰتَهُمْ عِندَ رَسُولِ ٱللَّهِ أُو۟لَـٰٓئِكَ ٱلَّذِينَ ٱمْتَحَنَ ٱللَّهُ قُلُوبَهُمْ لِلتَّقْوَىٰ ۚ لَهُم مَّغْفِرَةٌ وَأَجْرٌ عَظِيمٌ (٣) إِنَّ ٱلَّذِينَ يُنَادُونَكَ مِن وَرَآءِ ٱلْحُجُرَٰتِ أَكْثَرُهُمْ لَا يَعْقِلُونَ (٤) وَلَوْ أَنَّهُمْ صَبَرُوا۟ حَتَّىٰ تَخْرُجَ إِلَيْهِمْ لَكَانَ خَيْرًا لَّهُمْ ۚ وَٱللَّهُ غَفُورٌ رَّحِيمٌ (٥) يَـٰٓأَيُّهَا ٱلَّذِينَ ءَامَنُوٓا۟ إِن جَآءَكُمْ فَاسِقٌۢ بِنَبَإٍ فَتَبَيَّنُوٓا۟ أَن تُصِيبُوا۟ قَوْمًۢا بِجَهَـٰلَةٍ فَتُصْبِحُوا۟ عَلَىٰ مَا فَعَلْتُمْ نَـٰدِمِينَ (٦)

O you who believe! Make not (a decision) in advance before Allâh and His Messenger, and fear Allâh. Verily! Allâh is All-Hearing, All-Knowing. (1) O you who believe! Raise not your voices above the voice of the Prophet, nor speak aloud to him in talk as you speak aloud to one another, lest your deeds may be rendered fruitless while you perceive not. (2) Verily, those who lower their voices in the presence of Allâh's Messenger, they are the ones whose hearts Allâh has tested for piety. For them is forgiveness and a great reward. (3) Verily, those who call you from behind the dwellings, most of them have no sense. (4) And if they had patience till you could come out to them, it would have been better for them. And Allâh is Oft-Forgiving, Most Merciful. (5) O you who believe! If a Fasiq (liar — evil person) comes to you with any news, verify it, lest you should harm people in ignorance, and afterwards you become regretful for what you have done. (6)

Quran 49:9-12

وَإِن طَآئِفَتَانِ مِنَ ٱلْمُؤْمِنِينَ ٱقْتَتَلُوا۟ فَأَصْلِحُوا۟ بَيْنَهُمَا ۖ فَإِنۢ بَغَتْ إِحْدَىٰهُمَا عَلَى ٱلْأُخْرَىٰ فَقَـٰتِلُوا۟ ٱلَّتِى تَبْغِى حَتَّىٰ تَفِىٓءَ إِلَىٰٓ أَمْرِ ٱللَّهِ ۚ فَإِن فَآءَتْ فَأَصْلِحُوا۟ بَيْنَهُمَا بِٱلْعَدْلِ وَأَقْسِطُوٓا۟ ۖ إِنَّ ٱللَّهَ يُحِبُّ ٱلْمُقْسِطِينَ (٩) إِنَّمَا ٱلْمُؤْمِنُونَ إِخْوَةٌ فَأَصْلِحُوا۟ بَيْنَ أَخَوَيْكُمْ ۚ وَٱتَّقُوا۟ ٱللَّهَ لَعَلَّكُمْ تُرْحَمُونَ (١٠) يَـٰٓأَيُّهَا ٱلَّذِينَ ءَامَنُوا۟ لَا يَسْخَرْ قَوْمٌ مِّن قَوْمٍ عَسَىٰٓ أَن يَكُونُوا۟ خَيْرًا مِّنْهُمْ وَلَا نِسَآءٌ مِّن نِّسَآءٍ عَسَىٰٓ أَن يَكُنَّ خَيْرًا مِّنْهُنَّ ۖ وَلَا تَلْمِزُوٓا۟ أَنفُسَكُمْ وَلَا تَنَابَزُوا۟ بِٱلْأَلْقَـٰبِ ۖ بِئْسَ ٱلِٱسْمُ ٱلْفُسُوقُ بَعْدَ ٱلْإِيمَـٰنِ ۚ وَمَن لَّمْ يَتُبْ فَأُو۟لَـٰٓئِكَ هُمُ ٱلظَّـٰلِمُونَ (١١) يَـٰٓأَيُّهَا ٱلَّذِينَ ءَامَنُوا۟ ٱجْتَنِبُوا۟ كَثِيرًا مِّنَ ٱلظَّنِّ إِنَّ بَعْضَ ٱلظَّنِّ إِثْمٌ ۖ وَلَا تَجَسَّسُوا۟ وَلَا يَغْتَب بَّعْضُكُم بَعْضًا ۚ أَيُحِبُّ أَحَدُكُمْ أَن يَأْكُلَ لَحْمَ أَخِيهِ مَيْتًا فَكَرِهْتُمُوهُ ۚ وَٱتَّقُوا۟ ٱللَّهَ ۚ إِنَّ ٱللَّهَ تَوَّابٌ رَّحِيمٌ (١٢)

And if two parties or groups among the believers fall to fighting, then make peace between them both, But if one of them outrages against the other, then fight you (all) against the one that which outrages till it complies with the Command of Allâh; then if it complies, then make reconciliation between them justly, and be equitable. Verily! Allâh loves those who are equitable. (9) The believers are nothing else than brothers (in Islâmic religion). So make reconciliation between your brothers, and fear Allâh, that you may receive mercy. (10) O you who believe! Let not a group scoff at another group, it may be that the latter are better than the former; Nor let (some) women scoff at other women, it may be that the latter are better than the former, Nor defame one another, nor insult one another by nicknames. How bad is it, to insult one's brother after having Faith. And whosoever does not repent, then such are indeed Zâlimûn (wrong-doers). (11) O you who believe! Avoid much suspicion, indeed some suspicions are sins. And spy not, neither backbite one another. Would one of you like to eat the flesh of his dead brother? You would hate it (so hate backbiting) . And fear Allâh. Verily, Allâh is the One Who forgives and accepts repentance, Most Merciful. (12)

Quran 49:14-17

۞ قَالَتِ ٱلْأَعْرَابُ ءَامَنَّا ۖ قُل لَّمْ تُؤْمِنُوا۟ وَلَـٰكِن قُولُوٓا۟ أَسْلَمْنَا وَلَمَّا يَدْخُلِ ٱلْإِيمَـٰنُ فِى قُلُوبِكُمْ ۖ وَإِن تُطِيعُوا۟ ٱللَّهَ وَرَسُولَهُۥ لَا يَلِتْكُم مِّنْ أَعْمَـٰلِكُمْ شَيْـًٔا ۚ إِنَّ ٱللَّهَ غَفُورٌ رَّحِيمٌ (١٤) إِنَّمَا ٱلْمُؤْمِنُونَ ٱلَّذِينَ ءَامَنُوا۟ بِٱللَّهِ وَرَسُولِهِۦ ثُمَّ لَمْ يَرْتَابُوا۟ وَجَـٰهَدُوا۟ بِأَمْوَٰلِهِمْ وَأَنفُسِهِمْ فِى سَبِيلِ ٱللَّهِ ۚ أُو۟لَـٰٓئِكَ هُمُ ٱلصَّـٰدِقُونَ (١٥) قُلْ أَتُعَلِّمُونَ ٱللَّهَ بِدِينِكُمْ وَٱللَّهُ يَعْلَمُ مَا فِى ٱلسَّمَـٰوَٰتِ وَمَا فِى ٱلْأَرْضِ ۚ وَٱللَّهُ بِكُلِّ شَىْءٍ عَلِيمٌ (١٦) يَمُنُّونَ عَلَيْكَ أَنْ أَسْلَمُوا۟ ۖ قُل لَّا تَمُنُّوا۟ عَلَىَّ إِسْلَـٰمَكُم ۖ بَلِ ٱللَّهُ يَمُنُّ عَلَيْكُمْ أَنْ هَدَىٰكُمْ لِلْإِيمَـٰنِ إِن كُنتُمْ صَـٰدِقِينَ (١٧)

The bedouins say: "We believe." Say: "You believe not but you only say, 'We have surrendered (in Islâm),' for Faith has not yet entered your hearts. But if you obey Allâh and His Messenger, He will not decrease anything in reward for your deeds. Verily, Allâh is Oft-Forgiving, Most

Merciful." (14) Only those are the believers who have believed in Allâh and His Messenger, and afterward doubt not but strive with their wealth and their lives for the Cause of Allâh. Those! They are the truthful. (15) Say: "Will you inform Allâh of your religion While Allâh knows all that is in the heavens and all that is in the earth, and Allâh is All-Aware of everything. (16) They regard as favour to you that they have embraced Islâm. Say: "Count not your Islâm as a favour to me. Nay, but Allâh has conferred a favour upon you, that He has guided you to the Faith, if you indeed are true. (17)

Quran 51:35-36

فَأَخْرَجْنَا مَن كَانَ فِيهَا مِنَ ٱلْمُؤْمِنِينَ (٣٥) فَمَا وَجَدْنَا فِيهَا غَيْرَ بَيْتٍ مِّنَ ٱلْمُسْلِمِينَ (٣٦)

So We brought out from therein the believers. (35) But We found not there any household of the Muslims except one. (36)

Quran 57:7-8

ءَامِنُوا۟ بِٱللَّهِ وَرَسُولِهِۦ وَأَنفِقُوا۟ مِمَّا جَعَلَكُم مُّسْتَخْلَفِينَ فِيهِ ۖ فَٱلَّذِينَ ءَامَنُوا۟ مِنكُمْ وَأَنفَقُوا۟ لَهُمْ أَجْرٌ كَبِيرٌ (٧) وَمَا لَكُمْ لَا تُؤْمِنُونَ بِٱللَّهِ وَٱلرَّسُولُ يَدْعُوكُمْ لِتُؤْمِنُوا۟ بِرَبِّكُمْ وَقَدْ أَخَذَ مِيثَـٰقَكُمْ إِن كُنتُم مُّؤْمِنِينَ (٨)

Believe in Allâh and His Messenger (Muhammad), and spend of that whereof He has made you trustees. And such of you as believe and spend (in Allâh's Way), theirs will be a great reward. (7) And what is the matter with you that you believe not in Allâh! While the Messenger

(Muhammad) invites you to believe in your Lord (Allâh), and He (Allâh) has indeed taken your covenant, if you are real believers. (8)

Quran 57:16

أَلَمْ يَأْنِ لِلَّذِينَ ءَامَنُوٓاْ أَن تَخْشَعَ قُلُوبُهُمْ لِذِكْرِ ٱللَّهِ وَمَا نَزَلَ مِنَ ٱلْحَقِّ وَلَا يَكُونُواْ كَٱلَّذِينَ أُوتُواْ ٱلْكِتَـٰبَ مِن قَبْلُ فَطَالَ عَلَيْهِمُ ٱلْأَمَدُ فَقَسَتْ قُلُوبُهُمْ وَكَثِيرٌ مِّنْهُمْ فَـٰسِقُونَ

Has not the time come for the hearts of those who believe (in the Oneness of Allâh - Islâmic Monotheism) to be affected by Allâh's Reminder (this Qur'ân), and that which has been revealed of the truth, lest they become as those who received the Scripture [the Taurât (Torah) and the Injeel] before (i.e. Jews and Christians), and the term was prolonged for them and so their hearts were hardened? And many of them were Fâsiqûn (the rebellious, the disobedient to Allâh). (16)

Quran 57:19

وَٱلَّذِينَ ءَامَنُواْ بِٱللَّهِ وَرُسُلِهِۦٓ أُوْلَـٰٓئِكَ هُمُ ٱلصِّدِّيقُونَ وَٱلشُّهَدَآءُ عِندَ رَبِّهِمْ لَهُمْ أَجْرُهُمْ وَنُورُهُمْ وَٱلَّذِينَ كَفَرُواْ وَكَذَّبُواْ بِـَٔايَـٰتِنَآ أُوْلَـٰٓئِكَ أَصْحَـٰبُ ٱلْجَحِيمِ

And those who believe in (the Oneness of) Allâh and His Messengers, they are the Siddiqûn (i.e. those followers of the Prophets who were first and foremost to believe in them), and the martyrs with their Lord, they shall have their reward and their light. But those who disbelieve (in the Oneness of Allâh - Islâmic Monotheism) and deny

Our Ayât (proofs, evidences, verses, lessons, signs, revelations, etc.), they shall be the dwellers of the blazing Fire. (19)

Quran 57:28

يَـٰٓأَيُّهَا ٱلَّذِينَ ءَامَنُوا۟ ٱتَّقُوا۟ ٱللَّهَ وَءَامِنُوا۟ بِرَسُولِهِۦ يُؤْتِكُمْ كِفْلَيْنِ مِن رَّحْمَتِهِۦ وَيَجْعَل لَّكُمْ نُورًا تَمْشُونَ بِهِۦ وَيَغْفِرْ لَكُمْ ۚ وَٱللَّهُ غَفُورٌ رَّحِيمٌ

O you who believe! Fear Allâh, and believe in His Messenger (Muhammad), He will give you a double portion of His Mercy, and He will give you a light by which you shall walk (straight), and He will forgive you. And Allâh is Oft-Forgiving, Most Merciful. (28)

Quran 58:9-13

يَـٰٓأَيُّهَا ٱلَّذِينَ ءَامَنُوٓا۟ إِذَا تَنَـٰجَيْتُمْ فَلَا تَتَنَـٰجَوْا۟ بِٱلْإِثْمِ وَٱلْعُدْوَٰنِ وَمَعْصِيَتِ ٱلرَّسُولِ وَتَنَـٰجَوْا۟ بِٱلْبِرِّ وَٱلتَّقْوَىٰ ۖ وَٱتَّقُوا۟ ٱللَّهَ ٱلَّذِىٓ إِلَيْهِ تُحْشَرُونَ (٩) إِنَّمَا ٱلنَّجْوَىٰ مِنَ ٱلشَّيْطَـٰنِ لِيَحْزُنَ ٱلَّذِينَ ءَامَنُوا۟ وَلَيْسَ بِضَآرِّهِمْ شَيْـًٔا إِلَّا بِإِذْنِ ٱللَّهِ ۚ وَعَلَى ٱللَّهِ فَلْيَتَوَكَّلِ ٱلْمُؤْمِنُونَ (١٠) يَـٰٓأَيُّهَا ٱلَّذِينَ ءَامَنُوٓا۟ إِذَا قِيلَ لَكُمْ تَفَسَّحُوا۟ فِى ٱلْمَجَـٰلِسِ فَٱفْسَحُوا۟ يَفْسَحِ ٱللَّهُ لَكُمْ ۖ وَإِذَا قِيلَ ٱنشُزُوا۟ فَٱنشُزُوا۟ يَرْفَعِ ٱللَّهُ ٱلَّذِينَ ءَامَنُوا۟ مِنكُمْ وَٱلَّذِينَ أُوتُوا۟ ٱلْعِلْمَ دَرَجَـٰتٍ ۚ وَٱللَّهُ بِمَا تَعْمَلُونَ خَبِيرٌ (١١) يَـٰٓأَيُّهَا ٱلَّذِينَ ءَامَنُوٓا۟ إِذَا نَـٰجَيْتُمُ ٱلرَّسُولَ فَقَدِّمُوا۟ بَيْنَ يَدَىْ نَجْوَىٰكُمْ صَدَقَةً ۚ ذَٰلِكَ خَيْرٌ لَّكُمْ وَأَطْهَرُ ۚ فَإِن لَّمْ تَجِدُوا۟ فَإِنَّ ٱللَّهَ غَفُورٌ رَّحِيمٌ (١٢) ءَأَشْفَقْتُمْ أَن تُقَدِّمُوا۟ بَيْنَ يَدَىْ نَجْوَىٰكُمْ صَدَقَـٰتٍ ۚ فَإِذْ لَمْ تَفْعَلُوا۟ وَتَابَ ٱللَّهُ عَلَيْكُمْ فَأَقِيمُوا۟ ٱلصَّلَوٰةَ وَءَاتُوا۟ ٱلزَّكَوٰةَ وَأَطِيعُوا۟ ٱللَّهَ وَرَسُولَهُۥ ۚ وَٱللَّهُ خَبِيرٌۢ بِمَا تَعْمَلُونَ (١٣)

O you who believe! When you hold secret counsel, do it not for sin and wrong-doing, and disobedience towards the Messenger but do it for Al-Birr (righteousness) and Taqwa (virtues and piety); and fear Allâh unto Whom you shall be gathered. (9) Secret counsels (conspiracies) are only from Shaitân (Satan), in order that he may cause grief to the believers. But he cannot harm them in the least, except as Allâh permits, and in Allâh let the believers put their trust (10) O you who believe! When you are told to make room in the assemblies, (spread out and) make room. Allâh will give you (ample) room (from His Mercy). And when you are told to rise up [for prayers, Jihâd (holy fighting in Allâh's Cause), or for any other good deed], rise up. Allâh will exalt in degree those of you who believe, and those who have been granted knowledge. And Allâh is Well-Acquainted with what you do. (11) O you who believe! When you (want to) consult the Messenger (Muhammad) in private, spend something in charity before your private consultation. That will be better and purer for you. But if you find not (the means for it), then verily, Allâh is Oft-Forgiving, Most Merciful. (12) Are you afraid of spending in charity before your private consultation (with him)? If then you do it not, and Allâh has forgiven you, then (at least) perform Salât (Iqâmat¬as¬Salât) and give Zakât and obey Allâh (i.e. do all that Allâh and His Messenger order you to do). And Allâh is All-Aware of what you do. (13)

Quran 58:22

لَّا تَجِدُ قَوْمًا يُؤْمِنُونَ بِٱللَّهِ وَٱلْيَوْمِ ٱلْأَخِرِ يُوَآدُّونَ مَنْ حَآدَّ ٱللَّهَ وَرَسُولَهُۥ وَلَوْ كَانُوٓا۟ ءَابَآءَهُمْ أَوْ أَبْنَآءَهُمْ أَوْ إِخْوَٰنَهُمْ أَوْ عَشِيرَتَهُمْ ۚ أُو۟لَٰٓئِكَ كَتَبَ

فِى قُلُوبِهِمُ ٱلْإِيمَٰنَ وَأَيَّدَهُم بِرُوحٍ مِّنْهُ وَيُدْخِلُهُمْ جَنَّٰتٍ تَجْرِى مِن تَحْتِهَا ٱلْأَنْهَٰرُ خَٰلِدِينَ فِيهَا رَضِىَ ٱللَّهُ عَنْهُمْ وَرَضُوا۟ عَنْهُ أُو۟لَٰٓئِكَ حِزْبُ ٱللَّهِ أَلَآ إِنَّ حِزْبَ ٱللَّهِ هُمُ ٱلْمُفْلِحُونَ

You will not find any people who believe in Allâh and the Last Day, making friendship with those who oppose Allâh and His Messenger (Muhammad), even though they were their fathers or their sons or their brothers or their kindred (people). For such He has written Faith in their hearts, and strengthened them with Rûh (proofs, light and true guidance) from Himself. And He will admit them to Gardens (Paradise) under which rivers flow to dwell therein (forever). Allâh is pleased with them, and they with Him. They are the Party of Allâh. Verily, it is the Party of Allâh that will be the successful. (22)

Quran 59:10

وَٱلَّذِينَ جَآءُو مِنۢ بَعْدِهِمْ يَقُولُونَ رَبَّنَا ٱغْفِرْ لَنَا وَلِإِخْوَٰنِنَا ٱلَّذِينَ سَبَقُونَا بِٱلْإِيمَٰنِ وَلَا تَجْعَلْ فِى قُلُوبِنَا غِلًّا لِّلَّذِينَ ءَامَنُوا۟ رَبَّنَآ إِنَّكَ رَءُوفٌ رَّحِيمٌ

And those who came after them say: "Our Lord! Forgive us and our brethren who have preceded us in Faith, and put not in our hearts any hatred against those who have believed. Our Lord! You are indeed full of kindness, Most Merciful. (10)

Quran 59:18-21

يَٰٓأَيُّهَا ٱلَّذِينَ ءَامَنُوا۟ ٱتَّقُوا۟ ٱللَّهَ وَلْتَنظُرْ نَفْسٌ مَّا قَدَّمَتْ لِغَدٍ وَٱتَّقُوا۟ ٱللَّهَ إِنَّ ٱللَّهَ خَبِيرٌۢ بِمَا تَعْمَلُونَ (١٨) وَلَا تَكُونُوا۟ كَٱلَّذِينَ نَسُوا۟ ٱللَّهَ فَأَنسَىٰهُمْ أَنفُسَهُمْ أُو۟لَٰٓئِكَ

هُمُ ٱلْفَٰسِقُونَ (١٩) لَا يَسْتَوِىٓ أَصْحَٰبُ ٱلنَّارِ وَأَصْحَٰبُ ٱلْجَنَّةِ أَصْحَٰبُ ٱلْجَنَّةِ هُمُ ٱلْفَآئِزُونَ (٢٠) لَوْ أَنزَلْنَا هَٰذَا ٱلْقُرْءَانَ عَلَىٰ جَبَلٍ لَّرَأَيْتَهُۥ خَٰشِعًا مُّتَصَدِّعًا مِّنْ خَشْيَةِ ٱللَّهِ وَتِلْكَ ٱلْأَمْثَٰلُ نَضْرِبُهَا لِلنَّاسِ لَعَلَّهُمْ يَتَفَكَّرُونَ (٢١)

O you who believe! Fear Allâh and keep your duty to Him. And let every person look to what he has sent forth for the tomorrow, and fear Allâh. Verily, Allâh is All-Aware of what you do. (18) And be not like those who forgot Allâh (i.e. became disobedient to Allâh) and He caused them to forget their ownselves, (let them to forget to do righteous deeds). Those are the Fâsiqûn (rebellious, disobedient to Allâh). (19) Not equal are the dwellers of the Fire and the dwellers of the Paradise. It is the dwellers of Paradise that will be successful. (20) Had We sent down this Qur'ân on a mountain, you would surely have seen it humbling itself and rendt asunder by the fear of Allâh. Such are the parables which We put forward to mankind that they may reflect. (21)

Quran 60:1-11

يَٰٓأَيُّهَا ٱلَّذِينَ ءَامَنُوا۟ لَا تَتَّخِذُوا۟ عَدُوِّى وَعَدُوَّكُمْ أَوْلِيَآءَ تُلْقُونَ إِلَيْهِم بِٱلْمَوَدَّةِ وَقَدْ كَفَرُوا۟ بِمَا جَآءَكُم مِّنَ ٱلْحَقِّ يُخْرِجُونَ ٱلرَّسُولَ وَإِيَّاكُمْ أَن تُؤْمِنُوا۟ بِٱللَّهِ رَبِّكُمْ إِن كُنتُمْ خَرَجْتُمْ جِهَٰدًا فِى سَبِيلِى وَٱبْتِغَآءَ مَرْضَاتِى تُسِرُّونَ إِلَيْهِم بِٱلْمَوَدَّةِ وَأَنَا۠ أَعْلَمُ بِمَآ أَخْفَيْتُمْ وَمَآ أَعْلَنتُمْ وَمَن يَفْعَلْهُ مِنكُمْ فَقَدْ ضَلَّ سَوَآءَ ٱلسَّبِيلِ (١) إِن يَثْقَفُوكُمْ يَكُونُوا۟ لَكُمْ أَعْدَآءً وَيَبْسُطُوٓا۟ إِلَيْكُمْ أَيْدِيَهُمْ وَأَلْسِنَتَهُم بِٱلسُّوٓءِ وَوَدُّوا۟ لَوْ تَكْفُرُونَ (٢) لَن تَنفَعَكُمْ أَرْحَامُكُمْ وَلَآ أَوْلَٰدُكُمْ يَوْمَ ٱلْقِيَٰمَةِ يَفْصِلُ بَيْنَكُمْ وَٱللَّهُ بِمَا تَعْمَلُونَ بَصِيرٌ (٣) قَدْ كَانَتْ لَكُمْ أُسْوَةٌ حَسَنَةٌ فِىٓ إِبْرَٰهِيمَ وَٱلَّذِينَ مَعَهُۥٓ إِذْ قَالُوا۟ لِقَوْمِهِمْ إِنَّا بُرَءَٰٓؤُا۟ مِنكُمْ وَمِمَّا تَعْبُدُونَ

مِن دُونِ ٱللَّهِ كَفَرْنَا بِكُمْ وَبَدَا بَيْنَنَا وَبَيْنَكُمُ ٱلْعَدَٰوَةُ وَٱلْبَغْضَآءُ أَبَدًا حَتَّىٰ تُؤْمِنُوا۟ بِٱللَّهِ وَحْدَهُۥٓ إِلَّا قَوْلَ إِبْرَٰهِيمَ لِأَبِيهِ لَأَسْتَغْفِرَنَّ لَكَ وَمَآ أَمْلِكُ لَكَ مِنَ ٱللَّهِ مِن شَىْءٍ ۖ رَّبَّنَا عَلَيْكَ تَوَكَّلْنَا وَإِلَيْكَ أَنَبْنَا وَإِلَيْكَ ٱلْمَصِيرُ (٤) رَبَّنَا لَا تَجْعَلْنَا فِتْنَةً لِّلَّذِينَ كَفَرُوا۟ وَٱغْفِرْ لَنَا رَبَّنَآ ۖ إِنَّكَ أَنتَ ٱلْعَزِيزُ ٱلْحَكِيمُ (٥) لَقَدْ كَانَ لَكُمْ فِيهِمْ أُسْوَةٌ حَسَنَةٌ لِّمَن كَانَ يَرْجُوا۟ ٱللَّهَ وَٱلْيَوْمَ ٱلْءَاخِرَ ۚ وَمَن يَتَوَلَّ فَإِنَّ ٱللَّهَ هُوَ ٱلْغَنِىُّ ٱلْحَمِيدُ (٦) ۞ عَسَى ٱللَّهُ أَن يَجْعَلَ بَيْنَكُمْ وَبَيْنَ ٱلَّذِينَ عَادَيْتُم مِّنْهُم مَّوَدَّةً ۚ وَٱللَّهُ قَدِيرٌ ۚ وَٱللَّهُ غَفُورٌ رَّحِيمٌ (٧) لَّا يَنْهَىٰكُمُ ٱللَّهُ عَنِ ٱلَّذِينَ لَمْ يُقَٰتِلُوكُمْ فِى ٱلدِّينِ وَلَمْ يُخْرِجُوكُم مِّن دِيَٰرِكُمْ أَن تَبَرُّوهُمْ وَتُقْسِطُوٓا۟ إِلَيْهِمْ ۚ إِنَّ ٱللَّهَ يُحِبُّ ٱلْمُقْسِطِينَ (٨) إِنَّمَا يَنْهَىٰكُمُ ٱللَّهُ عَنِ ٱلَّذِينَ قَٰتَلُوكُمْ فِى ٱلدِّينِ وَأَخْرَجُوكُم مِّن دِيَٰرِكُمْ وَظَٰهَرُوا۟ عَلَىٰٓ إِخْرَاجِكُمْ أَن تَوَلَّوْهُمْ ۚ وَمَن يَتَوَلَّهُمْ فَأُو۟لَٰٓئِكَ هُمُ ٱلظَّٰلِمُونَ (٩) يَٰٓأَيُّهَا ٱلَّذِينَ ءَامَنُوٓا۟ إِذَا جَآءَكُمُ ٱلْمُؤْمِنَٰتُ مُهَٰجِرَٰتٍ فَٱمْتَحِنُوهُنَّ ۖ ٱللَّهُ أَعْلَمُ بِإِيمَٰنِهِنَّ ۖ فَإِنْ عَلِمْتُمُوهُنَّ مُؤْمِنَٰتٍ فَلَا تَرْجِعُوهُنَّ إِلَى ٱلْكُفَّارِ ۖ لَا هُنَّ حِلٌّ لَّهُمْ وَلَا هُمْ يَحِلُّونَ لَهُنَّ ۖ وَءَاتُوهُم مَّآ أَنفَقُوا۟ ۚ وَلَا جُنَاحَ عَلَيْكُمْ أَن تَنكِحُوهُنَّ إِذَآ ءَاتَيْتُمُوهُنَّ أُجُورَهُنَّ ۚ وَلَا تُمْسِكُوا۟ بِعِصَمِ ٱلْكَوَافِرِ وَسْـَٔلُوا۟ مَآ أَنفَقْتُمْ وَلْيَسْـَٔلُوا۟ مَآ أَنفَقُوا۟ ۚ ذَٰلِكُمْ حُكْمُ ٱللَّهِ ۖ يَحْكُمُ بَيْنَكُمْ ۚ وَٱللَّهُ عَلِيمٌ حَكِيمٌ (١٠) وَإِن فَاتَكُمْ شَىْءٌ مِّنْ أَزْوَٰجِكُمْ إِلَى ٱلْكُفَّارِ فَعَاقَبْتُمْ فَـَٔاتُوا۟ ٱلَّذِينَ ذَهَبَتْ أَزْوَٰجُهُم مِّثْلَ مَآ أَنفَقُوا۟ ۚ وَٱتَّقُوا۟ ٱللَّهَ ٱلَّذِىٓ أَنتُم بِهِۦ مُؤْمِنُونَ (١١)

O you who believe! Take not My enemies and your enemies (i.e. disbelievers and polytheists) as friends, showing affection towards them, while they have disbelieved in what has come to you of the truth, and have driven out the Messenger and yourselves (from your homeland) because you believe in Allâh your Lord! If you have come forth to strive in My Cause and to seek My Good Pleasure, (then take not these disbelievers and polytheists, as your friends). You show friendship to them in secret, while I am All-Aware of what you conceal and what you reveal. And whosoever of you (Muslims) does that, then indeed he has gone (far) astray, from the Straight Path. (1) Should they gain the upper hand over you, they would behave to you as enemies, and stretch forth their hands and their tongues against you with evil, and they desire that you should disbelieve. (2) Neither your relatives nor your children will benefit you on the Day of Resurrection (against Allâh). He will judge between you. And Allâh is the All-Seer of what you do. (3) Indeed there has been an excellent example for you in Ibrâhim (Abraham) and those with him, when they said to their people: "Verily, we are free from you and whatever you worship besides Allâh, we have rejected you, and there has started between us and you, hostility and hatred for ever, until you believe in Allâh Alone," except the saying of Ibrâhim (Abraham) to his father: "Verily, I will ask forgiveness (from Allâh) for you, but I have no power to do anything for you before Allâh ." Our Lord! In You (Alone) we put our trust, and to You (Alone) we turn in repentance, and to You (Alone) is (our) final Return, (4) "Our Lord! Make us not a trial for the disbelievers, and forgive us, Our Lord! Verily, You, only You are the All-Mighty, the All-Wise." (5) Certainly, there has been in them an excellent example for you to follow — for those who look forward to (the Meeting with) Allâh and the Last Day. And whosoever turns away, then verily, Allâh is Rich (Free of all needs), Worthy of all Praise. (6) Perhaps Allâh will make friendship between you and those whom you hold as enemies. And Allâh has power (over all things), and Allâh is Oft-Forgiving, Most Merciful. (7) Allâh does not forbid you to deal justly and kindly with those who fought not against you on account of religion nor drove you out of your homes. Verily, Allâh loves those who deal with equity. (8) It is only as regards those who fought against you on account of religion, and have driven you out of your homes, and helped to drive you out, that Allâh forbids you to befriend them. And whosoever will befriend them, then such are the Zâlimûn (wrong-doers those who disobey Allâh). (9) O you who believe! When believing women come to you as emigrants, examine them, Allâh knows best as to their Faith, then if you ascertain that they are true believers, send them not back to the disbelievers, They are not lawful (wives) for the disbelievers nor are the disbelievers lawful (husbands) for them. But give (the disbelievers) that (amount of money) which they have spent [as their Mahr] to them. And there will be no sin on you to marry them if you have paid their Mahr to them. Likewise hold not the disbelieving women as wives, and ask for (the return of) that which you have spent (as Mahr) and let them (the disbelievers) ask back for that which they have spent. That is the Judgement of Allâh. He judges between you. And Allâh is All-Knowing, All-Wise. (10) And if any of your wives have gone from you to the disbelievers, (as apostates and you asked them to retrun back your Mahr but they refused) — then you went out for a Ghazwah (military expedition) (against them and) gained booty;

then pay from that booty to those whose wives have gone, the equivalent of what they had spent (on their Mahr). And fear Allâh in Whom you believe. (11)

Quran 60:13

يَـٰٓأَيُّهَا ٱلَّذِينَ ءَامَنُوا۟ لَا تَتَوَلَّوْا۟ قَوْمًا غَضِبَ ٱللَّهُ عَلَيْهِمْ قَدْ يَئِسُوا۟ مِنَ ٱلْأَخِرَةِ كَمَا يَئِسَ ٱلْكُفَّارُ مِنْ أَصْحَـٰبِ ٱلْقُبُورِ

O you who believe! Take not as friends the people who incurred the Wrath of Allâh. Surely, they have despaired of (receiveing any good in) the Hereafter, just as the disbelievers have despaired of those (buried) in graves (that they will not be resurrected on the Day of Resurrection). (13)

Quran 61:2-4

يَـٰٓأَيُّهَا ٱلَّذِينَ ءَامَنُوا۟ لِمَ تَقُولُونَ مَا لَا تَفْعَلُونَ (٢) كَبُرَ مَقْتًا عِندَ ٱللَّهِ أَن تَقُولُوا۟ مَا لَا تَفْعَلُونَ (٣) إِنَّ ٱللَّهَ يُحِبُّ ٱلَّذِينَ يُقَـٰتِلُونَ فِى سَبِيلِهِ صَفًّا كَأَنَّهُم بُنْيَـٰنٌ مَّرْصُوصٌ (٤)

O you who believe! Why do you say that which you do not do? (2) Most hateful it is with Allâh that you say that which you do not do. (3) Verily, Allâh loves those who fight in His Cause in rows (ranks) as if they were a solid structure. (4)

Quran 61:10-14

يَـٰٓأَيُّهَا ٱلَّذِينَ ءَامَنُوا۟ هَلْ أَدُلُّكُمْ عَلَىٰ تِجَـٰرَةٍ تُنجِيكُم مِّنْ عَذَابٍ أَلِيمٍ (١٠) تُؤْمِنُونَ بِٱللَّهِ وَرَسُولِهِ وَتُجَـٰهِدُونَ فِى سَبِيلِ ٱللَّهِ بِأَمْوَٰلِكُمْ وَأَنفُسِكُمْ ذَٰلِكُمْ خَيْرٌ لَّكُمْ إِن كُنتُمْ تَعْلَمُونَ (١١) يَغْفِرْ لَكُمْ ذُنُوبَكُمْ وَيُدْخِلْكُمْ جَنَّـٰتٍ

تَجْرِى مِن تَحْتِهَا ٱلْأَنْهَٰرُ وَمَسَٰكِنَ طَيِّبَةً فِى جَنَّٰتِ عَدْنٍ ذَٰلِكَ ٱلْفَوْزُ ٱلْعَظِيمُ (١٢) وَأُخْرَىٰ تُحِبُّونَهَا نَصْرٌ مِّنَ ٱللَّهِ وَفَتْحٌ قَرِيبٌ وَبَشِّرِ ٱلْمُؤْمِنِينَ (١٣) يَٰٓأَيُّهَا ٱلَّذِينَ ءَامَنُوا۟ كُونُوٓا۟ أَنصَارَ ٱللَّهِ كَمَا قَالَ عِيسَى ٱبْنُ مَرْيَمَ لِلْحَوَارِيِّۦنَ مَنْ أَنصَارِىٓ إِلَى ٱللَّهِ قَالَ ٱلْحَوَارِيُّونَ نَحْنُ أَنصَارُ ٱللَّهِ فَـَٔامَنَت طَّآئِفَةٌ مِّنۢ بَنِىٓ إِسْرَٰٓءِيلَ وَكَفَرَت طَّآئِفَةٌ فَأَيَّدْنَا ٱلَّذِينَ ءَامَنُوا۟ عَلَىٰ عَدُوِّهِمْ فَأَصْبَحُوا۟ ظَٰهِرِينَ (١٤)

O You who believe! Shall I guide you to a trade that will save you from a painful torment? (10) That you believe in Allâh and His Messenger (Muhammad), and that you strive hard and fight in the Cause of Allâh with your wealth and your lives, that will be better for you, if you but know! (11) (If you do so) He will forgive you your sins, and admit you into Gardens under which rivers flow, and pleasant dwellings in Adn (Edn) Paradise; that is indeed the great success. (12) And also (He will give you) another (blessing) which you love, help from Allâh (against your enemies) and a near victory. And give glad tidings (O Muhammad) to the believers. (13) O you who believe! Be you helpers (in the Cause) of Allâh as said 'Īsā (Jesus), son of Maryam (Mary), to the Hawârîyyun (the disciples) : "Who are my helpers (in the Cause) of Allâh?" The Hawârîyyun (the disciples) said: "We are Allâh's helpers" (i.e. we will strive in His Cause!). Then a group of the Children of Israel believed and a group disbelieved. So We gave power to those who believed against their enemies, and they became the victorious (uppermost). (14)

Quran 62:9

يَـٰٓأَيُّهَا ٱلَّذِينَ ءَامَنُوٓاْ إِذَا نُودِىَ لِلصَّلَوٰةِ مِن يَوْمِ ٱلْجُمُعَةِ فَٱسْعَوْاْ إِلَىٰ ذِكْرِ ٱللَّهِ وَذَرُواْ ٱلْبَيْعَ ۚ ذَٰلِكُمْ خَيْرٌ لَّكُمْ إِن كُنتُمْ تَعْلَمُونَ

O you who believe! When the call is proclaimed for the Salât (prayer) on Friday (Jumu'ah prayer), come to the remembrance of Allâh [Jumu'ah religious talk (Khutbah) and Salât (prayer)] and leave off business (and every other thing), That is better for you if you did but know! (9)

Quran 63:9-10

يَـٰٓأَيُّهَا ٱلَّذِينَ ءَامَنُواْ لَا تُلْهِكُمْ أَمْوَٰلُكُمْ وَلَآ أَوْلَـٰدُكُمْ عَن ذِكْرِ ٱللَّهِ ۚ وَمَن يَفْعَلْ ذَٰلِكَ فَأُوْلَـٰٓئِكَ هُمُ ٱلْخَـٰسِرُونَ (٩) وَأَنفِقُواْ مِن مَّا رَزَقْنَـٰكُم مِّن قَبْلِ أَن يَأْتِىَ أَحَدَكُمُ ٱلْمَوْتُ فَيَقُولَ رَبِّ لَوْلَآ أَخَّرْتَنِىٓ إِلَىٰٓ أَجَلٍ قَرِيبٍ فَأَصَّدَّقَ وَأَكُن مِّنَ ٱلصَّـٰلِحِينَ (١٠)

O you who believe! Let not your properties or your children divert you from the remembrance of Allâh. And whosoever does that, then they are the losers. (9) And spend (in charity) of that with which We have provided you, before death comes to one of you and he says: "My Lord! If only You would give me respite for a little while (i.e. return to the worldly life), then I should give Sadaqah (i.e. Zakât) of my wealth, and be among the righteous [i.e. perform Hajj (pilgrimage to Makkah)] and other good deeds. (10)

Quran 64:12-17

وَأَطِيعُواْ ٱللَّهَ وَأَطِيعُواْ ٱلرَّسُولَ ۚ فَإِن تَوَلَّيْتُمْ فَإِنَّمَا عَلَىٰ رَسُولِنَا ٱلْبَلَـٰغُ ٱلْمُبِينُ (١٢) ٱللَّهُ لَآ إِلَـٰهَ إِلَّا هُوَ ۚ وَعَلَى ٱللَّهِ فَلْيَتَوَكَّلِ ٱلْمُؤْمِنُونَ (١٣) يَـٰٓأَيُّهَا ٱلَّذِينَ

ءَامَنُوٓا۟ إِنَّ مِنْ أَزْوَٰجِكُمْ وَأَوْلَٰدِكُمْ عَدُوًّا لَّكُمْ فَٱحْذَرُوهُمْ ۚ وَإِن تَعْفُوا۟ وَتَصْفَحُوا۟ وَتَغْفِرُوا۟ فَإِنَّ ٱللَّهَ غَفُورٌ رَّحِيمٌ (١٤) إِنَّمَآ أَمْوَٰلُكُمْ وَأَوْلَٰدُكُمْ فِتْنَةٌ ۚ وَٱللَّهُ عِندَهُۥٓ أَجْرٌ عَظِيمٌ (١٥) فَٱتَّقُوا۟ ٱللَّهَ مَا ٱسْتَطَعْتُمْ وَٱسْمَعُوا۟ وَأَطِيعُوا۟ وَأَنفِقُوا۟ خَيْرًا لِّأَنفُسِكُمْ ۗ وَمَن يُوقَ شُحَّ نَفْسِهِۦ فَأُو۟لَٰٓئِكَ هُمُ ٱلْمُفْلِحُونَ (١٦) إِن تُقْرِضُوا۟ ٱللَّهَ قَرْضًا حَسَنًا يُضَٰعِفْهُ لَكُمْ وَيَغْفِرْ لَكُمْ ۚ وَٱللَّهُ شَكُورٌ حَلِيمٌ (١٧)

Obey Allâh, and obey the Messenger (Muhammad), but if you turn away, then the duty of Our Messenger is only to convey (the Message) clearly. (12) Allâh! Lâ ilâha illa Huwa (none has the right to be worshipped but He), And in Allâh (Alone), therefore, let the believers put their trust. (13) O you who believe! Verily, among your wives and your children are your enemies (who may stop you from the obedience of Allâh), therefore beware of them! But if you pardon (them) and overlook, and forgive (their faults), then verily, Allâh is Oft-Forgiving, Most Merciful. (14) Your wealth and your children are only a trial, whereas Allâh! With Him is a great reward (Paradise). (15) So keep your duty to Allâh and fear Him as much as you can; listen and obey; and spend in charity, that is better for yourselves. And whosoever is saved from his own covetousness, then they are the successful ones. (16) If you lend Allâh a goodly loan (i.e. spend in Allâh's Cause) He will double it for you, and will forgive you. And Allâh is Most Ready to appreciate and to reward, Most Forbearing, (17)

Quran 65:2-3

فَإِذَا بَلَغْنَ أَجَلَهُنَّ فَأَمْسِكُوهُنَّ بِمَعْرُوفٍ أَوْ فَارِقُوهُنَّ بِمَعْرُوفٍ وَأَشْهِدُواْ ذَوَىْ عَدْلٍ مِّنكُمْ وَأَقِيمُواْ ٱلشَّهَـٰدَةَ لِلَّهِ ذَٰلِكُمْ يُوعَظُ بِهِۦ مَن كَانَ يُؤْمِنُ بِٱللَّهِ وَٱلْيَوْمِ ٱلْـَٔاخِرِ وَمَن يَتَّقِ ٱللَّهَ يَجْعَل لَّهُۥ مَخْرَجًا (٢) وَيَرْزُقْهُ مِنْ حَيْثُ لَا يَحْتَسِبُ وَمَن يَتَوَكَّلْ عَلَى ٱللَّهِ فَهُوَ حَسْبُهُۥٓ إِنَّ ٱللَّهَ بَـٰلِغُ أَمْرِهِۦ قَدْ جَعَلَ ٱللَّهُ لِكُلِّ شَىْءٍ قَدْرًا (٣)

Then when they are about to attain their term appointed, either take them back in a good manner or part with them in a good manner. And take as witness two just persons from among you (Muslims). And establish the testimony for Allâh. That will be an admonition given to him who believes in Allâh and the Last Day. And whosoever fears Allâh and keeps his duty to Him, He will make a way for him to get out (from every difficulty). (2) And He will provide him from (sources) he never could imagine. And whosoever puts his trust in Allâh, then He will suffice him. Verily, Allâh will accomplish his purpose. Indeed Allâh has set a measure for all things. (3)

Quran 66:6-8

يَـٰٓأَيُّهَا ٱلَّذِينَ ءَامَنُواْ قُوٓاْ أَنفُسَكُمْ وَأَهْلِيكُمْ نَارًا وَقُودُهَا ٱلنَّاسُ وَٱلْحِجَارَةُ عَلَيْهَا مَلَـٰٓئِكَةٌ غِلَاظٌ شِدَادٌ لَّا يَعْصُونَ ٱللَّهَ مَآ أَمَرَهُمْ وَيَفْعَلُونَ مَا يُؤْمَرُونَ (٦) يَـٰٓأَيُّهَا ٱلَّذِينَ كَفَرُواْ لَا تَعْتَذِرُواْ ٱلْيَوْمَ إِنَّمَا تُجْزَوْنَ مَا كُنتُمْ تَعْمَلُونَ (٧) يَـٰٓأَيُّهَا ٱلَّذِينَ ءَامَنُواْ تُوبُوٓاْ إِلَى ٱللَّهِ تَوْبَةً نَّصُوحًا عَسَىٰ رَبُّكُمْ أَن يُكَفِّرَ عَنكُمْ سَيِّـَٔاتِكُمْ وَيُدْخِلَكُمْ جَنَّـٰتٍ تَجْرِى مِن تَحْتِهَا ٱلْأَنْهَـٰرُ يَوْمَ لَا يُخْزِى ٱللَّهُ ٱلنَّبِىَّ وَٱلَّذِينَ ءَامَنُواْ مَعَهُۥ نُورُهُمْ يَسْعَىٰ بَيْنَ أَيْدِيهِمْ وَبِأَيْمَـٰنِهِم يَقُولُونَ رَبَّنَآ أَتْمِمْ لَنَا نُورَنَا وَٱغْفِرْ لَنَآ إِنَّكَ عَلَىٰ كُلِّ شَىْءٍ قَدِيرٌ (٨)

O you who believe! Ward off from yourselves and your families against a Fire (Hell) whose fuel is men and stones, over which are (appointed) angels stern (and) severe, who disobey not, (from executing) the Commands they receive from Allâh, but do that which they are commanded. (6) (It will be said in the Hereafter) O you who disbelieve (in the Oneness of Allâh - Islâmic Monotheism)! Make no excuses this Day! You are being requited only for what you used to do. (7) O you who believe! Turn to Allâh with sincere repentance! It may be that your Lord will expiate from you your sins, and admit you into Gardens under which rivers flow (Paradise) the Day that Allâh will not disgrace the Prophet (Muhammad) and those who believe with him, Their Light will run forward before them and (with their Records — Books of deeds) in their right hands They will say: "Our Lord! Keep perfect our Light for us [and do not put it off till we cross over the Sirât (a slippery bridge over the Hell) safely] and grant us forgiveness. Verily, You are Able to do all things." (8)

Quran 84:25

إِلَّا ٱلَّذِينَ ءَامَنُواْ وَعَمِلُواْ ٱلصَّٰلِحَٰتِ لَهُمْ أَجْرٌ غَيْرُ مَمْنُونٍ

Save those who believe and do righteous good deeds, for them is a reward that will never come to an end (i.e. Paradise). (25)

Quran 85:7-8

وَهُمْ عَلَىٰ مَا يَفْعَلُونَ بِٱلْمُؤْمِنِينَ شُهُودٌ (٧) وَمَا نَقَمُوا۟ مِنْهُمْ إِلَّآ أَن يُؤْمِنُوا۟ بِٱللَّهِ ٱلْعَزِيزِ ٱلْحَمِيدِ (٨)

And they witnessed what they were doing against the believers. (7) And they had no fault except that they believed in Allâh, the All-Mighty, Worthy of all Praise! (8)

Quran 85:11

إِنَّ ٱلَّذِينَ ءَامَنُوا۟ وَعَمِلُوا۟ ٱلصَّٰلِحَٰتِ لَهُمْ جَنَّٰتٌ تَجْرِى مِن تَحْتِهَا ٱلْأَنْهَٰرُ ۚ ذَٰلِكَ ٱلْفَوْزُ ٱلْكَبِيرُ

Verily, those who believe and do righteous good deeds, for them will be Gardens under which rivers flow (Paradise). That is the great success. (11)

Quran 90:17

ثُمَّ كَانَ مِنَ ٱلَّذِينَ ءَامَنُوا۟ وَتَوَاصَوْا۟ بِٱلصَّبْرِ وَتَوَاصَوْا۟ بِٱلْمَرْحَمَةِ

Then he became one of those who believed, and recommended one another to perseverance and patience, and (also) recommended one another to pity and compassion. (17)

Quran 95:6

إِلَّا ٱلَّذِينَ ءَامَنُوا۟ وَعَمِلُوا۟ ٱلصَّٰلِحَٰتِ فَلَهُمْ أَجْرٌ غَيْرُ مَمْنُونٍ

Save those who believe (in Islâmic Monotheism) and do righteous deeds, Then they shall have a reward without end (Paradise). (6)

Quran 98:7-8

إِنَّ ٱلَّذِينَ ءَامَنُوا۟ وَعَمِلُوا۟ ٱلصَّٰلِحَٰتِ أُو۟لَٰٓئِكَ هُمْ خَيْرُ ٱلْبَرِيَّةِ (٧) جَزَآؤُهُمْ عِندَ رَبِّهِمْ جَنَّٰتُ عَدْنٍ تَجْرِى مِن تَحْتِهَا ٱلْأَنْهَٰرُ خَٰلِدِينَ فِيهَآ أَبَدًا ۖ رَّضِىَ ٱللَّهُ عَنْهُمْ وَرَضُوا۟ عَنْهُ ۚ ذَٰلِكَ لِمَنْ خَشِىَ رَبَّهُۥ (٨)

Verily, those who believe and do righteous good deeds, they are the best of creatures (7) Their reward with their Lord is 'Adn (Eden) Paradise (Gardens of Eternity), underneath which rivers flow, They will abide therein forever, Allâh will be pleased with them, and they with Him. That is for him who fears his Lord. (8)

Quran 103:1-3

وَٱلْعَصْرِ (١) إِنَّ ٱلْإِنسَٰنَ لَفِى خُسْرٍ (٢) إِلَّا ٱلَّذِينَ ءَامَنُوا۟ وَعَمِلُوا۟ ٱلصَّٰلِحَٰتِ وَتَوَاصَوْا۟ بِٱلْحَقِّ وَتَوَاصَوْا۟ بِٱلصَّبْرِ (٣)

By Al-'Asr (the time). (1) Verily, man is in loss, (2) Except those who believe and do righteous good deeds, and recommend one another to the truth (i.e. order one another to perform all kinds of good deeds (Al-Ma'ruf) which Allâh has ordained, and abstain from all kinds of sins and evil deeds (Al-Munkar) which Allâh has forbidden), and recommend one another to patience (for the sufferings, harms, and injuries which one may encounter in Allâh's Cause during preaching His religion of Islâmic Monotheism or Jihâd). (3)

Narrated Abu Hurairah:

The Prophet (ﷺ) said: The believer is the believer's mirror, and the believer is the believer's brother who guards him against loss and protects him when he is absent.

Source: Sunan Abi Dawud 4918

Graded: Hasan by Albani

It is narrated by Jabir that he heard:

the Messenger of Allah (ﷺ) say, "If a believing man or a believing woman or a Muslim man or Muslim woman falls ill then Allah, the exalted, forgives them their sins (because of their illness)."

Source: Al-Adab Al-Mufrad 508

Narrated Abu Hurairah:

that the Messenger of Allah (ﷺ) said: "The Muslim is the one from (the harm of) whose tongue and hand (other) Muslims are safe, and the believer is the one with whom the people trust their blood and their wealth."

Source: Jami` at-Tirmidhi 2627 Graded: Sahih

Abu Hurairah reported:

God's Messenger as saying, "God most high is jealous of His honor, and the believer is jealous. God's jealousy is to the effect that a believer should not commit what God has prohibited."

Reported by Bukhari and Muslim

Narrated Abu Qatada:

The Prophet (ﷺ) said, "Relieved or relieving. And a believer is relieved (by death).

Source: Sahih al-Bukhari 6513

It was narrated that 'Abdullah said:

"Fighting a believer is Kufr and defaming him is evildoing."

Source: Sunan an-Nasa'i 4113 Graded: Sahih

It was narrated that Abu Hurairah said:

"The Messenger of Allah said: 'The adulterer is not a believer at the moment when he is committing adultery, and the wine drinker is not a believer at the moment when he is drinking wine, and the thief is not a believer at the moment when he is stealing, and the robber is not a believer at the moment when he is robbing and people are looking on.'"

Source: Sunan an-Nasa'i 5659 Graded: Sahih

Abu Hurairah reported the Messenger of Allah as saying :

When one commits fornication, one is not a believer ; when one steals, one is not a believer ; when one drinks, one is not a believer ; and repentance is placed before him.

Source: Sunan Abi Dawud 4689 Graded: Sahih

Abdullah said:

"The most blameworthy thing in a believer's character is coarseness."

Source: Al-Adab Al-Mufrad 314 Graded: Sahih by Albani

Narrated Abu Musa:

The Prophet (ﷺ) said, "A faithful believer to a faithful believer is like the bricks of a wall, enforcing each other." While (saying that) the Prophet (ﷺ) clasped his hands, by interlacing his fingers.

Source: Sahih al-Bukhari 481

Abu Hurairah reported Allah's Messenger (ﷺ) as saying:

The world is a prison-house for a believer and Paradise for a non-believer.

Source: Sahih Muslim 2956

Atiyyah Al-'Awfi narrated from Abu Sa'eed Al-Khudri, that The Messenger of Allah said:

"Whichever believer feeds a hungry believer, Allah feeds him from the fruits of Paradise on the Day of Resurrection. Whichever believer gives drink to a thirsty believer, Allah gives him to drink from the 'sealed nectar' on the Day of Resurrection. Whichever believer clothes a naked believer, Allah clothes him from the green garments of Paradise."

Source: Jami` at-Tirmidhi 2449

Graded: Daif by Darussalam

It was narrated from 'Ali that The Prophet (ﷺ) said:

'No one (truly) believes until he believes in four things; until he believes that there is no god but Allah and that I am the Messenger of Allah Who sent me with the truth, and until he believes in the resurrection after death, and until he believes in the divine will and decree."

Source: Musnad Ahmed 758 Graded: Sahih

Abu Hurairah reported:

The Prophet (ﷺ) said, "By Allah, he is not a believer! By Allah, he is not a believer! By Allah, he is not a believer." It was asked, "Who is that, O Messenger of Allah?" He said, "One whose neighbor does not feel safe from his evil".

Source: Bukhari and Muslim

Tamim al-Dari reported the Prophet as saying:

Religion conduct; religion consists in sincere conduct. The people asked; to whom should it be directed, Messenger of Allah? He replied :

To Allah, his book, his Apostle, the leaders (public authorities) of the believers and all the believers, and the leaders (public authorities) of Muslim and the Muslims and the Muslims in general.

Source: Sunan Abi Dawud 4944 Graded Sahih by Albani

Abu Huraira reported God's messenger as saying:

"He who believes in God and the last day should honor his guest; he who believes in God and the last day should not annoy his neighbor; and he who believes in God and the last day should say what is good, or keep silent." In a version instead of speaking of the neighbor he said, "He who believes in God and the last day should join ties of relationship."

Source: Bukhari and Muslim

Uqba b. 'Amir said on the pulpit that Allah's Messenger (ﷺ) said:

A believer is the brother of a believer, so it is not lawful for a believer to outbid his brother, and he should not propose an engagement when his brother has thus proposed until he gives it up.

Source: Sahih Muslim 1414

Malik related to me that Safwan ibn Sulaym said:

"The Messenger of Allah, may Allah bless him and grant him peace, was asked, 'Can the believer be a coward?' He said, 'Yes.' He was asked, 'Can the believer be a miser?' He said, 'Yes.' He was asked, 'Can the believer be a liar?' He said, 'No.'"

Source: Muwatta Imam Malik Hadith 1832

Narrated Jabir:

that the Prophet (ﷺ) said: "Whoever believes in Allah and the Last Day, then he is not to let his wife enter the public bathhouse, and whoever believes in Allah and the Last Day, then he is not to enter the public bathhouse without a loincloth. And whoever believes in Allah and the Last Day, then he is not to sit at a spread in which intoxicants are circulated."

Source: Jami at-Tirmidhi Hadith 3031 Graded: Hasan

Abu Hurairah reported:

Messenger of Allah (ﷺ) said, "A believer must not hate (his wife) believing woman; if he dislikes one of her characteristics he will be pleased with another".

Source: Muslim and Riyad as-Saliheen

Abu Hurairah reported God's messenger as saying:

"The believer is like a plant which is continually swayed by the wind, for the believer is continually afflicted by trial; but the hypocrite is like a cedar tree which does not shake till it is cut down."

Source: Bukhari and Muslim

Abu Hurairah reported that the Prophet said,

"A believer is the mirror of his brother. A believer is the brother of another believer. He protects him against loss and defends him behind his back."

Source: Al-Adab Al-Mufrad 239

Ruaifi' bin Thabit narrated that The Messenger of Allah (ﷺ) said:

"He who believes in Allah and the Hereafter must not ride on an animal belonging to the booty of the Muslims and put it back when he has emaciated it, or wear a garment belonging to the booty of the Muslims and put it back when it is worn."

Source: Abu Dawud and Ad-Darimi

Narrated Abu Hurairah:

A man used to eat much, but when he embraced Islam, he started eating less. That was mentioned to the Prophet (ﷺ) who then said, "A believer eats in one intestine (is satisfied with a little food) and a Kafir eats in seven intestines (eats much)."

Source: Sahih al-Bukhari 5397

Abu Hurairah narrated that the Messenger of Allah said:

"Trials will not cease afflicting the believing man and the believing woman in their self, children, and wealth, until they meet Allah without having any sin."

Source: Jami` at-Tirmidhi 2399 Graded Hasan

Abu Hurairah reported:

The Prophet (ﷺ) said, "He who believes in Allah and the Last Day must either speak good or remain silent."

Source: Riyad as-Salihin 1511 Graded Sahih

Abu Hurairah said:

The Prophet (ﷺ) said, "A believer should not be stung twice from the same hole."

Source: Bukhari and Muslim

Ibn 'Umar reported the Messenger of Allah as saying :

If any believing man calls another believing man an unbeliever, if he is actually an infidel, it is all right; if not, he will become an infidel.

Source: Sunan Abi Dawud 4687 Graded Sahih by Albani

Anas reported God's messenger as saying:

"None of you believes till I am dearer to him than his father, his child, and all mankind."

Source: Bukhari and Muslim

Narrated Abu Hurairah:

Allah's Messenger (ﷺ) said, "They say Al-Karm (the generous), and in fact Al-Karm is the heart of a believer."

Source: Sahih al-Bukhari 6183

Abu Hurrairah narrated that the Messenger of Allah said:

"In the end of time, the dreams of a believer will hardly ever fail to come true, and the most truthful of them in dreams will be the truest in speech among them. And dreams are three types: The good dreams wihich is glad tidings from Allah, dreams about something that has happened to the man himself, and dreams in which the Shaitan frightens someone. So when one of you sees what he dislikes, then he should get up and perform Salat."

Abu Hurairah said: "I like fetters and dislikes, the iron collar. And fetters refers to being firm in the religion." He said: "The Prophet said: 'Dreams are a portion among the forty-six portions of Prophethood."

Source: Jami` at-Tirmidhi 2291 Graded: Sahih

Abdullah bin Buraidah narrated from his father, that:

The Prophet said: "The believer dies with sweat on his brow."

Source: Jami` at-Tirmidhi 982 Graded: Sahih

Abu Hurairah narrated that:

The Messenger of Allah said: "The believer's soul is suspended by his debt until it is settled for him."

Source: Jami` at-Tirmidhi 1078 Graded: Hasan

Abu Sa'eed Al-Khudri narrated that the Messenger of Allah said:

"Two traits are not combined in a believer: Stinginess and bad manners."

Source: Jami` at-Tirmidhi 1962

Graded: Daif by Darussalam

Abu Hurairah narrated that the Messenger of Allah said:

"The believer is naively noble and the stingy person is deceitfully treacherous."

Source: Jami` at-Tirmidhi 1964

Graded: Daif by Darussalam

Ibn 'Umar narrated that the Messenger of Allah said:

"The believer is not one who curses others."

Source: Jami` at-Tirmidhi 2019 Graded: Hasan

Narrated Ibn 'Abbas:

"The Prophet (ﷺ) said to me: 'A man who believes in Allah and the Last Day does not hate the Ansar."

Source: Jami at-Tirmidhi 4283 Graded: Sahih

Abu Hurairah reported:

Messenger of Allah (ﷺ) said, "He who believes in Allah and the Last Day let him not harm his neighbour; and he who believes in Allah and the Last Day let him show hospitality to his guest; and he who believes in Allah and the Last Day let him speak good or remain silent".

Source: Bukhari and Muslim

Narrated Abdullah ibn Mas'ud:

The Prophet (ﷺ) said: The most merciful of the people in respect of killing are believers (in Allah).

Source: Sunan Abi Dawud 2666 Graded: Daif by Albani

Narrated Abu Hurairah:

The Prophet (ﷺ) said: Faith prevented assassination. A believer should not assassinate.

Source: Sunan Abi Dawud 2769 Graded: Sahih

Narrated Abu Hurairah:

The Prophet (ﷺ) said: The most perfect believer in respect of faith is he who is best of them in manners.

Source: Sunan Abi Dawud 4682

Graded: Hasan Sahih by Albani

Narrated Abu Salamah; Abu Hurairah:

The Prophet (ﷺ) said: The believer is simple and generous, but the profligate is deceitful and ignoble.

Source: Sunan Abi Dawud 4790 Graded: Hasan

Narrated Abu Hurairah:

The Prophet (ﷺ) as saying: How good is the believers meal of dates shortly before dawn.

Source: Sunan Abi Dawud 2345 Graded: Sahih

Mu'awiyah said:

"I heard the Messenger of Allah (ﷺ) say: 'Every intoxicant is unlawful for every believer.'"

Source: Sunan Ibn Majah 3389 Graded: Sahih

Abu Hurairah reported:

Messenger of Allah (ﷺ) said, "A believer owes another believer five rights: responding to greetings, visiting him in illness, following his funeral, accepting his invitation, and saying 'Yarhamuk-Allah (May Allah have mercy on you),' when he says 'Al-hamdu lillah (Praise be to Allah)' after sneezing".

Source: Bukhari and Muslim

Narrated Abu Huraira:

The Prophet (ﷺ) said, "I am more closer to the believers than their own selves, so whoever (of them) dies while being in debt and leaves nothing for its repayment, then we are to pay his debts on his behalf and whoever (among the believers) dies leaving some property, then that property is for his heirs."

Source: Sahih al-Bukhari 6731

Narrated Um Habiba:

The Prophet (ﷺ) said, "It is not lawful for a Muslim woman who believes in Allah and the Last Day to mourn for more than three days, except for her husband, for whom she should mourn for four months and ten days."

Source: Sahih al-Bukhari 5339

Jabir bin 'Abdullah narrated that the Messenger of Allah said:

'A slave (of Allah) shall not believe until he believes in Al-Qadar, its good and its bad, such that he knows that what struck him would not have missed him, and that what missed him would not have struck him."

Source: Jami at-Tirmidhi 2294 Graded: Hasan

Abu Sa'id and Abu Hurairah reported that the Prophet (ﷺ) said:

"Never a believer is stricken with a discomfort, an illness, an anxiety, a grief or mental worry or even the pricking of a thorn but Allah will expiate his sins on account of his patience".

Source: Bukhari and Muslim

Anas reported:

The Prophet (ﷺ) said, "No one of you becomes a true believer until he likes for his brother what he likes for himself".

Source: Bukhari and Muslim

Nu'man bin Bashir reported:

Messenger of Allah (ﷺ) said, "The believers in their mutual kindness, compassion and sympathy are just like one body. When one of the limbs suffers, the whole body responds to it with wakefulness and fever".

Source: Bukhari and Muslim

Al-Bara' bin 'Azib reported:

The Prophet (ﷺ) said about the Ansar: "Only a believer loves them, and only a hypocrite hates them. Allah loves him who loves them and Allah hates him who hates them".

Source: Bukhari and Muslim

Abu Hurairah reported:

Messenger of Allah (ﷺ) said, "If a believer had full knowledge of the chastisement of Allah, none would covet His Paradise; and were an infidel to know the Mercy Allah has, none would despair of His Paradise".

Source: Riyad as-Saliheen 443 Graded: Sahih

Abu Dharr said:

The Messenger of Allah (ﷺ) was asked: "Tell us about a person who does some good deed and people praise him, will this be considered as showing off?" He replied, "This is the glad tidings which a believer receives (in this life)."

Source: Riyad as-Salihin 1621 Graded: Sahih

Abu Hurairah reported:

I heard my Khalil (the Messenger of Allah (ﷺ)) as saying, "The adornment of the believer (in Jannah) will reach the places where the water of Wudu' reaches (his body)."

Source: Riyad as-Salihin 1025 Graded: Sahih

It was narrated from 'Ali, that the Prophet said:

"The lives of the believers are equal in value, and they are one against others, and they hasten to support the asylum granted by the least of them. But no believer may be killed in return for a disbeliever, nor one with a covenant while his covenant is in effect."

Source: Sunan an-Nasa'i 4735 Graded: Sahih

It was narrated from Ibn 'Umar that the Messenger of Allah (ﷺ) said:

"The believer who mixes with people and bears their annoyance with patience will have a greater reward than the believer who does not mix with people and does not put up with their annoyance."

Source: Sunan Ibn Majah 4032 Graded: Sahih

A'isha reported:

The believing women used to pray the morning prayer with the Messenger of Allah and then return wrapped in their mantles. No one could recognize them.

Source: Sahih Muslim 645a

Sa'd narrated it on the authority of his father (Abi Waqqas) that he observed:

The Messenger of Allah (ﷺ) distributed shares (of booty among his Companions). I said: Messenger of Allah! Give it to so and so, for verily he is a believer. Upon this the Messenger of Allah remarked: Or a Muslim. I (the narrator) repeated it (the word" believer") thrice and he (the Prophet) turned his back upon me (and substituted the word)" Muslim," and then observed: I bestow it (this share) to a man out of apprehension lest Allah should throw him prostrate into the fire (of Hell) whereas in fact the other man is dearer to me than he.

Source: Sahih Muslim 150a

Narrated Abu Huraira:

The Prophet said, "It is not permissible for a woman who believes in Allah and the Last Day to travel for one day and night except with a Mahram."

Source: Sahih al-Bukhari 1088

Ruwaifi bin Thabit narrated that :

the Prophet said: "Whoever believes in Allah and the Last Day, then he does not levy his water on someone else's child."

Source: Jami` at-Tirmidhi 1131 Graded: Hasan

Abdullah narrated that the Messenger of Allah said:

"The believer does not insult the honor of others, nor curse, nor commit Fahishah, nor is he foul."

Source: Jami` at-Tirmidhi 1977 Graded: Hasan

Narrated 'Aishah:

that the Messenger of Allah (ﷺ) said: "Indeed among the believers with the most complete faith is the one who is the best in conduct, and the most kind to his family."

Source: Jami` at-Tirmidhi 2612

Graded: Daif by Darussalam

Narrated Abu Sa'eed Al-Khudri:

that the Messenger of Allah (ﷺ) said: "The believer will never be satisfied with the good he hears, until he ends up in Paradise."

Source: Jami` at-Tirmidhi 2686

Graded: Daif by Darussalam

Narrated Abu Hurairah:

the Messenger of Allah (ﷺ) said: "The wise statement is the lost property of the believer, so wherever he finds it, then he is more worthy of it."

Source: Jami` at-Tirmidhi 2687

Graded: Daif by Darussalam

It was narrated that 'Ali said:

"The Prophet made a covenant with me that none would love me but a believer, and none would hate me but a hypocrite."

Source: Sunan an-Nasa'i 5022 Graded: Sahih

Narrated AbuSa'id al-Khudri:

The Prophet (ﷺ) said: Associate only with a believer, and let only a God-fearing man eat your meals.

Source: Sunan Abi Dawud 4832 Graded: Hasan

It was narrated from Abu Hurairah that the Messenger of Allah (ﷺ) said:

"The believer is more precious to Allah, the Mighty and Sublime, than some of His angels."

Source: Sunan Ibn Majah 3947

Graded: Daif by Darussalam

It was narrated from Abu Hurairah that the Messenger of Allah (ﷺ) said:

"The poor believers will enter Paradise half a day – five hundred years – before the rich.'"

Source: Sunan Ibn Majah 4122 Graded: Hasan

Ibn Mas'ud reported God's messenger as saying:

"There was no prophet whom God raised up among his people before me who did not have from among his people apostles and companions who held to his sunna and followed what he commanded; then they were succeeded by people who said what they did not practice and did things they were not commanded to do. So he who strives against them with his hand is a believer, he who strives against them with his tongue is a believer, and he who strives against them with his heart is a believer. Beyond that there is not so much faith as a grain of mustard seed."

Source: Mishkat al-Masabih 157 Graded: Sahih

Abū Mūsa al-Ash'ari reported God's messenger as saying:

"A believer who recites the Qur'ān is like a citron whose fragrance is sweet and whose taste is sweet, a believer who does not recite the Qur'ān is like a date which has no fragrance but has a sweet state, a hypocrite who does not recite the Qur'ān is like the colocynth which has no fragrance and has a better taste, and the hypocrite who recites the Qur'ān is like basil whose fragrance is sweet but whose taste is bitter." A version has, "A believer who recites the Qur'ān and acts according to it is like a citron, and a believer who does not recite the Qur'ān but acts according to it is like a date."

Source: Bukhari and Muslim

It is reported by Aishah that the Prophet said:

"When a Believer falls ill, Allah cleans him of sin as a kiln removes the rust from iron".

Source: Al-Adab Al-Mufrad 497

Abu Yahya Suhaib bin Sinan reported that:

The Messenger of Allah (ﷺ) said, "How wonderful is the case of a believer; there is good for him in everything and this applies only to a believer. If prosperity attends him, he expresses gratitude to Allah and that is good for him; and if adversity befalls him, he endures it patiently and that is better for him".

Source: Riyad as-Salihin 27 Graded: Sahih

Abu Hurairah reported:

Messenger of Allah (ﷺ) said, "By Him in Whose Hand my soul is! You will not enter Paradise until you believe, and you shall not believe until you love one another. May I inform you of something, if you do, you love each other. Promote greeting amongst you (by saying As-salamu 'alaikum to one another)".

Source: Riyad as-Salihin 378 Graded: Sahih

Narrated Zaid bin Khalid Al-Juhani:

Allah's Messenger (ﷺ) led the morning prayer in Al-Hudaibiya and it had rained the previous night. When the Prophet had finished the prayer he faced the people and said, "Do you know what your Lord has said?" They replied, "Allah and His Apostle know better." (The Prophet (ﷺ) said), "Allah says, 'In this morning some of My worshipers remained as true believers and some became non-believers; he who said that it had rained with the blessing and mercy of Allah is the one who believes in Me and does not believe in star, but he who said it had rained because of such and such (star) is a disbeliever in Me and is a believer in star.' "

Source: Sahih al-Bukhari 1038

It was narrated from Muhammad bin Jubair bin Mut'im that his father said:

"The Messenger of Allah (ﷺ) stood up in Khaif in Mina, and said: 'May Allah make his face shine, the man who hears my words and conveys them. It may be that the bearer of knowledge does not understand it, and it may be that he takes it to one who will understand it more than he does. There are three things in which the heart of the believer does not betray: sincerity of action for the sake of Allah, offering sincere advice to the rulers of the Muslims, and adhering to the Jama'ah (main body of the Muslims). Their supplication is answered (i.e. encompassing every good, and all of the people)."

Source: Sunan Ibn Majah 3056 Graded: Hasan

It has been narrated on the authority of Abu Hurairah that the Messenger Allah (ﷺ) said:

A disbeliever and a believer who killed him will never be gathered together in Hell.

Source: Sahih Muslim 1891a

A'isha reported:

I heard Allah's Messenger (ﷺ) as saying: There is nothing (in the form of trouble) that comes to a believer even if it is the pricking of a thorn that there is decreed for him by Allah good or his sins are obliterated.

Source: Sahih Muslim 2572g

Salim, the freed slave of Nasriyyin, said:

I heard Abu Huraira as saying that he heard Allah's Messenger (ﷺ) as saying: O Allah, Muhammad is a human being. I lose my temper just as human beings lose temper, and I have held a covenant with Thee which

Thou wouldst not break: For a believer whom I give any trouble or invoke curse or beat, make that an expiation (of his sins and a source of) his nearness to Thee on the Day of Resurrection.

Source: Sahih Muslim 2601e

Abu Hurairah narrated that The Messenger of Allah said:

"The most complete of the believers in faith, is the one with the best character among them. And the best of you are those who are best to your women."

Source: Jami` at-Tirmidhi 1162 Graded: Hasan

Abu Ad-Dardh narrated that the Messenger of Allah said:

"Nothing is heavier on the believer's Scale on the Day of Judgment than good character. For indeed Allah, Most High, is angered by the shameless obscene person."

Source: Jami` at-Tirmidhi 2002 Graded: Sahih

It was narrated from Hudhaifah, that the Messenger of Allah said:

"It is not for the believer to humiliate himself." They said: "How does he humiliate himself?" He said: "By taking on a trial which he can not bear."

Source: Jami` at-Tirmidhi 2254 Graded: Daif

Abu Shuraih Khuwailid bin 'Amr Al-Khuza'i reported:

I heard Messenger of Allah (ﷺ) saying, "He who believes in Allah and the Last Day, should accommodate his guest according to his right." He was asked: "What is his right, O Messenger of Allah?" He (ﷺ) replied: "It is (to accommodate him) for a day and a night, and hospitality extends for three days, and what is beyond that is charity."

Source: Bukhari and Muslim

It was narrated that 'Abdullah bin 'Amr bin Al-'As said:

"The Messenger of Allah said: 'By the One in Whose Hand is my soul, killing a believer is more grievous before Allah than the extinction of the whole world.'"

Source: Sunan an-Nasa'i 3986 Graded: Hasan

Narrated Aisha, Ummul Mu'minin:

The Messenger of Allah (ﷺ) said: By his good character a believer will attain the degree of one who prays during the night and fasts during the day.

Source: Sunan Abi Dawud 4798 Graded: Sahih

It was narrated from Sulaiman bin Buraidah that his father said:

"The Messenger of Allah (ﷺ) used to teach them, when they went out to the graveyard, to say: As-salamu 'alaykum ahlad-diyar minal-mu'minina wal- muslimin, wa inna insha' Allah bikum lahiqun, nas'alul-laha lana wa lakumul-'afiyah (Peace be upon you, O inhabitants of the abodes, believers and Muslims, and we will join you soon if Allah wills. We ask Allah for well-being for us and for you).'"

Source: Sunan Ibn Majah 1547 Graded: Sahih

It was narrated from 'Amr bin Sh'uaib from his father, that his grandfather said:

"The Messenger of Allah(ﷺ) forbade plucking out white hairs and said: 'It is the light of the believer.'"

Source: Sunan Ibn Majah 3721 Graded: Hasan

It was narrated that Qais bin 'Ubad said:

"Al-Ashtar and I went to 'Ali, may Allah be pleased with him, and said: Did the Prophet of Allah tell you anything that he did not tell to all the people?' He said: 'No, except what is in this letter of mine.' He brought out a letter from the sheath of his sword and it said therein: "The lives of the believers are equal in value, and they are one against others, and they hasten to support the asylum granted by the least of them. But no believer may be killed in return for a disbeliever, nor one with a covenant while his covenant is in effect. Whoever commits an offense then the blame is on himself, and whoever gives sanctuary to an offender, then upon him will be the curse of Allah, the angels and all the people."

Source: Sunan an-Nasa'i 4734 Graded: Sahih

It was narrated from 'Imran bin Husain that the Messenger of Allah (ﷺ) said:

"Allah loves His believing slave who is poor, does not beg and has many children."

Source: Sunan Ibn Majah 4121

Graded: Daif by Darussalam

Abdullah reported that the Prophet said:

"A believer is not a defamer nor a curser nor coarse nor obscene."

Source: Al-Adab Al-Mufrad 312 Graded: Sahih by Albani

Abu Hurairah reported that the Messenger of Allah said:

"The believer is guileless and generous while the corrupt is a swindler and miserly."

Source: Al-Adab Al-Mufrad 418 Graded: Sahih by Albani

Anas b. Malik reported that Allah's Messenger (ﷺ) thus told him:

When a non-believer does good he is made to taste Its reward in this world. And so far as the believer is concerned, Allah stores (the reward) of his virtues for the Hereafter and provides him sustenance in accordance with his obedience to Him.

Source: Sahih Muslim 2808b

Suhaib reported that Allah's Messenger (ﷺ) said:

Strange are the ways of a believer for there is good in every affair of his and this is not the case with anyone else except in the case of a believer for if he has an occasion to feel delight, he thanks (God), thus there is a good for him in it, and if he gets into trouble and shows resignation (and endures it patiently), there is a good for him in it.

Source: Sahih Muslim 2999

Narrated Abu Sa`id Al-Khudri:

Somebody asked, "O Allah's Messenger (ﷺ)! Who is the best among the people?" Allah's Messenger (ﷺ) replied "A believer who strives his utmost in Allah's Cause with his life and property." They asked, "Who is next?" He replied, "A believer who stays in one of the mountain paths worshipping Allah and leaving the people secure from his mischief."

Source: Sahih al-Bukhari 2786

Narrated Abu Sa`id Al-Khudri:

The Prophet (ﷺ) said, "The people of Paradise will look at the dwellers of the lofty mansions (i.e. a superior place in Paradise) in the same way as one looks at a brilliant star far away in the East or in the West on the horizon; all that is because of their superiority over one another (in rewards)." On that the people said, "O Allah's Messenger (ﷺ)! Are these lofty mansions for the prophets which nobody else can reach? The Prophet (ﷺ) replied," No! "By Allah in whose Hands my life is, these are for the men who believed in Allah and also believed in the Apostles(Prophets)."

Source: Sahih al-Bukhari 3256

Narrated `Aisha:

(the wife of the Prophet) I asked Allah's Messenger (ﷺ) about the plague. He told me that it was a Punishment sent by Allah on whom he wished, and Allah made it a source of mercy for the believers, for if one in the time of an epidemic plague stays in his country patiently hoping for Allah's Reward and believing that nothing will befall him except what Allah has written for him, he will get the reward of a martyr."

Source: Sahih al-Bukhari 3474

Narrated Abu Burda's father:

Allah's Messenger (ﷺ) said, any man who has a slave girl whom he educates properly, teaches good manners, manumits and marries her, will get a double reward And if any man of the people of the Scriptures believes in his own prophet and then believes in me too, he will (also) get a double reward And any slave who fulfills his duty to his master and to his Lord, will (also) get a double reward."

Source: Sahih al-Bukhari 5083

Abu Umamah reported:

Messenger of Allah (ﷺ) said, "Allah decrees the (Hell) Fire and debars Paradise for the one who usurps the rights of a believer by taking a false oath." One man asked: "O Messenger of Allah! Even if it should be for an insignificant thing?" He said, "Even if it be a stick of the Arak tree (i.e., the tree from which Miswak sticks are taken)".

Source: Riyad as-Salihin 214 Graded: Sahih

Abu Abdullah 'Amr bin Al-'as said:

I heard Messenger of Allah (ﷺ) saying openly not secretly, "The family of so-and-so (i.e., Abu Talib) are not my supporters. My supporter is Allah and the righteous believing people. But they (that family) have kinship (Rahm) with whom I will maintain good the ties of kinship".

Source: Bukhari and Muslim

It was narrated from Abu Hurairah that The Messenger of Allah (ﷺ) said:

"Two will never be gathered together in the Fire: A Muslim who killed a disbeliever then tried his best and did not deviate. And two will never be gathered together in the lungs of a believer: Dust in the cause of Allah, and the odor of Hell. And two will never be gathered in the heart of a slave: Faith and envy."

Source: Sunan an-Nasa'i 3109 Graded: Hasan

Narrated Abu Hurairah:

The Prophet (ﷺ) said: Striving in the path of Allah (jihad) is incumbent on you along with every ruler, whether he is pious or impious; the prayer is obligatory on you behind every believer, pious or impious, even if he commits grave sins; the (funeral) prayer is incumbent upon every Muslim, pious and impious, even if he commits major sins.

Source: Sunan Abi Dawud 2533 Graded: Daif by Albani

Narrated Mu'adh ibn Anas:

The Prophet (ﷺ) said: If anyone guards a believer from a hypocrite, Allah will send an angel who will guard his flesh on the Day of Resurrection from the fire of Jahannam; but if anyone attacks a Muslim saying something by which he wishes to disgrace him, he will be restrained by Allah on the bridge over Jahannam till he is acquitted of what he said.

Source: Sunan Abi Dawud 4883 Graded: Hasan

It was narrated that Abu Hurairah said:

"The Messenger of Allah (ﷺ) said: 'The strong believer is better and more beloved to Allah than the weak believer, although both are good. Strive for that which will benefit you, seek the help of Allah, and do not feel helpless. If anything befalls you, do not say, "if only I had done such and such" rather say "Qaddara Allahu wa ma sha'a fa'ala (Allah has decreed and whatever he wills, He does)." For (saying) 'If' opens (the door) to the deeds of Satan.'"

Source: Sunan Ibn Majah 79 Graded: Sahih

It was narrated from Abu Hurairah that the Messenger of Allah (ﷺ) said:

"O Abu Hurairah, be cautious, and you will be the most devoted of people to Allah. Be content, and you will be the most grateful of people to Allah. Love for people what you love for yourself, and you will be a (true) believer. Be a good neighbor to your neighbors, and you will be a (true) Muslim. And laugh little, for laughing a lot deadens the heart."

Source: Sunan Ibn Majah 4217

Graded: Daif by Darussalam

Abu Huraira (Allah be pleased with him) reported:

I heard Allah's Messenger (ﷺ) as saying: He who emancipates a believing slave. Allah will set free from Fire his every limb for every limb of his (slave's), even his private parts for his.

Source: Sahih Muslim 1509c

Narrated Anas bin Malik:

The Prophet (ﷺ) said, "A faithful believer while in prayer is speaking in private to his Lord, so he should neither spit in front of him nor to his right side but he could spit either on his left or under his foot."

Source: Sahih al-Bukhari 413

Narrated Abu Hurairah:

that the Messenger of Allah (ﷺ) said: "Allah has removed the pride of Jahiliyyah from you and boasting about lineage. (A person is either) a pious believer or a miserable sinner, and the people are the children of Adam, and Adam is from dirt."

Source: Jami at-Tirmidhi 4337 Graded: Hasan

Ibn 'Umar reported:

Messenger of Allah (ﷺ) said, "A believer continues to guard his Faith (and thus hopes for Allah's Mercy) so long as he does not shed blood unjustly".

Source: Riyad as-Salihin 220 Graded: Sahih

It was narrated that Abu Qatadah said:

"We were sitting with the Messenger of Allah when a funeral appeared. The Messenger of Allah said: 'He is relieved and others are relieved of him. When the believer dies he is relieved of the calamities, hardships and troubles of this world, and when the evildoer dies, the people, the land, the trees and the animals are relieved of him.'"

Source: Sunan an-Nasa'i 1931 Graded: Sahih

Abu Hurairah said:

By Allah, I shall offer prayer like that of the Messenger of Allah (ﷺ). The narrator said: Abu Hurairah used to recite the supplication in the last rak'ah of the noon, night and dawn prayers. He would supplicate for the believers and curse the disbelievers.

Source: Sunan Abi Dawud 1440 Graded: Sahih

It was narrated that 'Abdullah bin 'Amr said:

"The Messenger of Allah said: 'Adhere to righteousness even though you will not be able to do all acts of virtue. Know that among the best of your deeds is prayer and that no one maintains his ablution except a believer.'"

Source: Sunan Ibn Majah 278 Graded: Hasan

It was narrated from Abu Hurairah that the Prophet (ﷺ) visited a sick person, due to an illness that he was suffering from and Abu Hurairah was with him. The Messenger of Allah (ﷺ) said:

"Be of good cheer, for Allah says: 'It is My fire which I have causes to overwhelm My believing slave in this world, to be his share of the Fire in the Hereafter."

Source: Sunan Ibn Majah 3470 Graded: Hasan

It was narrated from 'Abdullah bin Mas'ud that the Messenger of Allah (ﷺ) said:

"There is no believing slave who sheds tears, even if they are like the head of a fly, out of fear of Allah, and they roll down his cheeks, but Allah will forbid him to the Fire."

Source: Sunan Ibn Majah 4197

Graded: Daif by Darussalam

It was narrated from Anas that the Messenger of Allah (ﷺ) said:

"Envy consumes good deeds just as fire consumes wood, and charity extinguishes bad deeds just as water extinguishes fire. Prayer is the light of the believer and fasting is a shield against the Fire."

Source: Sunan Ibn Majah 4210

Graded: Daif by Darussalam

Fadalah bin 'Ubaid said:

I heard 'Umar bin al Khattab رضي الله عنه say: I heard the Messenger of Allah ﷺ say: ` The martyrs are four: a man who believes and has good faith, who meets the enemy and shows sincerity to Allah until he is killed - he is the one at whom people will look like this`- and he raised his head until the hat of the Messenger of Allah ﷺ or 'Umar's hat fell of. ` The second is a man who is a believer and has good faith, who meets the enemy and it is as if his back was beaten with the thorns of an acacia tree, then a stray arrow comes and kills him- he will be in a the second rank. The third is a man who is a believer, but he mixes good and bad deeds, and he meets the enemy and shows sincerity to Allah until he is killed- he will be in the third rank. The fourth is a believing man who transgresses against himself by committing a great deal of evil deeds and sins, who meets the enemy and shows sincerity to Allah until he is killed- he will be in the fourth rank.`

Source: Musnad Ahmad 150 Graded: Daif by Darussalam

Abu Umama reported:

that a man asked God's messenger what faith was, to which he replied, "When your good deed pleases you and your evil deed grieves you, you are a believer." He then asked what sin was and received the reply, "When you have a besetting sin, give it up."

Source: Mishkat al-Masabih 45 Graded: Sahih

Imran ibn Abi Anas reported from a man of Aslam who was one of the Companions of the Prophet, that the Prophet said:

"Snubbing a believer for a year is like spilling his blood."

Source: Al-Adab Al-Mufrad 405 Graded: Sahih

It was narrated that Kuraib the freed slave of 'Abdullah bin 'Abbas said:

"A son of 'Abdullah bin 'Abbas died, and he said to me: 'O Kuraib! Get up and see if anyone has assembled (to pray) for my son.' I said: 'Yes.' He said: 'Woe to you, how many do you see? Forty?' I said: 'No, rather there are more.' He said: 'Take my son out, for I bear witness that I heard the Messenger of Allah (ﷺ) say: "No (group of) forty believers intercede for a believer, but Allah will accept their intercession."

Source: Sunan Ibn Majah 1489 Graded: Sahih

Safwan b. Muhriz reported that a person said to Ibn 'Umar:

How did you hear Allah's Messenger (ﷺ) as saying something about intimate conversation? He said: I heard him say: A believer will be brought to his Lord, the Exalted and Glorious, on the Day of Resurrection and He would place upon him His veil (of Light) and make him confess his faults and say: Do you recognize (your faults)? He would say: My Lord, I do recognize (them). He (the Lord) would say: I concealed them for you in the world. And today I forgive them. And he would then be given the Book containing (the account of his) good deeds. And so far as the non-believers and hypocrites are concerned, there would be general announcement about them before all creation telling them that these (people, i. e. non-believers and hypocrites) told a lie about Allah.

Source: Sahih Muslim 2768

Hammam b. Munabbih said:

Abu Huraira narrated to us ahadith from Allah's Messenger (ﷺ) and out of these one is that Allah's Messenger (ﷺ) said: None amongst you should make a request for death, and do not call for it before it comes, for when any one of you dies, he ceases (to do good) deeds and the life of a believer is not prolonged but for goodness.

Source: Sahih Muslim 2682

Narrated Mu'awiyah b. al-Hakam al-Sulami:

I said: Messenger of Allah, I have a slave girl whom I slapped. This grieved the Messenger of Allah (ﷺ). I said to him: Should I not emancipate her? He said: Bring her to me. He said: Then I brought her. He asked: Where is Allah? She replied: In the heaven. He said: Who am I? She replied: You are the Messenger of Allah. He said: Emancipate her, she is a believer.

Source: Sunan Abi Dawud 3282 Graded Sahih

Narrated Abdur Rahman:

I asked Abu Sa'id al-Khudri about wearing lower garment. He said: You have come to the man who knows it very well. The Messenger of Allah (ﷺ) said: The way for a believer to wear a lower garment is to have it halfway down his legs and he is guilty of no sin if it comes halfway between that and the ankles, but what comes lower than the ankles is in Hell. On the day of Resurrection. Allah will not look at him who trails his lower garment conceitedly.

Source: Sunan Abi Dawud 4093 Graded: Sahih

It was narrated that:

Thawban said: "When the Verse concerning silver and gold was revealed, they said: 'What kind of wealth should we acquire?' Umar said: 'I will tell you about that.' So he rode on his camel and caught up with the Prophet, and I followed him. He said: 'O Messenger of Allah what kind of wealth should we acquire?' He said: 'Let one of you acquire a thankful heart, a tongue that remembers Allah and a believing wife who will help him with regard to the Hereafter.'"

Source: Sunan Ibn Majah 1856 Graded: Hasan

It was narrated from Abu Umamah that:

the Prophet used to say: "Nothing is of more benefit to the believer after Taqwa of Allah than a righteous wife whom, if he commands her she obeys him, if he looks at her he is pleased, if he swears an oath concerning her she fulfills it, and when he is away from her she is sincere towards him with regard to herself and his wealth."

Source: Sunan Ibn Majah 1857

Graded: Daif by Darussalam

It was narrated that Anas bin Malik said:

"A funeral (procession) passed by the Prophet (ﷺ) and they praised (the deceased) and spoke well of him. He said: '(Paradise is) guaranteed for him.' Then another funeral passed by and they spoke badly of him, and he (the Prophet (ﷺ)) said: '(Hell is) guaranteed for him.' It was said: 'O Messenger of Allah, you said that (Paradise was) guaranteed for this one and that (Hell was) guaranteed for the other one.' He said: 'It is the testimony of the people, and the believers are the witnesses of Allah on earth.'"

Source: Sunan Ibn Majah 1491 Graded: Sahih

Qais, Abu 'Umarah, the freed slave of the Ansar, said:

"I heard 'Abdullah bin Abu Bakr bin Muhammad bin 'Amr bin Hazm narrating from his father, from his grandfather, that the Prophet (ﷺ) said: 'There is no believer who consoles for his brother for a calamity, but Allah will clothe him with garments of honor on the Day of Resurrection.'"

Source: Sunan Ibn Majah 1601

Graded: Daif by Darussalam

It was narrated from Abu Hurairah that the Messenger of Allah (ﷺ) said:

"When the believer commits sin, a black spot appears on his heart. If he repents and gives up that sin and seeks forgiveness, his heart will be polished. But if (the sin) increases, (the black spot) increases. That is the Ran that Allah mentions in His Book: "Nay! But on their hearts is the Ran (covering of sins and evil deeds) which they used to earn." [83:14]

Source: Sunan Ibn Majah 4244 Graded: Hasan

Abu Hurairah reported that the Prophet said:

"No believer turns his face to Allah and asks Him for something but that He gives it to him, either by giving it to him sooner in this world or storing it up for him in the Next World, as long as he does not try to make it come quickly." They asked, "Messenger of Allah, what does 'making it come quickly' mean?" He said, "He says, 'I asked and asked and do not think that I will be answered.'"

Source: Al-Adab Al-Mufrad 711 Graded: Sahih

Abu Huraira reported:

I invited my mother, who was a polytheist, to Islam. I invited her one day and she said to me something about Allah's Messenger (ﷺ) which I hated. I came to Allah's Messenger (ﷺ) weeping and said: Allah's Messenger, I invited my mother to Islam but she did not accept (my invitation). I invited her today but she said to me something which I did not like. (Kindly) supplicate Allah that He may set the mother of Abu Huraira right. Thereupon Allah's Messenger (ﷺ) said: O Allah, set the mother of Abu Huraira on the right path. I came out quite pleased with the supplication of Allah's Apostle (ﷺ) and when I came near the door it was closed from within. My mother heard the noise of my footsteps and she said: Abu Huraira, just wait. And I heard the noise of falling of water. She took a bath and put on the shirt and quickly covered her head with a headdress and opened the door and then said: Abu Huraira, I bear witness to the fact that there is no god but Allah and Muhammad is His bondsman and His Messenger. He (Abu Huraira) said: I went back to Allah's Messenger (ﷺ) and (this time) I was shedding the tears of joy. I said: Allah's Messenger, be happy, for Allah has responded to your supplication and

He has set on the right path the mother of Abu Huraira. He (the Prophet) praised Allah, and extolled Him and uttered good words. I said: Allah's Messenger, supplicate to Allah so that He may instill love of mine and that of my mother too in the believing servants and let our hearts be filled with their love, whereupon Allah's Messenger (ﷺ) said: O Allah, let there be love of these servants of yours, i.e. Abu Huraira and his mother, in the hearts of the believing servants and let their hearts be filled with the love of the believing servants. (Abu Huraira said: This prayer) was so well granted by Allah that no believer was ever born who heard of me and who saw me but did not love me.

Source: Sahih Muslim 2491

Ibn Umar reported that Allah's Messenger (ﷺ) one day said to his Companions:

Tell me about a tree which has resemblance with a believer. The people began to mention (different) trees of the forest. Ibn 'Umar said: It was instilled in my mind or in my heart and it stuck therein that it implied the date-palm tree. I made up my mind to make a mention of that but could not do that because of the presence of the elderly people there. When there was a hush amongst them (after they had expressed their views), Allah's Messenger (ﷺ) said: It Is the date-palm tree.

Source: Sahih Muslim 2811b

Narrated 'Ubada bin As-Samit, The Prophet (ﷺ) said:

"Who-ever loves to meet Allah, Allah (too) loves to meet him and who-ever hates to meet Allah, Allah (too) hates to meet him". `Aisha, or some of the wives of the Prophet (ﷺ) said, "But we dislike death." He said: It is not like this, but it is meant that when the time of the death of a believer approaches, he receives the good news of Allah's pleasure with him and His blessings upon him, and so at that time nothing is dearer to him than what is in front of him. He therefore loves the meeting with Allah, and Allah (too) loves the meeting with him. But when the time of the death of a disbeliever approaches, he receives the evil news of Allah's torment and His Requital, whereupon nothing is more hateful to him than what is before him. Therefore, he hates the meeting with Allah, and Allah too, hates the meeting with him."

Source: Sahih al-Bukhari 6507

Ibn 'Umar narrated:

" 'Umar delivered a Khutbah to us at Al-Jabiyah. He said: 'O you people! Indeed I have stood among you as the Messenger of Allah stood among us, and he said: "I order you (to stick to) my Companions, then those who come after them, then those who come after them. Then lying will spread until a man will take an oath when no oath was sought from him, and a witness will testify when his testimony was not sought. Behold! A man is not alone with a woman but the third of them is Ash-Shaitan. Adhere to the Jama'ah, beware of separation, for indeed Ash-Shaitan is with one, and he is further away from two.

Whoever wants the best place in Paradise, then let him stick to the Jama'ah. Whoever rejoices with his good deeds and grieves over his evil deeds, then that is the believer among you.'"

Source: Jami` at-Tirmidhi 2165 Graded: Sahih

Amr bin sa'eed bin Abi Husain told us that:

'Amr bin Shu'aib wrote to 'Abdullah bin 'Abdur-Rahman bin Abi Husain to offer condolences for a son of his who had died. In his letter he mentioned that he had heard his father narrate, that his grandfather, 'Abdullah bin 'Amr bin Al-As said: "The Messenger of Allah said: 'Allah does not approve for His believing slave, if He takes away his loved one from among the people of the Earth, and he bears that with patience and seeks reward, and says that which he is commanded any reward less than Paradise.'"

Source: Sunan an-Nasa'i 1871 Graded: Sahih

It was narrated that Ibn 'Abbas said:

"When a young daughter of the Messenger of Allah was dying, the Messenger of Allah picked her up and held her to his chest, then he put his hand on her, and she died in front of the Messenger of Allah. Umm Ayman wept and the Messenger of Allah said 'Oh Umm Ayman, do you weep while the Messenger of Allah is with you?' She said: 'Why shouldn't I weep when the Messenger of Allah is weeping." So the Messenger of Allah said "Verily, I am not weeping. Rather it is compassion.' Then the

Messenger of Allah said: 'The believer is fine whatever the situation; even when his soul is being pulled from his body and he praises Allah, the Mighty and Sublime'"

Source: Sunan an-Nasa'i 1843 Graded: Hasan

It was narrated that Abu Hurairah and Abu Dharr said:

"The Messenger of Allah would sit among his Companions and if a stranger came, he would not know which of them was he (the Prophet) until he asked. So we suggested to the Messenger of Allah that we should make a dais for him so that any stranger would know him if he came to him. So we built for him a bench made of clay on which he used to sit. (One day) we were sitting and the Messenger of Allah was sitting in his spot, when a man came along who was the most handsome and good-smelling of all people, and it was as if no dirt had ever touched his garments. He came near the edge of the rug and greeted him, saying: 'Peace be upon you, O Muhammad!' He returned the greeting, and he said: 'Shall I come closer, O Muhammad?' He came a little closer, and he kept telling him to come closer, until he put his hands on the knees of the Messenger of Allah. He said: 'O Muhammad, tell me, what is Islam?' He said: 'Islam means to worship Allah and not associate anything with Him; to establish Salah, to pay Zakah, to perform Hajj to the House, and to fast Ramadan.' He said: 'If I do that, will I have submitted (be a Muslim)?' He said: 'Yes.' He said: 'You have spoken the truth,' we found it odd. He said: 'O Muhammad, tell me, what is faith?' He said: 'To believe in Allah, His Angels, the Book, the Prophets, and to believe in the Divine Decree.' He said: 'If I do that, will I have believed?' The Messenger of Allah said: 'Yes.' He said: 'You have spoken the truth.' He said: 'O Muhammad, tell me, what is Al-Ihsan?' He said: 'To worship Allah as if you can see Him, for although you cannot see Him, He can see you.' He said: 'You have spoken the truth.' He said: 'O Muhammad, tell me about the Hour.' He lowered his head and did not answer. Then he repeated the question, and he did not answer. Then he repeated the question (a third time) and he did not answer. Then he raised his head and said: 'The one who is being asked does not know more than the one who is asking. But it has signs, by which it may be known. When you see the herdsmen competing in building tall buildings, when you see the barefoot and naked ruling the Earth, when you see a woman giving birth to her mistress. Five things which no one knows except Allah. Verily, Allah, with Him (alone) is the knowledge of the Hour up to His saying: 'Verily, Allah is All-Knower, All-Aware (of things).' Then he said: 'No, by the One who sent Muhammad with the truth, with guidance and glad tidings, I did not know him more than any man among you. That was Jibril, peace be upon you, who came down in the form of Dihyah Al-Kalbi.'"

Source: Sunan an-Nasa'i 4991 Graded: Sahih

It was narrated that Salamah bin Nufail Al-Kindi said:

"I was sitting with the Messenger of Allah when a man said: 'O Messenger of Allah! The people have lost interest in horses and put down their weapons, and they say there is no Jihad, and that war has ended.' The Messenger of Allah turned to face him and said: 'They are lying, now the fighting is to come. There will always be a group among my Ummah who will fight for the truth, for whom Allah will cause some people to deviate, and grant them provision from them, until the Hour begins and until the promise of Allah comes. Goodness is tied to the forelocks of horses until the Day of Resurrection. It has been revealed to me that I am going to die and will not stay long, and you will follow me group after group, striking one another's necks. And the place of safety for the believers is Ash-Sham.'"

Source: Sunan an-Nasa'i 3561 Graded: Sahih

It was narrated from 'Abdur-Rahman bin 'Amr As-Sulami that:

He heard Al-'Irbad bin Sariyah say: "The Messenger of Allah (ﷺ) delivered a moving speech to us which made our eyes flow with tears and made our hearts melt. We said: 'O Messenger of Allah. This is a speech of farewell. What did you enjoin upon us?' He said: 'I am leaving you upon a (path of) brightness whose night is like its day. No one will deviate from it after I am gone but one who is doomed. Whoever among you lives will see great conflict. I urge you to adhere to what you know of my Sunnah and the path of the Rightly-Guided Caliphs, and cling stubbornly to it. And you must obey, even if (your leader is) an Abyssinian leader. For the true believer is like a camel with a ring in its nose; wherever it is driven, it complies."

Source: Sunan Ibn Majah 43 Graded: Sahih

It was narrated from 'Abdullah As-Sunabihi that the Messenger of Allah (ﷺ) said:

"When the believing slave performs Wudu' and rinses his mouth, his sins come out from his mouth. When he sniffs water into his nose and blows it out, his sins come from his nose. When he washes his face, his sins come out from his face, even from beneath his eyelashes. When he washes his hands, his sins come out from his hands, even from beneath his fingernails. When he wipes his head, his sins come out from his head, even from his ears. When washes his feet, his sins come from his feet, even from beneath his toenails. Then his walking to the Masjid and his Salah will earn extra merit for him."

Source: Sunan an-Nasai 103 Graded: Hasan

Narrated Al-Abbas bin Abdul-Muttalib:

that he heard the Messenger of Allah (ﷺ) say: "Whoever is pleased with Allah as (his) Lord, and Islam as (his) religion, and Muhammad as (his) Prophet, then he has tasted the sweetness of faith."

Source: Jami` at-Tirmidhi 2623 Graded: Sahih

Narrated Ibn `Umar:

Allah's Messenger (ﷺ) said, "A faithful believer remains at liberty regarding his religion unless he kills somebody unlawfully."

Source: Sahih al-Bukhari 6862

Mus'ab bin Sa'd narrated from his father that a man said:

"O Messenger of Allah! Which of the people is tried most severely?" He said: "The Prophets, then those nearest to them, then those nearest to them. A man is tried according to his religion; if he is firm in his religion, then his trials are more severe, and if he is frail in his religion, then he is tried according to the strength of his religion. The servant shall continue to be tried until he is left walking upon the earth without any sins."

Source: Jami` at-Tirmidhi 2398 Graded: Hasan

Narrated Abu Hurairah, The Prophet (ﷺ) said:

A man follows the religion of his friend; so each one should consider whom he makes his friend.

Source: Sunan Abi Dawud 4833 Graded: Hasan

Narrated Abu Musa:

Some people asked Allah's Messenger (ﷺ), "Whose Islam is the best? i.e. (Who is a very good Muslim)?" He replied, "One who avoids harming the Muslims with his tongue and hands."

Source: Sahih al-Bukhari 11

Amr b. Shu'aib, on his father's authority, told that his grandfather reported the Messenger of Allah (ﷺ) said:

Do not pluck out grey hair. If any believer grows a grey hair in Islam, he will have light on the Day of Resurrection. (This is Sufyan's version). Yahya's version says: Allah will record on his behalf a good deed for it, and will blot out a sin for it.

Source: Sunan Abi Dawud 4202

Graded Hasan Sahih by Albani

It is narrated on the authority of Abu Huraira that the Messenger of Allah said:

Faith has over seventy branches or over sixty branches, the most excellent of which is the declaration that there is no god but Allah, and the humblest of which is the, removal of what is injurious from the path: and modesty is the branch of faith.

Source: Sahih Muslim 35b

Narrated Abu Hurairah:

The Prophet (ﷺ) said: The most perfect believer in respect of faith is he who is best of them in manners.

Source: Sunan Abi Dawud 4682 Graded: Hasan Sahih by Albani

Narrated Abu Umamah Ilyas ibn Tha'labah:

The Companions of the Messenger of Allah (ﷺ) mentioned this word before him. The Messenger of Allah (ﷺ) said: Listen, listen! Wearing old clothes is a part of faith, wearing old clothes is a part of faith.

Source: Sunan Abi Dawud 4161 Graded: Sahih

Narrated Anas:

The Prophet (ﷺ) said "None of you will have faith till he loves me more than his father, his children and all mankind."

Source: Sahih al-Bukhari 15

Narrated Abu Umamah:

The Prophet (ﷺ) said: If anyone loves for Allah's sake, hates for Allah's sake, gives for Allah's sake and withholds for Allah's sake, he will have perfect faith.

Source: Sunan Abi Dawud 4681 Graded: Sahih

It was narrated from Anas bin Malik that the Messenger of Allah (ﷺ) said:

"There are three things, whoever has them has found the taste of faith (One of the narrators) Bundar said: 'The sweetness of faith; When he loves a man and only loves him for the sake of Allah. When Allah and His Messenger are more beloved to him than anything else; and when being thrown into the fire is dearer to him than going back to disbelief after Allah has saved him from it."

Source: Sunan Ibn Majah 4033 Graded: Sahih

Sahl bin Mu'adh[bin Anas] Al-Juhni narrated from his father that the Prophet said:

"Whoever gives for the sake of Allah, withholds for the sake of Allah, loves for the sake of Allah, hates for the sake of Allah, and marries for the sake of Allah, he has indeed perfected his faith."

Source: Jami at-Tirmidhi 2521 Graded: Hasan

Abu Sa'eed said:

"I heard the Messenger of Allah say: 'Whoever among you sees an evil, let him change it with his hand; if he cannot, then with his tongue; if he cannot, then with his heart- and that is the weakest of Faith.'"

Source: Sunan an-Nasa'i 5008 Graded: Sahih

It is reported on the authority of Abu Mu'awiya that (the Prophet) said:

Every new-born babe is born on the millat (of Islam and he) remains on this until his tongue is enabled to express himself. This hadith has been narratted on the authority of Abu Mu'awiya through another chain of transmitters (and the words are):" Every child is born but on this Fitra so long as he does not express himself with his tongue."

Source: Sahih Muslim 2658f

Narrated Abu Huraira:

Allah's Messenger (ﷺ) said, "Every child is born with a true faith of Islam (i.e. to worship none but Allah Alone) but his parents convert him to Judaism, Christianity or Magainism, as an animal delivers a perfect baby animal. Do you find it mutilated?" Then Abu Huraira recited the verses: "The pure Allah's Islamic nature (true faith of Islam) (i.e. worshipping none but Allah) with which He has created human beings. No change let there be in the religion of Allah (i.e. joining none in worship with Allah). That is the straight religion (Islam) but most of men know, not." (30.30)

Source: Sahih al-Bukhari 1359

'Amr bin Shu'aib, from his father, from his grandfather, that the Messenger of Allah (ﷺ) said:

"People of two different religions do not inherit from one another."

Source: Sunan Ibn Majah 2731 Graded: Sahih

Narrated 'Usama bin Zaid:

I asked, "O Allah's Messenger (ﷺ)! Where will you stay in Mecca? Will you stay in your house in Mecca?" He replied, "Has `Aqil left any property or house?" `Aqil along with Talib had inherited the property of Abu Talib. Jafar and `Ali did not inherit anything as they were Muslims and the other two were non-believers. `Umar bin Al-Khattab used to say, "A believer cannot inherit (anything from an) infidel." Ibn Shihab, (a sub-narrator) said, "They (`Umar and others) derived the above verdict from Allah's Statement: "Verily! those who believed and

Emigrated and strove with their life And property in Allah's Cause, And those who helped (the emigrants) And gave them their places to live in, These are (all) allies to one another." (8.72)

Source: Sahih al-Bukhari 1588

It was narrated from Abu Musa Al-Ash'ari that the Messenger of Allah (ﷺ) said:

"Before the Hour comes, there will be tribulation like pieces of black night, when a man will wake up as a believer but be a disbeliever by evening, or he will be a believer in the evening but will be a disbeliever by morning. And the one who is sitting will be better than the one who is standing, and the one who is standing will be better than the one who is walking, and the one who is walking will be better than the one who is running. So break your bows, cut their strings and strike your swords against rocks, and if anyone enters upon anyone of you, let him be like the better of the two sons of Adam. (i.e. the one killed, not the killer)."

Source: Sunan Ibn Majah 3961 Graded: Hasan

Ibn 'Umar narrated the Messenger of Allah (ﷺ) said:

"He who imitates any people (in their actions) is considered to be one of them."

Source: Bulugh al Maram and Abu Dawood

Graded: Sahih by Ibn Hibban

It was narrated that Hudhaifah said The Messenger of Allah said:

'I know what the Dajjal (Antichrist) will have with him. He will have two flowing rivers, one that appears to the eye to be clear water, and one that appears to the eye to be flaming fire. If anyone sees that, let him go to the river which he thinks is fire and close his eyes, then lower his head and drink from it, for it is cool water. The Dajjal has one blind eye, with a layer of thick skin over it, and between his eyes is written "disbeliever," which every believer will read, whether he is literate or illiterate.'

Source: Sahih Muslim 2934b

Distinctions of Disbelievers

Quran 2:6-14

إِنَّ ٱلَّذِينَ كَفَرُواْ سَوَآءٌ عَلَيْهِمْ ءَأَنذَرْتَهُمْ أَمْ لَمْ تُنذِرْهُمْ لَا يُؤْمِنُونَ (٦) خَتَمَ ٱللَّهُ عَلَىٰ قُلُوبِهِمْ وَعَلَىٰ سَمْعِهِمْ وَعَلَىٰٓ أَبْصَٰرِهِمْ غِشَٰوَةٌ وَلَهُمْ عَذَابٌ عَظِيمٌ (٧) وَمِنَ ٱلنَّاسِ مَن يَقُولُ ءَامَنَّا بِٱللَّهِ وَبِٱلْيَوْمِ ٱلْءَاخِرِ وَمَا هُم بِمُؤْمِنِينَ (٨) يُخَٰدِعُونَ ٱللَّهَ وَٱلَّذِينَ ءَامَنُواْ وَمَا يَخْدَعُونَ إِلَّآ أَنفُسَهُمْ وَمَا يَشْعُرُونَ (٩) فِى قُلُوبِهِم مَّرَضٌ فَزَادَهُمُ ٱللَّهُ مَرَضًا وَلَهُمْ عَذَابٌ أَلِيمٌ بِمَا كَانُواْ يَكْذِبُونَ (١٠) وَإِذَا قِيلَ لَهُمْ لَا تُفْسِدُواْ فِى ٱلْأَرْضِ قَالُوٓاْ إِنَّمَا نَحْنُ مُصْلِحُونَ (١١) أَلَآ إِنَّهُمْ هُمُ ٱلْمُفْسِدُونَ وَلَٰكِن لَّا يَشْعُرُونَ (١٢) وَإِذَا قِيلَ لَهُمْ ءَامِنُواْ كَمَآ ءَامَنَ ٱلنَّاسُ قَالُوٓاْ أَنُؤْمِنُ كَمَآ ءَامَنَ ٱلسُّفَهَآءُ أَلَآ إِنَّهُمْ هُمُ ٱلسُّفَهَآءُ وَلَٰكِن لَّا يَعْلَمُونَ (١٣) وَإِذَا لَقُواْ ٱلَّذِينَ ءَامَنُواْ قَالُوٓاْ ءَامَنَّا وَإِذَا خَلَوْاْ إِلَىٰ شَيَٰطِينِهِمْ قَالُوٓاْ إِنَّا مَعَكُمْ إِنَّمَا نَحْنُ مُسْتَهْزِءُونَ (١٤)

Verily, those who disbelieve, it is the same to them whether you warn them or do not warn them, they will not believe. (6) Allâh has set a seal on their hearts and on their hearings, (i.e. they are closed from accepting Allâh's Guidance), and on their eyes there is a covering. Theirs will be a great torment. (7) And of mankind, there are some (hypocrites) who say: "We believe in Allâh and the Last Day" while in fact they believe not. (8) They (think to) deceive Allâh and those who believe, while they only deceive themselves, and perceive (it) not! (9) In their hearts is a disease (of doubt and hypocrisy) and Allâh has increased their disease. A painful torment is theirs because they used to tell lies. (10) And when it is said to them: "Make not mischief on the earth," they say: "We are only peacemakers." (11) Verily! They are the ones who make mischief, but they perceive not. (12) And when it is said to them (hypocrites): "Believe as the people (followers of Muhammad, Al-Ansâr and Al-Muhajirûn) have believed," they say: "Shall we believe as the fools have believed?" Verily, they are the fools, but they know not (13) And when they meet those who believe, they say: "We believe," but when they are alone with their Shayâtin (devils - polytheists, hypocrites), they say: "Truly, we are with you; verily, we were but mocking." (14)

Quran 2:26-27

﴿إِنَّ ٱللَّهَ لَا يَسْتَحْىِۦٓ أَن يَضْرِبَ مَثَلًا مَّا بَعُوضَةً فَمَا فَوْقَهَا ۚ فَأَمَّا ٱلَّذِينَ ءَامَنُوا۟ فَيَعْلَمُونَ أَنَّهُ ٱلْحَقُّ مِن رَّبِّهِمْ ۖ وَأَمَّا ٱلَّذِينَ كَفَرُوا۟ فَيَقُولُونَ مَاذَآ أَرَادَ ٱللَّهُ بِهَٰذَا مَثَلًا ۘ يُضِلُّ بِهِۦ كَثِيرًا وَيَهْدِى بِهِۦ كَثِيرًا ۚ وَمَا يُضِلُّ بِهِۦٓ إِلَّا ٱلْفَٰسِقِينَ (٢٦) ٱلَّذِينَ يَنقُضُونَ عَهْدَ ٱللَّهِ مِنۢ بَعْدِ مِيثَٰقِهِۦ وَيَقْطَعُونَ مَآ أَمَرَ ٱللَّهُ بِهِۦٓ أَن يُوصَلَ وَيُفْسِدُونَ فِى ٱلْأَرْضِ ۚ أُو۟لَٰٓئِكَ هُمُ ٱلْخَٰسِرُونَ (٢٧)

Verily, Allâh is not ashamed to set forth a parable even of a mosquito or so much more when it is bigger (or less when it is smaller) than it. And as for those who believe, they know that it is the Truth from their Lord, but as for those who disbelieve, they say: "What did Allâh intend by this parable?" By it He misleads many, and many He guides thereby. And He misleads thereby only those who are Al-Fâsiqûn (the rebellious, disobedient to Allâh). (26) Those who break Allâh's Covenant after ratifying it, and sever what Allâh has ordered to be joined, and do mischief on earth, it is they who are the losers. (27)

Quran 2:39

$$\text{وَٱلَّذِينَ كَفَرُوا۟ وَكَذَّبُوا۟ بِـَٔايَـٰتِنَآ أُو۟لَـٰٓئِكَ أَصْحَـٰبُ ٱلنَّارِ ۖ هُمْ فِيهَا خَـٰلِدُونَ}$$

But those who disbelieve and belie Our Ayât (proofs, evidences, verses, lessons, signs, revelations, etc.)- such are the dwellers of the Fire, They shall abide therein forever. (39)

Quran 2:75-81

$$\text{۞ أَفَتَطْمَعُونَ أَن يُؤْمِنُوا۟ لَكُمْ وَقَدْ كَانَ فَرِيقٌ مِّنْهُمْ يَسْمَعُونَ كَلَـٰمَ ٱللَّهِ ثُمَّ يُحَرِّفُونَهُۥ مِنۢ بَعْدِ مَا عَقَلُوهُ وَهُمْ يَعْلَمُونَ (٧٥) وَإِذَا لَقُوا۟ ٱلَّذِينَ ءَامَنُوا۟ قَالُوٓا۟ ءَامَنَّا وَإِذَا خَلَا بَعْضُهُمْ إِلَىٰ بَعْضٍ قَالُوٓا۟ أَتُحَدِّثُونَهُم بِمَا فَتَحَ ٱللَّهُ عَلَيْكُمْ لِيُحَآجُّوكُم بِهِۦ عِندَ رَبِّكُمْ ۚ أَفَلَا تَعْقِلُونَ (٧٦) أَوَلَا يَعْلَمُونَ أَنَّ ٱللَّهَ يَعْلَمُ مَا يُسِرُّونَ وَمَا يُعْلِنُونَ (٧٧) وَمِنْهُمْ أُمِّيُّونَ لَا يَعْلَمُونَ ٱلْكِتَـٰبَ إِلَّآ أَمَانِىَّ وَإِنْ هُمْ إِلَّا يَظُنُّونَ (٧٨) فَوَيْلٌ لِّلَّذِينَ يَكْتُبُونَ ٱلْكِتَـٰبَ بِأَيْدِيهِمْ ثُمَّ يَقُولُونَ هَـٰذَا مِنْ عِندِ ٱللَّهِ لِيَشْتَرُوا۟ بِهِۦ ثَمَنًا قَلِيلًا ۖ فَوَيْلٌ لَّهُم مِّمَّا كَتَبَتْ أَيْدِيهِمْ وَوَيْلٌ لَّهُم مِّمَّا يَكْسِبُونَ (٧٩) وَقَالُوا۟ لَن تَمَسَّنَا ٱلنَّارُ إِلَّآ أَيَّامًا مَّعْدُودَةً ۚ قُلْ أَتَّخَذْتُمْ عِندَ ٱللَّهِ عَهْدًا فَلَن يُخْلِفَ ٱللَّهُ عَهْدَهُۥٓ ۖ أَمْ تَقُولُونَ عَلَى ٱللَّهِ مَا لَا تَعْلَمُونَ (٨٠) بَلَىٰ مَن كَسَبَ سَيِّئَةً وَأَحَـٰطَتْ بِهِۦ خَطِيٓـَٔتُهُۥ فَأُو۟لَـٰٓئِكَ أَصْحَـٰبُ ٱلنَّارِ ۖ هُمْ فِيهَا خَـٰلِدُونَ (٨١)}$$

Do you (faithful believers) covet that they will believe in your religion inspite of the fact that a party of them (Jewish rabbis) used to hear the Word of Allâh [the Taurât (Torah)], then they used to change it knowingly after they understood it? (75) And when they (Jews) meet those who believe (Muslims), they say, "We believe", but when they meet one another in private, they say, "Shall you (Jews) tell them (Muslims) what Allâh has revealed to you [Jews, about the description and the qualities of Prophet Muhammad, that which are written in the Taurât

(Torah)], that they (Muslims) may argue with you (Jews) about it before your Lord?" Have you (Jews) then no understanding? (76) Know they (Jews) not that Allâh knows what they conceal and what they reveal? (77) And there are among them (Jews) unlettered people, who know not the Book, but they trust upon false desires and they but guess. (78) Then woe to those who write the Book with their own hands and then say, "This is from Allâh," to purchase with it a little price! Woe to them for what their hands have written and woe to them for that they earn thereby. (79) And they (Jews) say, "The Fire (i.e. Hell-fire on the Day of Resurrection) shall not touch us but for a few numbered days." Say (O Muhammad Peace be upon him to them): "Have you taken a covenant from Allâh, so that Allâh will not break His Covenant? Or is it that you say of Allâh what you know not?" (80) Yes! Whosoever earns evil and his sin has surrounded him, they are dwellers of the Fire (i.e. Hell); they will dwell therein forever. (81)

Quran 2:84-86

وَإِذْ أَخَذْنَا مِيثَٰقَكُمْ لَا تَسْفِكُونَ دِمَآءَكُمْ وَلَا تُخْرِجُونَ أَنفُسَكُم مِّن دِيَٰرِكُمْ ثُمَّ أَقْرَرْتُمْ وَأَنتُمْ تَشْهَدُونَ (٨٤) ثُمَّ أَنتُمْ هَٰٓؤُلَآءِ تَقْتُلُونَ أَنفُسَكُمْ وَتُخْرِجُونَ فَرِيقًا مِّنكُم مِّن دِيَٰرِهِمْ تَظَٰهَرُونَ عَلَيْهِم بِٱلْإِثْمِ وَٱلْعُدْوَٰنِ وَإِن يَأْتُوكُمْ أُسَٰرَىٰ تُفَٰدُوهُمْ وَهُوَ مُحَرَّمٌ عَلَيْكُمْ إِخْرَاجُهُمْ أَفَتُؤْمِنُونَ بِبَعْضِ ٱلْكِتَٰبِ وَتَكْفُرُونَ بِبَعْضٍ فَمَا جَزَآءُ مَن يَفْعَلُ ذَٰلِكَ مِنكُمْ إِلَّا خِزْىٌ فِى ٱلْحَيَوٰةِ ٱلدُّنْيَا وَيَوْمَ ٱلْقِيَٰمَةِ يُرَدُّونَ إِلَىٰٓ أَشَدِّ ٱلْعَذَابِ وَمَا ٱللَّهُ بِغَٰفِلٍ عَمَّا تَعْمَلُونَ (٨٥) أُوْلَٰٓئِكَ ٱلَّذِينَ ٱشْتَرَوُاْ ٱلْحَيَوٰةَ ٱلدُّنْيَا بِٱلْءَاخِرَةِ فَلَا يُخَفَّفُ عَنْهُمُ ٱلْعَذَابُ وَلَا هُمْ يُنصَرُونَ (٨٦)

And (remember) when We took your covenant (saying): Shed not the blood of your (people), nor turn out your own people from their dwellings. Then, (this) you ratified and (to this) you bear witness. (84) After this, it is you who kill one another and drive out a party of you from their homes, assist (their enemies) against them, in sin and transgression. And if they come to you as captives, you ransom them, although their expulsion was forbidden to you. Then do you believe in a part of the Scripture and reject the rest? Then what is the recompense of those who do so among you, except disgrace in the life of this world, and on the Day of Resurrection they shall be consigned to the most grievous torment. And Allâh is not unaware of what you do. (85) Those are they who have bought the life of this world at the price of the Hereafter. Their torment shall not be lightened nor shall they be helped. (86)

Quran 2:87-93

وَلَقَدْ ءَاتَيْنَا مُوسَى ٱلْكِتَٰبَ وَقَفَّيْنَا مِنۢ بَعْدِهِۦ بِٱلرُّسُلِۖ وَءَاتَيْنَا عِيسَى ٱبْنَ مَرْيَمَ ٱلْبَيِّنَٰتِ وَأَيَّدْنَٰهُ بِرُوحِ ٱلْقُدُسِۗ أَفَكُلَّمَا جَآءَكُمْ رَسُولٌۢ بِمَا لَا تَهْوَىٰٓ أَنفُسُكُمُ ٱسْتَكْبَرْتُمْ فَفَرِيقًا كَذَّبْتُمْ وَفَرِيقًا تَقْتُلُونَ (٨٧) وَقَالُوا۟ قُلُوبُنَا غُلْفٌۢ ۚ بَل لَّعَنَهُمُ ٱللَّهُ بِكُفْرِهِمْ فَقَلِيلًا مَّا يُؤْمِنُونَ (٨٨) وَلَمَّا جَآءَهُمْ كِتَٰبٌ مِّنْ عِندِ ٱللَّهِ مُصَدِّقٌ لِّمَا مَعَهُمْ وَكَانُوا۟ مِن قَبْلُ يَسْتَفْتِحُونَ عَلَى ٱلَّذِينَ كَفَرُوا۟ فَلَمَّا جَآءَهُم مَّا عَرَفُوا۟ كَفَرُوا۟ بِهِۦ ۚ فَلَعْنَةُ ٱللَّهِ عَلَى ٱلْكَٰفِرِينَ (٨٩) بِئْسَمَا ٱشْتَرَوْا۟ بِهِۦٓ أَنفُسَهُمْ أَن يَكْفُرُوا۟ بِمَآ أَنزَلَ ٱللَّهُ بَغْيًا أَن يُنَزِّلَ ٱللَّهُ مِن فَضْلِهِۦ عَلَىٰ مَن يَشَآءُ مِنْ عِبَادِهِۦ ۖ فَبَآءُو بِغَضَبٍ عَلَىٰ غَضَبٍ ۚ وَلِلْكَٰفِرِينَ عَذَابٌ مُّهِينٌ (٩٠) وَإِذَا قِيلَ لَهُمْ ءَامِنُوا۟ بِمَآ أَنزَلَ ٱللَّهُ قَالُوا۟ نُؤْمِنُ بِمَآ أُنزِلَ عَلَيْنَا وَيَكْفُرُونَ بِمَا وَرَآءَهُۥ وَهُوَ ٱلْحَقُّ مُصَدِّقًا لِّمَا مَعَهُمْ ۗ قُلْ فَلِمَ تَقْتُلُونَ أَنۢبِيَآءَ ٱللَّهِ مِن قَبْلُ إِن كُنتُم مُّؤْمِنِينَ

﴿ ٩١ ﴾ ۞ وَلَقَدْ جَاءَكُم مُّوسَىٰ بِٱلْبَيِّنَـٰتِ ثُمَّ ٱتَّخَذْتُمُ ٱلْعِجْلَ مِنۢ بَعْدِهِۦ وَأَنتُمْ ظَـٰلِمُونَ ﴿ ٩٢ ﴾ وَإِذْ أَخَذْنَا مِيثَـٰقَكُمْ وَرَفَعْنَا فَوْقَكُمُ ٱلطُّورَ خُذُوا۟ مَآ ءَاتَيْنَـٰكُم بِقُوَّةٍ وَٱسْمَعُوا۟ ۖ قَالُوا۟ سَمِعْنَا وَعَصَيْنَا وَأُشْرِبُوا۟ فِى قُلُوبِهِمُ ٱلْعِجْلَ بِكُفْرِهِمْ ۚ قُلْ بِئْسَمَا يَأْمُرُكُم بِهِۦٓ إِيمَـٰنُكُمْ إِن كُنتُم مُّؤْمِنِينَ ﴿ ٩٣ ﴾

And indeed, We gave Mûsa (Moses) the Book and followed him up with a succession of Messengers. And We gave 'Īsā (Jesus), the son of Maryam (Mary), clear signs and supported him with Rûh-ul-Qudus [Jibrael (Gabriel)]. Is it that whenever there came to you a Messenger with what you yourselves desired not, you grew arrogant? Some you disbelieved and some you killed. (87) And they say, "Our hearts are wrapped (i.e. do not hear or understand Allâh's Word)." Nay, Allâh has cursed them for their disbelief, so little is that which they believe. (88) And when there came to them (the Jews), a Book (this Qur'ân) from Allâh confirming what is with them, although aforetime they had invoked Allâh (for the coming of Muhammad) in order to gain victory over those who disbelieved, then when there came to them that which they had recognized, they disbelieved in it. So let the Curse of Allâh be on the disbelievers. (89) How bad is that for which they have sold their ownselves, that they should disbelieve in that which Allâh has revealed (the Qur'ân), grudging that Allâh should reveal of His Grace unto whom He wills of His slaves. So they have drawn on themselves wrath upon wrath. And for the disbelievers, there is disgracing torment. (90) And when it is said to them (the Jews), "Believe in what Allâh has sent down," they say, "We believe in what was sent down to us." And they disbelieve in that which came after it, while it is the truth confirming what is with them. Say (to them): "Why then have you killed the Prophets of Allâh aforetime, if you indeed have been believers?" (91) And indeed Mûsa (Moses) came to you with clear proofs, yet you worshipped the calf after he left, and you were Zâlimûn (polytheists and wrong-doers). (92) And (remember) when We took your covenant and We raised above you the Mount (saying), "Hold firmly to what We have given you and hear (Our Word). They said, "We have heard and disobeyed." And their hearts absorbed (the worship of) the calf because of their disbelief. Say: "Worst indeed is that which your faith enjoins on you if you are believers." (93)

Quran 2:97-103

قُلْ مَن كَانَ عَدُوًّا لِّجِبْرِيلَ فَإِنَّهُ نَزَّلَهُ عَلَىٰ قَلْبِكَ بِإِذْنِ ٱللَّهِ مُصَدِّقًا لِّمَا بَيْنَ يَدَيْهِ وَهُدًى وَبُشْرَىٰ لِلْمُؤْمِنِينَ (٩٧) مَن كَانَ عَدُوًّا لِّلَّهِ وَمَلَـٰٓئِكَتِهِۦ وَرُسُلِهِۦ وَجِبْرِيلَ وَمِيكَىٰلَ فَإِنَّ ٱللَّهَ عَدُوٌّ لِّلْكَـٰفِرِينَ (٩٨) وَلَقَدْ أَنزَلْنَآ إِلَيْكَ ءَايَـٰتٍۭ بَيِّنَـٰتٍ وَمَا يَكْفُرُ بِهَآ إِلَّا ٱلْفَـٰسِقُونَ (٩٩) أَوَكُلَّمَا عَـٰهَدُوا۟ عَهْدًا نَّبَذَهُۥ فَرِيقٌ مِّنْهُم بَلْ أَكْثَرُهُمْ لَا يُؤْمِنُونَ (١٠٠) وَلَمَّا جَآءَهُمْ رَسُولٌ مِّنْ عِندِ ٱللَّهِ مُصَدِّقٌ لِّمَا مَعَهُمْ نَبَذَ فَرِيقٌ مِّنَ ٱلَّذِينَ أُوتُوا۟ ٱلْكِتَـٰبَ كِتَـٰبَ ٱللَّهِ وَرَآءَ ظُهُورِهِمْ كَأَنَّهُمْ لَا يَعْلَمُونَ (١٠١) وَٱتَّبَعُوا۟ مَا تَتْلُوا۟ ٱلشَّيَـٰطِينُ عَلَىٰ مُلْكِ سُلَيْمَـٰنَ وَمَا كَفَرَ سُلَيْمَـٰنُ وَلَـٰكِنَّ ٱلشَّيَـٰطِينَ كَفَرُوا۟ يُعَلِّمُونَ ٱلنَّاسَ ٱلسِّحْرَ وَمَآ أُنزِلَ عَلَى ٱلْمَلَكَيْنِ بِبَابِلَ هَـٰرُوتَ وَمَـٰرُوتَ وَمَا يُعَلِّمَانِ مِنْ أَحَدٍ حَتَّىٰ يَقُولَآ إِنَّمَا نَحْنُ فِتْنَةٌ فَلَا تَكْفُرْ فَيَتَعَلَّمُونَ مِنْهُمَا مَا يُفَرِّقُونَ بِهِۦ بَيْنَ ٱلْمَرْءِ وَزَوْجِهِۦ وَمَا هُم بِضَآرِّينَ بِهِۦ مِنْ أَحَدٍ إِلَّا بِإِذْنِ ٱللَّهِ وَيَتَعَلَّمُونَ مَا يَضُرُّهُمْ وَلَا يَنفَعُهُمْ وَلَقَدْ عَلِمُوا۟ لَمَنِ ٱشْتَرَىٰهُ مَا لَهُۥ فِى ٱلْـَٔاخِرَةِ مِنْ خَلَـٰقٍ وَلَبِئْسَ مَا شَرَوْا۟ بِهِۦٓ أَنفُسَهُمْ

لَوْ كَانُوا۟ يَعْلَمُونَ ﴿١٠٢﴾ وَلَوْ أَنَّهُمْ ءَامَنُوا۟ وَٱتَّقَوْا۟ لَمَثُوبَةٌ مِّنْ عِندِ ٱللَّهِ خَيْرٌ ۖ لَّوْ كَانُوا۟ يَعْلَمُونَ ﴿١٠٣﴾

Say: "Whoever is an enemy to Jibrael (Gabriel) (let him die in his fury), for indeed he has brought it (this Qur'ân) down to your heart by Allâh's Permission, confirming what came before it [i.e. the Taurât (Torah) and the Injeel] and guidance and glad tidings for the believers. (97) "Whoever is an enemy to Allâh, His Angels, His Messengers, Jibrael (Gabriel) and Mikael (Michael), then verily, Allâh is an enemy to the disbelievers." (98) And indeed We have sent down to you manifest Ayât (these Verses of the Qur'ân which inform in detail about the news of the Jews and their secret intentions, etc.), and none disbelieve in them but Fâsiqûn (those who rebel against Allâh's Command). (99) Is it not (the case) that every time they make a covenant, some party among them throw it aside? Nay! (the truth) is most of them believe not. (100) And when there came to them a Messenger from Allâh (i.e. Muhammad) confirming what was with them, a party of those who were given the Scripture threw away the Book of Allâh behind their backs as if they did not know! (101) They followed what the Shayâtin (devils) gave out (falsely of the magic) in the lifetime of Sulaimân (Solomon). Sulaimân did not disbelieve, but the Shayâtin (devils) disbelieved, teaching men magic and such things that came down at Babylon to the two (angels,) Hârût and Mârût, but neither of these two angels taught anyone (such things) till they had said, "We are only for trial, so disbelieve not (by learning this magic from us)." And from these (angels) people learn that by which they cause separation between man and his wife, but they could not thus harm anyone except by Allâh's Leave. And they learn that which harms them and profits them not. And indeed they knew that the buyers of it (magic) would have no share in the Hereafter. And how bad indeed was that for which they sold their ownselves, if they but knew. (102) And if they had believed and guarded themselves from evil and kept their duty to Allâh, far better would have been the reward from their Lord, if they but knew! (103)

Quran 2:114

وَمَنْ أَظْلَمُ مِمَّن مَّنَعَ مَسَٰجِدَ ٱللَّهِ أَن يُذْكَرَ فِيهَا ٱسْمُهُۥ وَسَعَىٰ فِى خَرَابِهَآ أُو۟لَٰٓئِكَ مَا كَانَ لَهُمْ أَن يَدْخُلُوهَآ إِلَّا خَآئِفِينَ ۚ لَهُمْ فِى ٱلدُّنْيَا خِزْىٌ وَلَهُمْ فِى ٱلْءَاخِرَةِ عَذَابٌ عَظِيمٌ

And who are more unjust than those who forbid that Allâh's Name be glorified and mentioned much (i.e. prayers and invocations, etc.) in Allâh's mosques and strive for their ruin? It was not fitting that such should themselves enter them (Allâh's Mosques) except in fear. For them there is disgrace in this world, and they will have a great torment in the Hereafter. (114)

Quran 2:121

ٱلَّذِينَ ءَاتَيْنَٰهُمُ ٱلْكِتَٰبَ يَتْلُونَهُۥ حَقَّ تِلَاوَتِهِۦٓ أُو۟لَٰٓئِكَ يُؤْمِنُونَ بِهِۦ ۗ وَمَن يَكْفُرْ بِهِۦ فَأُو۟لَٰٓئِكَ هُمُ ٱلْخَٰسِرُونَ

Those (who embraced Islâm from Banî Israel) to whom We gave the Book [the Taurât (Torah)] [or those (Muhammad's companions) to whom We have given the Book (the Qur'ân)] recite it (i.e. obey its orders and follow its teachings) as it should be recited (i.e. followed), they are the ones that believe therein. And whoso disbelieves in it (the Qur'ân), those are they who are the losers.

Quran 2:145-146

وَلَئِنْ أَتَيْتَ ٱلَّذِينَ أُوتُوا۟ ٱلْكِتَٰبَ بِكُلِّ ءَايَةٍ مَّا تَبِعُوا۟ قِبْلَتَكَ وَمَآ أَنتَ بِتَابِعٍ قِبْلَتَهُمْ وَمَا بَعْضُهُم بِتَابِعٍ قِبْلَةَ بَعْضٍ وَلَئِنِ ٱتَّبَعْتَ أَهْوَآءَهُم مِّنۢ بَعْدِ مَا جَآءَكَ مِنَ ٱلْعِلْمِ إِنَّكَ إِذًۭا لَّمِنَ ٱلظَّٰلِمِينَ ﴿١٤٥﴾ ٱلَّذِينَ ءَاتَيْنَٰهُمُ ٱلْكِتَٰبَ يَعْرِفُونَهُۥ كَمَا يَعْرِفُونَ أَبْنَآءَهُمْ وَإِنَّ فَرِيقًۭا مِّنْهُمْ لَيَكْتُمُونَ ٱلْحَقَّ وَهُمْ يَعْلَمُونَ ﴿١٤٦﴾

And even if you were to bring to the people of the Scripture (Jews and Christians) all the Ayât (proofs, evidences, verses, lessons, signs, revelations, etc.), they would not follow your Qiblah (prayer direction), nor are you going to follow their Qiblah (prayer direction). And they will not follow each other's Qiblah (prayer direction). Verily, if you follow their desires after that which you have received of knowledge (from Allâh), then indeed you will be one of the Zâlimûn (polytheists, wrong-doers.) (145) Those to whom We gave the Scripture (Jews and Christians) recognise him (Muhammad) as they recongise their sons. But verily, a party of them conceal the truth while they know it - [i.e. the qualities of Muhammad which are written in the Taurât (Torah) and the Injeel]. (146)

Quran 2:159-161

إِنَّ ٱلَّذِينَ يَكْتُمُونَ مَآ أَنزَلْنَا مِنَ ٱلْبَيِّنَٰتِ وَٱلْهُدَىٰ مِنۢ بَعْدِ مَا بَيَّنَّٰهُ لِلنَّاسِ فِى ٱلْكِتَٰبِ أُو۟لَٰٓئِكَ يَلْعَنُهُمُ ٱللَّهُ وَيَلْعَنُهُمُ ٱللَّٰعِنُونَ (١٥٩) إِلَّا ٱلَّذِينَ تَابُوا۟ وَأَصْلَحُوا۟ وَبَيَّنُوا۟ فَأُو۟لَٰٓئِكَ أَتُوبُ عَلَيْهِمْ وَأَنَا ٱلتَّوَّابُ ٱلرَّحِيمُ (١٦٠) إِنَّ ٱلَّذِينَ كَفَرُوا۟ وَمَاتُوا۟ وَهُمْ كُفَّارٌ أُو۟لَٰٓئِكَ عَلَيْهِمْ لَعْنَةُ ٱللَّهِ وَٱلْمَلَٰٓئِكَةِ وَٱلنَّاسِ أَجْمَعِينَ (١٦١)

Verily, those who conceal the clear proofs, evidences and the guidance, which We have sent down, after We have made it clear for the people in the Book, they are the ones cursed by Allâh and cursed by the cursers. (159) Except those who repent and do righteous deeds, and openly declare (the truth which they concealed). These, I will accept their repentance. And I am the One Who accepts repentance, the Most Merciful. (160) Verily, those who disbelieve, and die while they are disbelievers, it is they on whom is the Curse of Allâh and of the angels and of mankind, combined. (161)

Quran 2:165-167

وَمِنَ ٱلنَّاسِ مَن يَتَّخِذُ مِن دُونِ ٱللَّهِ أَندَادًا يُحِبُّونَهُمْ كَحُبِّ ٱللَّهِ وَٱلَّذِينَ ءَامَنُوٓا۟ أَشَدُّ حُبًّا لِّلَّهِ وَلَوْ يَرَى ٱلَّذِينَ ظَلَمُوٓا۟ إِذْ يَرَوْنَ ٱلْعَذَابَ أَنَّ ٱلْقُوَّةَ لِلَّهِ جَمِيعًا وَأَنَّ ٱللَّهَ شَدِيدُ ٱلْعَذَابِ (١٦٥) إِذْ تَبَرَّأَ ٱلَّذِينَ ٱتُّبِعُوا۟ مِنَ ٱلَّذِينَ ٱتَّبَعُوا۟ وَرَأَوُا۟ ٱلْعَذَابَ وَتَقَطَّعَتْ بِهِمُ ٱلْأَسْبَابُ (١٦٦) وَقَالَ ٱلَّذِينَ ٱتَّبَعُوا۟ لَوْ أَنَّ لَنَا كَرَّةً فَنَتَبَرَّأَ مِنْهُمْ كَمَا تَبَرَّءُوا۟ مِنَّا كَذَٰلِكَ يُرِيهِمُ ٱللَّهُ أَعْمَٰلَهُمْ حَسَرَٰتٍ عَلَيْهِمْ وَمَا هُم بِخَٰرِجِينَ مِنَ ٱلنَّارِ (١٦٧)

And of mankind are some who take (for worship) others besides Allâh as rivals (to Allâh). They love them as they love Allâh. But those who believe, love Allâh more (than anything else). If only, those who do wrong could see, when they will see the torment, that all power belongs to Allâh and that Allâh is Severe in punishment. (165) When those who were followed, disown (declare themselves innocent of) those who followed (them), and they see the torment, then all their relations will be cut off from them. (166) And those who followed will say: "If only we had one more chance to return (to the worldly life), we would disown (declare ourselves as innocent from) them as they have disowned (declared themselves as innocent from) us." Thus Allâh will show them their deeds as regrets for them. And they will never get out of the Fire. (167)

Quran 2:170-171

وَإِذَا قِيلَ لَهُمُ ٱتَّبِعُواْ مَآ أَنزَلَ ٱللَّهُ قَالُواْ بَلْ نَتَّبِعُ مَآ أَلْفَيْنَا عَلَيْهِ ءَابَآءَنَآ أَوَلَوْ كَانَ ءَابَآؤُهُمْ لَا يَعْقِلُونَ شَيْئًا وَلَا يَهْتَدُونَ (١٧٠) وَمَثَلُ ٱلَّذِينَ كَفَرُواْ كَمَثَلِ ٱلَّذِى يَنْعِقُ بِمَا لَا يَسْمَعُ إِلَّا دُعَآءً وَنِدَآءً صُمٌّ بُكْمٌ عُمْىٌ فَهُمْ لَا يَعْقِلُونَ (١٧١)

When it is said to them: "Follow what Allâh has sent down." They say: "Nay! We shall follow what we found our fathers following." even though their fathers did not understand anything nor were they guided? (170) And the example of those who disbelieve, is as that of him who shouts to those (flock of sheep) that hears nothing but calls and cries. (They are) deaf, dumb and blind. So they do not understand.

Quran 2:174-176

إِنَّ ٱلَّذِينَ يَكْتُمُونَ مَآ أَنزَلَ ٱللَّهُ مِنَ ٱلْكِتَٰبِ وَيَشْتَرُونَ بِهِۦ ثَمَنًا قَلِيلًا أُو۟لَٰٓئِكَ مَا يَأْكُلُونَ فِى بُطُونِهِمْ إِلَّا ٱلنَّارَ وَلَا يُكَلِّمُهُمُ ٱللَّهُ يَوْمَ ٱلْقِيَٰمَةِ وَلَا يُزَكِّيهِمْ وَلَهُمْ عَذَابٌ أَلِيمٌ (١٧٤) أُو۟لَٰٓئِكَ ٱلَّذِينَ ٱشْتَرَوُا۟ ٱلضَّلَٰلَةَ بِٱلْهُدَىٰ وَٱلْعَذَابَ بِٱلْمَغْفِرَةِ ۚ فَمَآ أَصْبَرَهُمْ عَلَى ٱلنَّارِ (١٧٥) ذَٰلِكَ بِأَنَّ ٱللَّهَ نَزَّلَ ٱلْكِتَٰبَ بِٱلْحَقِّ ۗ وَإِنَّ ٱلَّذِينَ ٱخْتَلَفُوا۟ فِى ٱلْكِتَٰبِ لَفِى شِقَاقٍۭ بَعِيدٍ (١٧٦)

Verily, those who conceal what Allâh has sent down of the Book, and purchase a small gain therewith (of worldly things), they eat into their bellies nothing but fire. Allâh will not speak to them on the Day of Resurrection, nor purify them, and theirs will be a painful torment. (174) Those are they who have purchased error at the price of Guidance, and torment at the price of Forgiveness. So how bold they are (for evil deeds which will push them) to the Fire. (175) That is because Allâh has sent down the Book (the Qur'ân) in truth. And verily, those who disputed as regards the Book are far away in opposition. (176)

Quran 2:212

زُيِّنَ لِلَّذِينَ كَفَرُوا۟ ٱلْحَيَوٰةُ ٱلدُّنْيَا وَيَسْخَرُونَ مِنَ ٱلَّذِينَ ءَامَنُوا۟ ۘ وَٱلَّذِينَ ٱتَّقَوْا۟ فَوْقَهُمْ يَوْمَ ٱلْقِيَٰمَةِ ۗ وَٱللَّهُ يَرْزُقُ مَن يَشَآءُ بِغَيْرِ حِسَابٍ

Beautified is the life of this world for those who disbelieve, and they mock at those who believe. But those who obey Allâh's Orders and keep away from what He has forbidden, will be above them on the Day of Resurrection. And Allâh gives (of His Bounty, Blessings, Favours, Honours, on the Day of Resurrection) to whom He wills without limit. (212)

Quran 2:257

ٱللَّهُ وَلِىُّ ٱلَّذِينَ ءَامَنُواْ يُخْرِجُهُم مِّنَ ٱلظُّلُمَٰتِ إِلَى ٱلنُّورِۖ وَٱلَّذِينَ كَفَرُوٓاْ أَوْلِيَآؤُهُمُ ٱلطَّٰغُوتُ يُخْرِجُونَهُم مِّنَ ٱلنُّورِ إِلَى ٱلظُّلُمَٰتِۗ أُوْلَٰٓئِكَ أَصْحَٰبُ ٱلنَّارِۖ هُمْ فِيهَا خَٰلِدُونَ

Allâh is the Walî (Protector or Guardian) of those who believe. He brings them out from darkness into light. But as for those who disbelieve, their Auliyâ (supporters and helpers) are Tâghût [false deities and false leaders], they bring them out from light into darkness. Those are the dwellers of the Fire, and they will abide therein forever. (257)

Quran 3:10-12

إِنَّ ٱلَّذِينَ كَفَرُواْ لَن تُغْنِىَ عَنْهُمْ أَمْوَٰلُهُمْ وَلَآ أَوْلَٰدُهُم مِّنَ ٱللَّهِ شَيْـًٔاۖ وَأُوْلَٰٓئِكَ هُمْ وَقُودُ ٱلنَّارِ (١٠) كَدَأْبِ ءَالِ فِرْعَوْنَ وَٱلَّذِينَ مِن قَبْلِهِمْۚ كَذَّبُواْ بِـَٔايَٰتِنَا فَأَخَذَهُمُ ٱللَّهُ بِذُنُوبِهِمْۗ وَٱللَّهُ شَدِيدُ ٱلْعِقَابِ (١١) قُل لِّلَّذِينَ كَفَرُواْ سَتُغْلَبُونَ وَتُحْشَرُونَ إِلَىٰ جَهَنَّمَۚ وَبِئْسَ ٱلْمِهَادُ (١٢)

Verily, those who disbelieve, neither their properties nor their offspring will avail them whatsoever against Allâh; and it is they who will be fuel of the Fire. (10) Like the behaviour of the people of Fir'aun (Pharaoh) and those before them; they belied Our Ayât (proofs, evidences, verses, lessons, signs, revelations, etc.), so Allâh seized (destroyed) them for their sins. And Allâh is Severe in punishment. (11) Say to those who disbelieve: "You will be defeated and gathered together to Hell, and worst indeed is that place to rest." (12)

Quran 3:21

إِنَّ ٱلَّذِينَ يَكْفُرُونَ بِـَٔايَٰتِ ٱللَّهِ وَيَقْتُلُونَ ٱلنَّبِيِّـۧنَ بِغَيْرِ حَقٍّ وَيَقْتُلُونَ ٱلَّذِينَ يَأْمُرُونَ بِٱلْقِسْطِ مِنَ ٱلنَّاسِ فَبَشِّرْهُم بِعَذَابٍ أَلِيمٍ

Verily! Those who disbelieve in the Ayât (proofs, evidences, verses, lessons, signs, revelations, etc.) of Allâh and kill the Prophets without right, and kill those men who order just dealings, ... then announce to them a painful torment. (21)

Quran 3:32

قُلْ أَطِيعُوا۟ ٱللَّهَ وَٱلرَّسُولَ ۖ فَإِن تَوَلَّوْا۟ فَإِنَّ ٱللَّهَ لَا يُحِبُّ ٱلْكَٰفِرِينَ

Say: "Obey Allâh and the Messenger (Muhammad)." But if they turn away, then Allâh does not like the disbelievers (32)

Quran 3:69-73

وَدَّت طَّآئِفَةٌ مِّنْ أَهْلِ ٱلْكِتَٰبِ لَوْ يُضِلُّونَكُمْ وَمَا يُضِلُّونَ إِلَّآ أَنفُسَهُمْ وَمَا يَشْعُرُونَ (٦٩) يَٰٓأَهْلَ ٱلْكِتَٰبِ لِمَ تَكْفُرُونَ بِـَٔايَٰتِ ٱللَّهِ وَأَنتُمْ تَشْهَدُونَ (٧٠) يَٰٓأَهْلَ ٱلْكِتَٰبِ لِمَ تَلْبِسُونَ ٱلْحَقَّ بِٱلْبَٰطِلِ وَتَكْتُمُونَ ٱلْحَقَّ وَأَنتُمْ تَعْلَمُونَ (٧١) وَقَالَت طَّآئِفَةٌ مِّنْ أَهْلِ ٱلْكِتَٰبِ ءَامِنُوا۟ بِٱلَّذِىٓ أُنزِلَ عَلَى ٱلَّذِينَ ءَامَنُوا۟ وَجْهَ ٱلنَّهَارِ وَٱكْفُرُوٓا۟ ءَاخِرَهُۥ لَعَلَّهُمْ يَرْجِعُونَ (٧٢) وَلَا تُؤْمِنُوٓا۟ إِلَّا لِمَن تَبِعَ دِينَكُمْ قُلْ إِنَّ ٱلْهُدَىٰ هُدَى ٱللَّهِ أَن يُؤْتَىٰٓ أَحَدٌ مِّثْلَ مَآ أُوتِيتُمْ أَوْ يُحَآجُّوكُمْ عِندَ رَبِّكُمْ ۗ قُلْ إِنَّ ٱلْفَضْلَ بِيَدِ ٱللَّهِ يُؤْتِيهِ مَن يَشَآءُ ۗ وَٱللَّهُ وَٰسِعٌ عَلِيمٌ (٧٣)

A party of the people of the Scripture (Jews and Christians) wish to lead you astray. But they shall not lead astray anyone except themselves, and they perceive not. (69) O people of the Scripture! (Jews and Christians):

"Why do you disbelieve in the Ayât of Allâh, [the Verses about Prophet Muhammad present in the Taurât (Torah) and the Injeel] while you (yourselves) bear witness (to their truth)." (70) O people of the Scripture (Jews and Christians): "Why do you mix truth with falsehood and conceal the truth while you know?" (71) And a party of the people of the Scripture say: "Believe in the morning in that which is revealed to the believers (Muslims), and reject it at the end of the day, so that they may turn back. (72) And believe no one except the one who follows your religion. Say (O Muhammad): "Verily! Right guidance is the Guidance of Allâh" and do not believe that anyone can receive like that which you have received (of Revelation) except when he follows your religion, otherwise they would engage you in argument before your Lord. Say (O Muhammad): "All the bounty is in the Hand of Allâh; He grants to whom He wills. And Allâh is All-Sufficient for His creatures' needs, the All-Knower." (73)

Quran 3:77-80

إِنَّ ٱلَّذِينَ يَشْتَرُونَ بِعَهْدِ ٱللَّهِ وَأَيْمَٰنِهِمْ ثَمَنًا قَلِيلًا أُو۟لَٰٓئِكَ لَا خَلَٰقَ لَهُمْ فِى ٱلْءَاخِرَةِ وَلَا يُكَلِّمُهُمُ ٱللَّهُ وَلَا يَنظُرُ إِلَيْهِمْ يَوْمَ ٱلْقِيَٰمَةِ وَلَا يُزَكِّيهِمْ وَلَهُمْ عَذَابٌ أَلِيمٌ (٧٧) وَإِنَّ مِنْهُمْ لَفَرِيقًا يَلْوُۥنَ أَلْسِنَتَهُم بِٱلْكِتَٰبِ لِتَحْسَبُوهُ مِنَ ٱلْكِتَٰبِ وَمَا هُوَ مِنَ ٱلْكِتَٰبِ وَيَقُولُونَ هُوَ مِنْ عِندِ ٱللَّهِ وَمَا هُوَ مِنْ عِندِ ٱللَّهِ وَيَقُولُونَ عَلَى ٱللَّهِ ٱلْكَذِبَ وَهُمْ يَعْلَمُونَ (٧٨) مَا كَانَ لِبَشَرٍ أَن يُؤْتِيَهُ ٱللَّهُ ٱلْكِتَٰبَ وَٱلْحُكْمَ وَٱلنُّبُوَّةَ ثُمَّ يَقُولَ لِلنَّاسِ كُونُوا۟ عِبَادًا لِّى مِن دُونِ ٱللَّهِ وَلَٰكِن كُونُوا۟ رَبَّٰنِيِّۦنَ بِمَا كُنتُمْ تُعَلِّمُونَ ٱلْكِتَٰبَ وَبِمَا كُنتُمْ تَدْرُسُونَ (٧٩) وَلَا

يَأْمُرَكُمْ أَن تَتَّخِذُوا۟ ٱلْمَلَـٰٓئِكَةَ وَٱلنَّبِيِّـۧنَ أَرْبَابًا ۗ أَيَأْمُرُكُم بِٱلْكُفْرِ بَعْدَ إِذْ أَنتُم مُّسْلِمُونَ (٨٠)

Verily, those who purchase a small gain at the cost of Allâh's Covenant and their oaths, they shall have no portion in the Hereafter (Paradise). Neither will Allâh speak to them, nor look at them on the Day of Resurrection, nor will He purify them, and they shall have a painful torment. (77) And verily, among them is a party who distort the Book with their tongues (as they read), so that you may think it is from the Book, but it is not from the Book, and they say: "This is from Allâh," but it is not from Allâh; and they speak a lie against Allâh while they know it. (78) It is not for any human being to whom Allâh has given the Book and Al-Hukm (the knowledge and understanding of the laws of religion) and Prophethood to say to the people: "Be my worshippers rather than Allâh's." On the contrary (he would say): "Be you Rabbaniyyun (learned men of religion who practice what they know and also preach to others), because you are teaching the Book, and you are studying it." (79) Nor would he order you to take angels and Prophets for lords (gods). Would he order you to disbelieve after you have submitted to Allâh's Will? (80)

Quran 3:99

قُلْ يَـٰٓأَهْلَ ٱلْكِتَـٰبِ لِمَ تَصُدُّونَ عَن سَبِيلِ ٱللَّهِ مَنْ ءَامَنَ تَبْغُونَهَا عِوَجًا وَأَنتُمْ شُهَدَآءُ ۗ وَمَا ٱللَّهُ بِغَـٰفِلٍ عَمَّا تَعْمَلُونَ

Say: "O people of the Scripture (Jews and Christians)! Why do you stop those who have believed, from the Path of Allâh, seeking to make it seem crooked, while you (yourselves) are witnesses [to Muhammad as a Messenger of Allâh and Islâm (Allâh's Religion, i.e. to worship none but Him Alone)]? And Allâh is not unaware of what you do." (99)

Quran 3:151

سَنُلْقِى فِى قُلُوبِ ٱلَّذِينَ كَفَرُوا۟ ٱلرُّعْبَ بِمَآ أَشْرَكُوا۟ بِٱللَّهِ مَا لَمْ يُنَزِّلْ بِهِۦ سُلْطَٰنًا ۖ وَمَأْوَىٰهُمُ ٱلنَّارُ ۚ وَبِئْسَ مَثْوَى ٱلظَّٰلِمِينَ

We shall cast terror into the hearts of those who disbelieve, because they joined others in worship with Allâh, for which He had sent no authority; their abode will be the Fire and how evil is the abode of the Zâlimûn (polytheists and wrong¬doers). (151)

Quran 3:177-178

إِنَّ ٱلَّذِينَ ٱشْتَرَوُا۟ ٱلْكُفْرَ بِٱلْإِيمَٰنِ لَن يَضُرُّوا۟ ٱللَّهَ شَيْـًٔا وَلَهُمْ عَذَابٌ أَلِيمٌ (١٧٧) وَلَا يَحْسَبَنَّ ٱلَّذِينَ كَفَرُوٓا۟ أَنَّمَا نُمْلِى لَهُمْ خَيْرٌ لِّأَنفُسِهِمْ ۚ إِنَّمَا نُمْلِى لَهُمْ لِيَزْدَادُوٓا۟ إِثْمًا ۚ وَلَهُمْ عَذَابٌ مُّهِينٌ (١٧٨)

Verily, those who purchase disbelief at the price of Faith, not the least harm will they do to Allâh. For them, there is a painful torment. (177) And let not the disbelievers think that Our postponing of their punishment is good for them. We postpone the punishment only so that they may increase in sinfulness. And for them is a disgracing torment. (178)

Quran 3:180-181

وَلَا يَحْسَبَنَّ ٱلَّذِينَ يَبْخَلُونَ بِمَآ ءَاتَىٰهُمُ ٱللَّهُ مِن فَضْلِهِۦ هُوَ خَيْرًا لَّهُم ۖ بَلْ هُوَ شَرٌّ لَّهُمْ ۖ سَيُطَوَّقُونَ مَا بَخِلُوا۟ بِهِۦ يَوْمَ ٱلْقِيَٰمَةِ ۗ وَلِلَّهِ مِيرَٰثُ ٱلسَّمَٰوَٰتِ وَٱلْأَرْضِ ۗ وَٱللَّهُ بِمَا تَعْمَلُونَ خَبِيرٌ (١٨٠) لَّقَدْ سَمِعَ ٱللَّهُ قَوْلَ ٱلَّذِينَ قَالُوٓا۟ إِنَّ ٱللَّهَ فَقِيرٌ وَنَحْنُ أَغْنِيَآءُ ۘ سَنَكْتُبُ مَا قَالُوا۟ وَقَتْلَهُمُ ٱلْأَنۢبِيَآءَ بِغَيْرِ حَقٍّ وَنَقُولُ ذُوقُوا۟ عَذَابَ ٱلْحَرِيقِ (١٨١)

And let not those who covetously withhold of that which Allâh has bestowed on them of His Bounty (Wealth) think that it is good for them (and so they do not pay the obligatory Zakât). Nay, it will be worse for them; the things which they covetously withheld shall be tied to their necks like a collar on the Day of Resurrection[]. And to Allâh belongs the heritage of the heavens and the earth; and Allâh is Well¬Acquainted with all that you do. (180) Indeed, Allâh has heard the statement of those who say: "Truly, Allâh is poor and we are rich!" We shall record what they have said and their killing of the Prophets unjustly, and We shall say: "Taste you the torment of the burning (Fire)." (181)

Quran 3:196-197

لَا يَغُرَّنَّكَ تَقَلُّبُ ٱلَّذِينَ كَفَرُوا۟ فِى ٱلْبِلَٰدِ (١٩٦) مَتَٰعٌ قَلِيلٌ ثُمَّ مَأْوَىٰهُمْ جَهَنَّمُ ۚ وَبِئْسَ ٱلْمِهَادُ (١٩٧)

Let not the free disposal (and affluence) of the disbelievers throughout the land deceive you. (196) A brief enjoyment; then, their ultimate abode is Hell; and worst indeed is that place for rest. (197)

Quran 4:17-18

إِنَّمَا ٱلتَّوْبَةُ عَلَى ٱللَّهِ لِلَّذِينَ يَعْمَلُونَ ٱلسُّوٓءَ بِجَهَٰلَةٍ ثُمَّ يَتُوبُونَ مِن قَرِيبٍ فَأُو۟لَٰٓئِكَ يَتُوبُ ٱللَّهُ عَلَيْهِمْ ۗ وَكَانَ ٱللَّهُ عَلِيمًا حَكِيمًا (١٧) وَلَيْسَتِ ٱلتَّوْبَةُ لِلَّذِينَ يَعْمَلُونَ ٱلسَّيِّـَٔاتِ حَتَّىٰٓ إِذَا حَضَرَ أَحَدَهُمُ ٱلْمَوْتُ قَالَ إِنِّى تُبْتُ ٱلْـَٰٔنَ وَلَا ٱلَّذِينَ يَمُوتُونَ وَهُمْ كُفَّارٌ ۚ أُو۟لَٰٓئِكَ أَعْتَدْنَا لَهُمْ عَذَابًا أَلِيمًا (١٨)

Allâh accepts only the repentance of those who do evil in ignorance and foolishness and repent soon afterwards; it is they whom Allâh will forgive and Allâh is Ever All¬Knower, All¬Wise. (17) And of no effect is the repentance of those who continue to do evil deeds until death faces one of them and he says: "Now I repent;" nor of those who die while they are disbelievers. For them We have prepared a painful torment. (18)

Quran 4:37-39

ٱلَّذِينَ يَبْخَلُونَ وَيَأْمُرُونَ ٱلنَّاسَ بِٱلْبُخْلِ وَيَكْتُمُونَ مَآ ءَاتَىٰهُمُ ٱللَّهُ مِن فَضْلِهِۦ ۗ وَأَعْتَدْنَا لِلْكَٰفِرِينَ عَذَابًا مُّهِينًا (٣٧) وَٱلَّذِينَ يُنفِقُونَ أَمْوَٰلَهُمْ رِئَآءَ ٱلنَّاسِ وَلَا يُؤْمِنُونَ بِٱللَّهِ وَلَا بِٱلْيَوْمِ ٱلْـَٔاخِرِ ۗ وَمَن يَكُنِ ٱلشَّيْطَٰنُ لَهُۥ قَرِينًا فَسَآءَ قَرِينًا (٣٨) وَمَاذَا عَلَيْهِمْ لَوْ ءَامَنُوا۟ بِٱللَّهِ وَٱلْيَوْمِ ٱلْـَٔاخِرِ وَأَنفَقُوا۟ مِمَّا رَزَقَهُمُ ٱللَّهُ ۚ وَكَانَ ٱللَّهُ بِهِم عَلِيمًا (٣٩)

Those who are miserly and enjoin miserliness on other men and hide what Allâh has bestowed upon them of His Bounties. And We have prepared for the disbelievers a disgraceful torment. (37) And (also) those who spend of their substance to be seen of men, and believe not in Allâh and the Last Day [they are the friends of Shaitân (Satan)], and whoever takes Shaitân (Satan) as an intimate; then what a dreadful intimate he has! (38) And what loss have they if they had believed in Allâh and in the Last Day, and they spend out of what Allâh has given them for sustenance? And Allâh is Ever All¬Knower of them (39)

Quran 4:42

يَوْمَئِذٍ يَوَدُّ ٱلَّذِينَ كَفَرُواْ وَعَصَوُاْ ٱلرَّسُولَ لَوْ تُسَوَّىٰ بِهِمُ ٱلْأَرْضُ وَلَا يَكْتُمُونَ ٱللَّهَ حَدِيثًا

On that day those who disbelieved and disobeyed the Messenger (Muhammad) will wish that they were buried in the earth, but they will never be able to hide a single fact from Allâh. (42)

Quran 4:44-46

أَلَمْ تَرَ إِلَى ٱلَّذِينَ أُوتُواْ نَصِيبًا مِّنَ ٱلْكِتَبِ يَشْتَرُونَ ٱلضَّلَـٰلَةَ وَيُرِيدُونَ أَن تَضِلُّواْ ٱلسَّبِيلَ (٤٤) وَٱللَّهُ أَعْلَمُ بِأَعْدَآئِكُمْ وَكَفَىٰ بِٱللَّهِ وَلِيًّا وَكَفَىٰ بِٱللَّهِ نَصِيرًا (٤٥) مِّنَ ٱلَّذِينَ هَادُواْ يُحَرِّفُونَ ٱلْكَلِمَ عَن مَّوَاضِعِهِ وَيَقُولُونَ سَمِعْنَا وَعَصَيْنَا وَٱسْمَعْ غَيْرَ مُسْمَعٍ وَرَٰعِنَا لَيًّۢا بِأَلْسِنَتِهِمْ وَطَعْنًا فِى ٱلدِّينِ وَلَوْ أَنَّهُمْ قَالُواْ سَمِعْنَا وَأَطَعْنَا وَٱسْمَعْ وَٱنظُرْنَا لَكَانَ خَيْرًا لَّهُمْ وَأَقْوَمَ وَلَـٰكِن لَّعَنَهُمُ ٱللَّهُ بِكُفْرِهِمْ فَلَا يُؤْمِنُونَ إِلَّا قَلِيلًا (٤٦)

Have you not seen those who were given a portion of the book (the Jews), purchasing the wrong path, and wish that you should go astray from the Right Path. (44) Allâh has full knowledge of your enemies, and Allâh is Sufficient as a Walî (Protector), and Allâh is Sufficient as a Helper. (45) Among those who are Jews, there are some who displace words from (their) right places and say: "We hear your word (O Muhammad) and disobey," and

"Hear and let you (O Muhammad) hear nothing." And Râ'ina with a twist of their tongues and as a mockery of the religion (Islâm). And if only they had said: "We hear and obey", and "Do make us understand," it would have been better for them, and more proper, but Allâh has cursed them for their disbelief, so they believe not except a few. (46)

Quran 4:49-56

أَلَمْ تَرَ إِلَى ٱلَّذِينَ يُزَكُّونَ أَنفُسَهُم بَلِ ٱللَّهُ يُزَكِّى مَن يَشَآءُ وَلَا يُظْلَمُونَ فَتِيلًا (٤٩) ٱنظُرْ كَيْفَ يَفْتَرُونَ عَلَى ٱللَّهِ ٱلْكَذِبَ وَكَفَىٰ بِهِۦٓ إِثْمًا مُّبِينًا (٥٠) أَلَمْ تَرَ إِلَى ٱلَّذِينَ أُوتُوا۟ نَصِيبًا مِّنَ ٱلْكِتَـٰبِ يُؤْمِنُونَ بِٱلْجِبْتِ وَٱلطَّـٰغُوتِ وَيَقُولُونَ لِلَّذِينَ كَفَرُوا۟ هَـٰٓؤُلَآءِ أَهْدَىٰ مِنَ ٱلَّذِينَ ءَامَنُوا۟ سَبِيلًا (٥١) أُو۟لَـٰٓئِكَ ٱلَّذِينَ لَعَنَهُمُ ٱللَّهُ وَمَن يَلْعَنِ ٱللَّهُ فَلَن تَجِدَ لَهُۥ نَصِيرًا (٥٢) أَمْ لَهُمْ نَصِيبٌ مِّنَ ٱلْمُلْكِ فَإِذًا لَّا يُؤْتُونَ ٱلنَّاسَ نَقِيرًا (٥٣) أَمْ يَحْسُدُونَ ٱلنَّاسَ عَلَىٰ مَآ ءَاتَىٰهُمُ ٱللَّهُ مِن فَضْلِهِۦ فَقَدْ ءَاتَيْنَآ ءَالَ إِبْرَٰهِيمَ ٱلْكِتَـٰبَ وَٱلْحِكْمَةَ وَءَاتَيْنَـٰهُم مُّلْكًا عَظِيمًا (٥٤) فَمِنْهُم مَّنْ ءَامَنَ بِهِۦ وَمِنْهُم مَّن صَدَّ عَنْهُ وَكَفَىٰ بِجَهَنَّمَ سَعِيرًا (٥٥) إِنَّ ٱلَّذِينَ كَفَرُوا۟ بِـَٔايَـٰتِنَا سَوْفَ نُصْلِيهِمْ نَارًا كُلَّمَا نَضِجَتْ جُلُودُهُم بَدَّلْنَـٰهُمْ جُلُودًا غَيْرَهَا لِيَذُوقُوا۟ ٱلْعَذَابَ إِنَّ ٱللَّهَ كَانَ عَزِيزًا حَكِيمًا (٥٦)

Have you not seen those (Jews and Christians) who claim sanctity for themselves. Nay, but Allâh sanctifies whom He wills, and they will not be dealt with injustice even equal to the extent of a scalish thread in the long slit of a date-stone. (49) Look, how they invent a lie against Allâh, and enough is that as a manifest sin. (50) Have you not seen those who were given a portion of the Scripture? They believe in Jibt and Tâghût and say to the disbelievers that they are better guided as regards the way than the believers (Muslims). (51) They are those whom Allâh has cursed, and he whom Allâh curses, you will not find for him (any) helper, (52) Or have they a share in the dominion? Then in that case they would not give mankind even a speck on the back of a date-stone. (53) Or do they envy men (Muhammad and his followers) for what Allâh has given them of His Bounty? Then We had already given the family of Ibrâhim (Abraham) the Book and Al¬Hikmah, and conferred upon them a great kingdom (54) Of them were (some) who believed in him (Muhammad), and of them were (some) who averted their faces from him (Muhammad); and enough is Hell for burning (them). (55) Surely! Those who disbelieved in Our Ayât (proofs, evidences, verses, lessons, signs, revelations, etc.) We shall burn them in Fire. As often as their skins are roasted through, We shall change them for other skins that they may taste the punishment. Truly, Allâh is Ever Most Powerful, All¬Wise. (56)

Quran 4:60-65

أَلَمْ تَرَ إِلَى ٱلَّذِينَ يَزْعُمُونَ أَنَّهُمْ ءَامَنُواْ بِمَآ أُنزِلَ إِلَيْكَ وَمَآ أُنزِلَ مِن قَبْلِكَ يُرِيدُونَ أَن يَتَحَاكَمُوٓاْ إِلَى ٱلطَّٰغُوتِ وَقَدْ أُمِرُوٓاْ أَن يَكْفُرُواْ بِهِۦ وَيُرِيدُ ٱلشَّيْطَٰنُ أَن يُضِلَّهُمْ ضَلَٰلَۢا بَعِيدًا (٦٠) وَإِذَا قِيلَ لَهُمْ تَعَالَوْاْ إِلَىٰ مَآ أَنزَلَ ٱللَّهُ وَإِلَى ٱلرَّسُولِ رَأَيْتَ ٱلْمُنَٰفِقِينَ يَصُدُّونَ عَنكَ صُدُودًا (٦١) فَكَيْفَ إِذَآ أَصَٰبَتْهُم مُّصِيبَةٌۢ بِمَا قَدَّمَتْ أَيْدِيهِمْ ثُمَّ جَآءُوكَ يَحْلِفُونَ بِٱللَّهِ إِنْ أَرَدْنَآ إِلَّآ إِحْسَٰنًا وَتَوْفِيقًا (٦٢) أُوْلَٰٓئِكَ ٱلَّذِينَ يَعْلَمُ ٱللَّهُ مَا فِى قُلُوبِهِمْ فَأَعْرِضْ عَنْهُمْ وَعِظْهُمْ وَقُل لَّهُمْ فِىٓ أَنفُسِهِمْ قَوْلَۢا بَلِيغًا (٦٣) وَمَآ أَرْسَلْنَا مِن رَّسُولٍ إِلَّا لِيُطَاعَ بِإِذْنِ ٱللَّهِ وَلَوْ أَنَّهُمْ إِذ ظَّلَمُوٓاْ أَنفُسَهُمْ جَآءُوكَ فَٱسْتَغْفَرُواْ ٱللَّهَ وَٱسْتَغْفَرَ لَهُمُ ٱلرَّسُولُ لَوَجَدُواْ ٱللَّهَ تَوَّابًا رَّحِيمًا (٦٤) فَلَا وَرَبِّكَ لَا يُؤْمِنُونَ حَتَّىٰ

يُحَكِّمُوكَ فِيمَا شَجَرَ بَيْنَهُمْ ثُمَّ لَا يَجِدُواْ فِى أَنفُسِهِمْ حَرَجًا مِّمَّا قَضَيْتَ وَيُسَلِّمُواْ تَسْلِيمًا ﴿٦٥﴾

Have you seen those (hyprocrites) who claim that they believe in that which has been sent down to you, and that which was sent down before you, and they wish to go for judgement (in their disputes) to the Tâghût (false judges) while they have been ordered to reject them. But Shaitân (Satan) wishes to lead them far astray. (60) And when it is said to them: "Come to what Allâh has sent down and to the Messenger (Muhammad)," you see the hypocrites turn away from you with aversion (61) How then, when a catastrophe befalls them because of what their hands have sent forth, they come to you swearing by Allâh, "We meant no more than goodwill and conciliation!" (62) They (hypocrites) are those of whom Allâh knows what is in their hearts; so turn aside from them (do not punish them) but admonish them, and speak to them an effective word (i.e. to believe in Allâh, worship Him, obey Him, and be afraid of Him) to reach their innerselves (63) We sent no Messenger, but to be obeyed by Allâh's Leave. If they (hypocrites), when they had been unjust to themselves, had come to you (Muhammad) and begged Allâh's Forgiveness, and the Messenger had begged forgiveness for them: indeed, they would have found Allâh All-Forgiving (One Who forgives and accepts repentance), Most Merciful. (64) But no, by your Lord, they can have no Faith, until they make you (O Muhammad) judge in all disputes between them, and find in themselves no resistance against your decisions, and accept (them) with full submission. (65)

Quran 4:97

إِنَّ ٱلَّذِينَ تَوَفَّىٰهُمُ ٱلْمَلَـٰٓئِكَةُ ظَالِمِىٓ أَنفُسِهِمْ قَالُوا۟ فِيمَ كُنتُمْ ۖ قَالُوا۟ كُنَّا مُسْتَضْعَفِينَ فِى ٱلْأَرْضِ ۚ قَالُوٓا۟ أَلَمْ تَكُنْ أَرْضُ ٱللَّهِ وَٰسِعَةً فَتُهَاجِرُوا۟ فِيهَا ۚ فَأُو۟لَـٰٓئِكَ مَأْوَىٰهُمْ جَهَنَّمُ ۖ وَسَآءَتْ مَصِيرًا

Verily! As for those whom the angels take (in death) while they are wronging themselves (as they stayed among the disbelievers even though emigration was obligatory for them), they (angels) say (to them): "In what (condition) were you?" They reply: "We were weak and oppressed on earth." They (angels) say: "Was not the earth of Allâh spacious enough for you to emigrate therein?" Such men will find their abode in Hell - What an evil destination! (97)

Quran 4:101

وَإِذَا ضَرَبْتُمْ فِى ٱلْأَرْضِ فَلَيْسَ عَلَيْكُمْ جُنَاحٌ أَن تَقْصُرُوا۟ مِنَ ٱلصَّلَوٰةِ إِنْ خِفْتُمْ أَن يَفْتِنَكُمُ ٱلَّذِينَ كَفَرُوٓا۟ ۚ إِنَّ ٱلْكَـٰفِرِينَ كَانُوا۟ لَكُمْ عَدُوًّا مُّبِينًا

And when you (Muslims) travel in the land, there is no sin on you if you shorten As-Salât (the prayer) if you fear that the disbelievers may put you in trial (attack you etc.), verily, the disbelievers are ever unto you open enemies. (101)

Quran 4:138-143

بَشِّرِ ٱلْمُنَٰفِقِينَ بِأَنَّ لَهُمْ عَذَابًا أَلِيمًا ﴿١٣٨﴾ ٱلَّذِينَ يَتَّخِذُونَ ٱلْكَٰفِرِينَ أَوْلِيَآءَ مِن دُونِ ٱلْمُؤْمِنِينَ ۚ أَيَبْتَغُونَ عِندَهُمُ ٱلْعِزَّةَ فَإِنَّ ٱلْعِزَّةَ لِلَّهِ جَمِيعًا ﴿١٣٩﴾ وَقَدْ نَزَّلَ عَلَيْكُمْ فِى ٱلْكِتَٰبِ أَنْ إِذَا سَمِعْتُمْ ءَايَٰتِ ٱللَّهِ يُكْفَرُ بِهَا وَيُسْتَهْزَأُ بِهَا فَلَا تَقْعُدُوا۟ مَعَهُمْ حَتَّىٰ يَخُوضُوا۟ فِى حَدِيثٍ غَيْرِهِ ۚ إِنَّكُمْ إِذًا مِّثْلُهُمْ ۗ إِنَّ ٱللَّهَ جَامِعُ ٱلْمُنَٰفِقِينَ وَٱلْكَٰفِرِينَ فِى جَهَنَّمَ جَمِيعًا ﴿١٤٠﴾ ٱلَّذِينَ يَتَرَبَّصُونَ بِكُمْ فَإِن كَانَ لَكُمْ فَتْحٌ مِّنَ ٱللَّهِ قَالُوٓا۟ أَلَمْ نَكُن مَّعَكُمْ وَإِن كَانَ لِلْكَٰفِرِينَ نَصِيبٌ قَالُوٓا۟ أَلَمْ نَسْتَحْوِذْ عَلَيْكُمْ وَنَمْنَعْكُم مِّنَ ٱلْمُؤْمِنِينَ ۚ فَٱللَّهُ يَحْكُمُ بَيْنَكُمْ يَوْمَ ٱلْقِيَٰمَةِ ۗ وَلَن يَجْعَلَ ٱللَّهُ لِلْكَٰفِرِينَ عَلَى ٱلْمُؤْمِنِينَ سَبِيلًا ﴿١٤١﴾ إِنَّ ٱلْمُنَٰفِقِينَ يُخَٰدِعُونَ ٱللَّهَ وَهُوَ خَٰدِعُهُمْ وَإِذَا قَامُوٓا۟ إِلَى ٱلصَّلَوٰةِ قَامُوا۟ كُسَالَىٰ يُرَآءُونَ ٱلنَّاسَ وَلَا يَذْكُرُونَ ٱللَّهَ إِلَّا قَلِيلًا ﴿١٤٢﴾ مُّذَبْذَبِينَ بَيْنَ ذَٰلِكَ لَآ إِلَىٰ هَٰٓؤُلَآءِ وَلَآ إِلَىٰ هَٰٓؤُلَآءِ ۚ وَمَن يُضْلِلِ ٱللَّهُ فَلَن تَجِدَ لَهُۥ سَبِيلًا ﴿١٤٣﴾

Give to the hypocrites the tidings that there is for them a painful torment. (138) Those who take disbelievers for Auliyâ' (protectors or helpers or friends) instead of believers, do they seek honor, power and glory with them? Verily, then to Allâh belongs all honor, power and glory. (139) And it has already been revealed to you in the Book (this Qur'ân) that when you hear the Verses of Allâh being denied and mocked at, then sit not with them, until they engage in a talk other than that; (but if you stayed with them) certainly in that case you would be like them. Surely, Allâh will collect the hypocrites and disbelievers all together in Hell, (140) Those (hyprocrites) who wait and watch about you; if you gain a victory from Allâh, they say: "Were we not with you?" But if the disbelievers gain a success, they say (to them): "Did we not gain mastery over you and did we not protect you from the believers?" Allâh will judge between you (all) on the Day of Resurrection. And never will Allâh grant to the disbelievers a way (to triumph) over the believers. (141) Verily, the hypocrites seek to deceive Allâh, but it is He Who deceives them. And when they stand up for As-Salât (the prayer), they stand with laziness and to be seen of men, and they do not remember Allâh but little. (142) (They are) swaying between this and that, belonging neither to these nor to those, and he whom Allâh sends astray, you will not find for him a way (to the truth - Islâm). (143)

Quran 4:150-151

إِنَّ ٱلَّذِينَ يَكْفُرُونَ بِٱللَّهِ وَرُسُلِهِ وَيُرِيدُونَ أَن يُفَرِّقُوا۟ بَيْنَ ٱللَّهِ وَرُسُلِهِ وَيَقُولُونَ نُؤْمِنُ بِبَعْضٍ وَنَكْفُرُ بِبَعْضٍ وَيُرِيدُونَ أَن يَتَّخِذُوا۟ بَيْنَ ذَٰلِكَ سَبِيلًا (١٥٠) أُو۟لَٰٓئِكَ هُمُ ٱلْكَٰفِرُونَ حَقًّا وَأَعْتَدْنَا لِلْكَٰفِرِينَ عَذَابًا مُّهِينًا (١٥١)

Verily, those who disbelieve in Allâh and His Messengers and wish to make distinction between Allâh and His Messengers (by believing in Allâh and disbelieving in His Messengers) saying, "We believe in some but reject others," and wish to adopt a way in between. (150) They are in truth disbelievers. And We have prepared for the disbelievers a humiliating torment. (151)

Quran 4:155-159

فَبِمَا نَقْضِهِم مِّيثَٰقَهُمْ وَكُفْرِهِم بِـَٔايَٰتِ ٱللَّهِ وَقَتْلِهِمُ ٱلْأَنۢبِيَآءَ بِغَيْرِ حَقٍّ وَقَوْلِهِمْ قُلُوبُنَا غُلْفٌۢ بَلْ طَبَعَ ٱللَّهُ عَلَيْهَا بِكُفْرِهِمْ فَلَا يُؤْمِنُونَ إِلَّا قَلِيلًا (١٥٥) وَبِكُفْرِهِمْ وَقَوْلِهِمْ عَلَىٰ مَرْيَمَ بُهْتَٰنًا عَظِيمًا (١٥٦) وَقَوْلِهِمْ إِنَّا قَتَلْنَا ٱلْمَسِيحَ عِيسَى ٱبْنَ مَرْيَمَ رَسُولَ ٱللَّهِ وَمَا قَتَلُوهُ وَمَا صَلَبُوهُ وَلَٰكِن شُبِّهَ لَهُمْ وَإِنَّ ٱلَّذِينَ ٱخْتَلَفُوا۟ فِيهِ لَفِى شَكٍّ مِّنْهُ مَا لَهُم بِهِۦ مِنْ عِلْمٍ إِلَّا ٱتِّبَاعَ ٱلظَّنِّ وَمَا

قَتَلُوهُ يَقِينًا (١٥٧) بَل رَّفَعَهُ ٱللَّهُ إِلَيْهِ وَكَانَ ٱللَّهُ عَزِيزًا حَكِيمًا (١٥٨) وَإِن مِّنْ أَهْلِ ٱلْكِتَـٰبِ إِلَّا لَيُؤْمِنَنَّ بِهِ قَبْلَ مَوْتِهِۦ وَيَوْمَ ٱلْقِيَـٰمَةِ يَكُونُ عَلَيْهِمْ شَهِيدًا (١٥٩)

Because of their breaking the covenant, and of their rejecting the Ayât (proofs, evidences, verses, lessons, signs, revelations, etc.) of Allâh, and of their killing the Prophets unjustly, and of their saying: "Our hearts are wrapped (with coverings, i.e. we do not understand what the Messengers say)" - nay, Allâh has set a seal upon their hearts because of their disbelief, so they believe not but a little. (155) And because of their (Jews) disbelief and uttering against Maryam (Mary) a grave false charge (that she has committed illegal sexual intercourse); (156) And because of their saying (in boast), "We killed Messiah 'Īsā (Jesus), son of Maryam (Mary), the Messenger of Allâh," - but they killed him not, nor crucified him, but the resemblance of 'Īsā (Jesus) was put over another man (and they killed that man), and those who differ therein are full of doubts. They have no (certain) knowledge, they follow nothing but conjecture. For surely; they killed him not [i.e. 'Īsā (Jesus), son of Maryam (Mary)]: (157) But Allâh raised him ['Īsā (Jesus)] up (with his body and soul) unto Himself (and he is in the heavens). And Allâh is Ever All-Powerful, All-Wise. (158) And there is none of the people of the Scripture (Jews and Christians), but must believe in him ['Īsā (Jesus), son of Maryam (Mary), as only a Messenger of Allâh and a human being], before his ['Īsā (Jesus) or a Jew's or a Christian's] death (at the time of the appearance of the angel of death). And on the Day of Resurrection, he ['Īsā (Jesus)] will be a witness against them (159)

Quran 4:167-172

إِنَّ ٱلَّذِينَ كَفَرُوا۟ وَصَدُّوا۟ عَن سَبِيلِ ٱللَّهِ قَدْ ضَلُّوا۟ ضَلَٰلًۢا بَعِيدًا (١٦٧) إِنَّ ٱلَّذِينَ كَفَرُوا۟ وَظَلَمُوا۟ لَمْ يَكُنِ ٱللَّهُ لِيَغْفِرَ لَهُمْ وَلَا لِيَهْدِيَهُمْ طَرِيقًا (١٦٨) إِلَّا طَرِيقَ جَهَنَّمَ خَٰلِدِينَ فِيهَآ أَبَدًا۬ۚ وَكَانَ ذَٰلِكَ عَلَى ٱللَّهِ يَسِيرًا (١٦٩) يَٰٓأَيُّهَا ٱلنَّاسُ قَدْ جَآءَكُمُ ٱلرَّسُولُ بِٱلْحَقِّ مِن رَّبِّكُمْ فَـَٔامِنُوا۟ خَيْرًا لَّكُمْۚ وَإِن تَكْفُرُوا۟ فَإِنَّ لِلَّهِ مَا فِى ٱلسَّمَٰوَٰتِ وَٱلْأَرْضِۚ وَكَانَ ٱللَّهُ عَلِيمًا حَكِيمًا (١٧٠) يَٰٓأَهْلَ ٱلْكِتَٰبِ لَا تَغْلُوا۟ فِى دِينِكُمْ وَلَا تَقُولُوا۟ عَلَى ٱللَّهِ إِلَّا ٱلْحَقَّۚ إِنَّمَا ٱلْمَسِيحُ عِيسَى ٱبْنُ مَرْيَمَ رَسُولُ ٱللَّهِ وَكَلِمَتُهُۥٓ أَلْقَىٰهَآ إِلَىٰ مَرْيَمَ وَرُوحٌۭ مِّنْهُۖ فَـَٔامِنُوا۟ بِٱللَّهِ وَرُسُلِهِۦۖ وَلَا تَقُولُوا۟ ثَلَٰثَةٌۚ ٱنتَهُوا۟ خَيْرًا لَّكُمْۚ إِنَّمَا ٱللَّهُ إِلَٰهٌۭ وَٰحِدٌۘ سُبْحَٰنَهُۥٓ أَن يَكُونَ لَهُۥ وَلَدٌۘ لَّهُۥ مَا فِى ٱلسَّمَٰوَٰتِ وَمَا فِى ٱلْأَرْضِۗ وَكَفَىٰ بِٱللَّهِ وَكِيلًۭا (١٧١) لَّن يَسْتَنكِفَ ٱلْمَسِيحُ أَن يَكُونَ عَبْدًۭا لِّلَّهِ وَلَا ٱلْمَلَٰٓئِكَةُ ٱلْمُقَرَّبُونَۚ وَمَن يَسْتَنكِفْ عَنْ عِبَادَتِهِۦ وَيَسْتَكْبِرْ فَسَيَحْشُرُهُمْ إِلَيْهِ جَمِيعًۭا (١٧٢)

Verily, those who disbelieve [by concealing the truth about Prophet Muhammad and his message of true Islâmic Monotheism written in the Taurât (Torah) and the Injeel] and prevent (mankind) from the Path of Allâh (Islâmic Monotheism), they have certainly strayed far away. (167) Verily, those who disbelieve and did wrong [by concealing the truth about Prophet Muhammad and his message of true Islâmic Monotheism written in the Taurât (Torah) and the Injeel], Allâh will not forgive them, nor will He guide them to any way. (168) Except the way of Hell, to dwell therein forever, and this is ever easy for Allâh. (169) O mankind! Verily, there has come to you the Messenger (Muhammad) with the truth from your Lord, so believe in him, it is better for you. But if you disbelieve, then certainly to Allâh belongs all that is in the heavens and the earth. And Allâh is Ever All-Knowing, All-Wise. (170) O people of the Scripture! Do not exceed the limits in your religion, nor say of Allâh aught but the truth. The Messiah Īsā(Jesus), son of Maryam (Mary), was (no more than) a Messenger of Allâh and His Word, ("Be!" - and he was) which He bestowed on Maryam (Mary) and a spirit (Rûh) created by Him; so believe in Allâh and His Messengers. Say not: "Three (trinity)!" Cease! (it is) better for you. For Allâh is (the only) One Ilâh (God), glory be to Him (Far Exalted is He) above having a son. To Him belongs all that is in the heavens and all that is in the earth. And Allâh is All¬Sufficient as a Disposer of affairs. (171) The Messiah will never be proud to reject to be a slave of Allâh, nor the angels who are near (to Allâh). And whosoever rejects His worship and is proud, then He will gather them all together unto Himself. (172)

Quran 5:12-14

۞ وَلَقَدْ أَخَذَ ٱللَّهُ مِيثَٰقَ بَنِىٓ إِسْرَٰٓءِيلَ وَبَعَثْنَا مِنْهُمُ ٱثْنَىْ عَشَرَ نَقِيبًاۖ وَقَالَ ٱللَّهُ إِنِّى مَعَكُمْۖ لَئِنْ أَقَمْتُمُ ٱلصَّلَوٰةَ وَءَاتَيْتُمُ ٱلزَّكَوٰةَ وَءَامَنتُم بِرُسُلِى وَعَزَّرْتُمُوهُمْ وَأَقْرَضْتُمُ ٱللَّهَ قَرْضًا حَسَنًا لَّأُكَفِّرَنَّ عَنكُمْ سَيِّـَٔاتِكُمْ وَلَأُدْخِلَنَّكُمْ جَنَّٰتٍ تَجْرِى مِن تَحْتِهَا ٱلْأَنْهَٰرُۚ فَمَن كَفَرَ بَعْدَ ذَٰلِكَ مِنكُمْ فَقَدْ ضَلَّ سَوَآءَ ٱلسَّبِيلِ (١٢) فَبِمَا نَقْضِهِم مِّيثَٰقَهُمْ لَعَنَّٰهُمْ وَجَعَلْنَا قُلُوبَهُمْ قَٰسِيَةًۖ يُحَرِّفُونَ ٱلْكَلِمَ عَن مَّوَاضِعِهِۦۙ وَنَسُواْ حَظًّا مِّمَّا ذُكِّرُواْ بِهِۦۚ وَلَا تَزَالُ تَطَّلِعُ عَلَىٰ خَآئِنَةٍ مِّنْهُمْ إِلَّا قَلِيلًا مِّنْهُمْۖ فَٱعْفُ عَنْهُمْ وَٱصْفَحْۚ إِنَّ ٱللَّهَ يُحِبُّ ٱلْمُحْسِنِينَ (١٣) وَمِنَ ٱلَّذِينَ قَالُوٓاْ إِنَّا نَصَٰرَىٰٓ أَخَذْنَا مِيثَٰقَهُمْ فَنَسُواْ حَظًّا مِّمَّا ذُكِّرُواْ

بِهِ فَأَغْرَيْنَا بَيْنَهُمُ ٱلْعَدَاوَةَ وَٱلْبَغْضَاءَ إِلَىٰ يَوْمِ ٱلْقِيَٰمَةِ وَسَوْفَ يُنَبِّئُهُمُ ٱللَّهُ بِمَا كَانُوا۟ يَصْنَعُونَ (١٤)

Indeed Allâh took the covenant from the Children of Israel (Jews), and We appointed twelve leaders among them. And Allâh said: "I am with you if you perform As-Salât (Iqâmat-as-Salât) and give Zakât and believe in My Messengers; honor and assist them, and lend a good loan to Allâh. Verily, I will expiate your sins and admit you to Gardens under which rivers flow (in Paradise). But if any of you after this, disbelieved, he has indeed gone astray from the Straight Path." (12) So because of their breach of their covenant, We cursed them, and made their hearts grow hard. They change the words from their (right) places and have abandoned a good part of the Message that was sent to them. And you will not cease to discover deceit in them, except a few of them. But forgive them, and overlook (their misdeeds). Verily, Allâh loves Al¬Muhsinûn (good¬doers). (13) And from those who call themselves Christians, We took their covenant, but they have abandoned a good part of the Message that was sent to them. So We planted amongst them enmity and hatred till the Day of Resurrection (when they discarded Allâh's Book, disobeyed Allâh's Messengers and His Orders and transgressed beyond bounds in Allâh's disobedience), and Allâh will inform them of what they used to do. (14)

Quran 5:17-18

لَقَدْ كَفَرَ ٱلَّذِينَ قَالُوٓا۟ إِنَّ ٱللَّهَ هُوَ ٱلْمَسِيحُ ٱبْنُ مَرْيَمَ ۚ قُلْ فَمَن يَمْلِكُ مِنَ ٱللَّهِ شَيْـًٔا إِنْ أَرَادَ أَن يُهْلِكَ ٱلْمَسِيحَ ٱبْنَ مَرْيَمَ وَأُمَّهُۥ وَمَن فِى ٱلْأَرْضِ جَمِيعًا ۗ وَلِلَّهِ مُلْكُ ٱلسَّمَٰوَٰتِ وَٱلْأَرْضِ وَمَا بَيْنَهُمَا ۚ يَخْلُقُ مَا يَشَآءُ ۚ وَٱللَّهُ عَلَىٰ كُلِّ شَىْءٍ قَدِيرٌ (١٧) وَقَالَتِ ٱلْيَهُودُ وَٱلنَّصَٰرَىٰ نَحْنُ أَبْنَٰٓؤُا۟ ٱللَّهِ وَأَحِبَّٰٓؤُهُۥ ۚ قُلْ فَلِمَ يُعَذِّبُكُم بِذُنُوبِكُم ۖ بَلْ أَنتُم بَشَرٌ مِّمَّنْ خَلَقَ ۚ يَغْفِرُ لِمَن يَشَآءُ وَيُعَذِّبُ مَن يَشَآءُ ۚ وَلِلَّهِ مُلْكُ ٱلسَّمَٰوَٰتِ وَٱلْأَرْضِ وَمَا بَيْنَهُمَا ۖ وَإِلَيْهِ ٱلْمَصِيرُ (١٨)

Surely, in disbelief are they who say that Allâh is the Messiah, son of Maryam (Mary). Say: "Who then has the least power against Allâh, if He were to destroy the Messiah, son of Maryam (Mary), his mother, and all those who are on the earth together?" And to Allâh belongs the dominion of the heavens and the earth, and all that is between them. He creates what He wills. And Allâh is Able to do all things. (17) And (both) the Jews and the Christians say: "We are the children of Allâh and His loved ones." Say: "Why then does He punish you for your sins?" Nay, you are but human beings, of those He has created, He forgives whom He wills and He punishes whom He wills. And to Allâh belongs the dominion of the heavens and the earth and all that is between them, and to Him is the return (of all). (18)

Quran 5:33-34

إِنَّمَا جَزَٰٓؤُا۟ ٱلَّذِينَ يُحَارِبُونَ ٱللَّهَ وَرَسُولَهُۥ وَيَسْعَوْنَ فِى ٱلْأَرْضِ فَسَادًا أَن يُقَتَّلُوٓا۟ أَوْ يُصَلَّبُوٓا۟ أَوْ تُقَطَّعَ أَيْدِيهِمْ وَأَرْجُلُهُم مِّنْ خِلَٰفٍ أَوْ يُنفَوْا۟ مِنَ ٱلْأَرْضِ ۚ ذَٰلِكَ لَهُمْ خِزْىٌ فِى ٱلدُّنْيَا ۖ وَلَهُمْ فِى ٱلْءَاخِرَةِ عَذَابٌ عَظِيمٌ (٣٣) إِلَّا ٱلَّذِينَ تَابُوا۟ مِن قَبْلِ أَن تَقْدِرُوا۟ عَلَيْهِمْ ۖ فَٱعْلَمُوٓا۟ أَنَّ ٱللَّهَ غَفُورٌ رَّحِيمٌ (٣٤)

The recompense of those who wage war against Allâh and His Messenger and do mischief in the land is only that they shall be killed or crucified or their hands and their feet be cut off from the opposite sides, or be exiled from the land. That is their disgrace in this world, and a great torment is theirs in the Hereafter. (33) Except for those who came back with repentance before they fall into your power; in that case, know that Allâh is Oft-Forgiving, Most Merciful. (34)

Quran 5:36-37

إِنَّ ٱلَّذِينَ كَفَرُوا۟ لَوْ أَنَّ لَهُم مَّا فِى ٱلْأَرْضِ جَمِيعًا وَمِثْلَهُۥ مَعَهُۥ لِيَفْتَدُوا۟ بِهِۦ مِنْ عَذَابِ يَوْمِ ٱلْقِيَٰمَةِ مَا تُقُبِّلَ مِنْهُمْ ۖ وَلَهُمْ عَذَابٌ أَلِيمٌ (٣٦) يُرِيدُونَ أَن يَخْرُجُوا۟ مِنَ ٱلنَّارِ وَمَا هُم بِخَٰرِجِينَ مِنْهَا ۖ وَلَهُمْ عَذَابٌ مُّقِيمٌ (٣٧)

Verily, those who disbelieve, if they had all that is in the earth, and as much again therewith to ransom themselves thereby from the torment on the Day of Resurrection, it would never be accepted of them, and theirs would be a painful torment. (36) They will long to get out of the Fire, but never will they get out therefrom, and theirs will be a lasting torment. (37)

Quran 5:41-44

يَٰٓأَيُّهَا ٱلرَّسُولُ لَا يَحْزُنكَ ٱلَّذِينَ يُسَٰرِعُونَ فِى ٱلْكُفْرِ مِنَ ٱلَّذِينَ قَالُوٓا۟ ءَامَنَّا بِأَفْوَٰهِهِمْ وَلَمْ تُؤْمِن قُلُوبُهُمْ ۛ وَمِنَ ٱلَّذِينَ هَادُوا۟ ۛ سَمَّٰعُونَ لِلْكَذِبِ سَمَّٰعُونَ لِقَوْمٍ ءَاخَرِينَ لَمْ يَأْتُوكَ ۖ يُحَرِّفُونَ ٱلْكَلِمَ مِنۢ بَعْدِ مَوَاضِعِهِۦ ۖ يَقُولُونَ إِنْ أُوتِيتُمْ هَٰذَا فَخُذُوهُ وَإِن لَّمْ تُؤْتَوْهُ فَٱحْذَرُوا۟ ۚ وَمَن يُرِدِ ٱللَّهُ فِتْنَتَهُۥ فَلَن تَمْلِكَ لَهُۥ مِنَ ٱللَّهِ شَيْـًٔا ۚ أُو۟لَٰٓئِكَ ٱلَّذِينَ لَمْ يُرِدِ ٱللَّهُ أَن يُطَهِّرَ قُلُوبَهُمْ ۚ لَهُمْ فِى ٱلدُّنْيَا خِزْىٌ ۖ

وَلَهُمْ فِى ٱلْأَخِرَةِ عَذَابٌ عَظِيمٌ (٤١) سَمَّٰعُونَ لِلْكَذِبِ أَكَّٰلُونَ لِلسُّحْتِ ۚ فَإِن جَآءُوكَ فَٱحْكُم بَيْنَهُمْ أَوْ أَعْرِضْ عَنْهُمْ ۖ وَإِن تُعْرِضْ عَنْهُمْ فَلَن يَضُرُّوكَ شَيْـًٔا ۖ وَإِنْ حَكَمْتَ فَٱحْكُم بَيْنَهُم بِٱلْقِسْطِ ۚ إِنَّ ٱللَّهَ يُحِبُّ ٱلْمُقْسِطِينَ (٤٢) وَكَيْفَ يُحَكِّمُونَكَ وَعِندَهُمُ ٱلتَّوْرَىٰةُ فِيهَا حُكْمُ ٱللَّهِ ثُمَّ يَتَوَلَّوْنَ مِنۢ بَعْدِ ذَٰلِكَ ۚ وَمَآ أُو۟لَٰٓئِكَ بِٱلْمُؤْمِنِينَ (٤٣) إِنَّآ أَنزَلْنَا ٱلتَّوْرَىٰةَ فِيهَا هُدًى وَنُورٌ ۚ يَحْكُمُ بِهَا ٱلنَّبِيُّونَ ٱلَّذِينَ أَسْلَمُوا۟ لِلَّذِينَ هَادُوا۟ وَٱلرَّبَّٰنِيُّونَ وَٱلْأَحْبَارُ بِمَا ٱسْتُحْفِظُوا۟ مِن كِتَٰبِ ٱللَّهِ وَكَانُوا۟ عَلَيْهِ شُهَدَآءَ ۚ فَلَا تَخْشَوُا۟ ٱلنَّاسَ وَٱخْشَوْنِ وَلَا تَشْتَرُوا۟ بِـَٔايَٰتِى ثَمَنًا قَلِيلًا ۚ وَمَن لَّمْ يَحْكُم بِمَآ أَنزَلَ ٱللَّهُ فَأُو۟لَٰٓئِكَ هُمُ ٱلْكَٰفِرُونَ (٤٤)

O Messenger! Let not those who hurry to fall into disbelief grieve you, of such who say: "We believe" with their mouths but their hearts have no faith. And of the Jews are men who listen much and eagerly to lies - listen to others who have not come to you. They change the words from their places; they say, "If you are given this, take it, but if you are not given this, then beware!" And whomsoever Allâh wants to put in Al¬Fitnah [error, because of his rejecting the Faith], you can do nothing for him against Allâh. Those are the ones whose hearts Allâh does not want to purify (from disbelief and hypocrisy); for them there is a disgrace in this world, and in the Hereafter a great torment. (41) (They like to) listen to falsehood, to devour anything forbidden. So if they come to you, either judge between them, or turn away from them. If you turn away from them, they cannot hurt you in the least. And if you judge, judge with justice between them. Verily, Allâh loves those who act justly. (42) But how do they come to you for decision while they have the Taurât (Torah), in which is the (plain) Decision of Allâh;

yet even after that, they turn away. For they are not (really) believers. (43) Verily, We did send down the Taurât (Torah) [to Mûsa (Moses)], therein was guidance and light, by which the Prophets, who submitted themselves to Allâh's Will, judged for the Jews. And the rabbis and the priests [too judged for the Jews by the Taurât (Torah) after those Prophets] for to them was entrusted the protection of Allâh's Book, and they were witnesses thereto. Therefore fear not men but fear Me (O Jews) and sell not My Verses for a miserable price. And whosoever does not judge by what Allâh has revealed, such are the Kâfirûn (i.e. disbelievers - of a lesser degree as they do not act on Allâh's Laws). (44)

Quran 5:61-64

وَإِذَا جَآءُوكُمْ قَالُوٓاْ ءَامَنَّا وَقَد دَّخَلُواْ بِٱلْكُفْرِ وَهُمْ قَدْ خَرَجُواْ بِهِۦ وَٱللَّهُ أَعْلَمُ بِمَا كَانُواْ يَكْتُمُونَ (٦١) وَتَرَىٰ كَثِيرًا مِّنْهُمْ يُسَٰرِعُونَ فِى ٱلْإِثْمِ وَٱلْعُدْوَٰنِ وَأَكْلِهِمُ ٱلسُّحْتَ لَبِئْسَ مَا كَانُواْ يَعْمَلُونَ (٦٢) لَوْلَا يَنْهَىٰهُمُ ٱلرَّبَّٰنِيُّونَ وَٱلْأَحْبَارُ عَن قَوْلِهِمُ ٱلْإِثْمَ وَأَكْلِهِمُ ٱلسُّحْتَ لَبِئْسَ مَا كَانُواْ يَصْنَعُونَ (٦٣) وَقَالَتِ ٱلْيَهُودُ يَدُ ٱللَّهِ مَغْلُولَةٌ غُلَّتْ أَيْدِيهِمْ وَلُعِنُواْ بِمَا قَالُواْ بَلْ يَدَاهُ مَبْسُوطَتَانِ يُنفِقُ كَيْفَ يَشَآءُ وَلَيَزِيدَنَّ كَثِيرًا مِّنْهُم مَّآ أُنزِلَ إِلَيْكَ مِن رَّبِّكَ طُغْيَٰنًا وَكُفْرًا وَأَلْقَيْنَا بَيْنَهُمُ ٱلْعَدَاوَةَ وَٱلْبَغْضَآءَ إِلَىٰ يَوْمِ ٱلْقِيَٰمَةِ كُلَّمَآ أَوْقَدُواْ نَارًا لِّلْحَرْبِ أَطْفَأَهَا ٱللَّهُ وَيَسْعَوْنَ فِى ٱلْأَرْضِ فَسَادًا وَٱللَّهُ لَا يُحِبُّ ٱلْمُفْسِدِينَ (٦٤)

When they come to you, they say: "We believe." But in fact they enter with (an intention of) disbelief and they go out with the same. And Allâh knows all what they were hiding (61) And you see many of them (Jews) hurrying towards sin and transgression, and eating illegal things [as bribes and Ribâ (usury), etc.]. Evil indeed is that which they have been doing (62) Why do not the rabbis and the religious learned men forbid them from uttering sinful words and from eating illegal things. Evil indeed is that which they have been performing. (63) The Jews say: "Allâh's Hand is tied up (i.e. He does not give and spend of His Bounty)." Be their hands tied up and be they accursed for what they uttered. Nay, both His Hands are widely outstretched. He spends (of His Bounty) as He wills. Verily, the Revelation that has come to you from your Lord (Allâh) increases in most of them (their) obstinate rebellion and disbelief. We have put enmity and hatred amongst them till the Day of Resurrection. Every time they kindled the fire of war, Allâh extinguished it; and they (ever) strive to make mischief on earth. And Allâh does not like the Mufsidûn (mischief-makers). (64)

Quran 5:68

قُلْ يَٰٓأَهْلَ ٱلْكِتَٰبِ لَسْتُمْ عَلَىٰ شَىْءٍ حَتَّىٰ تُقِيمُوا۟ ٱلتَّوْرَىٰةَ وَٱلْإِنجِيلَ وَمَآ أُنزِلَ إِلَيْكُم مِّن رَّبِّكُمْ وَلَيَزِيدَنَّ كَثِيرًا مِّنْهُم مَّآ أُنزِلَ إِلَيْكَ مِن رَّبِّكَ طُغْيَٰنًا وَكُفْرًا فَلَا تَأْسَ عَلَى ٱلْقَوْمِ ٱلْكَٰفِرِينَ

Say (O Muhammad) "O people of the Scripture (Jews and Christians)! You have nothing (as regards guidance) till you act according to the Taurât (Torah), the Injeel, and what has (now) been sent down to you from your Lord (the Qur'ân)." Verily, that which has been sent down to you (Muhammad) from your Lord increases in most of them (their) obstinate rebellion and disbelief. So be not sorrowful over the people who disbelieve. (68)

Quran 5:72-82

لَقَدْ كَفَرَ ٱلَّذِينَ قَالُوٓاْ إِنَّ ٱللَّهَ هُوَ ٱلْمَسِيحُ ٱبْنُ مَرْيَمَ وَقَالَ ٱلْمَسِيحُ يَٰبَنِىٓ إِسْرَٰٓءِيلَ ٱعْبُدُواْ ٱللَّهَ رَبِّى وَرَبَّكُمْ إِنَّهُۥ مَن يُشْرِكْ بِٱللَّهِ فَقَدْ حَرَّمَ ٱللَّهُ عَلَيْهِ ٱلْجَنَّةَ وَمَأْوَىٰهُ ٱلنَّارُ وَمَا لِلظَّٰلِمِينَ مِنْ أَنصَارٍ (٧٢) لَقَدْ كَفَرَ ٱلَّذِينَ قَالُوٓاْ إِنَّ ٱللَّهَ ثَالِثُ ثَلَٰثَةٍ وَمَا مِنْ إِلَٰهٍ إِلَّآ إِلَٰهٌ وَٰحِدٌ وَإِن لَّمْ يَنتَهُواْ عَمَّا يَقُولُونَ لَيَمَسَّنَّ ٱلَّذِينَ كَفَرُواْ مِنْهُمْ عَذَابٌ أَلِيمٌ (٧٣) أَفَلَا يَتُوبُونَ إِلَى ٱللَّهِ وَيَسْتَغْفِرُونَهُۥ وَٱللَّهُ غَفُورٌ رَّحِيمٌ (٧٤) مَّا ٱلْمَسِيحُ ٱبْنُ مَرْيَمَ إِلَّا رَسُولٌ قَدْ خَلَتْ مِن قَبْلِهِ ٱلرُّسُلُ وَأُمُّهُۥ صِدِّيقَةٌ كَانَا يَأْكُلَانِ ٱلطَّعَامَ ٱنظُرْ كَيْفَ نُبَيِّنُ لَهُمُ ٱلْءَايَٰتِ ثُمَّ ٱنظُرْ أَنَّىٰ يُؤْفَكُونَ (٧٥) قُلْ أَتَعْبُدُونَ مِن دُونِ ٱللَّهِ مَا لَا يَمْلِكُ لَكُمْ ضَرًّا وَلَا نَفْعًا وَٱللَّهُ هُوَ ٱلسَّمِيعُ ٱلْعَلِيمُ (٧٦) قُلْ يَٰٓأَهْلَ ٱلْكِتَٰبِ لَا تَغْلُواْ فِى دِينِكُمْ غَيْرَ ٱلْحَقِّ وَلَا تَتَّبِعُوٓاْ أَهْوَآءَ قَوْمٍ قَدْ ضَلُّواْ مِن قَبْلُ وَأَضَلُّواْ كَثِيرًا وَضَلُّواْ عَن سَوَآءِ ٱلسَّبِيلِ (٧٧) لُعِنَ ٱلَّذِينَ كَفَرُواْ مِنۢ بَنِىٓ إِسْرَٰٓءِيلَ عَلَىٰ لِسَانِ دَاوُۥدَ وَعِيسَى ٱبْنِ مَرْيَمَ ذَٰلِكَ بِمَا عَصَوا وَّكَانُواْ يَعْتَدُونَ (٧٨) كَانُواْ لَا يَتَنَاهَوْنَ عَن مُّنكَرٍ فَعَلُوهُ لَبِئْسَ مَا كَانُواْ يَفْعَلُونَ (٧٩) تَرَىٰ كَثِيرًا مِّنْهُمْ يَتَوَلَّوْنَ ٱلَّذِينَ كَفَرُواْ لَبِئْسَ مَا قَدَّمَتْ لَهُمْ أَنفُسُهُمْ أَن سَخِطَ ٱللَّهُ عَلَيْهِمْ وَفِى ٱلْعَذَابِ هُمْ خَٰلِدُونَ (٨٠) وَلَوْ كَانُواْ يُؤْمِنُونَ بِٱللَّهِ وَٱلنَّبِىِّ وَمَآ أُنزِلَ إِلَيْهِ مَا ٱتَّخَذُوهُمْ أَوْلِيَآءَ وَلَٰكِنَّ كَثِيرًا مِّنْهُمْ فَٰسِقُونَ (٨١) لَتَجِدَنَّ أَشَدَّ ٱلنَّاسِ عَدَٰوَةً لِّلَّذِينَ ءَامَنُواْ ٱلْيَهُودَ وَٱلَّذِينَ أَشْرَكُواْ وَلَتَجِدَنَّ أَقْرَبَهُم مَّوَدَّةً لِّلَّذِينَ ءَامَنُواْ ٱلَّذِينَ قَالُوٓاْ إِنَّا نَصَٰرَىٰ ذَٰلِكَ بِأَنَّ مِنْهُمْ قِسِّيسِينَ وَرُهْبَانًا وَأَنَّهُمْ لَا يَسْتَكْبِرُونَ (٨٢)

Surely, they have disbelieved who say: "Allâh is the Messiah Īsā (Jesus), son of Maryam (Mary)." But the Messiah Īsā (Jesus) said: "O Children of Israel! Worship Allâh, my Lord and your Lord." Verily, whosoever sets up partners (in worship) with Allâh, then Allâh has forbidden Paradise to him, and the Fire will be his abode. And for the Zâlimûn (polytheists and wrong-doers) there are no helpers (72) Surely, disbelievers are those who said: "Allâh is the third of the three (in a Trinity)." But there is no Ilâh (god) (none who has the right to be worshipped) but One Ilâh (God -Allâh). And if they cease not from what they say, verily, a painful torment will befall on the disbelievers among them (73) Will they not turn with repentance to Allâh and ask His Forgiveness? For Allâh is Oft-Forgiving, Most Merciful. (74) The Messiah ['Īsā (Jesus)], son of Maryam (Mary), was no more than a Messenger; many were the Messengers that passed away before him. His mother [Maryam (Mary)] was a Siddiqah [i.e. she believed in the words of Allâh and His Books]. They both used to eat food (as any other human being, while Allâh does not eat). Look how We make the Ayât (proofs, evidences, verses, lessons, signs, revelations, etc.) clear to them, yet look how they are deluded away (from the truth) (75) Say (O Muhammad to mankind): "How do you worship besides Allâh something which has no power either to harm or to benefit you? But it is Allâh Who is the All¬Hearer, All¬Knower." (76) Say: "O people of the Scripture (Jews and Christians)! Exceed not the limits in your religion (by believing in something) other than the truth, and do not follow the vain desires of people who went astray before, and who misled many, and strayed (themselves) from the Right Path." (77) Those among the Children of Israel who disbelieved were cursed by the tongue of Dawûd (David) and 'Īsā (Jesus), son of Maryam (Mary). That was because they disobeyed (Allâh and the Messengers) and were ever transgressing beyond bounds. (78) They used not to forbid one another from Al-Munkar (wrong, evil-doing, sins, polytheism, disbelief) which they committed. Vile indeed was what they used to do. (79) You see many of them taking the disbelievers as their Auliyâ' (protectors and helpers). Evil indeed is that which their ownselves have sent forward before them, for that (reason) Allâh's Wrath fell upon them and in torment they will abide. (80) And had they believed in Allâh, and in the Prophet (Muhammad) and in what has been revealed to him, never would they have taken them (the disbelievers) as Auliyâ' (protectors and helpers), but many of them are the Fâsiqûn (rebellious, disobedient to Allâh). (81) Verily, you will find the strongest among men in enmity to the believers (Muslims) the Jews and those who are Al-Mushrikûn, and you will find the nearest in love to the believers (Muslims) those who say: "We are Christians." That is because amongst them are priests and monks, and they are not proud. (82)

Quran 5:86

وَٱلَّذِينَ كَفَرُوا۟ وَكَذَّبُوا۟ بِـَٔايَـٰتِنَآ أُو۟لَـٰٓئِكَ أَصْحَـٰبُ ٱلْجَحِيمِ

But those who disbelieved and belied Our Ayât (proofs, evidences, verses, lessons, signs, revelations, etc.), they shall be the dwellers of the (Hell) Fire. (86)

Quran 5:103-104

$$\text{مَا جَعَلَ ٱللَّهُ مِنۢ بَحِيرَةٍ وَلَا سَآئِبَةٍ وَلَا وَصِيلَةٍ وَلَا حَامٍ وَلَٰكِنَّ ٱلَّذِينَ كَفَرُوا۟ يَفْتَرُونَ عَلَى ٱللَّهِ ٱلْكَذِبَ ۖ وَأَكْثَرُهُمْ لَا يَعْقِلُونَ (١٠٣) وَإِذَا قِيلَ لَهُمْ تَعَالَوْا۟ إِلَىٰ مَآ أَنزَلَ ٱللَّهُ وَإِلَى ٱلرَّسُولِ قَالُوا۟ حَسْبُنَا مَا وَجَدْنَا عَلَيْهِ ءَابَآءَنَآ ۚ أَوَلَوْ كَانَ ءَابَآؤُهُمْ لَا يَعْلَمُونَ شَيْـًٔا وَلَا يَهْتَدُونَ (١٠٤)}$$

Allâh has not instituted things like Bahîrah or a Sâ'ibah, or a Wasîlah or a Hâm (all these animals were liberated in honour of idols as practised by pagan Arabs in the pre-Islâmic period). But those who disbelieve invent lies against Allâh, and most of them have no understanding. (103) And when it is said to them: "Come to what Allâh has revealed and unto the Messenger." They say: "Enough for us is that which we found our fathers following," even though their fathers had no knowledge whatsoever and no guidance. (104)

Quran 6:1

$$\text{ٱلْحَمْدُ لِلَّهِ ٱلَّذِى خَلَقَ ٱلسَّمَٰوَٰتِ وَٱلْأَرْضَ وَجَعَلَ ٱلظُّلُمَٰتِ وَٱلنُّورَ ۖ ثُمَّ ٱلَّذِينَ كَفَرُوا۟ بِرَبِّهِمْ يَعْدِلُونَ}$$

All praises and thanks be to Allâh, Who (Alone) created the heavens and the earth, and originated the darkness and the light, yet those who disbelieve hold others as equal with their Lord. (1)

Quran 6:7-8

$$\text{وَلَوْ نَزَّلْنَا عَلَيْكَ كِتَٰبًا فِى قِرْطَاسٍ فَلَمَسُوهُ بِأَيْدِيهِمْ لَقَالَ ٱلَّذِينَ كَفَرُوٓا۟ إِنْ هَٰذَآ إِلَّا سِحْرٌ مُّبِينٌ (٧) وَقَالُوا۟ لَوْلَآ أُنزِلَ عَلَيْهِ مَلَكٌ ۖ وَلَوْ أَنزَلْنَا مَلَكًا لَّقُضِىَ ٱلْأَمْرُ ثُمَّ لَا يُنظَرُونَ (٨)}$$

And even if We had sent down unto you (O Muhammad) a Message written on paper so that they could touch it with their hands, the disbelievers would have said: "This is nothing but obvious magic!" (7) And they say: "Why has not an angel been sent down to him?" Had We sent down an angel, the matter would have been judged at once, and no respite would be granted to them. (8)

Quran 6:21-31

وَمَنْ أَظْلَمُ مِمَّنِ ٱفْتَرَىٰ عَلَى ٱللَّهِ كَذِبًا أَوْ كَذَّبَ بِـَٔايَٰتِهِۦٓ إِنَّهُۥ لَا يُفْلِحُ ٱلظَّٰلِمُونَ (٢١) وَيَوْمَ نَحْشُرُهُمْ جَمِيعًا ثُمَّ نَقُولُ لِلَّذِينَ أَشْرَكُوٓاْ أَيْنَ شُرَكَآؤُكُمُ ٱلَّذِينَ كُنتُمْ تَزْعُمُونَ (٢٢) ثُمَّ لَمْ تَكُن فِتْنَتُهُمْ إِلَّآ أَن قَالُواْ وَٱللَّهِ رَبِّنَا مَا كُنَّا مُشْرِكِينَ (٢٣) ٱنظُرْ كَيْفَ كَذَبُواْ عَلَىٰٓ أَنفُسِهِمْ وَضَلَّ عَنْهُم مَّا كَانُواْ يَفْتَرُونَ (٢٤) وَمِنْهُم مَّن يَسْتَمِعُ إِلَيْكَ وَجَعَلْنَا عَلَىٰ قُلُوبِهِمْ أَكِنَّةً أَن يَفْقَهُوهُ وَفِىٓ ءَاذَانِهِمْ وَقْرًا وَإِن يَرَوْاْ كُلَّ ءَايَةٍ لَّا يُؤْمِنُواْ بِهَا حَتَّىٰٓ إِذَا جَآءُوكَ يُجَٰدِلُونَكَ يَقُولُ ٱلَّذِينَ كَفَرُوٓاْ إِنْ هَٰذَآ إِلَّآ أَسَٰطِيرُ ٱلْأَوَّلِينَ (٢٥) وَهُمْ يَنْهَوْنَ عَنْهُ وَيَنْـَٔوْنَ عَنْهُ وَإِن يُهْلِكُونَ إِلَّآ أَنفُسَهُمْ وَمَا يَشْعُرُونَ (٢٦) وَلَوْ تَرَىٰٓ إِذْ وُقِفُواْ عَلَى ٱلنَّارِ فَقَالُواْ يَٰلَيْتَنَا نُرَدُّ وَلَا نُكَذِّبَ بِـَٔايَٰتِ رَبِّنَا وَنَكُونَ مِنَ ٱلْمُؤْمِنِينَ (٢٧) بَلْ بَدَا لَهُم مَّا كَانُواْ يُخْفُونَ مِن قَبْلُ وَلَوْ رُدُّواْ لَعَادُواْ لِمَا نُهُواْ عَنْهُ وَإِنَّهُمْ لَكَٰذِبُونَ (٢٨) وَقَالُوٓاْ إِنْ هِىَ إِلَّا حَيَاتُنَا ٱلدُّنْيَا وَمَا نَحْنُ بِمَبْعُوثِينَ (٢٩) وَلَوْ تَرَىٰٓ إِذْ وُقِفُواْ عَلَىٰ رَبِّهِمْ قَالَ أَلَيْسَ هَٰذَا بِٱلْحَقِّ قَالُواْ بَلَىٰ وَرَبِّنَا قَالَ فَذُوقُواْ ٱلْعَذَابَ بِمَا كُنتُمْ تَكْفُرُونَ (٣٠) قَدْ خَسِرَ ٱلَّذِينَ كَذَّبُواْ بِلِقَآءِ ٱللَّهِ حَتَّىٰٓ إِذَا جَآءَتْهُمُ ٱلسَّاعَةُ بَغْتَةً قَالُواْ يَٰحَسْرَتَنَا عَلَىٰ مَا فَرَّطْنَا فِيهَا وَهُمْ يَحْمِلُونَ أَوْزَارَهُمْ عَلَىٰ ظُهُورِهِمْ أَلَا سَآءَ مَا يَزِرُونَ (٣١)

And who does more wrong aggression and than he who invents a lie against Allâh or rejects His Ayât (proofs, evidences, verses, lessons, or revelations)? Verily, the Zâlimûn (polytheists and wrong-doers,) shall never be successful. (21) And on the Day when We shall gather them all together, We shall say to those who joined partners (in worship with Us): "Where are your partners (false deities) whom you used to assert (as partners in worship with Allâh)?" (22) There will then be (left) no Fitnah (excuses or statements or arguments) for them but to say: "By Allâh, our Lord, we were not those who joined others in worship with Allâh." (23) Look! How they lie against themselves! But the (lie) which they invented will disappear from them. (24) And of them there are some who listen to you; but We have set veils on their hearts, so they understand it not, and deafness in their ears; and even if they see every one of the Ayât (proofs, evidences, verses, lessons, signs, revelations, etc.) they will not believe therein; to the point that when they come to you to argue with you, the disbelievers say: "These are nothing but tales of the men of old." (25) And they prevent others from him (from following Prophet Muhammad) and they themselves keep away from him, and (by doing so) they destroy not but their ownselves, yet they perceive (it) not. (26) If you could but see when they will be held over the (Hell) Fire! They will say: "Would that we were but sent back (to the world)! Then we would not deny the Ayât (proofs, evidences, verses, lessons, revelations, etc.) of our Lord, and we would be of the believers!" (27) Nay, it has become manifest to them what they had been concealing before. But if they were returned (to the world), they would certainly revert to that which they were forbidden. And indeed they are liars. (28) And they said: "There is no (other life) but our (present) life of this world, and never shall we be resurrected (on the Day of Resurrection)." (29) If you could but see when they will be held (brought and made to stand) in front of their Lord! He will say: "Is not this (Resurrection and the taking of the accounts) the truth?" They will say: "Yes, by our Lord!" He will then say: "So taste you the torment because you used not to believe." (30) They indeed are losers who denied their Meeting with Allâh, until all of a sudden, the Hour (signs of death) is on them, and they say: "Alas for us that we gave no thought to it," while they will bear their burdens on their backs; and evil indeed are the burdens that they will bear! (31)

Quran 6:68

وَإِذَا رَأَيْتَ ٱلَّذِينَ يَخُوضُونَ فِىٓ ءَايَـٰتِنَا فَأَعْرِضْ عَنْهُمْ حَتَّىٰ يَخُوضُواْ فِى حَدِيثٍ غَيْرِهِۦ وَإِمَّا يُنسِيَنَّكَ ٱلشَّيْطَـٰنُ فَلَا تَقْعُدْ بَعْدَ ٱلذِّكْرَىٰ مَعَ ٱلْقَوْمِ ٱلظَّـٰلِمِينَ

And when you see those who engage in a false conversation about Our Verses (of the Qur'ân) by mocking at them, stay away from them till they turn to another topic. And if Shaitân (Satan) causes you to forget, then after the remembrance sit not you in the company of those people who are the Zâlimûn (polytheists and wrong-doers). (68)

Quran 6:70

وَذَرِ ٱلَّذِينَ ٱتَّخَذُواْ دِينَهُمْ لَعِبًا وَلَهْوًا وَغَرَّتْهُمُ ٱلْحَيَوٰةُ ٱلدُّنْيَاۚ وَذَكِّرْ بِهِۦٓ أَن تُبْسَلَ نَفْسٌۢ بِمَا كَسَبَتْ لَيْسَ لَهَا مِن دُونِ ٱللَّهِ وَلِىٌّ وَلَا شَفِيعٌ وَإِن تَعْدِلْ كُلَّ عَدْلٍ لَّا يُؤْخَذْ مِنْهَآۗ أُوْلَٰٓئِكَ ٱلَّذِينَ أُبْسِلُواْ بِمَا كَسَبُواْۖ لَهُمْ شَرَابٌ مِّنْ حَمِيمٍ وَعَذَابٌ أَلِيمٌۢ بِمَا كَانُواْ يَكْفُرُونَ

And leave alone those who take their religion as play and amusement, and whom the life of this world has deceived. But remind (them) with it (the Qur'ân) lest a person be given up to destruction for that which he has earned, when he will find for himself no protector or intercessor besides Allâh, and even if he offers every ransom, it will not be accepted from him. Such are they who are given up to destruction because of that which they have earned. For them will be a drink of boiling water and a painful torment because they used to disbelieve. (70)

Quran 6:88

ذَٰلِكَ هُدَى ٱللَّهِ يَهْدِى بِهِۦ مَن يَشَآءُ مِنْ عِبَادِهِۦۚ وَلَوْ أَشْرَكُواْ لَحَبِطَ عَنْهُم مَّا كَانُواْ يَعْمَلُونَ

This is the Guidance of Allâh with which He guides whomsoever He will of His slaves. But if they had joined in worship others with Allâh, all that they used to do would have been of no benefit to them. (88)

Quran 6:91

وَمَا قَدَرُواْ ٱللَّهَ حَقَّ قَدْرِهِۦٓ إِذْ قَالُواْ مَآ أَنزَلَ ٱللَّهُ عَلَىٰ بَشَرٍ مِّن شَىْءٍۗ قُلْ مَنْ أَنزَلَ ٱلْكِتَٰبَ ٱلَّذِى جَآءَ بِهِۦ مُوسَىٰ نُورًا وَهُدًى لِّلنَّاسِۖ تَجْعَلُونَهُۥ قَرَاطِيسَ

تُبْدُونَهَا وَتُخْفُونَ كَثِيرًا ۖ وَعُلِّمْتُم مَّا لَمْ تَعْلَمُوٓا أَنتُمْ وَلَآ ءَابَآؤُكُمْ ۖ قُلِ ٱللَّهُ ۖ ثُمَّ ذَرْهُمْ فِى خَوْضِهِمْ يَلْعَبُونَ

They (the Jews, Quraish pagans, idolaters) did not estimate Allâh with an estimation due to Him when they said: "Nothing did Allâh send down to any human being (by revelation)." Say (O Muhammad): "Who then sent down the Book which Mûsa (Moses) brought, a light and a guidance to mankind which you (the Jews) have made into (separate) papersheets, disclosing (some of it) and concealing much. And you (believers in Allâh and His Messenger Muhammad), were taught (through the Qur'ân) that which neither you nor your fathers knew." Say: "Allâh (sent it down)." Then leave them to play in their vain discussions. (91)

Quran 6:93-94

وَمَنْ أَظْلَمُ مِمَّنِ ٱفْتَرَىٰ عَلَى ٱللَّهِ كَذِبًا أَوْ قَالَ أُوحِىَ إِلَىَّ وَلَمْ يُوحَ إِلَيْهِ شَىْءٌ وَمَن قَالَ سَأُنزِلُ مِثْلَ مَآ أَنزَلَ ٱللَّهُ ۗ وَلَوْ تَرَىٰٓ إِذِ ٱلظَّٰلِمُونَ فِى غَمَرَٰتِ ٱلْمَوْتِ وَٱلْمَلَٰٓئِكَةُ بَاسِطُوٓا أَيْدِيهِمْ أَخْرِجُوٓا أَنفُسَكُمُ ۖ ٱلْيَوْمَ تُجْزَوْنَ عَذَابَ ٱلْهُونِ بِمَا كُنتُمْ تَقُولُونَ عَلَى ٱللَّهِ غَيْرَ ٱلْحَقِّ وَكُنتُمْ عَنْ ءَايَٰتِهِۦ تَسْتَكْبِرُونَ (٩٣) وَلَقَدْ جِئْتُمُونَا فُرَٰدَىٰ كَمَا خَلَقْنَٰكُمْ أَوَّلَ مَرَّةٍ وَتَرَكْتُم مَّا خَوَّلْنَٰكُمْ وَرَآءَ ظُهُورِكُمْ ۖ وَمَا نَرَىٰ مَعَكُمْ شُفَعَآءَكُمُ ٱلَّذِينَ زَعَمْتُمْ أَنَّهُمْ فِيكُمْ شُرَكَٰٓؤُا۟ ۚ لَقَد تَّقَطَّعَ بَيْنَكُمْ وَضَلَّ عَنكُم مَّا كُنتُمْ تَزْعُمُونَ (٩٤)

And who can be more unjust than he who invents a lie against Allâh, or says: "A revelation has come to me," whereas as no revelation has come to him in anything; and who says, "I will reveal the like of what Allâh has revealed." And if you could but see when the Zâlimûn (polytheists and wrong-doers) are in the agonies of death, while the angels are stretching forth their hands (saying): "Deliver your souls! This day you shall be recompensed with the torment of degradation because of what you used to utter against Allâh other than the truth. And you used to reject His Ayât (proofs, evidences, verses, lessons, signs, revelations etc.) with disrespect!" (93) And truly you have come unto Us alone (without wealth, companions or anything else) as We created you the first time. You have left behind you all that which We had bestowed on you. We see not with you your intercessors whom you claimed to be partners with Allâh. Now all relations between you and them have been cut off, and all that you used to claim has vanished from you. (94)

Quran 6:100-101

وَجَعَلُوا۟ لِلَّهِ شُرَكَآءَ ٱلْجِنَّ وَخَلَقَهُمْ وَخَرَقُوا۟ لَهُۥ بَنِينَ وَبَنَٰتٍۭ بِغَيْرِ عِلْمٍۢ سُبْحَٰنَهُۥ وَتَعَٰلَىٰ عَمَّا يَصِفُونَ (١٠٠) بَدِيعُ ٱلسَّمَٰوَٰتِ وَٱلْأَرْضِ أَنَّىٰ يَكُونُ لَهُۥ وَلَدٌۭ وَلَمْ تَكُن لَّهُۥ صَٰحِبَةٌۭ وَخَلَقَ كُلَّ شَىْءٍۢ وَهُوَ بِكُلِّ شَىْءٍ عَلِيمٌۭ (١٠١)

Yet, they join the jinn as partners in worship with Allâh, though He has created them (the jinn), and they attribute falsely without knowledge sons and daughters to Him. Be He Glorified and Exalted above all that (evil) they attribute to Him. (100) He is the Originator of the heavens and the earth. How can He have children when He has no wife? He created all things and He is the All-Knower of everything (101)

Quran 6:105-119

وَكَذَٰلِكَ نُصَرِّفُ ٱلْءَايَٰتِ وَلِيَقُولُوا۟ دَرَسْتَ وَلِنُبَيِّنَهُۥ لِقَوْمٍ يَعْلَمُونَ ﴿١٠٥﴾ ٱتَّبِعْ مَآ أُوحِىَ إِلَيْكَ مِن رَّبِّكَ ۖ لَآ إِلَٰهَ إِلَّا هُوَ ۖ وَأَعْرِضْ عَنِ ٱلْمُشْرِكِينَ ﴿١٠٦﴾ وَلَوْ شَآءَ ٱللَّهُ مَآ أَشْرَكُوا۟ ۗ وَمَا جَعَلْنَٰكَ عَلَيْهِمْ حَفِيظًا ۖ وَمَآ أَنتَ عَلَيْهِم بِوَكِيلٍ ﴿١٠٧﴾ وَلَا تَسُبُّوا۟ ٱلَّذِينَ يَدْعُونَ مِن دُونِ ٱللَّهِ فَيَسُبُّوا۟ ٱللَّهَ عَدْوًۢا بِغَيْرِ عِلْمٍ ۗ كَذَٰلِكَ زَيَّنَّا لِكُلِّ أُمَّةٍ عَمَلَهُمْ ثُمَّ إِلَىٰ رَبِّهِم مَّرْجِعُهُمْ فَيُنَبِّئُهُم بِمَا كَانُوا۟ يَعْمَلُونَ ﴿١٠٨﴾ وَأَقْسَمُوا۟ بِٱللَّهِ جَهْدَ أَيْمَٰنِهِمْ لَئِن جَآءَتْهُمْ ءَايَةٌ لَّيُؤْمِنُنَّ بِهَا ۚ قُلْ إِنَّمَا ٱلْءَايَٰتُ عِندَ ٱللَّهِ ۖ وَمَا يُشْعِرُكُمْ أَنَّهَآ إِذَا جَآءَتْ لَا يُؤْمِنُونَ ﴿١٠٩﴾ وَنُقَلِّبُ أَفْـِٔدَتَهُمْ وَأَبْصَٰرَهُمْ كَمَا لَمْ يُؤْمِنُوا۟ بِهِۦٓ أَوَّلَ مَرَّةٍ وَنَذَرُهُمْ فِى طُغْيَٰنِهِمْ يَعْمَهُونَ ﴿١١٠﴾ ۞ وَلَوْ أَنَّنَا نَزَّلْنَآ إِلَيْهِمُ ٱلْمَلَٰٓئِكَةَ وَكَلَّمَهُمُ ٱلْمَوْتَىٰ وَحَشَرْنَا عَلَيْهِمْ كُلَّ شَىْءٍ قُبُلًا مَّا كَانُوا۟ لِيُؤْمِنُوٓا۟ إِلَّآ أَن يَشَآءَ ٱللَّهُ وَلَٰكِنَّ أَكْثَرَهُمْ يَجْهَلُونَ ﴿١١١﴾ وَكَذَٰلِكَ جَعَلْنَا لِكُلِّ نَبِىٍّ عَدُوًّا شَيَٰطِينَ ٱلْإِنسِ وَٱلْجِنِّ يُوحِى بَعْضُهُمْ إِلَىٰ بَعْضٍ زُخْرُفَ ٱلْقَوْلِ غُرُورًا ۚ وَلَوْ شَآءَ رَبُّكَ مَا فَعَلُوهُ ۖ فَذَرْهُمْ وَمَا يَفْتَرُونَ ﴿١١٢﴾ وَلِتَصْغَىٰٓ إِلَيْهِ أَفْـِٔدَةُ ٱلَّذِينَ لَا يُؤْمِنُونَ بِٱلْءَاخِرَةِ وَلِيَرْضَوْهُ وَلِيَقْتَرِفُوا۟ مَا هُم مُّقْتَرِفُونَ ﴿١١٣﴾ أَفَغَيْرَ ٱللَّهِ أَبْتَغِى حَكَمًا وَهُوَ ٱلَّذِىٓ أَنزَلَ إِلَيْكُمُ ٱلْكِتَٰبَ مُفَصَّلًا ۚ وَٱلَّذِينَ ءَاتَيْنَٰهُمُ ٱلْكِتَٰبَ يَعْلَمُونَ أَنَّهُۥ مُنَزَّلٌ مِّن رَّبِّكَ بِٱلْحَقِّ ۖ فَلَا تَكُونَنَّ مِنَ ٱلْمُمْتَرِينَ ﴿١١٤﴾ وَتَمَّتْ كَلِمَتُ رَبِّكَ صِدْقًا وَعَدْلًا ۚ لَّا مُبَدِّلَ لِكَلِمَٰتِهِۦ ۚ وَهُوَ ٱلسَّمِيعُ ٱلْعَلِيمُ ﴿١١٥﴾ وَإِن تُطِعْ أَكْثَرَ مَن فِى ٱلْأَرْضِ يُضِلُّوكَ عَن سَبِيلِ ٱللَّهِ ۚ إِن يَتَّبِعُونَ إِلَّا ٱلظَّنَّ وَإِنْ هُمْ إِلَّا يَخْرُصُونَ ﴿١١٦﴾ إِنَّ رَبَّكَ هُوَ أَعْلَمُ مَن يَضِلُّ عَن سَبِيلِهِۦ ۖ وَهُوَ أَعْلَمُ بِٱلْمُهْتَدِينَ ﴿١١٧﴾ فَكُلُوا۟ مِمَّا ذُكِرَ ٱسْمُ ٱللَّهِ عَلَيْهِ إِن كُنتُم بِـَٔايَٰتِهِۦ مُؤْمِنِينَ ﴿١١٨﴾ وَمَا لَكُمْ أَلَّا تَأْكُلُوا۟ مِمَّا ذُكِرَ ٱسْمُ ٱللَّهِ عَلَيْهِ وَقَدْ فَصَّلَ لَكُم مَّا حَرَّمَ عَلَيْكُمْ إِلَّا مَا ٱضْطُرِرْتُمْ إِلَيْهِ ۗ وَإِنَّ كَثِيرًا لَّيُضِلُّونَ بِأَهْوَآئِهِم بِغَيْرِ عِلْمٍ ۗ إِنَّ رَبَّكَ هُوَ أَعْلَمُ بِٱلْمُعْتَدِينَ ﴿١١٩﴾

Thus We explain variously the Verses so that they (the disbelievers) may say: "You have studied (the Books of the people of the Scripture and brought this Qur'ân from that)" and that We may make the matter clear for the people who have knowledge. (105) Follow what has been revealed to you from your Lord, Lâ ilâha illa Huwa (none has the right to be worshipped but He) and turn aside from Al-Mushrikûn(polytheists). (106) Had Allâh willed, they would not have taken others besides Him in worship. And We have not made you a watcher over them nor are you a Wakil (disposer of affairs, guardian or trustee) over them. (107) And insult not those whom they (disbelievers) worship besides Allâh, lest they insult Allâh wrongfully without knowledge. Thus We have made fair¬seeming to each people its own doings; then to their Lord is their return and He shall then inform them of all that they used to do. (108) And they swear their strongest oaths by Allâh, that if there came to them a sign, they would surely believe therein. Say: "Signs are but with Allâh and what will make you (Muslims) perceive that (even) if it (the sign) came, they will not believe?" (109) And We shall turn their hearts and their eyes away (from guidance), as they refused to believe therein for the first time, and We shall leave them in their trespass to wander blindly. (110) And even if We had sent down unto them angels, and the dead had spoken unto them, and We had gathered together all things before their very eyes, they would not have believed, unless Allâh willed, but most of them behave ignorantly. (111) And so We have appointed for every Prophet enemies - Shayâtin (devils) among mankind and jinn, inspiring one another with adorned speech as a delusion (or by way of deception). If your Lord had so willed, they would not have done it, so leave them alone with their fabrications. (112) (And this is in order) that the hearts of those who disbelieve in the Hereafter may incline to such (deceit), and that they may remain pleased with it, and that they may commit what they are committing (all kinds of sins and evil deeds). (113) [Say (O Muhammad)] "Shall I seek a judge other than Allâh while it is He Who has sent down unto you the Book (the Qur'ân), explained in detail." Those unto whom We gave the Scripture [the Taurât (Torah) and the Injeel] know that it is revealed from your Lord in truth. So be not you of those who doubt. (114) And the Word of your Lord has been fulfilled in truth and in justice. None can change His Words. And He is the All¬Hearer, the All¬Knower. (115) And if you obey most of those on the earth, they will mislead you far away from Allâh's Path. They follow nothing but conjectures, and they do nothing but lie. (116) Verily, your Lord! It is He Who knows best who strays from His Way, and He knows best the rightly guided ones. (117) So eat of that (meat) on which Allâh's Name has been pronounced (while slaughtering the animal), if you are believers in His Ayât (proofs, evidences, verses, lessons, signs, revelations, etc.) (118) And why should you not eat of that (meat) on which Allâh's Name has been pronounced (at the time of slaughtering the animal), while He has explained to you in detail what is forbidden to you, except under compulsion of necessity? And surely many do lead (mankind) astray by their own desires through lack of knowledge. Certainly your Lord knows best the transgressors (119)

Quran 6:128-132

وَيَوْمَ يَحْشُرُهُمْ جَمِيعًا يَـٰمَعْشَرَ ٱلْجِنِّ قَدِ ٱسْتَكْثَرْتُم مِّنَ ٱلْإِنسِ ۖ وَقَالَ أَوْلِيَآؤُهُم مِّنَ ٱلْإِنسِ رَبَّنَا ٱسْتَمْتَعَ بَعْضُنَا بِبَعْضٍ وَبَلَغْنَآ أَجَلَنَا ٱلَّذِىٓ أَجَّلْتَ لَنَا ۚ قَالَ ٱلنَّارُ مَثْوَىٰكُمْ خَـٰلِدِينَ فِيهَآ إِلَّا مَا شَآءَ ٱللَّهُ ۗ إِنَّ رَبَّكَ حَكِيمٌ عَلِيمٌ (١٢٨) وَكَذَٰلِكَ نُوَلِّى بَعْضَ ٱلظَّـٰلِمِينَ بَعْضًۢا بِمَا كَانُوا۟ يَكْسِبُونَ (١٢٩) يَـٰمَعْشَرَ ٱلْجِنِّ وَٱلْإِنسِ أَلَمْ يَأْتِكُمْ رُسُلٌ مِّنكُمْ يَقُصُّونَ عَلَيْكُمْ ءَايَـٰتِى وَيُنذِرُونَكُمْ لِقَآءَ يَوْمِكُمْ هَـٰذَا ۚ قَالُوا۟ شَهِدْنَا عَلَىٰٓ أَنفُسِنَا ۖ وَغَرَّتْهُمُ ٱلْحَيَوٰةُ ٱلدُّنْيَا وَشَهِدُوا۟ عَلَىٰٓ أَنفُسِهِمْ أَنَّهُمْ كَانُوا۟ كَـٰفِرِينَ (١٣٠) ذَٰلِكَ أَن لَّمْ يَكُن رَّبُّكَ مُهْلِكَ ٱلْقُرَىٰ بِظُلْمٍ وَأَهْلُهَا غَـٰفِلُونَ (١٣١) وَلِكُلٍّ دَرَجَـٰتٌ مِّمَّا عَمِلُوا۟ ۚ وَمَا رَبُّكَ بِغَـٰفِلٍ عَمَّا يَعْمَلُونَ (١٣٢)

And on the Day when He will gather them (all) together (and say): "O you assembly of jinn! Many did you mislead of men," and their Auliyâ' (friends and helpers) amongst men will say: "Our Lord! We benefited one from the other, but now we have reached our appointed term which You did appoint for us." He will say: "The Fire be your dwelling¬place, you will dwell therein forever, except as Allâh may will. Certainly your Lord is All¬Wise, All¬Knowing." (128) And thus We do make the Zâlimûn (polytheists and wrong-doers) Auliyâ' (supporters and helpers) of one another (in committing crimes), because of that which they used to earn. (129) O you assembly of jinn and mankind! "Did not there come to you Messengers from amongst you, reciting unto you My Verses and warning you of the meeting of this Day of yours?" They will say: "We bear witness against ourselves." It was the life of this world that deceived them. And they will bear witness against themselves that they were disbelievers (130) This is because your Lord would not destroy the (populations of) towns for their wrong-doing (i.e. associating others in worship along with Allâh) while their people were unaware (so the Messengers were sent). (131) For all there will be degrees (or ranks) according to what they did. And your Lord is not unaware of what they do. (132)

Quran 6:136-140

وَجَعَلُواْ لِلَّهِ مِمَّا ذَرَأَ مِنَ ٱلْحَرْثِ وَٱلْأَنْعَٰمِ نَصِيبًا فَقَالُواْ هَٰذَا لِلَّهِ بِزَعْمِهِمْ وَهَٰذَا لِشُرَكَآئِنَا ۖ فَمَا كَانَ لِشُرَكَآئِهِمْ فَلَا يَصِلُ إِلَى ٱللَّهِ ۖ وَمَا كَانَ لِلَّهِ فَهُوَ يَصِلُ إِلَىٰ شُرَكَآئِهِمْ ۗ سَآءَ مَا يَحْكُمُونَ (١٣٦) وَكَذَٰلِكَ زَيَّنَ لِكَثِيرٍ مِّنَ ٱلْمُشْرِكِينَ قَتْلَ أَوْلَٰدِهِمْ شُرَكَآؤُهُمْ لِيُرْدُوهُمْ وَلِيَلْبِسُواْ عَلَيْهِمْ دِينَهُمْ ۖ وَلَوْ شَآءَ ٱللَّهُ مَا فَعَلُوهُ ۖ فَذَرْهُمْ وَمَا يَفْتَرُونَ (١٣٧) وَقَالُواْ هَٰذِهِۦٓ أَنْعَٰمٌ وَحَرْثٌ حِجْرٌ لَّا يَطْعَمُهَآ إِلَّا مَن نَّشَآءُ بِزَعْمِهِمْ وَأَنْعَٰمٌ حُرِّمَتْ ظُهُورُهَا وَأَنْعَٰمٌ لَّا يَذْكُرُونَ ٱسْمَ ٱللَّهِ عَلَيْهَا ٱفْتِرَآءً عَلَيْهِ ۚ سَيَجْزِيهِم بِمَا كَانُواْ يَفْتَرُونَ (١٣٨) وَقَالُواْ مَا فِى بُطُونِ هَٰذِهِ ٱلْأَنْعَٰمِ خَالِصَةٌ لِّذُكُورِنَا وَمُحَرَّمٌ عَلَىٰٓ أَزْوَٰجِنَا ۖ وَإِن يَكُن مَّيْتَةً فَهُمْ فِيهِ شُرَكَآءُ ۚ سَيَجْزِيهِمْ وَصْفَهُمْ ۚ إِنَّهُۥ حَكِيمٌ عَلِيمٌ (١٣٩) قَدْ خَسِرَ ٱلَّذِينَ قَتَلُوٓاْ أَوْلَٰدَهُمْ سَفَهًۢا بِغَيْرِ عِلْمٍ وَحَرَّمُواْ مَا رَزَقَهُمُ ٱللَّهُ ٱفْتِرَآءً عَلَى ٱللَّهِ ۚ قَدْ ضَلُّواْ وَمَا كَانُواْ مُهْتَدِينَ (١٤٠)

And they assign to Allâh a share of the tilth and cattle which He has created, and they say: "This is for Allâh according to their claim, and this is for our partners." But the share of their (Allâh's so-called) "partners" reaches not Allâh, while the share of Allâh reaches their (Allâh's so-called) "partners"! Evil is the way they judge! (136) And so to many of the Mushrikûn (polytheists) their (Allâh's so-called) "partners" have made fair-seeming the killing of their children, in order to lead them to their own destruction and cause confusion in their religion. And if Allâh had willed, they would not have done so. So leave them alone with their fabrications. (137) And according to their claim, they say that such and such cattle and crops are forbidden, and none should eat of them except those whom we allow. And (they say) there are cattle forbidden to be used for burden (or any other work), and cattle on which (at slaughtering) the Name of Allâh is not pronounced; lying against Him (Allâh). He will recompense them for what they used to fabricate. (138) And they say: "What is in the bellies of such and such cattle (milk or foetus) is for our males alone, and forbidden to our females (girls and women), but if it is born dead, then all have shares therein." He will punish them for their attribution (of such false orders to Allâh). Verily, He is All-Wise, All-Knower. (139) Indeed lost are they who have killed their children, foolishly, without knowledge, and have forbidden that which Allâh has provided for them, inventing a lie against Allâh. They have indeed gone astray and were not guided. (140)

Quran 6:148-150

سَيَقُولُ ٱلَّذِينَ أَشْرَكُوا۟ لَوْ شَآءَ ٱللَّهُ مَآ أَشْرَكْنَا وَلَآ ءَابَآؤُنَا وَلَا حَرَّمْنَا مِن شَىْءٍ ۚ كَذَٰلِكَ كَذَّبَ ٱلَّذِينَ مِن قَبْلِهِم حَتَّىٰ ذَاقُوا۟ بَأْسَنَا ۗ قُلْ هَلْ عِندَكُم مِّنْ عِلْمٍ فَتُخْرِجُوهُ لَنَآ ۖ إِن تَتَّبِعُونَ إِلَّا ٱلظَّنَّ وَإِنْ أَنتُمْ إِلَّا تَخْرُصُونَ (١٤٨) قُلْ

فَلِلَّهِ ٱلْحُجَّةُ ٱلْبَٰلِغَةُ ۖ فَلَوْ شَآءَ لَهَدَىٰكُمْ أَجْمَعِينَ (١٤٩) قُلْ هَلُمَّ شُهَدَآءَكُمُ ٱلَّذِينَ يَشْهَدُونَ أَنَّ ٱللَّهَ حَرَّمَ هَٰذَا ۖ فَإِن شَهِدُوا۟ فَلَا تَشْهَدْ مَعَهُمْ ۚ وَلَا تَتَّبِعْ أَهْوَآءَ ٱلَّذِينَ كَذَّبُوا۟ بِـَٔايَٰتِنَا وَٱلَّذِينَ لَا يُؤْمِنُونَ بِٱلْءَاخِرَةِ وَهُم بِرَبِّهِمْ يَعْدِلُونَ (١٥٠)

Those who took partners (in worship) with Allâh will say: "If Allâh had willed, we would not have taken partners (in worship) with Him, nor would our fathers, and we would not have forbidden anything (against His Will)." Likewise belied those who were before them, (they argued falsely with Allâh's Messengers), till they tasted Our Wrath. Say: "Have you any knowledge (proof) that you can produce before us? Verily, you follow nothing but guess and you do nothing but lie." (148) Say: "With Allâh is the perfect proof and argument, (i.e. the Oneness of Allâh, the sending of His Messengers and His Books to mankind), had He so willed, He would indeed have guided you all." (149) Say: "Bring forward your witnesses, who can testify that Allâh has forbidden this. Then if they testify, testify not you with them. And you should not follow the vain desires of such as treat Our Ayât (proofs, evidences, verses, lessons, signs, revelations, etc.) as falsehoods, and such as believe not in the Hereafter, and they hold others as equal (in worship) with their Lord." (150)

Quran 6:159

إِنَّ ٱلَّذِينَ فَرَّقُوا۟ دِينَهُمْ وَكَانُوا۟ شِيَعًا لَّسْتَ مِنْهُمْ فِى شَىْءٍ ۚ إِنَّمَآ أَمْرُهُمْ إِلَىٰ ٱللَّهِ ثُمَّ يُنَبِّئُهُم بِمَا كَانُوا۟ يَفْعَلُونَ

Verily, those who divide their religion and break up into sects (all kinds of religious sects), you (O Muhammad) have no concern in them in the least. Their affair is only with Allâh, Who then will tell them what they used to do. (159)

Quran 7:9

وَمَنْ خَفَّتْ مَوَازِينُهُ فَأُو۟لَٰٓئِكَ ٱلَّذِينَ خَسِرُوٓا۟ أَنفُسَهُم بِمَا كَانُوا۟ بِـَٔايَٰتِنَا يَظْلِمُونَ

And as for those whose scale will be light, they are those who will lose their ownselves (by entering Hell) because they denied and rejected Our Ayât (proofs, evidences, verses, lessons, signs, revelations, etc.). (9)

Quran 7:27-28

يَٰبَنِىٓ ءَادَمَ لَا يَفْتِنَنَّكُمُ ٱلشَّيْطَٰنُ كَمَآ أَخْرَجَ أَبَوَيْكُم مِّنَ ٱلْجَنَّةِ يَنزِعُ عَنْهُمَا لِبَاسَهُمَا لِيُرِيَهُمَا سَوْءَٰتِهِمَآ إِنَّهُۥ يَرَىٰكُمْ هُوَ وَقَبِيلُهُۥ مِنْ حَيْثُ لَا تَرَوْنَهُمْ إِنَّا جَعَلْنَا ٱلشَّيَٰطِينَ أَوْلِيَآءَ لِلَّذِينَ لَا يُؤْمِنُونَ (٢٧) وَإِذَا فَعَلُوا۟ فَٰحِشَةً قَالُوا۟ وَجَدْنَا عَلَيْهَآ ءَابَآءَنَا وَٱللَّهُ أَمَرَنَا بِهَا۟ قُلْ إِنَّ ٱللَّهَ لَا يَأْمُرُ بِٱلْفَحْشَآءِ أَتَقُولُونَ عَلَى ٱللَّهِ مَا لَا تَعْلَمُونَ (٢٨)

O Children of Adam! Let not Shaitân (Satan) deceive you, as he got your parents [Adam and Hawwa (Eve)] out of Paradise, stripping them of their raiments, to show them their private parts. Verily, he and Qabîluhu (his soldiers from the jinn or his tribe) see you from where you cannot see them. Verily, We made the Shayâtin (devils) Auliyâ' (protectors and helpers) for those who believe not. (27) And when they commit a Fâhishah (evil deed, going round the Ka'bah in naked state, and every kind of unlawful sexual intercourse), they say: "We found our fathers doing it, and Allâh has commanded it on us." Say: "Nay, Allâh never commands of Fâhishah. Do you say of Allâh what you know not? (28)

Quran 7:30

فَرِيقًا هَدَىٰ وَفَرِيقًا حَقَّ عَلَيْهِمُ ٱلضَّلَـٰلَةُ ۗ إِنَّهُمُ ٱتَّخَذُوا۟ ٱلشَّيَـٰطِينَ أَوْلِيَآءَ مِن دُونِ ٱللَّهِ وَيَحْسَبُونَ أَنَّهُم مُّهْتَدُونَ

A group He has guided, and a group deserved to be in error; (because) surely they took the Shayâtin (devils) as Auliyâ' (protectors and helpers) instead of Allâh, and think that they are guided. (30)

Quran 7:36-41

وَٱلَّذِينَ كَذَّبُوا۟ بِـَٔايَـٰتِنَا وَٱسْتَكْبَرُوا۟ عَنْهَآ أُو۟لَـٰٓئِكَ أَصْحَـٰبُ ٱلنَّارِ ۖ هُمْ فِيهَا خَـٰلِدُونَ (٣٦) فَمَنْ أَظْلَمُ مِمَّنِ ٱفْتَرَىٰ عَلَى ٱللَّهِ كَذِبًا أَوْ كَذَّبَ بِـَٔايَـٰتِهِۦٓ ۚ أُو۟لَـٰٓئِكَ يَنَالُهُمْ نَصِيبُهُم مِّنَ ٱلْكِتَـٰبِ ۖ حَتَّىٰٓ إِذَا جَآءَتْهُمْ رُسُلُنَا يَتَوَفَّوْنَهُمْ قَالُوٓا۟ أَيْنَ مَا كُنتُمْ تَدْعُونَ مِن دُونِ ٱللَّهِ ۖ قَالُوا۟ ضَلُّوا۟ عَنَّا وَشَهِدُوا۟ عَلَىٰٓ أَنفُسِهِمْ أَنَّهُمْ كَانُوا۟ كَـٰفِرِينَ (٣٧) قَالَ ٱدْخُلُوا۟ فِىٓ أُمَمٍ قَدْ خَلَتْ مِن قَبْلِكُم مِّنَ ٱلْجِنِّ وَٱلْإِنسِ فِى ٱلنَّارِ ۖ كُلَّمَا دَخَلَتْ أُمَّةٌ لَّعَنَتْ أُخْتَهَا ۖ حَتَّىٰٓ إِذَا ٱدَّارَكُوا۟ فِيهَا جَمِيعًا قَالَتْ أُخْرَىٰهُمْ لِأُولَىٰهُمْ رَبَّنَا هَـٰٓؤُلَآءِ أَضَلُّونَا فَـَٔاتِهِمْ عَذَابًا ضِعْفًا مِّنَ ٱلنَّارِ ۖ قَالَ لِكُلٍّ ضِعْفٌ وَلَـٰكِن لَّا تَعْلَمُونَ (٣٨) وَقَالَتْ أُولَىٰهُمْ لِأُخْرَىٰهُمْ فَمَا كَانَ لَكُمْ عَلَيْنَا مِن فَضْلٍ فَذُوقُوا۟ ٱلْعَذَابَ بِمَا كُنتُمْ تَكْسِبُونَ (٣٩) إِنَّ ٱلَّذِينَ كَذَّبُوا۟ بِـَٔايَـٰتِنَا وَٱسْتَكْبَرُوا۟ عَنْهَا لَا تُفَتَّحُ لَهُمْ أَبْوَٰبُ ٱلسَّمَآءِ وَلَا يَدْخُلُونَ ٱلْجَنَّةَ حَتَّىٰ يَلِجَ ٱلْجَمَلُ فِى سَمِّ ٱلْخِيَاطِ ۚ وَكَذَٰلِكَ نَجْزِى ٱلْمُجْرِمِينَ (٤٠) لَهُم مِّن جَهَنَّمَ مِهَادٌ وَمِن فَوْقِهِمْ غَوَاشٍ ۚ وَكَذَٰلِكَ نَجْزِى ٱلظَّـٰلِمِينَ (٤١)

But those who reject Our Ayât (proofs, evidences, verses, lessons, signs, revelations,) and treat them with arrogance, they are the dwellers of the (Hell) Fire, they will abide therein forever (36) Who is more unjust than one who invents a lie against Allâh or rejects His Ayât (proofs, evidences, verses, lessons, signs, revelations)? For such their appointed portion (good things of this worldly life and their period of stay therein) will reach them from the Book (of Decrees) until, when Our Messengers (the angel of death and his assistants) come to them to take their souls, they (the angels) will say: "Where are those whom you used to invoke and worship besides Allâh," they will reply, "They have vanished and deserted us." And they will bear witness against themselves, that they were disbelievers. (37) (Allâh) will say: "Enter you in the company of nations who passed away before you, of men and jinn, into the Fire." Every time a new nation enters, it curses its sister nation (that went before), until they will be gathered all together in the Fire. The last of them will say to the first of them: "Our Lord! These misled us, so give them a double torment of the Fire." He will say: "For each one there is double (torment), but you know not." (38) The first of them will say to the last of them: "You were not better than us, so taste the torment for what you used to earn." (39) Verily, those who belie Our Ayât (proofs, evidences, verses, lessons, signs, revelations) and treat them with arrogance, for them the gates of heaven will not be opened, and they will not enter Paradise until the camel goes through the eye of the needle (which is impossible). Thus do We recompense the Mujrimûn (criminals, polytheists, and sinners). (40) Theirs will be a bed of Hell (Fire), and over them coverings (of Hell-fire). Thus do We recompense the Zâlimûn (polytheists and wrong-doers). (41)

Quran 7:45

ٱلَّذِينَ يَصُدُّونَ عَن سَبِيلِ ٱللَّهِ وَيَبْغُونَهَا عِوَجًا وَهُم بِٱلْأَخِرَةِ كَٰفِرُونَ

Those who hindered (men) from the Path of Allâh, and would seek to make it crooked, and they were disbelievers in the Hereafter. (45)

Quran 7:50-53

وَنَادَىٰٓ أَصْحَٰبُ ٱلنَّارِ أَصْحَٰبَ ٱلْجَنَّةِ أَنْ أَفِيضُوا۟ عَلَيْنَا مِنَ ٱلْمَآءِ أَوْ مِمَّا رَزَقَكُمُ ٱللَّهُ قَالُوٓا۟ إِنَّ ٱللَّهَ حَرَّمَهُمَا عَلَى ٱلْكَٰفِرِينَ (٥٠) ٱلَّذِينَ ٱتَّخَذُوا۟ دِينَهُمْ لَهْوًا وَلَعِبًا وَغَرَّتْهُمُ ٱلْحَيَوٰةُ ٱلدُّنْيَا ۚ فَٱلْيَوْمَ نَنسَىٰهُمْ كَمَا نَسُوا۟ لِقَآءَ يَوْمِهِمْ هَٰذَا وَمَا كَانُوا۟ بِـَٔايَٰتِنَا يَجْحَدُونَ (٥١) وَلَقَدْ جِئْنَٰهُم بِكِتَٰبٍ فَصَّلْنَٰهُ عَلَىٰ عِلْمٍ هُدًى وَرَحْمَةً لِّقَوْمٍ يُؤْمِنُونَ (٥٢) هَلْ يَنظُرُونَ إِلَّا تَأْوِيلَهُۥ ۚ يَوْمَ يَأْتِى تَأْوِيلُهُۥ يَقُولُ ٱلَّذِينَ نَسُوهُ مِن قَبْلُ قَدْ جَآءَتْ رُسُلُ رَبِّنَا بِٱلْحَقِّ فَهَل لَّنَا مِن شُفَعَآءَ فَيَشْفَعُوا۟ لَنَآ أَوْ نُرَدُّ فَنَعْمَلَ غَيْرَ ٱلَّذِى كُنَّا نَعْمَلُ ۚ قَدْ خَسِرُوٓا۟ أَنفُسَهُمْ وَضَلَّ عَنْهُم مَّا كَانُوا۟ يَفْتَرُونَ (٥٣)

And the dwellers of the Fire will call to the dwellers of Paradise: "Pour on us some water or anything that Allâh has provided you with." They will say: "Both (water and provision) Allâh has forbidden to the disbelievers." (50) "Who took their religion as an amusement and play, and the life of the world deceived them." So this Day We shall forget them as they forgot their meeting of this Day, and as they used to reject Our Ayât (proofs, evidences, verses, lessons, signs, revelations). (51) Certainly, We have brought them a Book (the Qur'ân) which We have explained in detail with knowledge, - a guidance and a mercy to a people who believe. (52) Await they just for the final fullfilment of the event? On the Day the event is finally fulfilled (i.e. the Day of Resurrection), those who neglected it before will say: "Verily, the Messengers of our Lord did come with the truth, now are there any intercessors for us that they might intercede on our behalf? Or could we be sent back (to the first life of the world) so that we might do (good) deeds other than those (evil) deeds which we used to do?" Verily, they have lost their ownselves (i.e. destroyed themselves) and that which they used to fabricate (invoking and worshipping others besides Allâh) has gone away from them. (53)

Quran 8:31-40

وَإِذَا تُتْلَىٰ عَلَيْهِمْ ءَايَٰتُنَا قَالُوا۟ قَدْ سَمِعْنَا لَوْ نَشَآءُ لَقُلْنَا مِثْلَ هَٰذَآ إِنْ هَٰذَآ إِلَّآ أَسَٰطِيرُ ٱلْأَوَّلِينَ (٣١) وَإِذْ قَالُوا۟ ٱللَّهُمَّ إِن كَانَ هَٰذَا هُوَ ٱلْحَقَّ مِنْ عِندِكَ فَأَمْطِرْ عَلَيْنَا حِجَارَةً مِّنَ ٱلسَّمَآءِ أَوِ ٱئْتِنَا بِعَذَابٍ أَلِيمٍ (٣٢) وَمَا كَانَ ٱللَّهُ لِيُعَذِّبَهُمْ وَأَنتَ فِيهِمْ وَمَا كَانَ ٱللَّهُ مُعَذِّبَهُمْ وَهُمْ يَسْتَغْفِرُونَ (٣٣) وَمَا لَهُمْ أَلَّا يُعَذِّبَهُمُ ٱللَّهُ وَهُمْ يَصُدُّونَ عَنِ ٱلْمَسْجِدِ ٱلْحَرَامِ وَمَا كَانُوٓا۟ أَوْلِيَآءَهُۥٓ إِنْ أَوْلِيَآؤُهُۥٓ إِلَّا ٱلْمُتَّقُونَ وَلَٰكِنَّ أَكْثَرَهُمْ لَا يَعْلَمُونَ (٣٤) وَمَا كَانَ صَلَاتُهُمْ عِندَ ٱلْبَيْتِ إِلَّا مُكَآءً وَتَصْدِيَةً فَذُوقُوا۟ ٱلْعَذَابَ بِمَا كُنتُمْ تَكْفُرُونَ (٣٥) إِنَّ ٱلَّذِينَ كَفَرُوا۟ يُنفِقُونَ أَمْوَٰلَهُمْ لِيَصُدُّوا۟ عَن سَبِيلِ ٱللَّهِ فَسَيُنفِقُونَهَا ثُمَّ تَكُونُ عَلَيْهِمْ حَسْرَةً ثُمَّ يُغْلَبُونَ وَٱلَّذِينَ كَفَرُوٓا۟ إِلَىٰ جَهَنَّمَ يُحْشَرُونَ (٣٦) لِيَمِيزَ ٱللَّهُ ٱلْخَبِيثَ مِنَ ٱلطَّيِّبِ وَيَجْعَلَ ٱلْخَبِيثَ بَعْضَهُۥ عَلَىٰ بَعْضٍ فَيَرْكُمَهُۥ جَمِيعًا فَيَجْعَلَهُۥ فِى جَهَنَّمَ أُو۟لَٰٓئِكَ هُمُ ٱلْخَٰسِرُونَ (٣٧) قُل لِّلَّذِينَ كَفَرُوٓا۟ إِن يَنتَهُوا۟

يُغْفَرْ لَهُم مَّا قَدْ سَلَفَ وَإِن يَعُودُواْ فَقَدْ مَضَتْ سُنَّتُ ٱلْأَوَّلِينَ (٣٨) وَقَٰتِلُوهُمْ حَتَّىٰ لَا تَكُونَ فِتْنَةٌ وَيَكُونَ ٱلدِّينُ كُلُّهُۥ لِلَّهِۚ فَإِنِ ٱنتَهَوْاْ فَإِنَّ ٱللَّهَ بِمَا يَعْمَلُونَ بَصِيرٌ (٣٩) وَإِن تَوَلَّوْاْ فَٱعْلَمُوٓاْ أَنَّ ٱللَّهَ مَوْلَىٰكُمْۚ نِعْمَ ٱلْمَوْلَىٰ وَنِعْمَ ٱلنَّصِيرُ (٤٠)

And when Our Verses (of the Qur'ân) are recited to them, they say: "We have heard this (the Qur'ân); if we wish we can say the like of this. This is nothing but the tales of the ancients." (31) And (remember) when they said: "O Allâh! If this (the Qur'ân) is indeed the truth (revealed) from You, then rain down stones on us from the sky or bring on us a painful torment." (32) And Allâh would not punish them while you (Muhammad) are amongst them, nor will He punish them while they seek (Allâh's) Forgiveness (33) And why should not Allâh punish them while they hinder (men) from Al-Masjid-Al-Harâm, and they are not its guardians? None can be its guardian except Al-Muttaqûn (the pious), but most of them know not (34) Their Salât (prayer) at the House (of Allâh, i.e. the Ka'bah at Makkah) was nothing but whistling and clapping of hands. Therefore taste the punishment because you used to disbelieve (35) Verily, those who disbelieve spend their wealth to hinder (men) from the Path of Allâh, and so will they continue to spend it; but in the end it will become an anguish for them. Then they will be overcomed. And those who disbelieve will be gathered unto Hell (36) In order that Allâh may distinguish the wicked (disbelievers, polytheists and doers of evil deeds) from the good (believers of Islâmic

Monotheism and doers of righteous deeds), and put the wicked (disbelievers, polytheists and doers of evil deeds) one over another, heap them together and cast them into Hell. Those! it is they who are the losers. (37) Say to those who have disbelieved, if they cease (from disbelief) their past will be forgiven. But if they return (thereto), then the examples of those (punished) before them have already preceded (as a warning). (38) And fight them until there is no more Fitnah (disbelief and polytheism: i.e. worshipping others besides Allâh) and the religion (worship) will all be for Allâh Alone [in the whole of the world]. But if they cease (worshipping others besides Allâh), then certainly, Allâh is All-Seer of what they do. (39) And if they turn away, then know that Allâh is your Maulâ (Patron, Lord, Protector and Supporter), (what) an Excellent Maulâ, and (what) an Excellent Helper! (40)

Quran 8:55-57

إِنَّ شَرَّ ٱلدَّوَابِّ عِندَ ٱللَّهِ ٱلَّذِينَ كَفَرُوا۟ فَهُمْ لَا يُؤْمِنُونَ (٥٥) ٱلَّذِينَ عَٰهَدتَّ مِنْهُمْ ثُمَّ يَنقُضُونَ عَهْدَهُمْ فِى كُلِّ مَرَّةٍ وَهُمْ لَا يَتَّقُونَ (٥٦) فَإِمَّا تَثْقَفَنَّهُمْ فِى ٱلْحَرْبِ فَشَرِّدْ بِهِم مَّنْ خَلْفَهُمْ لَعَلَّهُمْ يَذَّكَّرُونَ (٥٧)

Verily, The worst of moving (living) creatures before Allâh are those who disbelieve, - so they shall not believe. (55) They are those with whom you made a covenant, but they break their covenant every time and they do not fear Allâh. (56) So if you gain the mastery over them in war, punish them severely in order to disperse those who are behind them, so that they may learn a lesson. (57)

Quran 9:37

إِنَّمَا النَّسِيءُ زِيَادَةٌ فِى الْكُفْرِ يُضَلُّ بِهِ الَّذِينَ كَفَرُواْ يُحِلُّونَهُ عَامًا وَيُحَرِّمُونَهُ عَامًا لِّيُوَاطِئُواْ عِدَّةَ مَا حَرَّمَ اللَّهُ فَيُحِلُّواْ مَا حَرَّمَ اللَّهُ زُيِّنَ لَهُمْ سُوءُ أَعْمَالِهِمْ وَاللَّهُ لَا يَهْدِى الْقَوْمَ الْكَافِرِينَ

The postponing (of a Sacred Month) is indeed an addition to disbelief: thereby the disbelievers are led astray, for they make it lawful one year and forbid it another year in order to adjust the number of months forbidden by Allâh, and make such forbidden ones lawful. The evil of their deeds is made fair-seeming pleasing to them. And Allâh guides not the people, who disbelieve. (37)

Quran 9:45-50

إِنَّمَا يَسْتَأْذِنُكَ الَّذِينَ لَا يُؤْمِنُونَ بِاللَّهِ وَالْيَوْمِ الْآخِرِ وَارْتَابَتْ قُلُوبُهُمْ فَهُمْ فِى رَيْبِهِمْ يَتَرَدَّدُونَ (٤٥) وَلَوْ أَرَادُواْ الْخُرُوجَ لَأَعَدُّواْ لَهُ عُدَّةً وَلَكِن كَرِهَ اللَّهُ انْبِعَاثَهُمْ فَثَبَّطَهُمْ وَقِيلَ اقْعُدُواْ مَعَ الْقَاعِدِينَ (٤٦) لَوْ خَرَجُواْ فِيكُم مَّا زَادُوكُمْ إِلَّا خَبَالاً وَلَأَوْضَعُواْ خِلَالَكُمْ يَبْغُونَكُمُ الْفِتْنَةَ وَفِيكُمْ سَمَّاعُونَ لَهُمْ وَاللَّهُ عَلِيمٌ بِالظَّالِمِينَ (٤٧) لَقَدِ ابْتَغَوُاْ الْفِتْنَةَ مِن قَبْلُ وَقَلَّبُواْ لَكَ الْأُمُورَ حَتَّى جَاءَ الْحَقُّ وَظَهَرَ أَمْرُ اللَّهِ وَهُمْ كَارِهُونَ (٤٨) وَمِنْهُم مَّن يَقُولُ ائْذَن لِّى وَلَا تَفْتِنِّى أَلَا فِى الْفِتْنَةِ سَقَطُواْ وَإِنَّ جَهَنَّمَ لَمُحِيطَةٌ بِالْكَافِرِينَ (٤٩) إِن تُصِبْكَ حَسَنَةٌ تَسُؤْهُمْ وَإِن تُصِبْكَ مُصِيبَةٌ يَقُولُواْ قَدْ أَخَذْنَا أَمْرَنَا مِن قَبْلُ وَيَتَوَلَّواْ وَّهُمْ فَرِحُونَ (٥٠)

It is only those who believe not in Allâh and the Last Day and whose hearts are in doubt that ask your leave (to be exempted from Jihâd). So in their doubts they waver. (45) And if they had intended to march out, certainly, they would have made some preparation for it, but Allâh was averse to their being sent forth, so He made them lag behind, and it was said (to them), "Sit you among those who sit (at home)." (46) Had they marched out with you, they would have added to you nothing except disorder, and they would have hurried about in your midst (spreading corruption) and sowing sedition among you, and there are some among you who would have listened to them. And Allâh is the All-Knower of the Zâlimûn (polytheists and wrong-doers). (47) Verily, they had plotted sedition before, and had upset matters for you, - until the truth (victory) came and the Decree of Allâh (His religion, Islâm) became manifest though they hated it (48) And among them is he who says: "Grant me leave (to be exempted from Jihâd) and put me not into trial." Surely, they have fallen into trial. And verily, Hell is surrounding the disbelievers. (49) If good befalls you, it grieves them, but if a calamity overtakes you, they say: "We took our precaution beforehand," and they turn away rejoicing. (50)

Quran 9:54-58

وَمَا مَنَعَهُمْ أَن تُقْبَلَ مِنْهُمْ نَفَقَٰتُهُمْ إِلَّآ أَنَّهُمْ كَفَرُوا۟ بِٱللَّهِ وَبِرَسُولِهِۦ وَلَا يَأْتُونَ ٱلصَّلَوٰةَ إِلَّا وَهُمْ كُسَالَىٰ وَلَا يُنفِقُونَ إِلَّا وَهُمْ كَٰرِهُونَ (٥٤) فَلَا تُعْجِبْكَ أَمْوَٰلُهُمْ وَلَآ أَوْلَٰدُهُمْ إِنَّمَا يُرِيدُ ٱللَّهُ لِيُعَذِّبَهُم بِهَا فِى ٱلْحَيَوٰةِ ٱلدُّنْيَا وَتَزْهَقَ أَنفُسُهُمْ وَهُمْ كَٰفِرُونَ (٥٥) وَيَحْلِفُونَ بِٱللَّهِ إِنَّهُمْ لَمِنكُمْ وَمَا هُم مِّنكُمْ وَلَٰكِنَّهُمْ قَوْمٌ يَفْرَقُونَ (٥٦) لَوْ يَجِدُونَ مَلْجَـًٔا أَوْ مَغَٰرَٰتٍ أَوْ مُدَّخَلًا لَّوَلَّوْا۟ إِلَيْهِ وَهُمْ يَجْمَحُونَ (٥٧) وَمِنْهُم مَّن يَلْمِزُكَ فِى ٱلصَّدَقَٰتِ فَإِنْ أُعْطُوا۟ مِنْهَا رَضُوا۟ وَإِن لَّمْ يُعْطَوْا۟ مِنْهَآ إِذَا هُمْ يَسْخَطُونَ (٥٨)

And nothing prevents their contributions from being accepted from them except that they disbelieved in Allâh and in His Messenger (Muhammad); and that they came not to As-Salât (the prayer) except in a lazy state; and that they offer not contributions but unwillingly. (54) So let not their wealth or their children amaze you; in reality Allâh's Plan is to punish them with these things in the life of the this world, and that their souls shall depart (die) while they are disbelievers. (55) They swear by Allâh that they are truly of you while they are not of you, but they are a people (hypocrites) who are afraid (that you may kill them). (56) Should they find a refuge, or caves, or a place of concealment, they would turn straightway thereto with a swift rush. (57) And of them are some who accuse you (O Muhammad) in the matter of (the distribution of) the alms. If they are given part thereof, they are pleased, but if they are not given thereof, behold! They are enraged! (58)

Quran 9:61-69

وَمِنْهُمُ ٱلَّذِينَ يُؤْذُونَ ٱلنَّبِيَّ وَيَقُولُونَ هُوَ أُذُنٌ قُلْ أُذُنُ خَيْرٍ لَّكُمْ يُؤْمِنُ بِٱللَّهِ وَيُؤْمِنُ لِلْمُؤْمِنِينَ وَرَحْمَةٌ لِّلَّذِينَ ءَامَنُواْ مِنكُمْ وَٱلَّذِينَ يُؤْذُونَ رَسُولَ ٱللَّهِ لَهُمْ عَذَابٌ أَلِيمٌ (٦١) يَحْلِفُونَ بِٱللَّهِ لَكُمْ لِيُرْضُوكُمْ وَٱللَّهُ وَرَسُولُهُ أَحَقُّ أَن يُرْضُوهُ إِن كَانُواْ مُؤْمِنِينَ (٦٢) أَلَمْ يَعْلَمُوٓاْ أَنَّهُۥ مَن يُحَادِدِ ٱللَّهَ وَرَسُولَهُۥ فَأَنَّ لَهُۥ نَارَ جَهَنَّمَ خَٰلِدًا فِيهَآ ذَٰلِكَ ٱلْخِزْىُ ٱلْعَظِيمُ (٦٣) يَحْذَرُ ٱلْمُنَٰفِقُونَ أَن تُنَزَّلَ عَلَيْهِمْ سُورَةٌ تُنَبِّئُهُم بِمَا فِى قُلُوبِهِمْ قُلِ ٱسْتَهْزِءُوٓاْ إِنَّ ٱللَّهَ مُخْرِجٌ مَّا تَحْذَرُونَ (٦٤) وَلَئِن سَأَلْتَهُمْ لَيَقُولُنَّ إِنَّمَا كُنَّا نَخُوضُ وَنَلْعَبُ قُلْ أَبِٱللَّهِ وَءَايَٰتِهِۦ وَرَسُولِهِۦ كُنتُمْ تَسْتَهْزِءُونَ (٦٥) لَا تَعْتَذِرُواْ قَدْ كَفَرْتُم بَعْدَ إِيمَٰنِكُمْ إِن نَّعْفُ عَن طَآئِفَةٍ مِّنكُمْ نُعَذِّبْ طَآئِفَةَۢ بِأَنَّهُمْ كَانُواْ مُجْرِمِينَ (٦٦) ٱلْمُنَٰفِقُونَ

وَٱلْمُنَفِقَتُ بَعْضُهُم مِّنْ بَعْضٍۚ يَأْمُرُونَ بِٱلْمُنكَرِ وَيَنْهَوْنَ عَنِ ٱلْمَعْرُوفِ وَيَقْبِضُونَ أَيْدِيَهُمْۚ نَسُوا۟ ٱللَّهَ فَنَسِيَهُمْۗ إِنَّ ٱلْمُنَفِقِينَ هُمُ ٱلْفَسِقُونَ (٦٧) وَعَدَ ٱللَّهُ ٱلْمُنَفِقِينَ وَٱلْمُنَفِقَتِ وَٱلْكُفَّارَ نَارَ جَهَنَّمَ خَلِدِينَ فِيهَاۚ هِىَ حَسْبُهُمْۚ وَلَعَنَهُمُ ٱللَّهُۖ وَلَهُمْ عَذَابٌ مُّقِيمٌ (٦٨) كَٱلَّذِينَ مِن قَبْلِكُمْ كَانُوٓا۟ أَشَدَّ مِنكُمْ قُوَّةً وَأَكْثَرَ أَمْوَٰلًا وَأَوْلَٰدًا فَٱسْتَمْتَعُوا۟ بِخَلَٰقِهِمْ فَٱسْتَمْتَعْتُم بِخَلَٰقِكُمْ كَمَا ٱسْتَمْتَعَ ٱلَّذِينَ مِن قَبْلِكُم بِخَلَٰقِهِمْ وَخُضْتُمْ كَٱلَّذِى خَاضُوٓا۟ۚ أُو۟لَٰٓئِكَ حَبِطَتْ أَعْمَٰلُهُمْ فِى ٱلدُّنْيَا وَٱلْءَاخِرَةِۖ وَأُو۟لَٰٓئِكَ هُمُ ٱلْخَٰسِرُونَ (٦٩)

And among them are men who annoy the Prophet (Muhammad) and say: "He is (lending his) ear (to every news)." Say: "He listens to what is best for you; he believes in Allâh; has faith in the believers; and is a mercy to those of you who believe." But those who hurt Allâh's Messenger (Muhammad) will have a painful torment. (61) They swear by Allâh to you (Muslims) in order to please you, but it is more fitting that they should please Allâh and His Messenger, if they are believers. (62) Know they not that whoever opposes and shows hostility to Allâh and His Messenger, certainly for him will be the Fire of Hell to abide therein. That is extreme disgrace. (63) The hypocrites fear lest a Sûrah (chapter of the Qur'ân) should be revealed about them, showing them what is in their hearts. Say: "(Go ahead and) mock! But certainly Allâh will bring to light all that you fear." (64) If you ask them (about this), they declare: "We were only talking idly and joking." Say: "Was it at Allâh, and His Ayât (proofs, evidences, verses, lessons, signs, revelations) and His Messenger that you were mocking?" (65) Make no excuse; you have disbelieved after you had believed. If We pardon some of you, We will punish others amongst you because they were Mujrimûn (disbelievers, polytheists, sinners, criminals). (66) The hypocrites, men and women, are one from another, they enjoin (on the people) Al-Munkar (i.e. disbelief and polytheism of all kinds and all that Islâm has forbidden), and forbid (people) from Al-Ma'rûf (i.e. Islâmic Monotheism and all that Islâm orders one to do), and they close their hands [from giving (spending in Allâh's Cause) alms]. They have forgotten Allâh, so He has forgotten them. Verily, the hypocrites are the Fâsiqûn (rebellious, disobedient to Allâh). (67) Allâh has promised the hypocrites — men and women — and the disbelievers, the Fire of Hell, therein shall they abide. It will suffice them. Allâh has cursed them and for them is the lasting torment. (68) Like those before you: they were mightier than you in power, and more abundant in wealth and children. They had enjoyed their portion (awhile), so enjoy your portion (awhile) as those before you enjoyed their portion (awhile); and you indulged in play and pastime (and in telling lies against Allâh and His Messenger Muhammad) as they indulged in play and pastime. Such are they whose deeds are in vain in this world and in the Hereafter. Such are they who are the losers. (69)

Quran 9:75-80

۞ وَمِنْهُم مَّنْ عَـٰهَدَ ٱللَّهَ لَئِنْ ءَاتَىٰنَا مِن فَضْلِهِۦ لَنَصَّدَّقَنَّ وَلَنَكُونَنَّ مِنَ ٱلصَّـٰلِحِينَ (٧٥) فَلَمَّآ ءَاتَىٰهُم مِّن فَضْلِهِۦ بَخِلُوا۟ بِهِۦ وَتَوَلَّوا۟ وَّهُم مُّعْرِضُونَ (٧٦) فَأَعْقَبَهُمْ نِفَاقًا فِى قُلُوبِهِمْ إِلَىٰ يَوْمِ يَلْقَوْنَهُۥ بِمَآ أَخْلَفُوا۟ ٱللَّهَ مَا وَعَدُوهُ

وَبِمَا كَانُوا۟ يَكْذِبُونَ (٧٧) أَلَمْ يَعْلَمُوٓا۟ أَنَّ ٱللَّهَ يَعْلَمُ سِرَّهُمْ وَنَجْوَىٰهُمْ وَأَنَّ ٱللَّهَ عَلَّـٰمُ ٱلْغُيُوبِ (٧٨) ٱلَّذِينَ يَلْمِزُونَ ٱلْمُطَّوِّعِينَ مِنَ ٱلْمُؤْمِنِينَ فِى ٱلصَّدَقَـٰتِ وَٱلَّذِينَ لَا يَجِدُونَ إِلَّا جُهْدَهُمْ فَيَسْخَرُونَ مِنْهُمْ سَخِرَ ٱللَّهُ مِنْهُمْ وَلَهُمْ عَذَابٌ أَلِيمٌ (٧٩) ٱسْتَغْفِرْ لَهُمْ أَوْ لَا تَسْتَغْفِرْ لَهُمْ إِن تَسْتَغْفِرْ لَهُمْ سَبْعِينَ مَرَّةً فَلَن يَغْفِرَ ٱللَّهُ لَهُمْ ذَٰلِكَ بِأَنَّهُمْ كَفَرُوا۟ بِٱللَّهِ وَرَسُولِهِۦ وَٱللَّهُ لَا يَهْدِى ٱلْقَوْمَ ٱلْفَـٰسِقِينَ (٨٠)

And of them are some who made a covenant with Allâh (saying): "If He bestowed on us of His Bounty, we will verily, give Sadaqâh (Zakât and voluntary charity in Allâh's Cause) and will be certainly among those who are righteous." (75) Then when He gave them of His Bounty, they became niggardly [refused to pay the Sadaqâh (Zakât or voluntary charity)], and turned away, averse. (76) So He punished them by putting hypocrisy into their hearts till the Day whereon they shall meet Him, because they broke that (covenant with Allâh) which they had promised to Him and because they used to tell lies. (77) Know they not that Allâh knows their secret ideas, and their Najwa (secret counsels), and that Allâh is the All-Knower of the unseen. (78) Those who defame such of the believers who give charity (in Allâh's Cause) voluntarily, and such who could not find to give charity (in Allâh's Cause) except what is available to them, so they mock at them (believers), Allâh will throw back their mockery on them, and they shall have a painful torment. (79) Whether you (O Muhammad) ask forgiveness for them (hypocrites) or ask not forgiveness for them … (and even) if you ask seventy times for their forgiveness … Allâh will not forgive them, because they have disbelieved in Allâh and His Messenger. And Allâh guides not those people who are Fâsiqûn (rebellious, disobedient to Allâh). (80)

Quran 9:84-87

وَلَا تُصَلِّ عَلَىٰٓ أَحَدٍ مِّنْهُم مَّاتَ أَبَدًا وَلَا تَقُمْ عَلَىٰ قَبْرِهِۦٓ إِنَّهُمْ كَفَرُواْ بِٱللَّهِ وَرَسُولِهِۦ وَمَاتُواْ وَهُمْ فَٰسِقُونَ (٨٤) وَلَا تُعْجِبْكَ أَمْوَٰلُهُمْ وَأَوْلَٰدُهُمْ إِنَّمَا يُرِيدُ ٱللَّهُ أَن يُعَذِّبَهُم بِهَا فِى ٱلدُّنْيَا وَتَزْهَقَ أَنفُسُهُمْ وَهُمْ كَٰفِرُونَ (٨٥) وَإِذَآ أُنزِلَتْ سُورَةٌ أَنْ ءَامِنُواْ بِٱللَّهِ وَجَٰهِدُواْ مَعَ رَسُولِهِ ٱسْتَـْٔذَنَكَ أُوْلُواْ ٱلطَّوْلِ مِنْهُمْ وَقَالُواْ ذَرْنَا نَكُن مَّعَ ٱلْقَٰعِدِينَ (٨٦) رَضُواْ بِأَن يَكُونُواْ مَعَ ٱلْخَوَالِفِ وَطُبِعَ عَلَىٰ قُلُوبِهِمْ فَهُمْ لَا يَفْقَهُونَ (٨٧)

And never pray (funeral prayer) for any of them (hypocrites) who dies, nor stand at his grave. Certainly they disbelieved in Allâh and His Messenger, and died while they were Fâsiqûn (rebellious, - disobedient to Allâh and His Messenger). (84) And let not their wealth or their children amaze you. Allâh's Plan is to punish them with these things in this world, and that their souls shall depart (die) while they are disbelievers. (85) And when a Sûrah (chapter from the Qur'ân) is revealed, enjoining them to believe in Allâh and to strive hard and fight along with His Messenger, the wealthy among them ask your leave to exempt them (from Jihâd) and say, "Leave us (behind), we would be with those who sit (at home)." (86) They are content to be with those (the women) who sit behind (at home). Their hearts are sealed up (from all kinds of goodness and right guidance), so they understand not. (87)

Quran 9:107

وَٱلَّذِينَ ٱتَّخَذُوا۟ مَسْجِدًا ضِرَارًا وَكُفْرًا وَتَفْرِيقًۢا بَيْنَ ٱلْمُؤْمِنِينَ وَإِرْصَادًا لِّمَنْ حَارَبَ ٱللَّهَ وَرَسُولَهُۥ مِن قَبْلُ ۚ وَلَيَحْلِفُنَّ إِنْ أَرَدْنَآ إِلَّا ٱلْحُسْنَىٰ ۖ وَٱللَّهُ يَشْهَدُ إِنَّهُمْ لَكَٰذِبُونَ

And as for those who put up a mosque by way of harm and disbelief, and to disunite the believers, and as an outpost for those who warred against Allâh and His Messenger aforetime, they will indeed swear that their intention is nothing but good. Allâh bears witness that they are certainly liars. (107)

Quran 10:7-8

إِنَّ ٱلَّذِينَ لَا يَرْجُونَ لِقَآءَنَا وَرَضُوا۟ بِٱلْحَيَوٰةِ ٱلدُّنْيَا وَٱطْمَأَنُّوا۟ بِهَا وَٱلَّذِينَ هُمْ عَنْ ءَايَٰتِنَا غَٰفِلُونَ (٧) أُو۟لَٰٓئِكَ مَأْوَىٰهُمُ ٱلنَّارُ بِمَا كَانُوا۟ يَكْسِبُونَ (٨)

Verily, those who hope not for their meeting with Us, but are pleased and satisfied with the life of the present world, and those who are heedless of Our Ayât (proofs, evidences, verses, lessons, signs, revelations, etc.), (7) Those, their abode will be the Fire, because of what they used to earn. (8)

Quran 10:15-21

وَإِذَا تُتْلَىٰ عَلَيْهِمْ ءَايَاتُنَا بَيِّنَٰتٍ ۙ قَالَ ٱلَّذِينَ لَا يَرْجُونَ لِقَآءَنَا ٱئْتِ بِقُرْءَانٍ غَيْرِ هَٰذَآ أَوْ بَدِّلْهُ ۚ قُلْ مَا يَكُونُ لِىٓ أَنْ أُبَدِّلَهُۥ مِن تِلْقَآئِ نَفْسِىٓ ۖ إِنْ أَتَّبِعُ إِلَّا مَا يُوحَىٰٓ إِلَىَّ ۖ إِنِّىٓ أَخَافُ إِنْ عَصَيْتُ رَبِّى عَذَابَ يَوْمٍ عَظِيمٍ (١٥) قُل لَّوْ شَآءَ ٱللَّهُ مَا تَلَوْتُهُۥ عَلَيْكُمْ وَلَآ أَدْرَىٰكُم بِهِۦ ۖ فَقَدْ لَبِثْتُ فِيكُمْ عُمُرًا مِّن قَبْلِهِۦٓ ۚ أَفَلَا تَعْقِلُونَ (١٦) فَمَنْ أَظْلَمُ مِمَّنِ ٱفْتَرَىٰ عَلَى ٱللَّهِ كَذِبًا أَوْ كَذَّبَ بِـَٔايَٰتِهِۦٓ ۚ إِنَّهُۥ لَا يُفْلِحُ

ٱلْمُجْرِمُونَ ﴿١٧﴾ وَيَعْبُدُونَ مِن دُونِ ٱللَّهِ مَا لَا يَضُرُّهُمْ وَلَا يَنفَعُهُمْ وَيَقُولُونَ هَٰؤُلَاءِ شُفَعَٰٓؤُنَا عِندَ ٱللَّهِ قُلْ أَتُنَبِّـُٔونَ ٱللَّهَ بِمَا لَا يَعْلَمُ فِى ٱلسَّمَٰوَٰتِ وَلَا فِى ٱلْأَرْضِ سُبْحَٰنَهُۥ وَتَعَٰلَىٰ عَمَّا يُشْرِكُونَ ﴿١٨﴾ وَمَا كَانَ ٱلنَّاسُ إِلَّآ أُمَّةً وَٰحِدَةً فَٱخْتَلَفُوا۟ وَلَوْلَا كَلِمَةٌ سَبَقَتْ مِن رَّبِّكَ لَقُضِىَ بَيْنَهُمْ فِيمَا فِيهِ يَخْتَلِفُونَ ﴿١٩﴾ وَيَقُولُونَ لَوْلَآ أُنزِلَ عَلَيْهِ ءَايَةٌ مِّن رَّبِّهِۦ فَقُلْ إِنَّمَا ٱلْغَيْبُ لِلَّهِ فَٱنتَظِرُوٓا۟ إِنِّى مَعَكُم مِّنَ ٱلْمُنتَظِرِينَ ﴿٢٠﴾ وَإِذَآ أَذَقْنَا ٱلنَّاسَ رَحْمَةً مِّنْ بَعْدِ ضَرَّآءَ مَسَّتْهُمْ إِذَا لَهُم مَّكْرٌ فِىٓ ءَايَاتِنَا قُلِ ٱللَّهُ أَسْرَعُ مَكْرًا إِنَّ رُسُلَنَا يَكْتُبُونَ مَا تَمْكُرُونَ ﴿٢١﴾

And when Our Clear Verses are recited unto them, those who hope not for their meeting with Us, say: Bring us a Qur'ân other than this, or change it." Say (O Muhammad): "It is not for me to change it on my own accord; I only follow that which is revealed unto me. Verily, I fear the torment of the Great Day (i.e. the Day of Resurrection). if I were to disobey my Lord." (15) Say (O Muhammad): "If Allâh had so willed, I should not have recited it to you nor would He have made it known to you. Verily, I have stayed amongst you a life time before this. Have you then no sense?" (16) So who does more wrong than he who forges a lie against Allâh or denies His Ayât (proofs, evidences, verses, lessons, signs, revelations, etc.)? Surely, the Mujrimûn (criminals, sinners, disbelievers and polytheists) will never be successful! (17) And they worship besides Allâh things that hurt them not, nor profit them, and they say: "These are our intercessors with Allâh." Say: "Do you inform Allâh of that which He knows not in the heavens and on the earth?" Glorified and Exalted is He above all that which they associate as partners (with Him)! (18) Mankind were but one community (i.e. on one religion - Islâmic Monotheism), then they differed (later), and had not it been for a Word that went forth before from your Lord, it would have been settled between them regarding what they differed (19) And they say: "How is it that not a sign is sent down on him from his Lord?" Say: "The unseen belongs to Allâh Alone, so wait you, verily I am with you among those who wait (for Allâh's Judgement)." (20) And when We let mankind taste mercy after some adversity has afflicted them, behold! they take to plotting against Our Ayât (proofs, evidences, verses, lessons, signs, revelations, etc.)! Say: "Allâh is more Swift in planning!" Certainly, Our Messengers (angels) record all of that which you plot. (21)

Quran 10:66

أَلَآ إِنَّ لِلَّهِ مَن فِى ٱلسَّمَٰوَٰتِ وَمَن فِى ٱلْأَرْضِ ۗ وَمَا يَتَّبِعُ ٱلَّذِينَ يَدْعُونَ مِن دُونِ ٱللَّهِ شُرَكَآءَ ۚ إِن يَتَّبِعُونَ إِلَّا ٱلظَّنَّ وَإِنْ هُمْ إِلَّا يَخْرُصُونَ

No doubt! Verily, to Allâh belongs whosoever is in the heavens and whosoever is in the earth. And those who worship and invoke others besides Allâh, in fact they follow not the (Allâh's so-called) partners, they follow only a conjecture and they only invent lies. (66)

Quran 10:68-70

قَالُوا۟ ٱتَّخَذَ ٱللَّهُ وَلَدًا ۗ سُبْحَٰنَهُ ۖ هُوَ ٱلْغَنِىُّ ۖ لَهُۥ مَا فِى ٱلسَّمَٰوَٰتِ وَمَا فِى ٱلْأَرْضِ ۚ إِنْ عِندَكُم مِّن سُلْطَٰنٍۭ بِهَٰذَآ ۚ أَتَقُولُونَ عَلَى ٱللَّهِ مَا لَا تَعْلَمُونَ (٦٨) قُلْ إِنَّ

ٱلَّذِينَ يَفْتَرُونَ عَلَى ٱللَّهِ ٱلْكَذِبَ لَا يُفْلِحُونَ (٦٩) مَتَـٰعٌ فِى ٱلدُّنْيَا ثُمَّ إِلَيْنَا مَرْجِعُهُمْ ثُمَّ نُذِيقُهُمُ ٱلْعَذَابَ ٱلشَّدِيدَ بِمَا كَانُوا۟ يَكْفُرُونَ (٧٠)

They (Jews, Christians and pagans) say: "Allâh has begotten a son (children)." Glory is to Him! He is Rich (Free of all needs). His is all that is in the heavens and all that is in the earth. No warrant you have for this. Do you say against Allâh what you know not. (68) Say: "Verily, those who invent a lie against Allâh will never be successful" - (69) (A brief) enjoyment in this world! - and then unto Us will be their return, then We shall make them taste the severest torment because they used to disbelieve [in Allâh, belie His Messengers, deny and challenge His Ayât (proofs, signs, verses, etc.)]. (70)

Quran 11:7-8

وَهُوَ ٱلَّذِى خَلَقَ ٱلسَّمَـٰوَٰتِ وَٱلْأَرْضَ فِى سِتَّةِ أَيَّامٍ وَكَانَ عَرْشُهُ عَلَى ٱلْمَآءِ لِيَبْلُوَكُمْ أَيُّكُمْ أَحْسَنُ عَمَلًا ۗ وَلَئِن قُلْتَ إِنَّكُم مَّبْعُوثُونَ مِنۢ بَعْدِ ٱلْمَوْتِ لَيَقُولَنَّ ٱلَّذِينَ كَفَرُوٓا۟ إِنْ هَـٰذَآ إِلَّا سِحْرٌ مُّبِينٌ (٧) وَلَئِنْ أَخَّرْنَا عَنْهُمُ ٱلْعَذَابَ إِلَىٰٓ أُمَّةٍ مَّعْدُودَةٍ لَّيَقُولُنَّ مَا يَحْبِسُهُ ۚ أَلَا يَوْمَ يَأْتِيهِمْ لَيْسَ مَصْرُوفًا عَنْهُمْ وَحَاقَ بِهِم مَّا كَانُوا۟ بِهِۦ يَسْتَهْزِءُونَ (٨)

And He it is Who has created the heavens and the earth in six Days and His Throne was on the water, that He might try you, which of you is the best in deeds. But if you were to say to them: "You shall indeed be raised up after death," those who disbelieve would be sure to say, "This is nothing but obvious magic." (7) And if We delay the torment for them till a determined term, they are sure to say, "What keeps it back?" Verily, on the day it reaches them, nothing will turn it away from them, and they will be surrounded by (or fall in) that at which they used to mock! (8)

Quran 11:18-22

وَمَنْ أَظْلَمُ مِمَّنِ ٱفْتَرَىٰ عَلَى ٱللَّهِ كَذِبًا أُوْلَٰٓئِكَ يُعْرَضُونَ عَلَىٰ رَبِّهِمْ وَيَقُولُ ٱلْأَشْهَٰدُ هَٰٓؤُلَآءِ ٱلَّذِينَ كَذَبُواْ عَلَىٰ رَبِّهِمْ أَلَا لَعْنَةُ ٱللَّهِ عَلَى ٱلظَّٰلِمِينَ (١٨) ٱلَّذِينَ يَصُدُّونَ عَن سَبِيلِ ٱللَّهِ وَيَبْغُونَهَا عِوَجًا وَهُم بِٱلْأَخِرَةِ هُمْ كَٰفِرُونَ (١٩) أُوْلَٰٓئِكَ لَمْ يَكُونُواْ مُعْجِزِينَ فِى ٱلْأَرْضِ وَمَا كَانَ لَهُم مِّن دُونِ ٱللَّهِ مِنْ أَوْلِيَآءَ يُضَٰعَفُ لَهُمُ ٱلْعَذَابُ مَا كَانُواْ يَسْتَطِيعُونَ ٱلسَّمْعَ وَمَا كَانُواْ يُبْصِرُونَ (٢٠) أُوْلَٰٓئِكَ ٱلَّذِينَ خَسِرُوٓاْ أَنفُسَهُمْ وَضَلَّ عَنْهُم مَّا كَانُواْ يَفْتَرُونَ (٢١) لَا جَرَمَ أَنَّهُمْ فِى ٱلْأَخِرَةِ هُمُ ٱلْأَخْسَرُونَ (٢٢)

And who does more wrong than he who invents a lie against Allâh. Such will be brought before their Lord, and the witnesses will say, "These are the ones who lied against their Lord!" No doubt! the curse of Allâh is on the Zâlimûn (polytheists, wrong-doers, oppressors) (18) Those who hinder (others) from the Path of Allâh (Islâmic Monotheism), and seek a crookedness therein, while they are disbelievers in the Hereafter. (19) By no means will they escape (from Allâh's Torment) on earth, nor have they protectors besides Allâh! Their torment will be doubled! They could not bear to hear (the preachers of the truth) and they used not to see (the truth because of their severe aversoin, inspite of the fact that they had the sense of hearing and sight). (20) They are those who have lost their ownselves, and their invented false deities will vanish from them. (21) Certainly, they are those who will be the greatest losers in the Hereafter. (22)

Quran 13:5-7

$$\text{وَإِن تَعْجَبْ فَعَجَبٌ قَوْلُهُمْ أَءِذَا كُنَّا تُرَابًا أَءِنَّا لَفِى خَلْقٍ جَدِيدٍ ۗ أُوْلَٰٓئِكَ الَّذِينَ كَفَرُواْ بِرَبِّهِمْ ۖ وَأُوْلَٰٓئِكَ الْأَغْلَٰلُ فِىٓ أَعْنَاقِهِمْ ۖ وَأُوْلَٰٓئِكَ أَصْحَٰبُ النَّارِ ۖ هُمْ فِيهَا خَٰلِدُونَ (٥) وَيَسْتَعْجِلُونَكَ بِالسَّيِّئَةِ قَبْلَ الْحَسَنَةِ وَقَدْ خَلَتْ مِن قَبْلِهِمُ الْمَثُلَٰتُ ۗ وَإِنَّ رَبَّكَ لَذُو مَغْفِرَةٍ لِّلنَّاسِ عَلَىٰ ظُلْمِهِمْ ۖ وَإِنَّ رَبَّكَ لَشَدِيدُ الْعِقَابِ (٦) وَيَقُولُ الَّذِينَ كَفَرُواْ لَوْلَآ أُنزِلَ عَلَيْهِ ءَايَةٌ مِّن رَّبِّهِۦٓ ۗ إِنَّمَآ أَنتَ مُنذِرٌ ۖ وَلِكُلِّ قَوْمٍ هَادٍ (٧)}$$

And if you wonder, then wondrous is their saying: "When we are dust, shall we indeed then be (raised) in a new creation?" They are those who disbelieved in their Lord! They are those who will have iron chains tying their hands to their necks. They will be dwellers of the Fire to abide therein. (5) They ask you to hasten the evil before the good, while (many) exemplary punishments have indeed occurred before them. But verily, your Lord is full of Forgiveness for mankind inspite of their wrong-doing. And verily, your Lord is (also) Severe in punishment. (6) And the disbelievers say: "Why is not a sign sent down to him from his Lord?" You are only a warner, and to every people there is a guide. (7)

Quran 13:27

$$\text{وَيَقُولُ الَّذِينَ كَفَرُواْ لَوْلَآ أُنزِلَ عَلَيْهِ ءَايَةٌ مِّن رَّبِّهِۦ ۗ قُلْ إِنَّ اللَّهَ يُضِلُّ مَن يَشَآءُ وَيَهْدِىٓ إِلَيْهِ مَنْ أَنَابَ}$$

And those who disbelieve say: "Why is not a sign sent down to him (Muhammad) from his Lord?" Say: "Verily, Allâh sends astray whom He wills and guides unto Himself those who turn to Him in repentance." (27)

Quran 13:32-34

وَلَقَدِ ٱسْتُهْزِئَ بِرُسُلٍ مِّن قَبْلِكَ فَأَمْلَيْتُ لِلَّذِينَ كَفَرُواْ ثُمَّ أَخَذْتُهُمْ فَكَيْفَ كَانَ عِقَابِ (٣٢) أَفَمَنْ هُوَ قَآئِمٌ عَلَىٰ كُلِّ نَفْسٍ بِمَا كَسَبَتْ وَجَعَلُواْ لِلَّهِ شُرَكَآءَ قُلْ سَمُّوهُمْ أَمْ تُنَبِّئُونَهُ بِمَا لَا يَعْلَمُ فِى ٱلْأَرْضِ أَم بِظَـٰهِرٍ مِّنَ ٱلْقَوْلِ بَلْ زُيِّنَ لِلَّذِينَ كَفَرُواْ مَكْرُهُمْ وَصُدُّواْ عَنِ ٱلسَّبِيلِ وَمَن يُضْلِلِ ٱللَّهُ فَمَا لَهُ مِنْ هَادٍ (٣٣) لَهُمْ عَذَابٌ فِى ٱلْحَيَوٰةِ ٱلدُّنْيَا وَلَعَذَابُ ٱلْأَخِرَةِ أَشَقُّ وَمَا لَهُم مِّنَ ٱللَّهِ مِن وَاقٍ (٣٤)

And indeed (many) Messengers were mocked at before you (O Muhammad), but I granted respite to those who disbelieved, and finally I punished them. Then how (terrible) was My Punishment! (32) Is then He (Allâh) Who takes charge (guards, maintains, provides) of every person and knows all that he has earned (like any other deities who know nothing)? Yet they ascribe partners to Allâh. Say: "Name them! Is it that you will inform Him of something He knows not in the earth or is it (just) a show of false words." Nay! To those who disbelieved, their plotting is made fairseeming, and they have been hindered from the Right Path, and whom Allâh sends astray, for him, there is no guide. (33) For them is a torment in the life of this world, and certainly, harder is the torment of the Hereafter. And they have no Waq (defender or protector) against Allâh (34)

Quran 13:43

وَيَقُولُ ٱلَّذِينَ كَفَرُوا۟ لَسْتَ مُرْسَلًا ۚ قُلْ كَفَىٰ بِٱللَّهِ شَهِيدًۢا بَيْنِى وَبَيْنَكُمْ وَمَنْ عِندَهُۥ عِلْمُ ٱلْكِتَٰبِ

And those who disbelieved, say: "You (O Muhammad) are not a Messenger." Say: "Sufficient as a witness between me and you is Allâh and those too who have knowledge of the Scripture (such as 'Abdullâh bin Salâm and other Jews and Christians who embraced Islâm)." (43)

Quran 14:2-3

ٱللَّهِ ٱلَّذِى لَهُۥ مَا فِى ٱلسَّمَٰوَٰتِ وَمَا فِى ٱلْأَرْضِ ۗ وَوَيْلٌ لِّلْكَٰفِرِينَ مِنْ عَذَابٍ شَدِيدٍ (٢) ٱلَّذِينَ يَسْتَحِبُّونَ ٱلْحَيَوٰةَ ٱلدُّنْيَا عَلَى ٱلْءَاخِرَةِ وَيَصُدُّونَ عَن سَبِيلِ ٱللَّهِ وَيَبْغُونَهَا عِوَجًا ۚ أُو۟لَٰٓئِكَ فِى ضَلَٰلٍۭ بَعِيدٍ (٣)

Allâh to Whom belongs all that is in the heavens and all that is in the earth! And woe unto the disbelievers from a severe torment. (2) Those who prefer the life of this world to of the Hereafter, and hinder (men) from the Path of Allâh (i.e. Islâm) and seek crookedness therein - they are far astray. (3)

Quran 14:13

وَقَالَ ٱلَّذِينَ كَفَرُوا۟ لِرُسُلِهِمْ لَنُخْرِجَنَّكُم مِّنْ أَرْضِنَآ أَوْ لَتَعُودُنَّ فِى مِلَّتِنَا ۖ فَأَوْحَىٰٓ إِلَيْهِمْ رَبُّهُمْ لَنُهْلِكَنَّ ٱلظَّٰلِمِينَ

And those who disbelieved, said to their Messengers: "Surely, we shall drive you out of our land, or you shall return to our religion." So their Lord revealed to them:

"Truly, We shall destroy the Zâlimûn (polytheists, disbelievers and wrong-doers.). (13)

Quran 15:2

رُّبَمَا يَوَدُّ ٱلَّذِينَ كَفَرُواْ لَوْ كَانُواْ مُسْلِمِينَ

How much will those who disbelieve desire that they were Muslims

Quran 16:22-29

إِلَٰهُكُمْ إِلَٰهٌ وَٰحِدٌ فَٱلَّذِينَ لَا يُؤْمِنُونَ بِٱلْأَخِرَةِ قُلُوبُهُم مُّنكِرَةٌ وَهُم مُّسْتَكْبِرُونَ (٢٢) لَا جَرَمَ أَنَّ ٱللَّهَ يَعْلَمُ مَا يُسِرُّونَ وَمَا يُعْلِنُونَ إِنَّهُۥ لَا يُحِبُّ ٱلْمُسْتَكْبِرِينَ (٢٣) وَإِذَا قِيلَ لَهُم مَّاذَآ أَنزَلَ رَبُّكُمْ قَالُوٓاْ أَسَٰطِيرُ ٱلْأَوَّلِينَ (٢٤) لِيَحْمِلُوٓاْ أَوْزَارَهُمْ كَامِلَةً يَوْمَ ٱلْقِيَٰمَةِ وَمِنْ أَوْزَارِ ٱلَّذِينَ يُضِلُّونَهُم بِغَيْرِ عِلْمٍ أَلَا سَآءَ مَا يَزِرُونَ (٢٥) قَدْ مَكَرَ ٱلَّذِينَ مِن قَبْلِهِمْ فَأَتَى ٱللَّهُ بُنْيَٰنَهُم مِّنَ ٱلْقَوَاعِدِ فَخَرَّ عَلَيْهِمُ ٱلسَّقْفُ مِن فَوْقِهِمْ وَأَتَىٰهُمُ ٱلْعَذَابُ مِنْ حَيْثُ لَا يَشْعُرُونَ (٢٦) ثُمَّ يَوْمَ ٱلْقِيَٰمَةِ يُخْزِيهِمْ وَيَقُولُ أَيْنَ شُرَكَآءِىَ ٱلَّذِينَ كُنتُمْ تُشَٰقُّونَ فِيهِمْ قَالَ ٱلَّذِينَ أُوتُواْ ٱلْعِلْمَ إِنَّ ٱلْخِزْىَ ٱلْيَوْمَ وَٱلسُّوٓءَ عَلَى ٱلْكَٰفِرِينَ (٢٧) ٱلَّذِينَ تَتَوَفَّىٰهُمُ ٱلْمَلَٰٓئِكَةُ ظَالِمِىٓ أَنفُسِهِمْ فَأَلْقَوُاْ ٱلسَّلَمَ مَا كُنَّا نَعْمَلُ مِن سُوٓءٍ بَلَىٰٓ إِنَّ ٱللَّهَ عَلِيمٌۢ بِمَا كُنتُمْ تَعْمَلُونَ (٢٨) فَٱدْخُلُوٓاْ أَبْوَٰبَ جَهَنَّمَ خَٰلِدِينَ فِيهَا فَلَبِئْسَ مَثْوَى ٱلْمُتَكَبِّرِينَ (٢٩)

Your Ilâh (God) is One Ilâh (God — Allâh, none has the right to be worshipped but He). But for those who believe not in the Hereafter, their hearts deny (the faith in the Oneness of Allâh), and they are proud. (22) Certainly, Allâh knows what they conceal and what they reveal. Truly, He likes not the proud. (23) And when it is said to them: "What is it that your Lord has sent down (unto Muhammad)?" They say: "Tales of the men of old!" (24)

They may bear their own burdens in full on the Day of Resurrection, and also of the burdens of those whom they misled without knowledge. Evil indeed is that which they shall bear! (25) Those before them indeed plotted, but Allâh struck at the foundation of their building, and then the roof fell down upon them, from above them, and the torment overtook them from directions they did not perceive. (26) Then, on the Day of Resurrection, He will disgrace them and will say: "Where are My (so called) 'partners' concerning whom you used to disagree and dispute (with the believers, by defying and disobeying Allâh)?" Those who have been given the knowledge (about the Torment of Allâh for the disbelievers) will say: "Verily! Disgrace this Day and misery this Day are upon the disbelievers. (27) "Those whose lives the angels take while they are doing wrong to themselves (by disbelief and by associating partners in worship with Allâh and by committing all kinds of crimes and evil deeds)." Then, they will make (false) submission (saying): "We used not to do any evil." (The angels will reply): "Yes! Truly, Allâh is All-Knower of what you used to do. (28) "So enter the gates of Hell, to abide therein, and indeed, what an evil abode will be for the arrogant." (29)

Quran 16:33-39

هَلْ يَنظُرُونَ إِلَّا أَن تَأْتِيَهُمُ ٱلْمَلَـٰٓئِكَةُ أَوْ يَأْتِىَ أَمْرُ رَبِّكَ كَذَٰلِكَ فَعَلَ ٱلَّذِينَ مِن قَبْلِهِمْ وَمَا ظَلَمَهُمُ ٱللَّهُ وَلَـٰكِن كَانُوٓا۟ أَنفُسَهُمْ يَظْلِمُونَ (٣٣) فَأَصَابَهُمْ سَيِّـَٔاتُ مَا عَمِلُوا۟ وَحَاقَ بِهِم مَّا كَانُوا۟ بِهِۦ يَسْتَهْزِءُونَ (٣٤) وَقَالَ ٱلَّذِينَ أَشْرَكُوا۟ لَوْ شَآءَ ٱللَّهُ مَا عَبَدْنَا مِن دُونِهِۦ مِن شَىْءٍ نَّحْنُ وَلَآ ءَابَآؤُنَا وَلَا حَرَّمْنَا مِن دُونِهِۦ

مِن شَىْءٍ كَذَٰلِكَ فَعَلَ ٱلَّذِينَ مِن قَبْلِهِمْ فَهَلْ عَلَى ٱلرُّسُلِ إِلَّا ٱلْبَلَـٰغُ ٱلْمُبِينُ (٣٥) وَلَقَدْ بَعَثْنَا فِى كُلِّ أُمَّةٍ رَّسُولًا أَنِ ٱعْبُدُواْ ٱللَّهَ وَٱجْتَنِبُواْ ٱلطَّـٰغُوتَ ۖ فَمِنْهُم مَّنْ هَدَى ٱللَّهُ وَمِنْهُم مَّنْ حَقَّتْ عَلَيْهِ ٱلضَّلَـٰلَةُ ۚ فَسِيرُواْ فِى ٱلْأَرْضِ فَٱنظُرُواْ كَيْفَ كَانَ عَـٰقِبَةُ ٱلْمُكَذِّبِينَ (٣٦) إِن تَحْرِصْ عَلَىٰ هُدَىٰهُمْ فَإِنَّ ٱللَّهَ لَا يَهْدِى مَن يُضِلُّ ۖ وَمَا لَهُم مِّن نَّـٰصِرِينَ (٣٧) وَأَقْسَمُواْ بِٱللَّهِ جَهْدَ أَيْمَـٰنِهِمْ ۙ لَا يَبْعَثُ ٱللَّهُ مَن يَمُوتُ ۚ بَلَىٰ وَعْدًا عَلَيْهِ حَقًّا وَلَـٰكِنَّ أَكْثَرَ ٱلنَّاسِ لَا يَعْلَمُونَ (٣٨) لِيُبَيِّنَ لَهُمُ ٱلَّذِى يَخْتَلِفُونَ فِيهِ وَلِيَعْلَمَ ٱلَّذِينَ كَفَرُواْ أَنَّهُمْ كَانُواْ كَـٰذِبِينَ (٣٩)

Do they (the disbelievers and polytheists) await but that the angels should come to them [to take away their souls (at death)], or there should come the command (i.e. the torment or the Day of Resurrection) of your Lord? Thus did those before them. And Allâh wronged them not, but they used to wrong themselves. (33) Then, the evil results of their deeds overtook them, and that at which they used to mock at surrounded them. (34) And those who joined others in worship with Allâh say: "If Allâh had so willed, neither we nor our fathers would have worshipped aught but Him, nor would we have forbidden anything without (Command from) Him." So did those before them. Then! Are the Messengers charged with anything but to convey clearly the Message? (35) And verily, We have sent among every Ummah (community, nation) a Messenger (proclaiming): "Worship Allâh (Alone), and avoid (or keep away from) Tâghût (all false deities, etc. i.e. do not worship Tâghût besides Allâh)." Then of them were some whom Allâh guided and of them were some upon whom the straying was justified. So travel through the land and see what was the end of those who denied (the truth). (36) If you covet for their guidance, then verily Allâh guides not those whom He makes to go astray (or none can guide him whom Allâh sends astray). And they will have no helpers. (37) And they swear by Allâh their strongest oaths, that Allâh will not raise up him who dies. Yes, (He will raise them up), a promise (binding) upon Him in truth, but most of mankind know not. (38) In order that He may make manifest to them the truth of that wherein they differ, and that those who disbelieved (in Resurrection, and in the Oneness of Allâh) may know that they were liars. (39)

Quran 16:83-88

يَعْرِفُونَ نِعْمَتَ ٱللَّهِ ثُمَّ يُنكِرُونَهَا وَأَكْثَرُهُمُ ٱلْكَٰفِرُونَ (٨٣) وَيَوْمَ نَبْعَثُ مِن كُلِّ أُمَّةٍ شَهِيدًا ثُمَّ لَا يُؤْذَنُ لِلَّذِينَ كَفَرُوا۟ وَلَا هُمْ يُسْتَعْتَبُونَ (٨٤) وَإِذَا رَءَا ٱلَّذِينَ ظَلَمُوا۟ ٱلْعَذَابَ فَلَا يُخَفَّفُ عَنْهُمْ وَلَا هُمْ يُنظَرُونَ (٨٥) وَإِذَا رَءَا ٱلَّذِينَ أَشْرَكُوا۟ شُرَكَآءَهُمْ قَالُوا۟ رَبَّنَا هَٰٓؤُلَآءِ شُرَكَآؤُنَا ٱلَّذِينَ كُنَّا نَدْعُوا۟ مِن دُونِكَ فَأَلْقَوْا۟ إِلَيْهِمُ ٱلْقَوْلَ إِنَّكُمْ لَكَٰذِبُونَ (٨٦) وَأَلْقَوْا۟ إِلَى ٱللَّهِ يَوْمَئِذٍ ٱلسَّلَمَ وَضَلَّ عَنْهُم مَّا كَانُوا۟ يَفْتَرُونَ (٨٧) ٱلَّذِينَ كَفَرُوا۟ وَصَدُّوا۟ عَن سَبِيلِ ٱللَّهِ زِدْنَٰهُمْ عَذَابًا فَوْقَ ٱلْعَذَابِ بِمَا كَانُوا۟ يُفْسِدُونَ (٨٨)

They recognize the Grace of Allâh, yet they deny it (by worshipping others besides Allâh) and most of them are disbelievers (deny the Prophethood of Muhammad). (83) And (remember) the Day when We shall raise up from each nation a witness (their Messenger), then, those who have disbelieved will not be given leave (to put forward excuses), nor will they be allowed (to return to the world) to repent and ask for Allâh's Forgiveness (of their sins). (84) And when those who did wrong (the disbelievers) will see the torment, then it will not be lightened unto them, nor will they be given respite. (85) And when those who associated partners with Allâh see their (Allâh's so-called) partners, they will say: "Our Lord! These are our partners whom we used to invoke besides you." But they will throw back their word at them (and say): "Surely! You indeed are liars!" (86) And they will offer (their full) submission to Allâh (Alone) on that Day, and their invented false deities [all that they used to invoke besides Allâh, e.g. idols, saints, priests, monks, angels, jinn, Jibrael (Gabriel), Messengers] will vanish from them. (87) Those who disbelieved and hinder (men) from the Path of Allâh, for them We will add torment to the torment; because they used to spread corruption [by disobeying Allâh themselves, as well as ordering others (mankind) to do so]. (88)

Quran 16:101-109

وَإِذَا بَدَّلْنَآ ءَايَةً مَّكَانَ ءَايَةٍ وَٱللَّهُ أَعْلَمُ بِمَا يُنَزِّلُ قَالُوٓا۟ إِنَّمَآ أَنتَ مُفْتَرٍۭ بَلْ أَكْثَرُهُمْ لَا يَعْلَمُونَ (١٠١) قُلْ نَزَّلَهُۥ رُوحُ ٱلْقُدُسِ مِن رَّبِّكَ بِٱلْحَقِّ لِيُثَبِّتَ ٱلَّذِينَ ءَامَنُوا۟ وَهُدًى وَبُشْرَىٰ لِلْمُسْلِمِينَ (١٠٢) وَلَقَدْ نَعْلَمُ أَنَّهُمْ يَقُولُونَ إِنَّمَا يُعَلِّمُهُۥ بَشَرٌ ۗ لِّسَانُ ٱلَّذِى يُلْحِدُونَ إِلَيْهِ أَعْجَمِىٌّ وَهَٰذَا لِسَانٌ عَرَبِىٌّ مُّبِينٌ (١٠٣) إِنَّ ٱلَّذِينَ لَا يُؤْمِنُونَ بِـَٔايَٰتِ ٱللَّهِ لَا يَهْدِيهِمُ ٱللَّهُ وَلَهُمْ عَذَابٌ أَلِيمٌ (١٠٤) إِنَّمَا يَفْتَرِى ٱلْكَذِبَ ٱلَّذِينَ لَا يُؤْمِنُونَ بِـَٔايَٰتِ ٱللَّهِ ۖ وَأُو۟لَٰٓئِكَ هُمُ ٱلْكَٰذِبُونَ (١٠٥) مَن كَفَرَ بِٱللَّهِ مِنۢ بَعْدِ إِيمَٰنِهِۦٓ إِلَّا مَنْ أُكْرِهَ وَقَلْبُهُۥ مُطْمَئِنٌّۢ بِٱلْإِيمَٰنِ وَلَٰكِن مَّن شَرَحَ بِٱلْكُفْرِ صَدْرًا فَعَلَيْهِمْ غَضَبٌ مِّنَ ٱللَّهِ وَلَهُمْ عَذَابٌ عَظِيمٌ (١٠٦) ذَٰلِكَ بِأَنَّهُمُ ٱسْتَحَبُّوا۟ ٱلْحَيَوٰةَ ٱلدُّنْيَا عَلَى ٱلْءَاخِرَةِ وَأَنَّ ٱللَّهَ

لَا يَهْدِى ٱلْقَوْمَ ٱلْكَـٰفِرِينَ (١٠٧) أُوْلَـٰٓئِكَ ٱلَّذِينَ طَبَعَ ٱللَّهُ عَلَىٰ قُلُوبِهِمْ وَسَمْعِهِمْ وَأَبْصَـٰرِهِمْ وَأُوْلَـٰٓئِكَ هُمُ ٱلْغَـٰفِلُونَ (١٠٨) لَا جَرَمَ أَنَّهُمْ فِى ٱلْآخِرَةِ هُمُ ٱلْخَـٰسِرُونَ (١٠٩)

And when We change a Verse [of the Qur'ân) in place of another, — and Allâh knows the best what He sends down, they (the disbelievers) say: "You (O Muhammad) are but a Muftari! (forger, liar)." Nay, but most of them know not (101) Say (O Muhammad) Ruh-ul-Qudus [Jibril (Gabriel)] has brought it (the Qur'an) down from your Lord with truth, that it may make firm and strengthen (the Faith of) those who believe and as a guidance and glad tidings to those who have submitted (to Allâh as Muslims). (102) And indeed We know that they (polytheists and pagans) say: "It is only a human being who teaches him (Muhammad)." The tongue of the man they refer to is foreign, while this (the Qur'ân) is a clear Arabic tongue. (103) Verily! Those who believe not in the Ayât (proofs, evidences, verses, lessons, signs, revelations, etc.) of Allâh, Allâh will not guide them and theirs will be a painful torment (104) It is only those who believe not in the Ayât (proofs, evidences, verses, lessons, signs, revelations, etc.) of Allâh, who fabricate falsehood, and it is they who are liars (105) Whoever disbelieved in Allâh after his belief, except him who is forced thereto and whose heart is at rest with Faith, but such as open their breasts to disbelief, on them is wrath from Allâh, and theirs will be a great torment. (106) That is because they loved and preferred the life of this world over that of the Hereafter. And Allâh guides not the people who disbelieve. (107) They are those upon whose hearts, hearing (ears) and sight (eyes) Allâh has set a seal. And they are the heedless! (108) No doubt, in the Hereafter, they will be the losers. (109)

Quran 17:10

وَأَنَّ ٱلَّذِينَ لَا يُؤْمِنُونَ بِٱلْآخِرَةِ أَعْتَدْنَا لَهُمْ عَذَابًا أَلِيمًا

And that those who believe not in the Hereafter, for them We have prepared a painful torment (Hell). (10)

Quran 17:45-51

وَإِذَا قَرَأْتَ ٱلْقُرْءَانَ جَعَلْنَا بَيْنَكَ وَبَيْنَ ٱلَّذِينَ لَا يُؤْمِنُونَ بِٱلْآخِرَةِ حِجَابًا مَّسْتُورًا (٤٥) وَجَعَلْنَا عَلَىٰ قُلُوبِهِمْ أَكِنَّةً أَن يَفْقَهُوهُ وَفِىٓ ءَاذَانِهِمْ وَقْرًا ۚ وَإِذَا ذَكَرْتَ رَبَّكَ فِى ٱلْقُرْءَانِ وَحْدَهُۥ وَلَّوْا۟ عَلَىٰٓ أَدْبَـٰرِهِمْ نُفُورًا (٤٦) نَّحْنُ أَعْلَمُ بِمَا يَسْتَمِعُونَ بِهِۦٓ إِذْ يَسْتَمِعُونَ إِلَيْكَ وَإِذْ هُمْ نَجْوَىٰٓ إِذْ يَقُولُ ٱلظَّـٰلِمُونَ إِن تَتَّبِعُونَ إِلَّا رَجُلًا مَّسْحُورًا (٤٧) ٱنظُرْ كَيْفَ ضَرَبُوا۟ لَكَ ٱلْأَمْثَالَ فَضَلُّوا۟ فَلَا يَسْتَطِيعُونَ سَبِيلًا (٤٨) وَقَالُوٓا۟ أَءِذَا كُنَّا عِظَـٰمًا وَرُفَـٰتًا أَءِنَّا لَمَبْعُوثُونَ خَلْقًا جَدِيدًا (٤٩) ۞ قُلْ كُونُوا۟ حِجَارَةً أَوْ حَدِيدًا (٥٠) أَوْ خَلْقًا مِّمَّا يَكْبُرُ فِى صُدُورِكُمْ ۚ فَسَيَقُولُونَ مَن يُعِيدُنَا ۖ قُلِ ٱلَّذِى فَطَرَكُمْ أَوَّلَ مَرَّةٍ ۚ فَسَيُنْغِضُونَ إِلَيْكَ رُءُوسَهُمْ وَيَقُولُونَ مَتَىٰ هُوَ ۖ قُلْ عَسَىٰٓ أَن يَكُونَ قَرِيبًا (٥١)

And when you (Muhammad) recite the Qur'ân, We put between you and those who believe not in the Hereafter, an invisible veil (or screen their hearts, so they hear or understand it not). (45) And We have put coverings over their hearts lest, they should understand it (the Qur'ân), and in their ears deafness. And when you make mention of your Lord Alone [Lâ ilâha ill-allâh (none has the right to be worshipped but Allâh) Islâmic Monotheism] in the

Qur'ân, they turn on their backs, fleeing in extreme disliken. (46) We know best of what they listen to, when they listen to you. And when they take secret counsel, then the Zâlimûn (polytheists and wrong-doers) say: "You follow none but a bewitched man." (47) See what examples they have put forward for you. So they have gone astray, and never can they find a way. (48) And they say: "When we are bones and fragments (destroyed), should we really be resurrected (to be) a new creation?" (49) Say "Be you stones or iron," (50) "Or some created thing that is yet greater (or harder) in your breasts (thoughts to be resurrected, even then you shall be resurrected)" Then, they will say: "Who shall bring us back (to life)?" Say: "He Who created you first!" Then, they will shake their heads at you and say: "When will that be ?" Say: "Perhaps it is near!" (51)

Quran 17:90-99

وَقَالُوا۟ لَن نُّؤْمِنَ لَكَ حَتَّىٰ تَفْجُرَ لَنَا مِنَ ٱلْأَرْضِ يَنۢبُوعًا (٩٠) أَوْ تَكُونَ لَكَ جَنَّةٌ مِّن نَّخِيلٍ وَعِنَبٍ فَتُفَجِّرَ ٱلْأَنْهَٰرَ خِلَٰلَهَا تَفْجِيرًا (٩١) أَوْ تُسْقِطَ ٱلسَّمَآءَ كَمَا زَعَمْتَ عَلَيْنَا كِسَفًا أَوْ تَأْتِىَ بِٱللَّهِ وَٱلْمَلَٰٓئِكَةِ قَبِيلًا (٩٢) أَوْ يَكُونَ لَكَ بَيْتٌ مِّن زُخْرُفٍ أَوْ تَرْقَىٰ فِى ٱلسَّمَآءِ وَلَن نُّؤْمِنَ لِرُقِيِّكَ حَتَّىٰ تُنَزِّلَ عَلَيْنَا كِتَٰبًا نَّقْرَؤُهُۥ ۗ قُلْ سُبْحَانَ رَبِّى هَلْ كُنتُ إِلَّا بَشَرًا رَّسُولًا (٩٣) وَمَا مَنَعَ ٱلنَّاسَ أَن يُؤْمِنُوٓا۟ إِذْ جَآءَهُمُ ٱلْهُدَىٰٓ إِلَّآ أَن قَالُوٓا۟ أَبَعَثَ ٱللَّهُ بَشَرًا رَّسُولًا (٩٤) قُل لَّوْ كَانَ فِى ٱلْأَرْضِ مَلَٰٓئِكَةٌ يَمْشُونَ مُطْمَئِنِّينَ لَنَزَّلْنَا عَلَيْهِم مِّنَ ٱلسَّمَآءِ مَلَكًا رَّسُولًا (٩٥) قُلْ كَفَىٰ بِٱللَّهِ شَهِيدًۢا بَيْنِى وَبَيْنَكُمْ ۚ إِنَّهُۥ كَانَ بِعِبَادِهِۦ خَبِيرًۢا بَصِيرًا (٩٦) وَمَن يَهْدِ ٱللَّهُ فَهُوَ ٱلْمُهْتَدِ ۖ وَمَن يُضْلِلْ فَلَن تَجِدَ لَهُمْ أَوْلِيَآءَ مِن دُونِهِۦ ۖ وَنَحْشُرُهُمْ يَوْمَ ٱلْقِيَٰمَةِ عَلَىٰ وُجُوهِهِمْ عُمْيًا وَبُكْمًا وَصُمًّا ۖ مَّأْوَىٰهُمْ جَهَنَّمُ ۖ كُلَّمَا خَبَتْ زِدْنَٰهُمْ سَعِيرًا (٩٧) ذَٰلِكَ جَزَآؤُهُم بِأَنَّهُمْ

كَفَرُواْ بِـَٔايَـٰتِنَا وَقَالُوٓاْ أَءِذَا كُنَّا عِظَـٰمًا وَرُفَـٰتًا أَءِنَّا لَمَبْعُوثُونَ خَلْقًا جَدِيدًا (٩٨) ۞ أَوَلَمْ يَرَوْاْ أَنَّ ٱللَّهَ ٱلَّذِى خَلَقَ ٱلسَّمَـٰوَٰتِ وَٱلْأَرْضَ قَادِرٌ عَلَىٰٓ أَن يَخْلُقَ مِثْلَهُمْ وَجَعَلَ لَهُمْ أَجَلًا لَّا رَيْبَ فِيهِ فَأَبَى ٱلظَّـٰلِمُونَ إِلَّا كُفُورًا (٩٩)

And they say: "We shall not believe in you (O Muhammad), until you cause a spring to gush forth from the earth for us; (90) "Or you have a garden of date-palms and grapes, and cause rivers to gush forth in their midst abundantly; (91) "Or you cause the heaven to fall upon us in pieces, as you have pretended, or you bring Allâh and the angels before (us) face to face; (92) "Or you have a house of Zukhruf (like silver and pure gold), or you ascend up into the sky, and even then we will put no faith in your ascension until you bring down for us a Book that we would read." Say (O Muhammad): "Glorified (and Exalted) is my Lord [(Allâh) above all that evil they (polytheists) associate with Him]! Am I anything but a man, sent as a Messenger?" (93) And nothing prevented men from believing when the guidance came to them, except that they said: "Has Allâh sent a man as (His) Messenger?" (94) Say: "If there were on the earth, angels walking about in peace and security, We should certainly have sent down for them from the heaven an angel as a Messenger." (95) Say: "Sufficient is Allâh for a witness between me and you. Verily! He is Ever the All-Knower, the All-Seer of His slaves." (96) And he whom Allâh guides, he is led aright; but he whom He sends astray for such you will find no Auliyâ' (helpers and protectors), besides Him, and We shall gather them together on the Day of Resurrection on their faces, blind, dumb and deaf, their abode will be Hell; whenever it abates, We shall increase for them the fierceness of the Fire (97) That is their recompense, because they denied Our Ayât (proofs, evidences, verses, lessons, signs, revelations, etc.) and said: "When we are bones and fragments, shall we really be raised up as a new creation?" (98) See they not that Allâh, Who created the heavens and the earth, is Able to create the like of them. And He has decreed for them an appointed term, whereof there is not doubt. But the Zâlimûn (polytheists and wrong-doers) refuse (the truth the Message of Islâmic Monotheism, and accept nothing) but disbelief. (99)

Quran 18:55-57

وَمَا مَنَعَ ٱلنَّاسَ أَن يُؤْمِنُوٓا۟ إِذْ جَآءَهُمُ ٱلْهُدَىٰ وَيَسْتَغْفِرُوا۟ رَبَّهُمْ إِلَّآ أَن تَأْتِيَهُمْ سُنَّةُ ٱلْأَوَّلِينَ أَوْ يَأْتِيَهُمُ ٱلْعَذَابُ قُبُلًا (٥٥) وَمَا نُرْسِلُ ٱلْمُرْسَلِينَ إِلَّا مُبَشِّرِينَ وَمُنذِرِينَ وَيُجَـٰدِلُ ٱلَّذِينَ كَفَرُوا۟ بِٱلْبَـٰطِلِ لِيُدْحِضُوا۟ بِهِ ٱلْحَقَّ وَٱتَّخَذُوٓا۟ ءَايَـٰتِى وَمَآ أُنذِرُوا۟ هُزُوًا (٥٦) وَمَنْ أَظْلَمُ مِمَّن ذُكِّرَ بِـَٔايَـٰتِ رَبِّهِۦ فَأَعْرَضَ عَنْهَا وَنَسِىَ مَا قَدَّمَتْ يَدَاهُ إِنَّا جَعَلْنَا عَلَىٰ قُلُوبِهِمْ أَكِنَّةً أَن يَفْقَهُوهُ وَفِىٓ ءَاذَانِهِمْ وَقْرًا وَإِن تَدْعُهُمْ إِلَى ٱلْهُدَىٰ فَلَن يَهْتَدُوٓا۟ إِذًا أَبَدًا (٥٧)

And nothing prevents men from believing, (now) when the guidance (the Qur'ân) has come to them, and from asking Forgiveness of their Lord, except that the ways of the ancients be repeated with them (i.e. their destruction decreed by Allâh), or the torment be brought to them face to face? (55) And We send not the Messengers except as givers of glad tidings and warners. But those who disbelieve, dispute with false argument, in order to refute the truth thereby. And they treat My Ayât (proofs, evidences, verses, lessons, signs, revelations, etc.), and that with which they are warned, as jest and mockery! (56) And who does more wrong than he who is reminded of the Ayât (proofs, evidences, verses, lessons, signs, revelations, etc.) of his Lord, but turns away from them forgetting what (deeds) his hands have sent forth. Truly, We have set veils over their hearts lest they should understand this (the Qur'ân), and in their ears, deafness. And if you call them to guidance, even then they will never be guided. (57)

Quran 18:101-106

ٱلَّذِينَ كَانَتْ أَعْيُنُهُمْ فِى غِطَآءٍ عَن ذِكْرِى وَكَانُواْ لَا يَسْتَطِيعُونَ سَمْعًا (١٠١) أَفَحَسِبَ ٱلَّذِينَ كَفَرُوٓاْ أَن يَتَّخِذُواْ عِبَادِى مِن دُونِىٓ أَوْلِيَآءَ إِنَّآ أَعْتَدْنَا جَهَنَّمَ لِلْكَـٰفِرِينَ نُزُلًا (١٠٢) قُلْ هَلْ نُنَبِّئُكُم بِٱلْأَخْسَرِينَ أَعْمَـٰلًا (١٠٣) ٱلَّذِينَ ضَلَّ سَعْيُهُمْ فِى ٱلْحَيَوٰةِ ٱلدُّنْيَا وَهُمْ يَحْسَبُونَ أَنَّهُمْ يُحْسِنُونَ صُنْعًا (١٠٤) أُوْلَـٰٓئِكَ ٱلَّذِينَ كَفَرُواْ بِـَٔايَـٰتِ رَبِّهِمْ وَلِقَآئِهِۦ فَحَبِطَتْ أَعْمَـٰلُهُمْ فَلَا نُقِيمُ لَهُمْ يَوْمَ ٱلْقِيَـٰمَةِ وَزْنًا (١٠٥) ذَٰلِكَ جَزَآؤُهُمْ جَهَنَّمُ بِمَا كَفَرُواْ وَٱتَّخَذُوٓاْ ءَايَـٰتِى وَرُسُلِى هُزُوًا (١٠٦)

(To) those whose eyes had been under a covering from My Reminder (this Qur'ân), and who could not bear to hear (it). (101) Do then those who disbelieved think that they can take My slaves [i.e., the angels, Allâh's Messengers, 'Īsā (Jesus), son of Maryam (Mary)] as Auliyâ' (lords, gods, protectors) besides Me? Verily, We have prepared Hell as an entertainment for the disbelievers (in the Oneness of Allâh, Islâmic Monotheism). (102) Say (O Muhammad): "Shall We tell you the greatest losers in respect of (their) deeds? (103) "Those whose efforts have been wasted in this life while they thought that they were acquiring good by their deeds! (104) "They are those who deny the Ayât (proofs, evidences, verses, lessons, signs, revelations, etc.) of their Lord and the Meeting with Him (in the Hereafter). So their works are in vain, and on the Day of Resurrection, We shall assign not weight for them. (105) "That shall be their recompense, Hell; because they disbelieved and took My Ayât (proofs, evidences, verses, lessons, signs, revelations, etc.) and My Messengers by way of jest and mockery. (106)

Quran 19:59

فَخَلَفَ مِنْ بَعْدِهِمْ خَلْفٌ أَضَاعُواْ ٱلصَّلَوٰةَ وَٱتَّبَعُواْ ٱلشَّهَوَٰتِ فَسَوْفَ يَلْقَوْنَ غَيًّا

Then, there has succeeded them a posterity who have given up As-Salât (the prayers) [i.e. made their Salât (prayers) to be lost, either by not offering them or by not offering them perfectly or by not offering them in their proper fixed times] and have followed lusts. So they will be thrown in Hell. (59)

Quran 19:73-83

وَإِذَا تُتْلَىٰ عَلَيْهِمْ ءَايَٰتُنَا بَيِّنَٰتٍ قَالَ ٱلَّذِينَ كَفَرُواْ لِلَّذِينَ ءَامَنُواْ أَىُّ ٱلْفَرِيقَيْنِ خَيْرٌ مَّقَامًا وَأَحْسَنُ نَدِيًّا (٧٣) وَكَمْ أَهْلَكْنَا قَبْلَهُم مِّن قَرْنٍ هُمْ أَحْسَنُ أَثَٰثًا وَرِءْيًا (٧٤) قُلْ مَن كَانَ فِى ٱلضَّلَٰلَةِ فَلْيَمْدُدْ لَهُ ٱلرَّحْمَٰنُ مَدًّا حَتَّىٰٓ إِذَا رَأَوْاْ مَا يُوعَدُونَ إِمَّا ٱلْعَذَابَ وَإِمَّا ٱلسَّاعَةَ فَسَيَعْلَمُونَ مَنْ هُوَ شَرٌّ مَّكَانًا وَأَضْعَفُ جُندًا (٧٥) وَيَزِيدُ ٱللَّهُ ٱلَّذِينَ ٱهْتَدَوْاْ هُدًى وَٱلْبَٰقِيَٰتُ ٱلصَّٰلِحَٰتُ خَيْرٌ عِندَ

رَبِّكَ ثَوَابًا وَخَيْرٌ مَّرَدًّا (٧٦) أَفَرَءَيْتَ ٱلَّذِى كَفَرَ بِـَٔايَـٰتِنَا وَقَالَ لَأُوتَيَنَّ مَالًا وَوَلَدًا (٧٧) أَطَّلَعَ ٱلْغَيْبَ أَمِ ٱتَّخَذَ عِندَ ٱلرَّحْمَـٰنِ عَهْدًا (٧٨) كَلَّا سَنَكْتُبُ مَا يَقُولُ وَنَمُدُّ لَهُۥ مِنَ ٱلْعَذَابِ مَدًّا (٧٩) وَنَرِثُهُۥ مَا يَقُولُ وَيَأْتِينَا فَرْدًا (٨٠) وَٱتَّخَذُواْ مِن دُونِ ٱللَّهِ ءَالِهَةً لِّيَكُونُواْ لَهُمْ عِزًّا (٨١) كَلَّا سَيَكْفُرُونَ بِعِبَادَتِهِمْ وَيَكُونُونَ عَلَيْهِمْ ضِدًّا (٨٢) أَلَمْ تَرَ أَنَّا أَرْسَلْنَا ٱلشَّيَـٰطِينَ عَلَى ٱلْكَـٰفِرِينَ تَؤُزُّهُمْ أَزًّا (٨٣)

And when Our Clear Verses are recited to them, those who disbelieve say to those who believe: "Which of the two groups (i.e. believers or disbelievers) is best in (point of) position and as regards station (place of council for consultation)." (73) And how many a generation (past nations) have We destroyed before them, who were better in wealth, goods and outward appearance? (74) Say whoever is in error, the Most Gracious (Allâh) will extend (the rope) to him, until, when they see that which they were promised, either the torment or the Hour, they will come to know who is worst in position, and who is weaker in forces. (75) And Allâh increases in guidance those who walk aright. And the righteous good deeds that last, are better with your Lord, for reward and better for resort. (76) Have you seen him who disbelieved in Our Ayât (this Qur'ân and Muhammad) and said: "I shall certainly be given wealth and children [if I will be alive (again)]," (77) Has he known the unseen or has he taken a covenant from the Most Gracious (Allâh)? (78) Nay! We shall record what he says, and We shall increase his torment (in the Hell); (79) And We shall inherit from him (at his death) all that he talks of (i.e. wealth and children which We have bestowed upon him in this world), and he shall come to Us alone (80) And they have taken (for worship) âlihah (gods) besides Allâh, that they might give them honour, power and glory (and also protect them from Allâh's Punishment). (81) Nay, but they (the so-called gods) will deny their worship of them, and become opponents to them (on the Day of Resurrection). (82) See you not that We have sent the Shayâtin (devils) against the disbelievers to push them to do evil. (83)

Quran 20:16

فَلَا يَصُدَّنَّكَ عَنْهَا مَن لَّا يُؤْمِنُ بِهَا وَاتَّبَعَ هَوَىٰهُ فَتَرْدَىٰ

"Therefore, let not the one who believes not therein (i.e. in the Day of Resurrection, Reckoning, Paradise and Hell), but follows his own lusts, divert you therefrom, lest you perish." (16)

Quran 21:97-99

وَاقْتَرَبَ الْوَعْدُ الْحَقُّ فَإِذَا هِيَ شَاخِصَةٌ أَبْصَارُ الَّذِينَ كَفَرُوا يَٰوَيْلَنَا قَدْ كُنَّا فِي غَفْلَةٍ مِّنْ هَٰذَا بَلْ كُنَّا ظَٰلِمِينَ (٩٧) إِنَّكُمْ وَمَا تَعْبُدُونَ مِن دُونِ اللَّهِ حَصَبُ جَهَنَّمَ أَنتُمْ لَهَا وَارِدُونَ (٩٨) لَوْ كَانَ هَٰؤُلَاءِ ءَالِهَةً مَّا وَرَدُوهَا وَكُلٌّ فِيهَا خَٰلِدُونَ (٩٩)

And the true promise (Day of Resurrection) shall draw near (of fulfillment). Then (when mankind is resurrected from their graves), you shall see the eyes of the disbelievers fixedly staring in horror. (They will say): "Woe to us! We were indeed heedless of this; nay, but we were Zâlimûn (polytheists and wrong-doers)." (97)

Certainly! You (disbelievers) and that which you are worshipping now besides Allâh, are (but) fuel for Hell! (Surely), you will enter it. (98) Had these (idols) been âlihah (gods), they would not have entered there (Hell), and all of them will abide therein. (99)

Quran 22:3-4

وَمِنَ ٱلنَّاسِ مَن يُجَٰدِلُ فِى ٱللَّهِ بِغَيْرِ عِلْمٍ وَيَتَّبِعُ كُلَّ شَيْطَٰنٍ مَّرِيدٍ (٣) كُتِبَ عَلَيْهِ أَنَّهُۥ مَن تَوَلَّاهُ فَأَنَّهُۥ يُضِلُّهُۥ وَيَهْدِيهِ إِلَىٰ عَذَابِ ٱلسَّعِيرِ (٤)

And among mankind is he who disputes concerning Allâh, without knowledge, and follows every rebellious (disobedient to Allâh) Shaitân (devil) (devoid of every kind of good). (3) For him (the devil) it is decreed that whosoever follows him, he will mislead him, and will drive him to the torment of the Fire. (4)

Quran 22:8-13

وَمِنَ ٱلنَّاسِ مَن يُجَٰدِلُ فِى ٱللَّهِ بِغَيْرِ عِلْمٍ وَلَا هُدًى وَلَا كِتَٰبٍ مُّنِيرٍ (٨) ثَانِىَ عِطْفِهِۦ لِيُضِلَّ عَن سَبِيلِ ٱللَّهِ ۖ لَهُۥ فِى ٱلدُّنْيَا خِزْىٌ ۖ وَنُذِيقُهُۥ يَوْمَ ٱلْقِيَٰمَةِ عَذَابَ ٱلْحَرِيقِ (٩) ذَٰلِكَ بِمَا قَدَّمَتْ يَدَاكَ وَأَنَّ ٱللَّهَ لَيْسَ بِظَلَّٰمٍ لِّلْعَبِيدِ (١٠) وَمِنَ ٱلنَّاسِ مَن يَعْبُدُ ٱللَّهَ عَلَىٰ حَرْفٍ ۖ فَإِنْ أَصَابَهُۥ خَيْرٌ ٱطْمَأَنَّ بِهِۦ ۖ وَإِنْ أَصَابَتْهُ فِتْنَةٌ ٱنقَلَبَ عَلَىٰ وَجْهِهِۦ خَسِرَ ٱلدُّنْيَا وَٱلْءَاخِرَةَ ۚ ذَٰلِكَ هُوَ ٱلْخُسْرَانُ ٱلْمُبِينُ (١١) يَدْعُواْ مِن دُونِ ٱللَّهِ مَا لَا يَضُرُّهُۥ وَمَا لَا يَنفَعُهُۥ ۚ ذَٰلِكَ هُوَ ٱلضَّلَٰلُ ٱلْبَعِيدُ (١٢) يَدْعُواْ لَمَن ضَرُّهُۥٓ أَقْرَبُ مِن نَّفْعِهِۦ ۚ لَبِئْسَ ٱلْمَوْلَىٰ وَلَبِئْسَ ٱلْعَشِيرُ (١٣)

And among men is he who disputes about Allâh, without knowledge or guidance, or a Book giving light (from Allâh), (8) Bending his neck in pride (far astray from the

Path of Allâh), and leading (others) too (far) astray from the Path of Allâh. For him there is disgrace in this worldly life, and on the Day of Resurrection We shall make him taste the torment of burning (Fire). (9) That is because of what your hands have sent forth, and verily, Allâh is not unjust to (His) slaves. (10) And among mankind is he who worships Allâh as it were, upon the edge (i.e. in doubt); if good befalls him, he is content therewith; but if a trial befalls him, he turns back on his face (i.e. reverts back to disbelief after embracing Islâm). He loses both this world and the Hereafter. That is the evident loss. (11) He calls besides Allâh unto that which hurts him not, nor profits him. That is a straying far away. (12) He calls unto him whose harm is nearer than his profit; certainly, an evil Maula (patron) and certainly an evil friend! (13)

Quran 22:55-57

وَلَا يَزَالُ ٱلَّذِينَ كَفَرُوا۟ فِى مِرْيَةٍ مِّنْهُ حَتَّىٰ تَأْتِيَهُمُ ٱلسَّاعَةُ بَغْتَةً أَوْ يَأْتِيَهُمْ عَذَابُ يَوْمٍ عَقِيمٍ (٥٥) ٱلْمُلْكُ يَوْمَئِذٍ لِّلَّهِ يَحْكُمُ بَيْنَهُمْ فَٱلَّذِينَ ءَامَنُوا۟ وَعَمِلُوا۟ ٱلصَّٰلِحَٰتِ فِى جَنَّٰتِ ٱلنَّعِيمِ (٥٦) وَٱلَّذِينَ كَفَرُوا۟ وَكَذَّبُوا۟ بِـَٔايَٰتِنَا فَأُو۟لَٰٓئِكَ لَهُمْ عَذَابٌ مُّهِينٌ (٥٧)

And those who disbelieved will not cease to be in doubt about it (this Qur'ân) until the Hour comes suddenly upon them, or there comes to them the torment of the Day after which there will be no night (i.e. the Day of Resurrection). (55) The sovereignty on that Day will be that of Allâh (the one Who has no partners). He will judge between them. So those who believed (in the Oneness of Allâh Islâmic Monotheism) and did righteous good deeds will be in Gardens of delight (Paradise). (56) And those who disbelieved and belied Our Verses (of this Qur'ân), for them will be a humiliating torment (in Hell). (57)

Quran 22:72-73

وَإِذَا تُتْلَىٰ عَلَيْهِمْ ءَايَـٰتُنَا بَيِّنَـٰتٍ تَعْرِفُ فِى وُجُوهِ ٱلَّذِينَ كَفَرُواْ ٱلْمُنكَرَ ۖ يَكَادُونَ يَسْطُونَ بِٱلَّذِينَ يَتْلُونَ عَلَيْهِمْ ءَايَـٰتِنَا ۗ قُلْ أَفَأُنَبِّئُكُم بِشَرٍّ مِّن ذَٰلِكُمُ ٱلنَّارُ وَعَدَهَا ٱللَّهُ ٱلَّذِينَ كَفَرُواْ ۖ وَبِئْسَ ٱلْمَصِيرُ (٧٢) يَـٰٓأَيُّهَا ٱلنَّاسُ ضُرِبَ مَثَلٌ فَٱسْتَمِعُواْ لَهُ ۚ إِنَّ ٱلَّذِينَ تَدْعُونَ مِن دُونِ ٱللَّهِ لَن يَخْلُقُواْ ذُبَابًا وَلَوِ ٱجْتَمَعُواْ لَهُ ۖ وَإِن يَسْلُبْهُمُ ٱلذُّبَابُ شَيْـًٔا لَّا يَسْتَنقِذُوهُ مِنْهُ ۚ ضَعُفَ ٱلطَّالِبُ وَٱلْمَطْلُوبُ (٧٣)

And when Our Clear Verses are recited to them, you will notice a denial on the faces of the disbelievers! They are nearly ready to attack with violence those who recite Our Verses to them. Say: "Shall I tell you of something worse than that? The Fire (of Hell) which Allâh has promised to those who disbelieved, and worst indeed is that destination!" (72) O mankind! A similitude has been coined, so listen to it (carefully): Verily! those on whom you call besides Allâh, cannot create (even) a fly, even though they combine together for the purpose. And if the fly snatches away a thing from them, they will have no power to release it from the fly. So weak are (both) the seeker and the sought. (73)

Quran 23:33-38

وَقَالَ ٱلْمَلَأُ مِن قَوْمِهِ ٱلَّذِينَ كَفَرُواْ وَكَذَّبُواْ بِلِقَآءِ ٱلْـَٔاخِرَةِ وَأَتْرَفْنَـٰهُمْ فِى ٱلْحَيَوٰةِ ٱلدُّنْيَا مَا هَـٰذَآ إِلَّا بَشَرٌ مِّثْلُكُمْ يَأْكُلُ مِمَّا تَأْكُلُونَ مِنْهُ وَيَشْرَبُ مِمَّا تَشْرَبُونَ (٣٣) وَلَئِنْ أَطَعْتُم بَشَرًا مِّثْلَكُمْ إِنَّكُمْ إِذًا لَّخَـٰسِرُونَ (٣٤) أَيَعِدُكُمْ أَنَّكُمْ إِذَا مِتُّمْ

وَكُنتُمْ تُرَابًا وَعِظَـٰمًا أَنَّكُم مُّخْرَجُونَ ﴿٣٥﴾ ۞ هَيْهَاتَ هَيْهَاتَ لِمَا تُوعَدُونَ ﴿٣٦﴾ إِنْ هِىَ إِلَّا حَيَاتُنَا ٱلدُّنْيَا نَمُوتُ وَنَحْيَا وَمَا نَحْنُ بِمَبْعُوثِينَ ﴿٣٧﴾ إِنْ هُوَ إِلَّا رَجُلٌ ٱفْتَرَىٰ عَلَى ٱللَّهِ كَذِبًا وَمَا نَحْنُ لَهُۥ بِمُؤْمِنِينَ ﴿٣٨﴾

And the chiefs of his people, who disbelieved and denied the Meeting in the Hereafter, and whom We had given the luxuries and comforts of this life, said: "He is no more than a human being like you, he eats of that which you eat, and drinks of what you drink (33) "If you were to obey a human being like yourselves, then verily! You indeed would be losers. (34) "Does he promise you that when you have died and have become dust and bones, you shall come out alive (resurrected)? (35) "Far, very far is that which you are promised! (36) "There is nothing but our life of this world! We die and we live! And we are not going to be resurrected! (37) "He is only a man who has invented a lie against Allâh, and we are not going to believe in him." (38)

Quran 23:63-77

بَلْ قُلُوبُهُمْ فِى غَمْرَةٍ مِّنْ هَـٰذَا وَلَهُمْ أَعْمَـٰلٌ مِّن دُونِ ذَٰلِكَ هُمْ لَهَا عَـٰمِلُونَ ﴿٦٣﴾ حَتَّىٰٓ إِذَآ أَخَذْنَا مُتْرَفِيهِم بِٱلْعَذَابِ إِذَا هُمْ يَجْـَٔرُونَ ﴿٦٤﴾ لَا تَجْـَٔرُوا۟ ٱلْيَوْمَ ۖ إِنَّكُم مِّنَّا لَا تُنصَرُونَ ﴿٦٥﴾ قَدْ كَانَتْ ءَايَـٰتِى تُتْلَىٰ عَلَيْكُمْ فَكُنتُمْ عَلَىٰٓ أَعْقَـٰبِكُمْ تَنكِصُونَ ﴿٦٦﴾ مُسْتَكْبِرِينَ بِهِۦ سَـٰمِرًا تَهْجُرُونَ ﴿٦٧﴾ أَفَلَمْ يَدَّبَّرُوا۟ ٱلْقَوْلَ أَمْ جَآءَهُم مَّا لَمْ يَأْتِ ءَابَآءَهُمُ ٱلْأَوَّلِينَ ﴿٦٨﴾ أَمْ لَمْ يَعْرِفُوا۟ رَسُولَهُمْ فَهُمْ لَهُۥ مُنكِرُونَ ﴿٦٩﴾ أَمْ يَقُولُونَ بِهِۦ جِنَّةٌ ۚ بَلْ جَآءَهُم بِٱلْحَقِّ وَأَكْثَرُهُمْ لِلْحَقِّ كَـٰرِهُونَ ﴿٧٠﴾ وَلَوِ ٱتَّبَعَ ٱلْحَقُّ أَهْوَآءَهُمْ لَفَسَدَتِ ٱلسَّمَـٰوَٰتُ وَٱلْأَرْضُ وَمَن فِيهِنَّ ۚ بَلْ أَتَيْنَـٰهُم بِذِكْرِهِمْ فَهُمْ عَن ذِكْرِهِم مُّعْرِضُونَ ﴿٧١﴾ أَمْ تَسْـَٔلُهُمْ خَرْجًا فَخَرَاجُ رَبِّكَ خَيْرٌ ۖ وَهُوَ خَيْرُ ٱلرَّٰزِقِينَ ﴿٧٢﴾ وَإِنَّكَ لَتَدْعُوهُمْ إِلَىٰ

صِرَٰطٍ مُّسْتَقِيمٍ (٧٣) وَإِنَّ ٱلَّذِينَ لَا يُؤْمِنُونَ بِٱلْـَٔاخِرَةِ عَنِ ٱلصِّرَٰطِ لَنَٰكِبُونَ (٧٤) ۞ وَلَوْ رَحِمْنَٰهُمْ وَكَشَفْنَا مَا بِهِم مِّن ضُرٍّ لَّلَجُّوا۟ فِى طُغْيَٰنِهِمْ يَعْمَهُونَ (٧٥) وَلَقَدْ أَخَذْنَٰهُم بِٱلْعَذَابِ فَمَا ٱسْتَكَانُوا۟ لِرَبِّهِمْ وَمَا يَتَضَرَّعُونَ (٧٦) حَتَّىٰٓ إِذَا فَتَحْنَا عَلَيْهِم بَابًا ذَا عَذَابٍ شَدِيدٍ إِذَا هُمْ فِيهِ مُبْلِسُونَ (٧٧)

Nay, but their hearts are covered from (understanding) this (the Qur'ân), and they have other (evil) deeds, besides, which they are doing. (63) Until, when We seize those of them who lead a luxurious life with punishment, behold! they make humble invocation with a loud voice. (64) Invoke not loudly this day! Certainly, you shall not be helped by Us. (65) Indeed My Verses used to be recited to you, but you used to turn back on your heels (denying them, and refusing with hatred to listen to them). (66) In pride (they Quraish pagans and polytheists of Makkah used to feel proud that they are the dwellers of Makkah sanctuary Haram), talking evil about it (the Qur'ân) by night. (67) Have they not pondered over the Word (of Allâh, i.e. what is sent down to the Prophet), or has there come to them what had not come to their fathers of old? (68) Or is it that they did not recognize their Messenger (Muhammad) so they deny him? (69) Or say they: "There is madness in him?" Nay, but he brought them the truth [i.e. "Tauhîd: Worshipping Allâh Alone in all aspects The Qur'ân and the religion of Islâm,"] but most of them (the disbelievers) are averse to the truth. (70) And if the truth had been in accordance with their desires, verily, the heavens and the earth, and whosoever is therein would have been corrupted! Nay, We have brought them their reminder, but they turn away from their reminder. (71) Or is it that you (O Muhammad) ask them for some wages? But the recompense of your Lord is better, and He is the Best of those who give sustenance. (72) And certainly, you (O Muhammad) call them to the Straight Path (true religion - Islâmic Monotheism). (73) And verily, those who believe not in the Hereafter are indeed deviating far astray from the Path (true religion - Islâmic Monotheism). (74) And though We had mercy on them and removed the distress which is on them, still they would obstinately persist in their transgression, wandering blindly. (75) And indeed We seized them with punishment, but they humbled not themselves to their Lord, nor did they invoke (Allâh) with submission to Him. (76) Until, when We open for them the gate of severe punishment, then lo! they will be plunged into destruction with deep regrets, sorrows and in despair. (77)

Quran 23:103-110

وَمَنْ خَفَّتْ مَوَازِينُهُ فَأُوْلَٰٓئِكَ ٱلَّذِينَ خَسِرُوٓاْ أَنفُسَهُمْ فِى جَهَنَّمَ خَٰلِدُونَ (١٠٣) تَلْفَحُ وُجُوهَهُمُ ٱلنَّارُ وَهُمْ فِيهَا كَٰلِحُونَ (١٠٤) أَلَمْ تَكُنْ ءَايَٰتِى تُتْلَىٰ عَلَيْكُمْ فَكُنتُم بِهَا تُكَذِّبُونَ (١٠٥) قَالُوا۟ رَبَّنَا غَلَبَتْ عَلَيْنَا شِقْوَتُنَا وَكُنَّا قَوْمًا ضَآلِّينَ (١٠٦) رَبَّنَآ أَخْرِجْنَا مِنْهَا فَإِنْ عُدْنَا فَإِنَّا ظَٰلِمُونَ (١٠٧) قَالَ ٱخْسَـُٔوا۟ فِيهَا وَلَا تُكَلِّمُونِ (١٠٨) إِنَّهُۥ كَانَ فَرِيقٌ مِّنْ عِبَادِى يَقُولُونَ رَبَّنَآ ءَامَنَّا فَٱغْفِرْ لَنَا وَٱرْحَمْنَا وَأَنتَ خَيْرُ ٱلرَّٰحِمِينَ (١٠٩) فَٱتَّخَذْتُمُوهُمْ سِخْرِيًّا حَتَّىٰٓ أَنسَوْكُمْ ذِكْرِى وَكُنتُم مِّنْهُمْ تَضْحَكُونَ (١١٠)

And those whose scales (of good deeds) are light, they are those who lose their ownselves, in Hell will they abide. (103) The Fire will burn their faces, and therein they will grin, with displaced lips (disfigured). (104) "Were not My Verses (this Qur'ân) recited to you, and then you used to deny them?" (105) They will say: "Our Lord! Our wretchedness overcame us, and we were (an) erring people. (106) "Our Lord! Bring us out of this; if ever we return (to evil), then indeed we shall be Zâlimûn: (polytheists, oppressors, unjust, and wrong-doers)." (107) He (Allâh) will say: "Remain you in it with ignominy! And speak you not to Me!" (108) Verily! there was a party of My slaves, who used to say: "Our Lord! We believe, so forgive us, and have mercy on us, for You are the Best of all who show mercy!" (109) But you took them for a laughingstock, so much so that they made you forget My Remembrance while you used to laugh at them! (110)

Quran 23:117

وَمَن يَدْعُ مَعَ ٱللَّهِ إِلَٰهًا ءَاخَرَ لَا بُرْهَٰنَ لَهُۥ بِهِۦ فَإِنَّمَا حِسَابُهُۥ عِندَ رَبِّهِۦٓ إِنَّهُۥ لَا يُفْلِحُ ٱلْكَٰفِرُونَ

And whoever invokes (or worships), besides Allâh, any other ilâh (god), of whom he has no proof, then his reckoning is only with his Lord. Surely! Al-Kâfirûn (the disbelievers in Allâh and in the Oneness of Allâh, polytheists, pagans, idolaters) will not be successful (117)

Quran 24:39-40

وَٱلَّذِينَ كَفَرُوٓا۟ أَعْمَٰلُهُمْ كَسَرَابٍۭ بِقِيعَةٍ يَحْسَبُهُ ٱلظَّمْـَٔانُ مَآءً حَتَّىٰٓ إِذَا جَآءَهُۥ لَمْ يَجِدْهُ شَيْـًٔا وَوَجَدَ ٱللَّهَ عِندَهُۥ فَوَفَّىٰهُ حِسَابَهُۥ ۗ وَٱللَّهُ سَرِيعُ ٱلْحِسَابِ (٣٩) أَوْ كَظُلُمَٰتٍ فِى بَحْرٍ لُّجِّىٍّ يَغْشَىٰهُ مَوْجٌ مِّن فَوْقِهِۦ مَوْجٌ مِّن فَوْقِهِۦ سَحَابٌ ۚ ظُلُمَٰتٌۢ بَعْضُهَا فَوْقَ بَعْضٍ إِذَآ أَخْرَجَ يَدَهُۥ لَمْ يَكَدْ يَرَىٰهَا ۗ وَمَن لَّمْ يَجْعَلِ ٱللَّهُ لَهُۥ نُورًا فَمَا لَهُۥ مِن نُّورٍ (٤٠)

As for those who disbelieve, their deeds are like a mirage in a desert. The thirsty one thinks it to be water, until he comes up to it, he finds it to be nothing, but he finds Allâh with him, Who will pay him his due (Hell). And Allâh is Swift in taking account. (39) Or [the state of a disbeliever] is like the darkness in a vast deep sea, overwhelmed with waves topped by waves, topped by dark clouds, (layers of) darkness upon darkness: if a man stretches out his hand, he can hardly see it! And he for whom Allâh has not appointed light, for him there is no light. (40)

Quran 24:47-50

وَيَقُولُونَ ءَامَنَّا بِٱللَّهِ وَبِٱلرَّسُولِ وَأَطَعْنَا ثُمَّ يَتَوَلَّىٰ فَرِيقٌ مِّنْهُم مِّنۢ بَعْدِ ذَٰلِكَ ۚ وَمَآ أُو۟لَٰٓئِكَ بِٱلْمُؤْمِنِينَ (٤٧) وَإِذَا دُعُوٓا۟ إِلَى ٱللَّهِ وَرَسُولِهِۦ لِيَحْكُمَ بَيْنَهُمْ إِذَا فَرِيقٌ مِّنْهُم مُّعْرِضُونَ (٤٨) وَإِن يَكُن لَّهُمُ ٱلْحَقُّ يَأْتُوٓا۟ إِلَيْهِ مُذْعِنِينَ (٤٩) أَفِى قُلُوبِهِم مَّرَضٌ أَمِ ٱرْتَابُوٓا۟ أَمْ يَخَافُونَ أَن يَحِيفَ ٱللَّهُ عَلَيْهِمْ وَرَسُولُهُۥ ۚ بَلْ أُو۟لَٰٓئِكَ هُمُ ٱلظَّٰلِمُونَ (٥٠)

They (hypocrites) say: "We have believed in Allâh and in the Messenger (Muhammad), and we obey," then a party of them turn away thereafter, such are not believers. (47) And when they are called to Allâh (i.e. His Words, the Qur'ân) and His Messenger, to judge between them, lo! a party of them refuse (to come) and turn away. (48) But if the truth is on their sides, they come to him willingly with submission. (49) Is there a disease in their hearts? Or do they doubt or fear lest Allâh and His Messenger should wrong them in judgement. Nay, it is they themselves who are the Zâlimûn (polytheists, hypocrites and wrong-doers). (50)

Quran 25:4-9

وَقَالَ ٱلَّذِينَ كَفَرُوٓا۟ إِنْ هَـٰذَآ إِلَّآ إِفْكٌ ٱفْتَرَىٰهُ وَأَعَانَهُۥ عَلَيْهِ قَوْمٌ ءَاخَرُونَۖ فَقَدْ جَآءُو ظُلْمًا وَزُورًا (٤) وَقَالُوٓا۟ أَسَـٰطِيرُ ٱلْأَوَّلِينَ ٱكْتَتَبَهَا فَهِىَ تُمْلَىٰ عَلَيْهِ بُكْرَةً وَأَصِيلًا (٥) قُلْ أَنزَلَهُ ٱلَّذِى يَعْلَمُ ٱلسِّرَّ فِى ٱلسَّمَـٰوَٰتِ وَٱلْأَرْضِۚ إِنَّهُۥ كَانَ غَفُورًا رَّحِيمًا (٦) وَقَالُوا۟ مَالِ هَـٰذَا ٱلرَّسُولِ يَأْكُلُ ٱلطَّعَامَ وَيَمْشِى فِى ٱلْأَسْوَاقِۙ لَوْلَآ أُنزِلَ إِلَيْهِ مَلَكٌ فَيَكُونَ مَعَهُۥ نَذِيرًا (٧) أَوْ يُلْقَىٰٓ إِلَيْهِ كَنزٌ أَوْ تَكُونُ لَهُۥ جَنَّةٌ يَأْكُلُ مِنْهَاۚ وَقَالَ ٱلظَّـٰلِمُونَ إِن تَتَّبِعُونَ إِلَّا رَجُلًا مَّسْحُورًا (٨) ٱنظُرْ كَيْفَ ضَرَبُوا۟ لَكَ ٱلْأَمْثَـٰلَ فَضَلُّوا۟ فَلَا يَسْتَطِيعُونَ سَبِيلًا (٩)

Those who disbelieve say: "This (the Qurân) is nothing but a lie that he (Muhammad) has invented, and others have helped him at it, in fact they have produced an unjust wrong (thing) and a lie." (4) And they say: "Tales of the ancients, which he has written down, and they are dictated to him morning and afternoon." (5) Say: "It (this Qur'ân) has been sent down by Him (Allâh) (the Real Lord of the heavens and earth) Who knows the secret of the heavens and the earth. Truly, He is Oft-Forgiving, Most Merciful." (6) And they say: "Why does this Messenger eat food, and walk about in the markets (as we). Why is not an angel sent down to him to be a warner with him? (7) "Or (why) has not a treasure been granted to him, or why has he not a garden whereof he may eat?" And the Zâlimûn (polytheists and wrong-doers) say: "You follow none but a man bewitched." (8) See how they coin similitudes for you, so they have gone astray, and they cannot find a (Right) Path (9)

Quran 25:11

بَلْ كَذَّبُوا۟ بِٱلسَّاعَةِ ۖ وَأَعْتَدْنَا لِمَن كَذَّبَ بِٱلسَّاعَةِ سَعِيرًا

Nay, they deny the Hour (the Day of Resurrection), and for those who deny the Hour, We have prepared a flaming Fire (i.e. Hell). (11)

Quran 25:26-32

ٱلْمُلْكُ يَوْمَئِذٍ ٱلْحَقُّ لِلرَّحْمَٰنِ ۚ وَكَانَ يَوْمًا عَلَى ٱلْكَٰفِرِينَ عَسِيرًا (٢٦) وَيَوْمَ يَعَضُّ ٱلظَّالِمُ عَلَىٰ يَدَيْهِ يَقُولُ يَٰلَيْتَنِى ٱتَّخَذْتُ مَعَ ٱلرَّسُولِ سَبِيلًا (٢٧) يَٰوَيْلَتَىٰ لَيْتَنِى لَمْ أَتَّخِذْ فُلَانًا خَلِيلًا (٢٨) لَّقَدْ أَضَلَّنِى عَنِ ٱلذِّكْرِ بَعْدَ إِذْ جَآءَنِى ۗ وَكَانَ ٱلشَّيْطَٰنُ لِلْإِنسَٰنِ خَذُولًا (٢٩) وَقَالَ ٱلرَّسُولُ يَٰرَبِّ إِنَّ قَوْمِى ٱتَّخَذُوا۟ هَٰذَا ٱلْقُرْءَانَ مَهْجُورًا (٣٠) وَكَذَٰلِكَ جَعَلْنَا لِكُلِّ نَبِىٍّ عَدُوًّا مِّنَ ٱلْمُجْرِمِينَ ۗ وَكَفَىٰ بِرَبِّكَ هَادِيًا وَنَصِيرًا (٣١) وَقَالَ ٱلَّذِينَ كَفَرُوا۟ لَوْلَا نُزِّلَ عَلَيْهِ ٱلْقُرْءَانُ جُمْلَةً وَٰحِدَةً ۚ كَذَٰلِكَ لِنُثَبِّتَ بِهِۦ فُؤَادَكَ ۖ وَرَتَّلْنَٰهُ تَرْتِيلًا (٣٢)

The sovereignty on that Day will be the true (sovereignty), belonging to the Most Gracious (Allâh), and it will be a hard Day for the disbelievers (those who disbelieve in the Oneness of Allâh Islâmic Monotheism). (26) And (remember) the Day when the Zâlim (wrong-doer, oppressor, polytheist) will bite at his hands, he will say: "Oh! Would that I had taken a path with the

Messenger (Muhammad). (27) "Ah! Woe to me! Would that I had never taken so-and-so as a Khalil (an intimate friend)! (28) "He indeed led me astray from the Reminder (this Qur'ân) after it had come to me. And Shaitân (Satan) is to man ever a deserter in the hour of need." (29) And the Messenger (Muhammad) will say: "O my Lord! Verily, my people deserted this Qur'ân (neither listened to it, nor acted on its laws and teachings). (30) Thus have We made for every Prophet an enemy among the Mujrimûn (disbelievers, polytheists, criminals). But Sufficient is your Lord as a Guide and Helper. (31) And those who disbelieve say: "Why is not the Qur'ân revealed to him all at once?" Thus (it is sent down in parts), that We may strengthen your heart thereby. And We have revealed it to you gradually, in stages. (32)

Quran 25:55

وَيَعْبُدُونَ مِن دُونِ ٱللَّهِ مَا لَا يَنفَعُهُمْ وَلَا يَضُرُّهُمْۗ وَكَانَ ٱلْكَافِرُ عَلَىٰ رَبِّهِۦ ظَهِيرًا

And they (disbelievers, polytheists) worship besides Allâh, that which can neither profit them nor harm them, and the disbeliever is ever a helper (of the Satan) against his Lord. (55)

Quran 27:4-5

إِنَّ ٱلَّذِينَ لَا يُؤْمِنُونَ بِٱلْآخِرَةِ زَيَّنَّا لَهُمْ أَعْمَٰلَهُمْ فَهُمْ يَعْمَهُونَ (٤) أُوْلَٰٓئِكَ ٱلَّذِينَ لَهُمْ سُوٓءُ ٱلْعَذَابِ وَهُمْ فِى ٱلْآخِرَةِ هُمُ ٱلْأَخْسَرُونَ (٥)

Verily, those who believe not in the Hereafter, We have made their deeds fair-seeming to them, so that they wander about blindly (4) They are those for whom there will be an evil torment (in this world). And in the Hereafter they will be the greatest losers. (5)

Quran 27:67-73

وَقَالَ ٱلَّذِينَ كَفَرُوٓاْ أَءِذَا كُنَّا تُرَٰبًا وَءَابَآؤُنَآ أَئِنَّا لَمُخْرَجُونَ (٦٧) لَقَدْ وُعِدْنَا هَٰذَا نَحْنُ وَءَابَآؤُنَا مِن قَبْلُ إِنْ هَٰذَآ إِلَّآ أَسَٰطِيرُ ٱلْأَوَّلِينَ (٦٨) قُلْ سِيرُواْ فِى ٱلْأَرْضِ فَٱنظُرُواْ كَيْفَ كَانَ عَٰقِبَةُ ٱلْمُجْرِمِينَ (٦٩) وَلَا تَحْزَنْ عَلَيْهِمْ وَلَا تَكُن فِى ضَيْقٍ مِّمَّا يَمْكُرُونَ (٧٠) وَيَقُولُونَ مَتَىٰ هَٰذَا ٱلْوَعْدُ إِن كُنتُمْ صَٰدِقِينَ (٧١) قُلْ عَسَىٰٓ أَن يَكُونَ رَدِفَ لَكُم بَعْضُ ٱلَّذِى تَسْتَعْجِلُونَ (٧٢) وَإِنَّ رَبَّكَ لَذُو فَضْلٍ عَلَى ٱلنَّاسِ وَلَٰكِنَّ أَكْثَرَهُمْ لَا يَشْكُرُونَ (٧٣)

And those who disbelieve say: "When we have become dust — we and our fathers — shall we really be brought forth (again)? (67) "Indeed we were promised this, we and our forefathers before (us), Verily, these are nothing but tales of ancients." (68) Say to them "Travel in the land and see how has been the end of the Mujrimun (criminals, those who denied Allâh's Messengers and disobeyed Allâh)." (69) And grieve you not over them, nor be straitened (in distress) because of what they plot. (70) And they (the disbelievers in the Oneness of Allâh) say: "When (will) this promise (be fulfilled), if you are truthful?" (71) Say: "Perhaps that which you wish to hasten on, may be close behind you (72) "Verily, your Lord is full of Grace for mankind, yet most of them do not give thanks." (73)

Quran 28:48-50

فَلَمَّا جَآءَهُمُ ٱلْحَقُّ مِنْ عِندِنَا قَالُوا۟ لَوْلَآ أُوتِىَ مِثْلَ مَآ أُوتِىَ مُوسَىٰٓ أَوَلَمْ يَكْفُرُوا۟ بِمَآ أُوتِىَ مُوسَىٰ مِن قَبْلُ قَالُوا۟ سِحْرَانِ تَظَـٰهَرَا وَقَالُوٓا۟ إِنَّا بِكُلٍّ كَـٰفِرُونَ (٤٨) قُلْ فَأْتُوا۟ بِكِتَـٰبٍ مِّنْ عِندِ ٱللَّهِ هُوَ أَهْدَىٰ مِنْهُمَآ أَتَّبِعْهُ إِن كُنتُمْ صَـٰدِقِينَ (٤٩) فَإِن لَّمْ يَسْتَجِيبُوا۟ لَكَ فَٱعْلَمْ أَنَّمَا يَتَّبِعُونَ أَهْوَآءَهُمْ وَمَنْ أَضَلُّ مِمَّنِ ٱتَّبَعَ هَوَىٰهُ بِغَيْرِ هُدًى مِّنَ ٱللَّهِ إِنَّ ٱللَّهَ لَا يَهْدِى ٱلْقَوْمَ ٱلظَّـٰلِمِينَ (٥٠)

But when the truth (i.e. Muhammad with his Message) has come to them from Us, they say: "Why is he not given the like of what was given to Mûsa (Moses)? Did they not disbelieve in that which was given to Mûsa (Moses) of old? They say: "Two kinds of magic [the Taurât (Torah) and the Qur'ân] each helping the other!" And they say: "Verily! In both we are disbelievers." (48) Say (to them, O Muhammad): "Then bring a Book from Allâh, which is a better guide than these two [the Taurât (Torah) and the Qur'ân], that I may follow it, if you are truthful." (49) But if they answer you not (i.e. do not bring the book nor believe in your doctrine of Islâmic Monotheism), then know that they only follow their own lusts. And who is more astray than one who follows his own lusts, without guidance from Allâh? Verily! Allâh guides not the people who are Zâlimûn (wrong-doers, disobedient to Allâh, and polytheists) (50)

Quran 29:10-13

وَمِنَ ٱلنَّاسِ مَن يَقُولُ ءَامَنَّا بِٱللَّهِ فَإِذَآ أُوذِىَ فِى ٱللَّهِ جَعَلَ فِتْنَةَ ٱلنَّاسِ كَعَذَابِ ٱللَّهِ وَلَئِن جَآءَ نَصْرٌ مِّن رَّبِّكَ لَيَقُولُنَّ إِنَّا كُنَّا مَعَكُمْ أَوَلَيْسَ ٱللَّهُ بِأَعْلَمَ بِمَا فِى صُدُورِ ٱلْعَـٰلَمِينَ (١٠) وَلَيَعْلَمَنَّ ٱللَّهُ ٱلَّذِينَ ءَامَنُوا۟ وَلَيَعْلَمَنَّ ٱلْمُنَـٰفِقِينَ

$$\text{(۱۱) وَقَالَ ٱلَّذِينَ كَفَرُواْ لِلَّذِينَ ءَامَنُواْ ٱتَّبِعُواْ سَبِيلَنَا وَلْنَحْمِلْ خَطَٰيَٰكُمْ وَمَا هُم بِحَٰمِلِينَ مِنْ خَطَٰيَٰهُم مِّن شَىْءٍۖ إِنَّهُمْ لَكَٰذِبُونَ (۱۲) وَلَيَحْمِلُنَّ أَثْقَالَهُمْ وَأَثْقَالًا مَّعَ أَثْقَالِهِمْۖ وَلَيُسْـَٔلُنَّ يَوْمَ ٱلْقِيَٰمَةِ عَمَّا كَانُواْ يَفْتَرُونَ (۱۳)}$$

Of mankind are some who say: "We believe in Allâh," but if they are made to suffer for the sake of Allâh, they consider the trial of mankind as Allâh's punishment, and if victory comes from your Lord, (the hypocrites) will say: "Verily! We were with you (helping you)." Is not Allâh Best Aware of what is in the breast of the 'Alamîn (mankind and jinn). (10) Verily, Allâh knows those who believe, and verily, He knows the hypocrites. (11) And those who disbelieve say to those who believe: "Follow our way and we will verily bear your sins," never will they bear anything of their sins. Surely, they are liars. (12) And verily, they shall bear their own loads, and other loads besides their own, and verily, they shall be questioned on the Day of Resurrection about that which they used to fabricate. (13)

Quran 29:23

$$\text{وَٱلَّذِينَ كَفَرُواْ بِـَٔايَٰتِ ٱللَّهِ وَلِقَآئِهِۦٓ أُوْلَٰٓئِكَ يَئِسُواْ مِن رَّحْمَتِى وَأُوْلَٰٓئِكَ لَهُمْ عَذَابٌ أَلِيمٌ}$$

And those who disbelieve in the Ayât (proofs, evidences, verses, lessons, signs, revelations, etc.) of Allâh and the Meeting with Him, it is they who have no hope of My Mercy, and it is they who will have a painful torment. (23)

Quran 29:47

وَكَذَٰلِكَ أَنزَلْنَآ إِلَيْكَ ٱلْكِتَٰبَ ۚ فَٱلَّذِينَ ءَاتَيْنَٰهُمُ ٱلْكِتَٰبَ يُؤْمِنُونَ بِهِۦ ۖ وَمِنْ هَٰٓؤُلَآءِ مَن يُؤْمِنُ بِهِۦ ۚ وَمَا يَجْحَدُ بِـَٔايَٰتِنَآ إِلَّا ٱلْكَٰفِرُونَ

And thus We have sent down the Book (i.e this Qur'an) to you, and those whom We gave the Scripture [the Taurât (Torah) and the Injeel aforetime] believe therein as also do some of these (who are present with you now like 'Abdullâh bin Salâm) and none but the disbelievers reject Our Ayât (proofs, signs, verses, lessons, etc.) (47)

Quran 29:52-54

قُلْ كَفَىٰ بِٱللَّهِ بَيْنِى وَبَيْنَكُمْ شَهِيدًا ۖ يَعْلَمُ مَا فِى ٱلسَّمَٰوَٰتِ وَٱلْأَرْضِ ۗ وَٱلَّذِينَ ءَامَنُوا۟ بِٱلْبَٰطِلِ وَكَفَرُوا۟ بِٱللَّهِ أُو۟لَٰٓئِكَ هُمُ ٱلْخَٰسِرُونَ (٥٢) وَيَسْتَعْجِلُونَكَ بِٱلْعَذَابِ ۚ وَلَوْلَآ أَجَلٌ مُّسَمًّى لَّجَآءَهُمُ ٱلْعَذَابُ وَلَيَأْتِيَنَّهُم بَغْتَةً وَهُمْ لَا يَشْعُرُونَ (٥٣) يَسْتَعْجِلُونَكَ بِٱلْعَذَابِ وَإِنَّ جَهَنَّمَ لَمُحِيطَةٌۢ بِٱلْكَٰفِرِينَ (٥٤)

Say (to them O Muhammad): "Sufficient is Allâh for a witness between me and you. He knows what is in the heavens and on earth." And those who believe in Bâtil (all false deities other than Allâh), and disbelieve in Allâh and (in His Oneness), it is they who are the losers. (52) And they ask you to hasten on the torment (for them), and had it not been for a term appointed, the torment would certainly have come to them. And surely, it will come upon them suddenly while they perceive not! (53) They ask you to hasten on the torment. And verily! Hell, of a surety, will encompass the disbelievers. (54)

Quran 29:68

وَمَنْ أَظْلَمُ مِمَّنِ ٱفْتَرَىٰ عَلَى ٱللَّهِ كَذِبًا أَوْ كَذَّبَ بِٱلْحَقِّ لَمَّا جَاءَهُ ۚ أَلَيْسَ فِى جَهَنَّمَ مَثْوًى لِّلْكَافِرِينَ

And who does more wrong than he who invents a lie against Allâh or denies the truth (Muhammad and his doctrine of Islâmic Monotheism and this Qur'ân), when it comes to him? Is there not a dwelling in Hell for disbelievers (in the Oneness of Allâh and in His Messenger Muhammad)? (68)

Quran 30:16

وَأَمَّا ٱلَّذِينَ كَفَرُواْ وَكَذَّبُواْ بِـَٔايَٰتِنَا وَلِقَآئِ ٱلْأَخِرَةِ فَأُوْلَٰٓئِكَ فِى ٱلْعَذَابِ مُحْضَرُونَ

And as for those who disbelieved and belied Our Ayât (proofs, evidences, verses, lessons, signs, revelations, Allâh's Messengers, Resurrection, etc.), and the Meeting of the Hereafter, such shall be brought forth to the torment (in the Hell-fire). (16)

Quran 30:44-45

مَن كَفَرَ فَعَلَيْهِ كُفْرُهُۥ ۖ وَمَنْ عَمِلَ صَٰلِحًا فَلِأَنفُسِهِمْ يَمْهَدُونَ (٤٤) لِيَجْزِىَ ٱلَّذِينَ ءَامَنُواْ وَعَمِلُواْ ٱلصَّٰلِحَٰتِ مِن فَضْلِهِۦٓ ۚ إِنَّهُۥ لَا يُحِبُّ ٱلْكَٰفِرِينَ (٤٥)

Whosoever disbelieves will suffer from his disbelief, and whosoever does righteous good deeds (by practising Islâmic Monotheism), then such will prepare a good place (in Paradise) for themselves (and will be saved by Allâh from His Torment). (44) That He may reward those who believe (in the Oneness of Allâh Islâmic Monotheism), and do righteous good deeds, out of His Bounty. Verily, He likes not the disbelievers. (45)

Quran 30:58-59

وَلَقَدْ ضَرَبْنَا لِلنَّاسِ فِى هَٰذَا ٱلْقُرْءَانِ مِن كُلِّ مَثَلٍ وَلَئِن جِئْتَهُم بِـَٔايَةٍ لَّيَقُولَنَّ ٱلَّذِينَ كَفَرُوٓاْ إِنْ أَنتُمْ إِلَّا مُبْطِلُونَ (٥٨) كَذَٰلِكَ يَطْبَعُ ٱللَّهُ عَلَىٰ قُلُوبِ ٱلَّذِينَ لَا يَعْلَمُونَ (٥٩)

And indeed We have set forth for mankind, in this Qur'ân every kind of parable. But if you (O Muhammad) bring to them any sign or proof, (as an evidence for the truth of your Prophethood), the disbelievers are sure to say (to the believers): "You follow nothing but falsehood, and magic." (58) Thus does Allâh seal up the hearts of those who know not. (59)

Quran 32:20-22

وَأَمَّا ٱلَّذِينَ فَسَقُواْ فَمَأْوَىٰهُمُ ٱلنَّارُ كُلَّمَآ أَرَادُوٓاْ أَن يَخْرُجُواْ مِنْهَآ أُعِيدُواْ فِيهَا وَقِيلَ لَهُمْ ذُوقُواْ عَذَابَ ٱلنَّارِ ٱلَّذِى كُنتُم بِهِۦ تُكَذِّبُونَ (٢٠) وَلَنُذِيقَنَّهُم مِّنَ ٱلْعَذَابِ ٱلْأَدْنَىٰ دُونَ ٱلْعَذَابِ ٱلْأَكْبَرِ لَعَلَّهُمْ يَرْجِعُونَ (٢١) وَمَنْ أَظْلَمُ مِمَّن ذُكِّرَ بِـَٔايَٰتِ رَبِّهِۦ ثُمَّ أَعْرَضَ عَنْهَآ إِنَّا مِنَ ٱلْمُجْرِمِينَ مُنتَقِمُونَ (٢٢)

And as for those who are Fâsiqûn (disbelievers and disobedient to Allâh), their abode will be the Fire, everytime they wish to get away therefrom, they will be put back thereto, and it will be said to them: "Taste you the torment of the Fire which you used to deny." (20) And verily, We will make them taste of the near torment (i.e. the torment in the life of this world, i.e. disasters, calamities, etc.) prior to the supreme torment (in the

Hereafter), in order that they may (repent and) return (i.e. accept Islâm). (21) And who does more wrong than he who is reminded of the Ayât (proofs, evidences, verses, lessons, signs, revelations, etc.) of his Lord, then turns aside therefrom? Verily, We shall exact retribution from the Mujrimûn (criminals, disbelievers, polytheists, sinners, etc.) (22)

Quran 32:28-29

وَيَقُولُونَ مَتَىٰ هَٰذَا ٱلْفَتْحُ إِن كُنتُمْ صَٰدِقِينَ (٢٨) قُلْ يَوْمَ ٱلْفَتْحِ لَا يَنفَعُ ٱلَّذِينَ كَفَرُوٓاْ إِيمَٰنُهُمْ وَلَا هُمْ يُنظَرُونَ (٢٩)

They say: "When will this Fath (Decision) be (between us and you, i.e. the Day of Resurrection), if you are telling the truth?" (28) Say: "On the Day of Al¬Fath (Decision), no profit will it be to those who disbelieve if they (then) believe! Nor will they be granted a respite." (29)

Quran 33:18-20

۞ قَدْ يَعْلَمُ ٱللَّهُ ٱلْمُعَوِّقِينَ مِنكُمْ وَٱلْقَآئِلِينَ لِإِخْوَٰنِهِمْ هَلُمَّ إِلَيْنَا ۖ وَلَا يَأْتُونَ ٱلْبَأْسَ إِلَّا قَلِيلًا (١٨) أَشِحَّةً عَلَيْكُمْ ۖ فَإِذَا جَآءَ ٱلْخَوْفُ رَأَيْتَهُمْ يَنظُرُونَ إِلَيْكَ تَدُورُ أَعْيُنُهُمْ كَٱلَّذِى يُغْشَىٰ عَلَيْهِ مِنَ ٱلْمَوْتِ ۖ فَإِذَا ذَهَبَ ٱلْخَوْفُ سَلَقُوكُم بِأَلْسِنَةٍ حِدَادٍ أَشِحَّةً عَلَى ٱلْخَيْرِ ۚ أُوْلَٰٓئِكَ لَمْ يُؤْمِنُواْ فَأَحْبَطَ ٱللَّهُ أَعْمَٰلَهُمْ ۚ وَكَانَ ذَٰلِكَ عَلَى ٱللَّهِ يَسِيرًا (١٩) يَحْسَبُونَ ٱلْأَحْزَابَ لَمْ يَذْهَبُواْ ۖ وَإِن يَأْتِ ٱلْأَحْزَابُ يَوَدُّواْ لَوْ أَنَّهُم بَادُونَ فِى ٱلْأَعْرَابِ يَسْـَٔلُونَ عَنْ أَنۢبَآئِكُمْ ۚ وَلَوْ كَانُواْ فِيكُم مَّا قَٰتَلُوٓاْ إِلَّا قَلِيلًا (٢٠)

Allâh already knows those among you who keep back (men) from fighting in Allâh's Cause, and those who say to their brethren "Come here towards us," while they (themselves) come not to the battle except a little. (18) Being miserly towards you (as regards help and aid in Allâh's Cause). Then when fear comes, you will see them looking to you, their eyes revolving like (those of) one over whom hovers death, but when the fear departs, they will smite you with sharp tongues, miserly towards (spending anything in any) good (and only covetous of booty and wealth). Such have not believed. Therefore Allâh makes their deeds fruitless, and that is ever easy for Allâh. (19) They think that Al¬Ahzâb (the Confederates) have not yet withdrawn, and if Al¬Ahzâb (the Confederates) should come (again), they would wish they were in the deserts (wandering) among the bedouins, seeking news about you (from a far place); and if they (happen) to be among you, they would not fight but little. (20)

Quran 33:57-58

إِنَّ ٱلَّذِينَ يُؤْذُونَ ٱللَّهَ وَرَسُولَهُ لَعَنَهُمُ ٱللَّهُ فِى ٱلدُّنْيَا وَٱلْأَخِرَةِ وَأَعَدَّ لَهُمْ عَذَابًا مُّهِينًا (٥٧) وَٱلَّذِينَ يُؤْذُونَ ٱلْمُؤْمِنِينَ وَٱلْمُؤْمِنَـٰتِ بِغَيْرِ مَا ٱكْتَسَبُوا۟ فَقَدِ ٱحْتَمَلُوا۟ بُهْتَـٰنًا وَإِثْمًا مُّبِينًا (٥٨)

Verily, those who annoy Allâh and His Messenger Allâh has cursed them in this world, and in the Hereafter, and has prepared for them a humiliating torment. (57) And those who annoy believing men and women undeservedly, they bear (on themselves) the crime of slander and plain sin. (58)

Quran 33:64-68

إِنَّ ٱللَّهَ لَعَنَ ٱلْكَٰفِرِينَ وَأَعَدَّ لَهُمْ سَعِيرًا (٦٤) خَٰلِدِينَ فِيهَآ أَبَدًا لَّا يَجِدُونَ وَلِيًّا وَلَا نَصِيرًا (٦٥) يَوْمَ تُقَلَّبُ وُجُوهُهُمْ فِى ٱلنَّارِ يَقُولُونَ يَٰلَيْتَنَآ أَطَعْنَا ٱللَّهَ وَأَطَعْنَا ٱلرَّسُولَا۠ (٦٦) وَقَالُوا۟ رَبَّنَآ إِنَّآ أَطَعْنَا سَادَتَنَا وَكُبَرَآءَنَا فَأَضَلُّونَا ٱلسَّبِيلَا۠ (٦٧) رَبَّنَآ ءَاتِهِمْ ضِعْفَيْنِ مِنَ ٱلْعَذَابِ وَٱلْعَنْهُمْ لَعْنًا كَبِيرًا (٦٨)

Verily, Allâh has cursed the disbelievers, and has prepared for them a flaming Fire (Hell). (64) Wherein they will abide for ever, and they will find neither a Walî (a protector) nor a helper. (65) On the Day when their faces will be turned over in the Fire, they will say: "Oh, would that we had obeyed Allâh and obeyed the Messenger (Muhammad)." (66) And they will say: "Our Lord! Verily, we obeyed our chiefs and our great ones, and they misled us from the (Right) Way. (67) Our Lord! Give them double torment and curse them with a mighty curse!" (68)

Quran 34:3

وَقَالَ ٱلَّذِينَ كَفَرُوا۟ لَا تَأْتِينَا ٱلسَّاعَةُ قُلْ بَلَىٰ وَرَبِّى لَتَأْتِيَنَّكُمْ عَٰلِمِ ٱلْغَيْبِ لَا يَعْزُبُ عَنْهُ مِثْقَالُ ذَرَّةٍ فِى ٱلسَّمَٰوَٰتِ وَلَا فِى ٱلْأَرْضِ وَلَآ أَصْغَرُ مِن ذَٰلِكَ وَلَآ أَكْبَرُ إِلَّا فِى كِتَٰبٍ مُّبِينٍ

Those who disbelieve say: "The Hour will not come to us." Say: "Yes, by my Lord, the All¬Knower of the unseen, it will come to you." not even the weight of an atom (or a small ant) or less than that or greater, escapes His Knowledge in the heavens or in the earth, but it is in a Clear Book (Al¬Lauh Al¬Mahfûz). (3)

Quran 34:7-8

وَقَالَ ٱلَّذِينَ كَفَرُوا۟ هَلْ نَدُلُّكُمْ عَلَىٰ رَجُلٍ يُنَبِّئُكُمْ إِذَا مُزِّقْتُمْ كُلَّ مُمَزَّقٍ إِنَّكُمْ لَفِى خَلْقٍ جَدِيدٍ (٧) أَفْتَرَىٰ عَلَى ٱللَّهِ كَذِبًا أَم بِهِۦ جِنَّةٌۢ بَلِ ٱلَّذِينَ لَا يُؤْمِنُونَ بِٱلْءَاخِرَةِ فِى ٱلْعَذَابِ وَٱلضَّلَٰلِ ٱلْبَعِيدِ (٨)

Those who disbelieve say: "Shall we direct you to a man (Muhammad) who will tell you (that) when you have become fully disintegrated into dust with full dispersion, then, you will be created (again) anew?" (7) Has he invented a lie against Allâh, or is there a madness in him? Nay, but those who disbelieve in the Hereafter are (themselves) in a torment, and in far error. (8)

Quran 34:31-35

وَقَالَ ٱلَّذِينَ كَفَرُوا۟ لَن نُّؤْمِنَ بِهَٰذَا ٱلْقُرْءَانِ وَلَا بِٱلَّذِى بَيْنَ يَدَيْهِ وَلَوْ تَرَىٰٓ إِذِ ٱلظَّٰلِمُونَ مَوْقُوفُونَ عِندَ رَبِّهِمْ يَرْجِعُ بَعْضُهُمْ إِلَىٰ بَعْضٍ ٱلْقَوْلَ يَقُولُ ٱلَّذِينَ ٱسْتُضْعِفُوا۟ لِلَّذِينَ ٱسْتَكْبَرُوا۟ لَوْلَآ أَنتُمْ لَكُنَّا مُؤْمِنِينَ (٣١) قَالَ ٱلَّذِينَ ٱسْتَكْبَرُوا۟ لِلَّذِينَ ٱسْتُضْعِفُوٓا۟ أَنَحْنُ صَدَدْنَٰكُمْ عَنِ ٱلْهُدَىٰ بَعْدَ إِذْ جَآءَكُم بَلْ كُنتُم مُّجْرِمِينَ (٣٢) وَقَالَ ٱلَّذِينَ ٱسْتُضْعِفُوا۟ لِلَّذِينَ ٱسْتَكْبَرُوا۟ بَلْ مَكْرُ ٱلَّيْلِ وَٱلنَّهَارِ إِذْ تَأْمُرُونَنَآ أَن نَّكْفُرَ بِٱللَّهِ وَنَجْعَلَ لَهُۥٓ أَندَادًا وَأَسَرُّوا۟ ٱلنَّدَامَةَ لَمَّا رَأَوُا۟ ٱلْعَذَابَ وَجَعَلْنَا ٱلْأَغْلَٰلَ فِىٓ أَعْنَاقِ ٱلَّذِينَ كَفَرُوا۟ هَلْ يُجْزَوْنَ إِلَّا مَا كَانُوا۟ يَعْمَلُونَ (٣٣) وَمَآ أَرْسَلْنَا فِى قَرْيَةٍ مِّن نَّذِيرٍ إِلَّا قَالَ مُتْرَفُوهَآ إِنَّا بِمَآ أُرْسِلْتُم بِهِۦ كَٰفِرُونَ (٣٤) وَقَالُوا۟ نَحْنُ أَكْثَرُ أَمْوَٰلًا وَأَوْلَٰدًا وَمَا نَحْنُ بِمُعَذَّبِينَ (٣٥)

And those who disbelieve say: "We believe not in this Qur'ân nor in that which was before it," but if you could see when the Zâlimûn (polytheists and wrong¬doers) will be made to stand before their Lord, how they will cast the (blaming) word one to another! Those who were deemed weak will say to those who were arrogant: "Had it not been for you, we should certainly have been believers!"

(31) And those who were arrogant will say to those who were deemed weak: "Did we keep you back from guidance after it had come to you? Nay, but you were Mujrimûn (polytheists, sinners, disbeliveres, criminals). (32) Those who were deemed weak will say to those who were arrogant: "Nay, but it was your plotting by night and day, when you ordered us to disbelieve in Allâh and set up rivals to Him!" And each of them (parties) will conceal their own regrets (for disobeying Allâh during this worldly life), when they behold the torment. And We shall put iron collars round the necks of those who disbelieved. Are they requited aught except what they used to do? (33) And We did not send a warner to a township, but those who were given the worldly wealth and luxuries among them said: "We believe not in the (Message) with which you have been sent." (34) And they say: "We are more in wealth and in children, and we are not going to be punished." (35)

Quran 34:43-45

وَإِذَا تُتْلَىٰ عَلَيْهِمْ ءَايَٰتُنَا بَيِّنَٰتٍ قَالُوا۟ مَا هَٰذَآ إِلَّا رَجُلٌ يُرِيدُ أَن يَصُدَّكُمْ عَمَّا كَانَ يَعْبُدُ ءَابَآؤُكُمْ وَقَالُوا۟ مَا هَٰذَآ إِلَّآ إِفْكٌ مُّفْتَرًى وَقَالَ ٱلَّذِينَ كَفَرُوا۟ لِلْحَقِّ لَمَّا جَآءَهُمْ إِنْ هَٰذَآ إِلَّا سِحْرٌ مُّبِينٌ (٤٣) وَمَآ ءَاتَيْنَٰهُم مِّن كُتُبٍ يَدْرُسُونَهَا وَمَآ أَرْسَلْنَآ إِلَيْهِمْ قَبْلَكَ مِن نَّذِيرٍ (٤٤) وَكَذَّبَ ٱلَّذِينَ مِن قَبْلِهِمْ وَمَا بَلَغُوا۟ مِعْشَارَ مَآ ءَاتَيْنَٰهُمْ فَكَذَّبُوا۟ رُسُلِى فَكَيْفَ كَانَ نَكِيرِ (٤٥)

And when Our Clear Verses are recited to them, they say: "This (Muhammad) is naught but a man who wishes to hinder you from that which your fathers used to worship." And they say: "This (the Quran) is nothing but an invented lie." And those who disbelieve say of the truth when it has come to them: "This is nothing but evident magic!" (43) And We had not given them Scriptures which they could study, nor sent to them before you (O Muhammad) any warner (Messenger) (44) And those before them belied; these have not received even a tenth of what We had granted to those (of old); yet they belied My Messengers, Then how (terrible) was My denial (punishment)! (45)

Quran 34:53-54

وَقَدْ كَفَرُواْ بِهِۦ مِن قَبْلُ وَيَقْذِفُونَ بِٱلْغَيْبِ مِن مَّكَانٍۭ بَعِيدٍ (٥٣) وَحِيلَ بَيْنَهُمْ وَبَيْنَ مَا يَشْتَهُونَ كَمَا فُعِلَ بِأَشْيَاعِهِم مِّن قَبْلُ إِنَّهُمْ كَانُواْ فِى شَكٍّ مُّرِيبٍ (٥٤)

Indeed they did disbelieve (in the Oneness of Allâh, Islâm, the Qur'ân and Muhammad) before (in this world), and they (used to) conjecture about the unseen [i.e. the Hereafter, Hell, Paradise, Resurrection and the Promise of Allâh (by saying) all that is untrue], from a far place. (53) And a barrier will be set between them and that which they desire [i.e. At-Taubah (turning to Allâh in repentance) and the accepting of Faith], as was done in the past with the people of their kind. Verily, they have been in grave doubt. (54)

Quran 35:25-26

وَإِن يُكَذِّبُوكَ فَقَدْ كَذَّبَ ٱلَّذِينَ مِن قَبْلِهِمْ جَآءَتْهُمْ رُسُلُهُم بِٱلْبَيِّنَٰتِ وَبِٱلزُّبُرِ وَبِٱلْكِتَٰبِ ٱلْمُنِيرِ (٢٥) ثُمَّ أَخَذْتُ ٱلَّذِينَ كَفَرُواْ فَكَيْفَ كَانَ نَكِيرِ (٢٦)

And if they belie you, those before them also belied. Their Messengers came to them with clear signs, and with the Scriptures, and the book giving light. (25) Then I took hold of those who disbelieved, and how terrible was My denial (punishment)! (26)

Quran 35:36-40

وَٱلَّذِينَ كَفَرُوا۟ لَهُمْ نَارُ جَهَنَّمَ لَا يُقْضَىٰ عَلَيْهِمْ فَيَمُوتُوا۟ وَلَا يُخَفَّفُ عَنْهُم مِّنْ عَذَابِهَا ۚ كَذَٰلِكَ نَجْزِى كُلَّ كَفُورٍ (٣٦) وَهُمْ يَصْطَرِخُونَ فِيهَا رَبَّنَآ أَخْرِجْنَا نَعْمَلْ صَٰلِحًا غَيْرَ ٱلَّذِى كُنَّا نَعْمَلُ ۚ أَوَلَمْ نُعَمِّرْكُم مَّا يَتَذَكَّرُ فِيهِ مَن تَذَكَّرَ وَجَآءَكُمُ ٱلنَّذِيرُ ۖ فَذُوقُوا۟ فَمَا لِلظَّٰلِمِينَ مِن نَّصِيرٍ (٣٧) إِنَّ ٱللَّهَ عَٰلِمُ غَيْبِ ٱلسَّمَٰوَٰتِ وَٱلْأَرْضِ ۚ إِنَّهُۥ عَلِيمٌۢ بِذَاتِ ٱلصُّدُورِ (٣٨) هُوَ ٱلَّذِى جَعَلَكُمْ خَلَٰٓئِفَ فِى ٱلْأَرْضِ ۚ فَمَن كَفَرَ فَعَلَيْهِ كُفْرُهُۥ ۖ وَلَا يَزِيدُ ٱلْكَٰفِرِينَ كُفْرُهُمْ عِندَ رَبِّهِمْ إِلَّا مَقْتًا ۖ وَلَا يَزِيدُ ٱلْكَٰفِرِينَ كُفْرُهُمْ إِلَّا خَسَارًا (٣٩) قُلْ أَرَءَيْتُمْ شُرَكَآءَكُمُ ٱلَّذِينَ تَدْعُونَ مِن دُونِ ٱللَّهِ أَرُونِى مَاذَا خَلَقُوا۟ مِنَ ٱلْأَرْضِ أَمْ لَهُمْ شِرْكٌ فِى ٱلسَّمَٰوَٰتِ أَمْ ءَاتَيْنَٰهُمْ كِتَٰبًا فَهُمْ عَلَىٰ بَيِّنَتٍ مِّنْهُ ۚ بَلْ إِن يَعِدُ ٱلظَّٰلِمُونَ بَعْضُهُم بَعْضًا إِلَّا غُرُورًا (٤٠)

But those who disbelieve, (in the Oneness of Allâh - Islâmic Monotheism) for them will be the Fire of Hell. Neither will it have a complete killing effect on them so that they die, nor shall its torment be lightened for them. Thus do We requite every disbeliever! (36) Therein they will cry: "Our Lord! Bring us out, we shall do righteous good deeds, not (the evil deeds) that we used to do." (Allâh will reply): "Did We not give you lives long enough, so that whosoever would receive admonition, could receive it? And the warner came to you. So taste you (the evil of your deeds). For the Zâlimûn (polytheists and wrong-doers) there is no helper." (37) Verily, Allâh is the All-Knower of the unseen of the heavens and the earth. Verily! He is the All-Knower of that is in the breasts. (38) He it is Who has made you successors generations after generations in the earth, so whosoever disbelieves (in Islâmic Monotheism) on him will be his disbelief. And the disbelief of the disbelievers adds nothing but hatred of their Lord. And the disbelief of the disbelievers adds nothing but loss. (39) Say: "Tell me or inform me (what) do you think about your (so-called) partner-gods to whom you call upon besides Allâh? show me, what they have created of the earth? Or have they any share in the heavens? Or have We given them a Book, so that they act on clear proof therefrom? Nay, the Zâlimûn (polytheists and wrong-doers) promise one another nothing but delusions." (40)

Quran 36:10

وَسَوَآءٌ عَلَيْهِمْ ءَأَنذَرْتَهُمْ أَمْ لَمْ تُنذِرْهُمْ لَا يُؤْمِنُونَ

It is the same to them whether you warn them or you warn them not, they will not believe. (10)

Quran 36:45-48

وَإِذَا قِيلَ لَهُمُ ٱتَّقُوا۟ مَا بَيْنَ أَيْدِيكُمْ وَمَا خَلْفَكُمْ لَعَلَّكُمْ تُرْحَمُونَ (٤٥) وَمَا تَأْتِيهِم مِّنْ ءَايَةٍ مِّنْ ءَايَـٰتِ رَبِّهِمْ إِلَّا كَانُوا۟ عَنْهَا مُعْرِضِينَ (٤٦) وَإِذَا قِيلَ لَهُمْ أَنفِقُوا۟ مِمَّا رَزَقَكُمُ ٱللَّهُ قَالَ ٱلَّذِينَ كَفَرُوا۟ لِلَّذِينَ ءَامَنُوٓا۟ أَنُطْعِمُ مَن لَّوْ يَشَآءُ ٱللَّهُ أَطْعَمَهُۥٓ إِنْ أَنتُمْ إِلَّا فِى ضَلَـٰلٍ مُّبِينٍ (٤٧) وَيَقُولُونَ مَتَىٰ هَـٰذَا ٱلْوَعْدُ إِن كُنتُمْ صَـٰدِقِينَ (٤٨)

And when it is said to them: "Fear of that which is before you (worldly torments), and that which is behind you (torments in the Hereafter), in order that you may receive Mercy." (45) And never came an Ayâh from among the Ayât (proofs, evidences, verses, lessons, signs, revelations, etc.) of their Lord to them, but they did turn away from it. (46) And when it is said to them: "Spend of that with which Allâh has provided you," those who disbelieve say to those who believe: "Shall we feed those whom, if Allâh willed, He (Himself) would have fed? You are only in a plain error." (47) And they say: "When will this promise (i.e. Resurrection) be fulfilled, if you are truthful?" (48)

Quran 37:14-36

وَإِذَا رَأَوْاْ ءَايَةً يَسْتَسْخِرُونَ (١٤) وَقَالُوٓاْ إِنْ هَٰذَآ إِلَّا سِحْرٌ مُّبِينٌ (١٥) أَءِذَا مِتْنَا وَكُنَّا تُرَابًا وَعِظَٰمًا أَءِنَّا لَمَبْعُوثُونَ (١٦) أَوَءَابَآؤُنَا ٱلْأَوَّلُونَ (١٧) قُلْ نَعَمْ وَأَنتُمْ دَٰخِرُونَ (١٨) فَإِنَّمَا هِىَ زَجْرَةٌ وَٰحِدَةٌ فَإِذَا هُمْ يَنظُرُونَ (١٩) وَقَالُوا۟ يَٰوَيْلَنَا هَٰذَا يَوْمُ ٱلدِّينِ (٢٠) هَٰذَا يَوْمُ ٱلْفَصْلِ ٱلَّذِى كُنتُم بِهِۦ تُكَذِّبُونَ (٢١) ۞ ٱحْشُرُوا۟ ٱلَّذِينَ ظَلَمُوا۟ وَأَزْوَٰجَهُمْ وَمَا كَانُوا۟ يَعْبُدُونَ (٢٢) مِن دُونِ ٱللَّهِ فَٱهْدُوهُمْ إِلَىٰ صِرَٰطِ ٱلْجَحِيمِ (٢٣) وَقِفُوهُمْ ۖ إِنَّهُم مَّسْـُٔولُونَ (٢٤) مَا لَكُمْ لَا تَنَاصَرُونَ (٢٥) بَلْ هُمُ ٱلْيَوْمَ مُسْتَسْلِمُونَ (٢٦) وَأَقْبَلَ بَعْضُهُمْ عَلَىٰ بَعْضٍ يَتَسَآءَلُونَ (٢٧) قَالُوٓاْ إِنَّكُمْ كُنتُمْ تَأْتُونَنَا عَنِ ٱلْيَمِينِ (٢٨) قَالُوا۟ بَل لَّمْ تَكُونُوا۟ مُؤْمِنِينَ (٢٩) وَمَا كَانَ لَنَا عَلَيْكُم مِّن سُلْطَٰنٍۭ ۖ بَلْ كُنتُمْ قَوْمًا طَٰغِينَ (٣٠) فَحَقَّ عَلَيْنَا قَوْلُ رَبِّنَآ ۖ إِنَّا لَذَآئِقُونَ (٣١) فَأَغْوَيْنَٰكُمْ إِنَّا كُنَّا غَٰوِينَ (٣٢) فَإِنَّهُمْ يَوْمَئِذٍ فِى ٱلْعَذَابِ مُشْتَرِكُونَ (٣٣) إِنَّا كَذَٰلِكَ نَفْعَلُ بِٱلْمُجْرِمِينَ (٣٤) إِنَّهُمْ كَانُوٓاْ إِذَا قِيلَ لَهُمْ لَآ إِلَٰهَ إِلَّا ٱللَّهُ يَسْتَكْبِرُونَ (٣٥) وَيَقُولُونَ أَئِنَّا لَتَارِكُوٓاْ ءَالِهَتِنَا لِشَاعِرٍ مَّجْنُونٍۭ (٣٦)

And when they see an Ayâh (a sign, a proof, or an evidence) from Allâh, they mock at it. (14) And they say: "This is nothing but evident magic! (15) "When we are dead and have become dust and bones, shall we (then) verily be resurrected? (16) "And also our fathers of old?" (17) Say (O Muhammad): "Yes, and you shall then be humiliated." (18) It will be a single Zajrah [shout (i.e. the second blowing of the Trumpet)], and behold, they will be staring! (19) They will say: "Woe to us! This is the Day of Recompense!" (20) (It will be said): "This is the Day of Judgement which you used to deny." (21) It will be said to the angels): "Assemble those who did wrong, together with their companions (from the devils) and what they used to worship (22) "Instead of Allâh, and lead them on to the way of flaming Fire (Hell); (23) "But stop them, verily they are to be questioned. (24) "What is the matter with you? Why do you not help one another (as you used to do in the world)?" (25) Nay, but that Day they shall surrender, (26) And they will turn to one another and question one another. (27) They will say: "It was you who used to come to us from the right side [i.e. from the right side of one of us and beautify for us every evil, enjoin on us polytheism, and stop us from the truth i.e. Islâmic Monotheism and from every good deed]." (28) They will reply: "Nay, you yourselves were not believers. (29) "And we had no authority over you. Nay! But you were Taghun (transgressing) people (polytheists, and disbelievers). (30) "So now the Word of our Lord has been justified against us, that we shall certainly (have to) taste (the torment). (31) "So we led you astray because we were ourselves astray." (32) Then verily, that Day, they will (all) share in the torment. (33) Certainly, that is how We deal with Al¬Mujrimûn (polytheists, sinners, disbelivers, criminals, the disobedient to Allâh). (34) Truly, when it was said to them: Lâ ilâha illallâh "(none has the right to be worshipped but Allâh)," they puffed themselves up with pride (i.e. denied it). (35) And (they) said: "Are we going to abandon our âlihah (gods) for the sake of a mad poet? (36)

Quran 38:2-8

بَلِ ٱلَّذِينَ كَفَرُوا۟ فِى عِزَّةٍ وَشِقَاقٍ (٢) كَمْ أَهْلَكْنَا مِن قَبْلِهِم مِّن قَرْنٍ فَنَادَوا۟ وَّلَاتَ حِينَ مَنَاصٍ (٣) وَعَجِبُوٓا۟ أَن جَآءَهُم مُّنذِرٌ مِّنْهُمْ ۖ وَقَالَ ٱلْكَـٰفِرُونَ هَـٰذَا سَـٰحِرٌ كَذَّابٌ (٤) أَجَعَلَ ٱلْـَٔالِهَةَ إِلَـٰهًا وَٰحِدًا ۖ إِنَّ هَـٰذَا لَشَىْءٌ عُجَابٌ (٥) وَٱنطَلَقَ ٱلْمَلَأُ مِنْهُمْ أَنِ ٱمْشُوا۟ وَٱصْبِرُوا۟ عَلَىٰٓ ءَالِهَتِكُمْ ۖ إِنَّ هَـٰذَا لَشَىْءٌ يُرَادُ (٦) مَا سَمِعْنَا بِهَـٰذَا فِى ٱلْمِلَّةِ ٱلْـَٔاخِرَةِ إِنْ هَـٰذَآ إِلَّا ٱخْتِلَـٰقٌ (٧) أَءُنزِلَ عَلَيْهِ ٱلذِّكْرُ مِنۢ بَيْنِنَا ۚ بَلْ هُمْ فِى شَكٍّ مِّن ذِكْرِى ۖ بَل لَّمَّا يَذُوقُوا۟ عَذَابِ (٨)

Nay, those who disbelieve are in false pride and opposition. (2) How many a generation We have destroyed before them, And they cried out when there was no longer time for escape! (3) And they (Arab pagans) wonder that a warner (Prophet Muhammad) has come to them from among themselves! And the disbelievers say: "This is a sorcerer, a liar. (4) "Has he made the âlihah (gods) (all) into One Ilâh (God - Allâh). Verily, this is a curious thing!" (5) And the leaders among them went about (saying): "Go on, and remain constant to your âliha (gods)! Verily, this is a thing designed (against you)! (6) "We have not heard (the like) of this in the religion of these later days. This is nothing but an invention! (7) "Has the Reminder been sent down to him (alone) from among us?" Nay! but they are in doubt about My Reminder (this Qur'ân)! Nay, but they have not tasted (My) Torment! (8)

Quran 38:27

وَمَا خَلَقْنَا ٱلسَّمَآءَ وَٱلْأَرْضَ وَمَا بَيْنَهُمَا بَـٰطِلًا ۚ ذَٰلِكَ ظَنُّ ٱلَّذِينَ كَفَرُوا۟ ۚ فَوَيْلٌ لِّلَّذِينَ كَفَرُوا۟ مِنَ ٱلنَّارِ

And We created not the heaven and the earth and all that is between them without purpose! That is the consideration of those who disbelieve! Then woe to those who disbelieve (in Islâmic Monotheism) from the Fire! (27)

Quran 39:3

أَلَا لِلَّهِ ٱلدِّينُ ٱلْخَالِصُ ۚ وَٱلَّذِينَ ٱتَّخَذُوا۟ مِن دُونِهِۦٓ أَوْلِيَآءَ مَا نَعْبُدُهُمْ إِلَّا لِيُقَرِّبُونَآ إِلَى ٱللَّهِ زُلْفَىٰٓ إِنَّ ٱللَّهَ يَحْكُمُ بَيْنَهُمْ فِى مَا هُمْ فِيهِ يَخْتَلِفُونَ ۗ إِنَّ ٱللَّهَ لَا يَهْدِى مَنْ هُوَ كَـٰذِبٌ كَفَّارٌ

Surely, the religion (i.e. the worship and the obedience) is for Allâh only. And those who take Auliyâ' (protectors, helpers, lords, gods) besides Him (say): "We worship them only that they may bring us near to Allâh." Verily, Allâh will judge between them concerning that wherein they differ. Truly, Allâh guides not him who is a liar, and a disbeliever. (3)

Quran 39:7-8

إِن تَكْفُرُوا۟ فَإِنَّ ٱللَّهَ غَنِىٌّ عَنكُمْ ۖ وَلَا يَرْضَىٰ لِعِبَادِهِ ٱلْكُفْرَ ۖ وَإِن تَشْكُرُوا۟ يَرْضَهُ لَكُمْ ۗ وَلَا تَزِرُ وَازِرَةٌ وِزْرَ أُخْرَىٰ ۗ ثُمَّ إِلَىٰ رَبِّكُم مَّرْجِعُكُمْ فَيُنَبِّئُكُم بِمَا كُنتُمْ تَعْمَلُونَ ۚ إِنَّهُۥ عَلِيمٌۢ بِذَاتِ ٱلصُّدُورِ (٧) وَإِذَا مَسَّ ٱلْإِنسَـٰنَ ضُرٌّ دَعَا رَبَّهُۥ مُنِيبًا إِلَيْهِ ثُمَّ إِذَا خَوَّلَهُۥ نِعْمَةً مِّنْهُ نَسِىَ مَا كَانَ يَدْعُوٓا۟ إِلَيْهِ مِن قَبْلُ وَجَعَلَ لِلَّهِ أَندَادًا لِّيُضِلَّ عَن سَبِيلِهِۦ ۚ قُلْ تَمَتَّعْ بِكُفْرِكَ قَلِيلًا ۖ إِنَّكَ مِنْ أَصْحَـٰبِ ٱلنَّارِ (٨)

If you disbelieve, then verily, Allâh is not in need of you, He likes not disbelief for His slaves. And if you are grateful (by being believers), He is pleased therewith for you. No bearer of burdens shall bear the burden of another. Then to your Lord is your return, and He will inform you what you used to do. Verily, He is the All-Knower of that which is in (men's) breasts. (7) And when some hurt touches man, he cries to his Lord (Allâh Alone), turning to Him in repentance, but when He bestows a favour upon him from Himself, he forgets that for which he cried for before, and he sets up rivals to Allâh, in order to mislead others from His Path. Say: "Take pleasure in your disbelief for a while: surely, you are (one) of the dwellers of the Fire!" (8)

Quran 39:32

فَمَنْ أَظْلَمُ مِمَّن كَذَبَ عَلَى ٱللَّهِ وَكَذَّبَ بِٱلصِّدْقِ إِذْ جَآءَهُۥ ۚ أَلَيْسَ فِى جَهَنَّمَ مَثْوًى لِّلْكَـٰفِرِينَ

Then, who does more wrong than one who utters a lie against Allâh, and denies the truth [this Qur'ân, the Prophet, and the Islâmic Monotheism] when it comes to him! Is there not in Hell an abode for the disbelievers? (32)

Quran 39:43-45

أَمِ ٱتَّخَذُوا۟ مِن دُونِ ٱللَّهِ شُفَعَآءَ ۚ قُلْ أَوَلَوْ كَانُوا۟ لَا يَمْلِكُونَ شَيْـًٔا وَلَا يَعْقِلُونَ (٤٣) قُل لِّلَّهِ ٱلشَّفَٰعَةُ جَمِيعًا ۖ لَّهُۥ مُلْكُ ٱلسَّمَٰوَٰتِ وَٱلْأَرْضِ ۖ ثُمَّ إِلَيْهِ تُرْجَعُونَ (٤٤) وَإِذَا ذُكِرَ ٱللَّهُ وَحْدَهُ ٱشْمَأَزَّتْ قُلُوبُ ٱلَّذِينَ لَا يُؤْمِنُونَ بِٱلْءَاخِرَةِ ۖ وَإِذَا ذُكِرَ ٱلَّذِينَ مِن دُونِهِۦٓ إِذَا هُمْ يَسْتَبْشِرُونَ (٤٥)

Have they taken (others) as intercessors besides Allâh? Say: "Even if they have power over nothing whatever and have no intelligence?" (43) Say: "To Allâh belongs all intercession. His is the Sovereignty of the heavens and the earth, Then to Him you shall be brought back." (44) And when Allâh Alone is mentioned, the hearts of those who believe not in the Hereafter are filled with disgust (from the Oneness of Allâh) and when those (whom they obey or worship) besides Him [like all false deities other than Allâh, it may be a Messenger, an angel, a pious man, a jinn, or any other creature even idols, graves of religious people, saints, priests, monks and others] are mentioned, behold, they rejoice! (45)

Quran 39:56-60

أَن تَقُولَ نَفْسٌ يَٰحَسْرَتَىٰ عَلَىٰ مَا فَرَّطتُ فِى جَنۢبِ ٱللَّهِ وَإِن كُنتُ لَمِنَ ٱلسَّٰخِرِينَ (٥٦) أَوْ تَقُولَ لَوْ أَنَّ ٱللَّهَ هَدَىٰنِى لَكُنتُ مِنَ ٱلْمُتَّقِينَ (٥٧) أَوْ تَقُولَ حِينَ تَرَى ٱلْعَذَابَ لَوْ أَنَّ لِى كَرَّةً فَأَكُونَ مِنَ ٱلْمُحْسِنِينَ (٥٨) بَلَىٰ قَدْ جَآءَتْكَ ءَايَٰتِى فَكَذَّبْتَ بِهَا وَٱسْتَكْبَرْتَ وَكُنتَ مِنَ ٱلْكَٰفِرِينَ (٥٩) وَيَوْمَ ٱلْقِيَٰمَةِ تَرَى ٱلَّذِينَ كَذَبُوا۟ عَلَى ٱللَّهِ وُجُوهُهُم مُّسْوَدَّةٌ ۚ أَلَيْسَ فِى جَهَنَّمَ مَثْوًى لِّلْمُتَكَبِّرِينَ (٦٠)

Lest a person should say: "Alas, my grief that I was undutiful to Allâh (i.e. I have not done what Allâh has ordered me to do), and I was indeed among those who mocked [at the truth! i.e. Lâ ilâha illallâh (none has the right to be worshipped but Allâh), the Qur'ân, and Muhammad and at the faithful believers] (56) Or (lest) he should say: "If only Allâh had guided me, I should indeed have been among the Muttaqûn (pious and righteous persons)." (57) Or (lest) he should say when he sees the torment: "If only I had another chance (to return to the world) then I should indeed be among the Muhsinûn (good-doers)." (58) Yes! Verily, there came to you My Ayât (proofs, evidences, verses, lessons, signs, revelations, etc.) and you denied them, and were proud and were among the disbelievers. (59) And on the Day of Resurrection you will see those who lied against Allâh (i.e. attributed to Him sons, partners) — their faces will be black. Is there not in Hell an abode for the arrogant? (60)

Quran 39:71-72

وَسِيقَ ٱلَّذِينَ كَفَرُوٓاْ إِلَىٰ جَهَنَّمَ زُمَرًاۖ حَتَّىٰٓ إِذَا جَآءُوهَا فُتِحَتْ أَبْوَٰبُهَا وَقَالَ لَهُمْ خَزَنَتُهَآ أَلَمْ يَأْتِكُمْ رُسُلٌ مِّنكُمْ يَتْلُونَ عَلَيْكُمْ ءَايَٰتِ رَبِّكُمْ وَيُنذِرُونَكُمْ لِقَآءَ يَوْمِكُمْ هَٰذَاۚ قَالُواْ بَلَىٰ وَلَٰكِنْ حَقَّتْ كَلِمَةُ ٱلْعَذَابِ عَلَى ٱلْكَٰفِرِينَ (٧١) قِيلَ ٱدْخُلُوٓاْ أَبْوَٰبَ جَهَنَّمَ خَٰلِدِينَ فِيهَاۖ فَبِئْسَ مَثْوَى ٱلْمُتَكَبِّرِينَ (٧٢)

And those who disbelieved will be driven to Hell in groups, till, when they reach it, the gates thereof will be opened (suddenly like a prison at the arrival of the prisoners). And its keepers will say, "Did not the Messengers come to you from yourselves, reciting to you the Verses of your Lord, and warning you of the Meeting of this Day of yours?" They will say: "Yes, but the Word of torment has been justified against the disbelievers!" (71) It will be said (to them): "Enter you the gates of Hell, to abide therein. And (indeed) what an evil abode of the arrogant!" (72)

Quran 40:4-6

مَا يُجَٰدِلُ فِىٓ ءَايَٰتِ ٱللَّهِ إِلَّا ٱلَّذِينَ كَفَرُوا۟ فَلَا يَغْرُرْكَ تَقَلُّبُهُمْ فِى ٱلْبِلَٰدِ (٤) كَذَّبَتْ قَبْلَهُمْ قَوْمُ نُوحٍ وَٱلْأَحْزَابُ مِنۢ بَعْدِهِمْ ۖ وَهَمَّتْ كُلُّ أُمَّةٍۭ بِرَسُولِهِمْ لِيَأْخُذُوهُ ۖ وَجَٰدَلُوا۟ بِٱلْبَٰطِلِ لِيُدْحِضُوا۟ بِهِ ٱلْحَقَّ فَأَخَذْتُهُمْ ۖ فَكَيْفَ كَانَ عِقَابِ (٥) وَكَذَٰلِكَ حَقَّتْ كَلِمَتُ رَبِّكَ عَلَى ٱلَّذِينَ كَفَرُوٓا۟ أَنَّهُمْ أَصْحَٰبُ ٱلنَّارِ (٦)

None disputes in the Ayât (proofs, evidences, verses, lessons, signs, revelations, etc.) of Allâh but those who disbelieve. So let not their ability of going about here and there through the land (for their purposes) deceive you! (4) The people of Nûh (Noah) and the confederates after them denied (their Messengers) before these, and every (disbelieving) nation plotted against their Messenger to seize him, and disputed by means of falsehood to refute therewith the truth. So I seized them (with punishment), and how (terrible) was My punishment! (5) Thus has the Word of your Lord been justified against those who disbelieved, that they will be the dwellers of the Fire (6)

Quran 40:10-12

إِنَّ ٱلَّذِينَ كَفَرُوا۟ يُنَادَوْنَ لَمَقْتُ ٱللَّهِ أَكْبَرُ مِن مَّقْتِكُمْ أَنفُسَكُمْ إِذْ تُدْعَوْنَ إِلَى ٱلْإِيمَٰنِ فَتَكْفُرُونَ (١٠) قَالُوا۟ رَبَّنَآ أَمَتَّنَا ٱثْنَتَيْنِ وَأَحْيَيْتَنَا ٱثْنَتَيْنِ فَٱعْتَرَفْنَا

بِذُنُوبِنَا فَهَلْ إِلَىٰ خُرُوجٍ مِّن سَبِيلٍ (١١) ذَٰلِكُم بِأَنَّهُۥ إِذَا دُعِىَ ٱللَّهُ وَحْدَهُۥ كَفَرْتُمْ ۚ وَإِن يُشْرَكْ بِهِۦ تُؤْمِنُوا۟ ۚ فَٱلْحُكْمُ لِلَّهِ ٱلْعَلِىِّ ٱلْكَبِيرِ (١٢)

Those who disbelieve will be addressed (at the time of entering the Fire): "Allâh's aversion was greater towards you (in the worldly life when you used to reject the Faith) than your aversion towards one another (now in the Fire of Hell, as you are now enemies to one another), when you were called to the Faith but you used to refuse." (10) They will say: "Our Lord! You have made us to die twice (i.e. we were dead in the loins of our fathers and dead after our life in this world), and You have given us life twice (i.e. life when we were born and life when we are Resurrected)! Now we confess our sins, then is there any way to get out (of the Fire)?" (11) (It will be said): "This is because, when Allâh Alone was invoked (in worship) you disbelieved, but when partners were joined to Him, you believed (denied)! So the judgement is only with Allâh, the Most High, the Most Great!" (12)

Quran 40:14

فَٱدْعُوا۟ ٱللَّهَ مُخْلِصِينَ لَهُ ٱلدِّينَ وَلَوْ كَرِهَ ٱلْكَٰفِرُونَ

So, call you upon (or invoke) Allâh making (your) worship pure for Him (Alone) (by worshipping none but Him and by doing religious deeds sincerely for Allâh's sake only and not to show off and not to set up rivals with Him in worship). however much the disbelievers (in the Oneness of Allâh) may hate (it). (14)

Quran 40:59-60

إِنَّ ٱلسَّاعَةَ لَآتِيَةٌ لَّا رَيْبَ فِيهَا وَلَٰكِنَّ أَكْثَرَ ٱلنَّاسِ لَا يُؤْمِنُونَ (٥٩) وَقَالَ رَبُّكُمُ ٱدْعُونِىٓ أَسْتَجِبْ لَكُمْ ۚ إِنَّ ٱلَّذِينَ يَسْتَكْبِرُونَ عَنْ عِبَادَتِى سَيَدْخُلُونَ جَهَنَّمَ دَاخِرِينَ (٦٠)

Verily, the Hour (Day of Judgement) is surely coming, there is no doubt it, yet most men believe not. (59) And your Lord said: "Invoke Me, [i.e. believe in My Oneness (Islâmic Monotheism)] (and ask Me for anything) I will respond to your (invocation). Verily! Those who scorn My worship [i.e. do not invoke Me, and do not believe in My Oneness, (Islâmic Monotheism)] they will surely enter Hell in humiliation!" (60)

Quran 40:69-76

أَلَمْ تَرَ إِلَى ٱلَّذِينَ يُجَٰدِلُونَ فِىٓ ءَايَٰتِ ٱللَّهِ أَنَّىٰ يُصْرَفُونَ (٦٩) ٱلَّذِينَ كَذَّبُوا۟ بِٱلْكِتَٰبِ وَبِمَآ أَرْسَلْنَا بِهِۦ رُسُلَنَا ۖ فَسَوْفَ يَعْلَمُونَ (٧٠) إِذِ ٱلْأَغْلَٰلُ فِىٓ أَعْنَٰقِهِمْ وَٱلسَّلَٰسِلُ يُسْحَبُونَ (٧١) فِى ٱلْحَمِيمِ ثُمَّ فِى ٱلنَّارِ يُسْجَرُونَ (٧٢) ثُمَّ قِيلَ لَهُمْ أَيْنَ مَا كُنتُمْ تُشْرِكُونَ (٧٣) مِن دُونِ ٱللَّهِ ۖ قَالُوا۟ ضَلُّوا۟ عَنَّا بَل لَّمْ نَكُن نَّدْعُوا۟ مِن قَبْلُ شَيْـًٔا ۚ كَذَٰلِكَ يُضِلُّ ٱللَّهُ ٱلْكَٰفِرِينَ (٧٤) ذَٰلِكُم بِمَا كُنتُمْ تَفْرَحُونَ فِى ٱلْأَرْضِ بِغَيْرِ ٱلْحَقِّ وَبِمَا كُنتُمْ تَمْرَحُونَ (٧٥) ٱدْخُلُوٓا۟ أَبْوَٰبَ جَهَنَّمَ خَٰلِدِينَ فِيهَا ۖ فَبِئْسَ مَثْوَى ٱلْمُتَكَبِّرِينَ (٧٦)

See you not those who dispute about the Ayât (proofs, evidences, verses, lessons, signs, revelations, etc.) of Allâh? How are they turning away (from the truth, i.e. Islâmic Monotheism to the falsehood (i.e. polytheism)? (69) Those who deny the Book (this Qur'ân), and that with which We sent Our Messengers (i.e. to worship none but Allâh Alone sincerely, and to reject all false deities and to confess resurrection after the death for recompense) they will come to know (when they will be cast into the Fire of Hell). (70) When iron collars will be rounded over their necks, and the chains, they shall be dragged along (71) In the boiling water, then they will be burned in the Fire. (72) Then it will be said to them: "Where are (all) those whom you used to join in worship as partners. (73) "Besides Allâh"? They will say: "They have vanished from us: Nay, we did not invoke (worship) anything before." Thus Allâh leads astray the disbelievers. (74) That was because you had been exulting in the earth without any right (by worshipping others instead of Allâh and by committing crimes), and that you used to rejoice extremely (in your error). (75) Enter the gates of Hell to abide therein, and (indeed) what an evil abode of the arrogant! (76)

Quran 41:5-7

وَقَالُوا۟ قُلُوبُنَا فِىٓ أَكِنَّةٍ مِّمَّا تَدْعُونَآ إِلَيْهِ وَفِىٓ ءَاذَانِنَا وَقْرٌ وَمِنۢ بَيْنِنَا وَبَيْنِكَ حِجَابٌ فَٱعْمَلْ إِنَّنَا عَـٰمِلُونَ (٥) قُلْ إِنَّمَآ أَنَا۠ بَشَرٌ مِّثْلُكُمْ يُوحَىٰٓ إِلَىَّ أَنَّمَآ إِلَـٰهُكُمْ إِلَـٰهٌ وَٰحِدٌ فَٱسْتَقِيمُوٓا۟ إِلَيْهِ وَٱسْتَغْفِرُوهُ ۗ وَوَيْلٌ لِّلْمُشْرِكِينَ (٦) ٱلَّذِينَ لَا يُؤْتُونَ ٱلزَّكَوٰةَ وَهُم بِٱلْءَاخِرَةِ هُمْ كَـٰفِرُونَ (٧)

And they say: "Our hearts are under coverings (screened) from that to which you invite us, and in our ears is deafness, and between us and you is a screen, so work you (on your way); verily, we are working (on our way)." (5) Say (O Muhammad): "I am only a human being like you. It is revealed to me that your Ilâh (God) is One Ilâh (God - Allâh), therefore take Straight Path to Him (with true Faith — Islâmic Monotheism) and obedience to Him, and seek forgiveness of Him. And woe to Al-Mushrikûn (the polytheists, idolaters, disbelievers in the Oneness of Allâh). (6) Those who give not the Zakât and they are disbelievers in the Hereafter. (7)

Quran 41:9

قُلْ أَئِنَّكُمْ لَتَكْفُرُونَ بِٱلَّذِى خَلَقَ ٱلْأَرْضَ فِى يَوْمَيْنِ وَتَجْعَلُونَ لَهُۥٓ أَندَادًا ۚ ذَٰلِكَ رَبُّ ٱلْعَٰلَمِينَ

Say: "Do you verily disbelieve in Him Who created the earth in two Days And you set up rivals (in worship) with Him? That is the Lord of the 'Alamîn (mankind, jinn and all that exists). (9)

Quran 41:19-29

وَيَوْمَ يُحْشَرُ أَعْدَآءُ ٱللَّهِ إِلَى ٱلنَّارِ فَهُمْ يُوزَعُونَ (١٩) حَتَّىٰٓ إِذَا مَا جَآءُوهَا شَهِدَ عَلَيْهِمْ سَمْعُهُمْ وَأَبْصَٰرُهُمْ وَجُلُودُهُم بِمَا كَانُوا۟ يَعْمَلُونَ (٢٠) وَقَالُوا۟ لِجُلُودِهِمْ لِمَ شَهِدتُّمْ عَلَيْنَا ۖ قَالُوٓا۟ أَنطَقَنَا ٱللَّهُ ٱلَّذِىٓ أَنطَقَ كُلَّ شَىْءٍ وَهُوَ خَلَقَكُمْ أَوَّلَ مَرَّةٍ وَإِلَيْهِ تُرْجَعُونَ (٢١) وَمَا كُنتُمْ تَسْتَتِرُونَ أَن يَشْهَدَ عَلَيْكُمْ سَمْعُكُمْ وَلَآ أَبْصَٰرُكُمْ وَلَا جُلُودُكُمْ وَلَٰكِن ظَنَنتُمْ أَنَّ ٱللَّهَ لَا يَعْلَمُ كَثِيرًا مِّمَّا تَعْمَلُونَ (٢٢) وَذَٰلِكُمْ ظَنُّكُمُ ٱلَّذِى ظَنَنتُم بِرَبِّكُمْ أَرْدَىٰكُمْ فَأَصْبَحْتُم مِّنَ ٱلْخَٰسِرِينَ (٢٣) فَإِن يَصْبِرُوا۟ فَٱلنَّارُ مَثْوًى لَّهُمْ ۖ وَإِن يَسْتَعْتِبُوا۟ فَمَا هُم مِّنَ ٱلْمُعْتَبِينَ (٢٤) ۞ وَقَيَّضْنَا لَهُمْ قُرَنَآءَ فَزَيَّنُوا۟ لَهُم مَّا بَيْنَ أَيْدِيهِمْ وَمَا خَلْفَهُمْ وَحَقَّ عَلَيْهِمُ ٱلْقَوْلُ فِىٓ أُمَمٍ قَدْ خَلَتْ مِن قَبْلِهِم مِّنَ ٱلْجِنِّ وَٱلْإِنسِ ۖ إِنَّهُمْ كَانُوا۟ خَٰسِرِينَ (٢٥) وَقَالَ ٱلَّذِينَ كَفَرُوا۟ لَا تَسْمَعُوا۟ لِهَٰذَا ٱلْقُرْءَانِ وَٱلْغَوْا۟ فِيهِ لَعَلَّكُمْ تَغْلِبُونَ (٢٦) فَلَنُذِيقَنَّ ٱلَّذِينَ كَفَرُوا۟ عَذَابًا شَدِيدًا وَلَنَجْزِيَنَّهُمْ أَسْوَأَ ٱلَّذِى كَانُوا۟ يَعْمَلُونَ (٢٧) ذَٰلِكَ جَزَآءُ أَعْدَآءِ ٱللَّهِ ٱلنَّارُ ۖ لَهُمْ فِيهَا دَارُ ٱلْخُلْدِ ۖ جَزَآءً بِمَا كَانُوا۟ بِـَٔايَٰتِنَا يَجْحَدُونَ (٢٨) وَقَالَ ٱلَّذِينَ كَفَرُوا۟ رَبَّنَآ أَرِنَا ٱلَّذَيْنِ أَضَلَّانَا مِنَ ٱلْجِنِّ وَٱلْإِنسِ نَجْعَلْهُمَا تَحْتَ أَقْدَامِنَا لِيَكُونَا مِنَ ٱلْأَسْفَلِينَ (٢٩)

And (remember) the Day that the enemies of Allâh will be gathered to the Fire, then they will be driven [(to the fire), former ones being withheld till their later ones will join them]. (19) Till, when they reach it (Hell-fire), their hearing (ears) and their eyes, and their skins will testify against them as to what they used to do. (20) And they will say to their skins, "Why do you testify against us?" They will say: "Allâh has caused us to speak," — He causes all things to speak, and He created you the first time, and to Him you are made to return." (21) And you have not been hiding yourselves (in the world), lest your ears, and your eyes, and your skins should testify against you, but you thought that Allâh knew not much of what you were doing. (22) And that thought of yours which you thought about your Lord, has brought you to destruction, and you have become (this Day) of those utterly lost! (23) Then, if they bear the torment patiently, then the Fire is the home for them, and if they seek to please Allâh, yet they are not of those who will ever be allowed to please Allâh. (24) And We have assigned them (devils) intimate companions (in this world), who have made fair-seeming to them, what was before them (evil deeds which they were doing in the present worldly life and disbelief in the Reckoning and the Resurrection) and what was behind them (denial of the matters in the coming life of the Hereafter as regards punishment or reward). And the Word (i.e. the torment) is justified against them as it was justified against those who were among the previous generations of jinn and men that had passed away before them. Indeed they (all) were the losers. (25) And those who disbelieve say: "Listen not to this Qur'ân, and make noise in the midst of its (recitation) that you may overcome." (26) But surely, We shall cause those who disbelieve to taste a severe torment, and certainly, We shall requite them the worst of what they used to do. (27) That is the recompense of the enemies of Allâh: the Fire. Therein will be for them the eternal home, a (deserving) recompense for that they used to deny Our Ayât (proofs, evidences, verses, lessons, signs, revelations, etc.). (28) And those who disbelieve will say: "Our Lord! Show us those among jinn and men who led us astray, that we may crush them under our feet so that they become the lowest." (29)

Quran 41:40-41

إِنَّ ٱلَّذِينَ يُلْحِدُونَ فِى ءَايَٰتِنَا لَا يَخْفَوْنَ عَلَيْنَآ أَفَمَن يُلْقَىٰ فِى ٱلنَّارِ خَيْرٌ أَم مَّن يَأْتِىٓ ءَامِنًا يَوْمَ ٱلْقِيَٰمَةِ ٱعْمَلُوا۟ مَا شِئْتُمْ إِنَّهُۥ بِمَا تَعْمَلُونَ بَصِيرٌ (٤٠) إِنَّ ٱلَّذِينَ كَفَرُوا۟ بِٱلذِّكْرِ لَمَّا جَآءَهُمْ وَإِنَّهُۥ لَكِتَٰبٌ عَزِيزٌ (٤١)

Verily, those who turn away from Our Ayât (proofs, evidences, verses, lessons, signs, revelations, etc. by attacking, distorting and denying them), are not hidden from Us. Is he who is cast into the Fire better or he who comes secure on the Day of Resurrection? Do what you will. Verily! He is All-Seer of what you do (40) Verily, those who disbelieved in the Reminder (i.e. the Qur'ân) when it came to them (shall receive the punishment). And verily, it is an honourable well-fortified respected Book (because it is Allâh's Speech, and He has protected it from corruption). (41)

Quran 41:47-54

﴿ إِلَيْهِ يُرَدُّ عِلْمُ ٱلسَّاعَةِ وَمَا تَخْرُجُ مِن ثَمَرَٰتٍ مِّنْ أَكْمَامِهَا وَمَا تَحْمِلُ مِنْ أُنثَىٰ وَلَا تَضَعُ إِلَّا بِعِلْمِهِۦ وَيَوْمَ يُنَادِيهِمْ أَيْنَ شُرَكَآءِى قَالُوٓا۟ ءَاذَنَّٰكَ مَا مِنَّا مِن شَهِيدٍ (٤٧) وَضَلَّ عَنْهُم مَّا كَانُوا۟ يَدْعُونَ مِن قَبْلُ ۖ وَظَنُّوا۟ مَا لَهُم مِّن مَّحِيصٍ (٤٨) لَّا يَسْـَٔمُ ٱلْإِنسَٰنُ مِن دُعَآءِ ٱلْخَيْرِ وَإِن مَّسَّهُ ٱلشَّرُّ فَيَـُٔوسٌ قَنُوطٌ (٤٩) وَلَئِنْ أَذَقْنَٰهُ رَحْمَةً مِّنَّا مِنْ بَعْدِ ضَرَّآءَ مَسَّتْهُ لَيَقُولَنَّ هَٰذَا لِى وَمَآ أَظُنُّ ٱلسَّاعَةَ قَآئِمَةً وَلَئِن رُّجِعْتُ إِلَىٰ رَبِّىٓ إِنَّ لِى عِندَهُۥ لَلْحُسْنَىٰ ۚ فَلَنُنَبِّئَنَّ ٱلَّذِينَ كَفَرُوا۟ بِمَا عَمِلُوا۟ وَلَنُذِيقَنَّهُم مِّنْ عَذَابٍ غَلِيظٍ (٥٠) وَإِذَآ أَنْعَمْنَا عَلَى ٱلْإِنسَٰنِ أَعْرَضَ وَنَـَٔا بِجَانِبِهِۦ وَإِذَا مَسَّهُ ٱلشَّرُّ فَذُو دُعَآءٍ عَرِيضٍ (٥١) قُلْ أَرَءَيْتُمْ إِن كَانَ مِنْ عِندِ ٱللَّهِ ثُمَّ كَفَرْتُم بِهِۦ مَنْ أَضَلُّ مِمَّنْ هُوَ فِى شِقَاقٍۭ بَعِيدٍ (٥٢) سَنُرِيهِمْ ءَايَٰتِنَا فِى ٱلْءَافَاقِ وَفِىٓ أَنفُسِهِمْ حَتَّىٰ يَتَبَيَّنَ لَهُمْ أَنَّهُ ٱلْحَقُّ ۗ أَوَلَمْ يَكْفِ بِرَبِّكَ أَنَّهُۥ عَلَىٰ كُلِّ شَىْءٍ شَهِيدٌ (٥٣) أَلَآ إِنَّهُمْ فِى مِرْيَةٍ مِّن لِّقَآءِ رَبِّهِمْ ۗ أَلَآ إِنَّهُۥ بِكُلِّ شَىْءٍ مُّحِيطٌۢ (٥٤) ﴾

To Him (Alone) is referred the knowledge of the Hour. No fruit comes out of its sheath, nor does a female conceive, nor brings forth (young), except by His Knowledge. And on the Day when He will call unto them (saying): "Where are My (so-called) partners (whom you did invent)?" They will say: "We inform You that none of us bears witness to it (that they are Your partners)!" (47) And those whom they used to invoke before (in this world) shall disappear from them, and they will perceive that they have no place of refuge (from Allâh's punishment). (48) Man (the disbeliever) does not get tired of asking good (things from Allâh), but if an evil touches him, then he gives up all hope and is lost in despair. (49) And truly, if We give him a taste of mercy from Us, after some adversity (severe poverty or disease, etc.) has touched him, he is sure to say: "This is due to me (merit), I think not that the Hour will be established. But if I am brought back to my Lord, surely, there will be for me the best (wealth) with Him. Then, We verily, will show to the disbelievers what they have done and We shall make them taste a severe torment. (50) And when We show favour to man, he withdraws and turns away; but when evil touches him, then he has recourse to long supplications. (51) Say: "Tell me, if it (the Qur'ân) is from Allâh, and you disbelieve in it, who is more astray than one who is in opposition far away (from Allâh's Right Path and His obedience). (52) We will show them Our Signs in the universe, and in their own selves, until it becomes manifest to them that this (the Qur'ân) is the truth. Is it not sufficient in regard to your Lord that He is a Witness over all things? (53) Verily, they are in doubt concerning the Meeting with their Lord? (i.e. Resurrection after their death, and their return to their Lord). Verily! He it is Who is surrounding all things! (54)

Quran 43:19-24

وَجَعَلُوا۟ ٱلْمَلَـٰٓئِكَةَ ٱلَّذِينَ هُمْ عِبَـٰدُ ٱلرَّحْمَـٰنِ إِنَـٰثًا ۚ أَشَهِدُوا۟ خَلْقَهُمْ ۚ سَتُكْتَبُ شَهَـٰدَتُهُمْ وَيُسْـَٔلُونَ (١٩) وَقَالُوا۟ لَوْ شَآءَ ٱلرَّحْمَـٰنُ مَا عَبَدْنَـٰهُم ۗ مَّا لَهُم بِذَٰلِكَ مِنْ عِلْمٍ ۖ إِنْ هُمْ إِلَّا يَخْرُصُونَ (٢٠) أَمْ ءَاتَيْنَـٰهُمْ كِتَـٰبًا مِّن قَبْلِهِۦ فَهُم بِهِۦ مُسْتَمْسِكُونَ (٢١) بَلْ قَالُوٓا۟ إِنَّا وَجَدْنَآ ءَابَآءَنَا عَلَىٰٓ أُمَّةٍ وَإِنَّا عَلَىٰٓ ءَاثَـٰرِهِم مُّهْتَدُونَ (٢٢) وَكَذَٰلِكَ مَآ أَرْسَلْنَا مِن قَبْلِكَ فِى قَرْيَةٍ مِّن نَّذِيرٍ إِلَّا قَالَ

مُتْرَفُوهَآ إِنَّا وَجَدْنَآ ءَابَآءَنَا عَلَىٰٓ أُمَّةٍ وَإِنَّا عَلَىٰٓ ءَاثَـٰرِهِم مُّقْتَدُونَ (٢٣) ۞ قَـٰلَ أَوَلَوْ جِئْتُكُم بِأَهْدَىٰ مِمَّا وَجَدتُّمْ عَلَيْهِ ءَابَآءَكُمْ ۖ قَالُوٓا۟ إِنَّا بِمَآ أُرْسِلْتُم بِهِۦ كَـٰفِرُونَ (٢٤)

And they make the angels who themselves are slaves of the Most Gracious (Allâh) females. Did they witness their creation? Their testimony will be recorded, and they will be questioned! (19) And they said: "If it had been the Will of the Most Gracious (Allâh), we should not have worshipped them (false deities)." They have no knowledge whatsoever of that. They do nothing but lie! (20) Or have We given them any Book before this (the Qur'ân), to which they are holding fast? (21) Nay! They say: "We found our fathers following a certain way and religion, and we guide ourselves by their footsteps." (22) And similarly, We sent not a warner before you (O Muhammad) to any town (people) but the luxurious ones among them said: "We found our fathers following a certain way and religion, and we will indeed follow their footsteps." (23) (The warner) said: "Even if I bring you better guidance than that which you found your fathers following?" They said: "Verily, We disbelieve in that with which you have been sent." (24)

Quran 45:7-11

وَيْلٌ لِّكُلِّ أَفَّاكٍ أَثِيمٍ (٧) يَسْمَعُ ءَايَـٰتِ ٱللَّهِ تُتْلَىٰ عَلَيْهِ ثُمَّ يُصِرُّ مُسْتَكْبِرًا كَأَن لَّمْ يَسْمَعْهَا ۖ فَبَشِّرْهُ بِعَذَابٍ أَلِيمٍ (٨) وَإِذَا عَلِمَ مِنْ ءَايَـٰتِنَا شَيْـًٔا ٱتَّخَذَهَا هُزُوًا ۚ أُو۟لَـٰٓئِكَ لَهُمْ عَذَابٌ مُّهِينٌ (٩) مِّن وَرَآئِهِمْ جَهَنَّمُ ۖ وَلَا يُغْنِى عَنْهُم مَّا كَسَبُوا۟

شَيْئًا وَلَا مَا ٱتَّخَذُوا۟ مِن دُونِ ٱللَّهِ أَوْلِيَآءَ وَلَهُمْ عَذَابٌ عَظِيمٌ (١٠) هَٰذَا هُدًى وَٱلَّذِينَ كَفَرُوا۟ بِـَٔايَٰتِ رَبِّهِمْ لَهُمْ عَذَابٌ مِّن رِّجْزٍ أَلِيمٌ (١١)

Woe to every sinful liar, (7) Who hears the Verses of Allâh (being) recited to him, yet persists with pride as if he heard them not. So announce to him a painful torment! (8) And when he learns something of Our Verses (this Qur'ân), he makes them a jest. For such there will be a humiliating torment. (9) In front of them there is Hell, and that which they have earned will be of no profit to them, nor (will be of any profit to them) those whom they have taken as Auliyâ' (protectors, helpers) besides Allâh. And theirs will be a great torment. (10) This (Qur'ân) is a guidance. And those who disbelieve in the Ayât (proofs, evidences, verses, lessons, signs, revelations) of their Lord, for them there is a painful torment of Rijz (a severe kind of punishment). (11)

Quran 45:31-35

وَأَمَّا ٱلَّذِينَ كَفَرُوٓا۟ أَفَلَمْ تَكُنْ ءَايَٰتِى تُتْلَىٰ عَلَيْكُمْ فَٱسْتَكْبَرْتُمْ وَكُنتُمْ قَوْمًا مُّجْرِمِينَ (٣١) وَإِذَا قِيلَ إِنَّ وَعْدَ ٱللَّهِ حَقٌّ وَٱلسَّاعَةُ لَا رَيْبَ فِيهَا قُلْتُم مَّا نَدْرِى مَا ٱلسَّاعَةُ إِن نَّظُنُّ إِلَّا ظَنًّا وَمَا نَحْنُ بِمُسْتَيْقِنِينَ (٣٢) وَبَدَا لَهُمْ سَيِّـَٔاتُ مَا عَمِلُوا۟ وَحَاقَ بِهِم مَّا كَانُوا۟ بِهِۦ يَسْتَهْزِءُونَ (٣٣) وَقِيلَ ٱلْيَوْمَ نَنسَىٰكُمْ كَمَا نَسِيتُمْ لِقَآءَ يَوْمِكُمْ هَٰذَا وَمَأْوَىٰكُمُ ٱلنَّارُ وَمَا لَكُم مِّن نَّٰصِرِينَ (٣٤) ذَٰلِكُم بِأَنَّكُمُ ٱتَّخَذْتُمْ ءَايَٰتِ ٱللَّهِ هُزُوًا وَغَرَّتْكُمُ ٱلْحَيَوٰةُ ٱلدُّنْيَا فَٱلْيَوْمَ لَا يُخْرَجُونَ مِنْهَا وَلَا هُمْ يُسْتَعْتَبُونَ (٣٥)

But as for those who disbelieved (it will be said to them): "Were not Our Verses recited to you? But you were proud, and you were a people who were Mujrimûn (polytheists, disbelievers, sinners, criminals)." (31) And when it was said: "Verily! Allâh's Promise is the truth, and there is no doubt about the coming of the Hour," you said;"We know not what is the Hour, we do not think it but as a conjecture, and we have no firm convincing belief (therein)." (32) And the evil of what they did will appear to them, and that which they used to mock at will completely encircle them. (33) And it will be said: "This Day We will forget you as you forgot the Meeting of this Day of yours. And your abode is the Fire, and there is none to help you." (34) This, because you took the revelations of Allâh (this Qur'ân) in mockery, and the life of the world deceived you. So this Day, they shall not be taken out from there (Hell), nor shall they be returned to the worldly life, (so that they repent to Allâh, and beg His Pardon for their sins). (35)

Quran 46:3-11

مَا خَلَقْنَا ٱلسَّمَٰوَٰتِ وَٱلْأَرْضَ وَمَا بَيْنَهُمَآ إِلَّا بِٱلْحَقِّ وَأَجَلٍ مُّسَمًّى ۚ وَٱلَّذِينَ كَفَرُوا۟ عَمَّآ أُنذِرُوا۟ مُعْرِضُونَ (٣) قُلْ أَرَءَيْتُم مَّا تَدْعُونَ مِن دُونِ ٱللَّهِ أَرُونِى مَاذَا خَلَقُوا۟ مِنَ ٱلْأَرْضِ أَمْ لَهُمْ شِرْكٌ فِى ٱلسَّمَٰوَٰتِ ۖ ٱئْتُونِى بِكِتَٰبٍ مِّن قَبْلِ هَٰذَآ أَوْ أَثَٰرَةٍ مِّنْ عِلْمٍ إِن كُنتُمْ صَٰدِقِينَ (٤) وَمَنْ أَضَلُّ مِمَّن يَدْعُوا۟ مِن دُونِ ٱللَّهِ مَن لَّا يَسْتَجِيبُ لَهُۥٓ إِلَىٰ يَوْمِ ٱلْقِيَٰمَةِ وَهُمْ عَن دُعَآئِهِمْ غَٰفِلُونَ (٥) وَإِذَا حُشِرَ ٱلنَّاسُ كَانُوا۟ لَهُمْ أَعْدَآءً وَكَانُوا۟ بِعِبَادَتِهِمْ كَٰفِرِينَ (٦) وَإِذَا تُتْلَىٰ عَلَيْهِمْ ءَايَٰتُنَا بَيِّنَٰتٍ قَالَ ٱلَّذِينَ كَفَرُوا۟ لِلْحَقِّ لَمَّا جَآءَهُمْ هَٰذَا سِحْرٌ مُّبِينٌ (٧) أَمْ يَقُولُونَ ٱفْتَرَىٰهُ ۖ قُلْ إِنِ ٱفْتَرَيْتُهُۥ فَلَا تَمْلِكُونَ لِى مِنَ ٱللَّهِ شَيْـًٔا ۖ هُوَ أَعْلَمُ بِمَا تُفِيضُونَ فِيهِ ۖ كَفَىٰ بِهِۦ شَهِيدًۢا بَيْنِى وَبَيْنَكُمْ ۖ وَهُوَ ٱلْغَفُورُ ٱلرَّحِيمُ (٨) قُلْ مَا كُنتُ بِدْعًا مِّنَ ٱلرُّسُلِ وَمَآ أَدْرِى مَا يُفْعَلُ بِى وَلَا بِكُمْ ۖ إِنْ أَتَّبِعُ إِلَّا مَا يُوحَىٰٓ إِلَىَّ وَمَآ أَنَا۠ إِلَّا نَذِيرٌ مُّبِينٌ (٩) قُلْ أَرَءَيْتُمْ إِن كَانَ مِنْ عِندِ

ٱللَّهِ وَكَفَرْتُم بِهِۦ وَشَهِدَ شَاهِدٌ مِّنۢ بَنِىٓ إِسْرَٰٓءِيلَ عَلَىٰ مِثْلِهِۦ فَـَٔامَنَ وَٱسْتَكْبَرْتُمْ إِنَّ ٱللَّهَ لَا يَهْدِى ٱلْقَوْمَ ٱلظَّٰلِمِينَ (١٠) وَقَالَ ٱلَّذِينَ كَفَرُوا۟ لِلَّذِينَ ءَامَنُوا۟ لَوْ كَانَ خَيْرًا مَّا سَبَقُونَآ إِلَيْهِ وَإِذْ لَمْ يَهْتَدُوا۟ بِهِۦ فَسَيَقُولُونَ هَٰذَآ إِفْكٌ قَدِيمٌ (١١)

We created not the heavens and the earth and all that is between them except with truth, and for an appointed term. But those who disbelieve turn away from that whereof they are warned. (3) Say: "Think you about all that you invoke besides Allâh? Show me. What have they created of the earth? Or have they a share in (the creation of) the heavens? Bring me a Book (revealed before this), or some trace of knowledge (in support of your claims), if you are truthful!" (4) And who is more astray than one who calls on (invokes) besides Allâh, such as will not answer him till the Day of Resurrection, and who are (even) unaware of their calls (invocations) to them? (5) And when mankind are gathered (on the Day of Resurrection), they (false deities) will become their enemies and will deny their worshipping. (6) And when Our Clear Verses are recited to them, the disbelievers say of the truth (this Qur'ân), when it reaches them: "This is plain magic!" (7) Or say they: "He (Muhammad) has fabricated it." Say: "If I have fabricated it? still you have no power to support me against Allâh. He knows best of what you say among yourselves concerning it (i.e. this Qur'ân)! Sufficient is He as a witness between me and you! And He is the Oft-Forgiving, the Most Merciful." (8) Say (O Muhammad):"I am not a new thing among the Messengers (of Allâh) (i.e. I am not the first Messenger) nor do I know what will be done with me or with you. I only follow that which is revealed to me, and I am but a plain warner." (9) Say: "Tell me! If this (Qur'ân) is from Allâh and you deny it, and a witness from among the Children of Israel ('Abdullâh bin Salâm) testifies that [this Qur'ân is from Allâh (like the Taurât (Torah)], and he believed (embraced Islâm) while you are too proud (to believe)." Verily, Allâh guides not the people who are Zâlimûn (polytheists, disbelievers and wrong-doers). (10) And those who disbelieve (strong and wealthy) say of those who believe (the weak and poor): "Had it (Islâmic Monotheism to which Muhammad is inviting mankind) been a good thing, they (the weak and poor) would not have preceded us thereto!" And when they have not let themselves be guided by it (this Qur'ân), they say: "This is an ancient lie!" (11)

Quran 46:20

وَيَوْمَ يُعْرَضُ ٱلَّذِينَ كَفَرُواْ عَلَى ٱلنَّارِ أَذْهَبْتُمْ طَيِّبَٰتِكُمْ فِى حَيَاتِكُمُ ٱلدُّنْيَا وَٱسْتَمْتَعْتُم بِهَا فَٱلْيَوْمَ تُجْزَوْنَ عَذَابَ ٱلْهُونِ بِمَا كُنتُمْ تَسْتَكْبِرُونَ فِى ٱلْأَرْضِ بِغَيْرِ ٱلْحَقِّ وَبِمَا كُنتُمْ تَفْسُقُونَ

On the Day when those who disbelieve (in the Oneness of Allâh Islâmic Monotheism) will be exposed to the Fire (it will be said): "You received your good things in the life of the world, and you took your pleasure therein. Now this Day you shall be recompensed with a torment of humiliation, because you were arrogant in the land without a right, and because you used to rebel against Allah's Command (disobey Allâh). (20)

Quran 46:34

وَيَوْمَ يُعْرَضُ ٱلَّذِينَ كَفَرُواْ عَلَى ٱلنَّارِ أَلَيْسَ هَٰذَا بِٱلْحَقِّ ۖ قَالُواْ بَلَىٰ وَرَبِّنَا ۚ قَالَ فَذُوقُواْ ٱلْعَذَابَ بِمَا كُنتُمْ تَكْفُرُونَ

And on the Day when those who disbelieve will be exposed to the Fire (it will be said to them): "Is this not the truth?" They will say: "Yes, By our Lord!" He will say: "Then taste the torment, because you used to disbelieve!" (34)

Quran 47:1

ٱلَّذِينَ كَفَرُواْ وَصَدُّواْ عَن سَبِيلِ ٱللَّهِ أَضَلَّ أَعْمَٰلَهُمْ

Those who disbelieve [in the Oneness of Allâh, and in the Message of Prophet Muhammad], and hinder (men) from the Path of Allâh (Islâmic Monotheism), He will render their deeds vain. (1)

Quran 47:3

ذَٰلِكَ بِأَنَّ ٱلَّذِينَ كَفَرُواْ ٱتَّبَعُواْ ٱلْبَٰطِلَ وَأَنَّ ٱلَّذِينَ ءَامَنُواْ ٱتَّبَعُواْ ٱلْحَقَّ مِن رَّبِّهِمْ ۚ كَذَٰلِكَ يَضْرِبُ ٱللَّهُ لِلنَّاسِ أَمْثَٰلَهُمْ

That is because those who disbelieve follow falsehood, while those who believe follow the truth from their Lord. Thus does Allâh set forth for mankind their parables. (3)

Quran 47:8-9

وَٱلَّذِينَ كَفَرُواْ فَتَعْسًا لَّهُمْ وَأَضَلَّ أَعْمَٰلَهُمْ (٨) ذَٰلِكَ بِأَنَّهُمْ كَرِهُواْ مَآ أَنزَلَ ٱللَّهُ فَأَحْبَطَ أَعْمَٰلَهُمْ (٩)

But those who disbelieve (in the Oneness of Allâh Islâmic Monotheism), for them is destruction, and (Allâh) will make their deeds vain. (8) That is because they hate that which Allâh has sent down (this Qur'ân and Islâmic laws etc.), so He has made their deeds fruitless. (9)

Quran 47:22-34

فَهَلْ عَسَيْتُمْ إِن تَوَلَّيْتُمْ أَن تُفْسِدُوا۟ فِى ٱلْأَرْضِ وَتُقَطِّعُوٓا۟ أَرْحَامَكُمْ (٢٢) أُو۟لَٰٓئِكَ ٱلَّذِينَ لَعَنَهُمُ ٱللَّهُ فَأَصَمَّهُمْ وَأَعْمَىٰٓ أَبْصَٰرَهُمْ (٢٣) أَفَلَا يَتَدَبَّرُونَ ٱلْقُرْءَانَ أَمْ عَلَىٰ قُلُوبٍ أَقْفَالُهَآ (٢٤) إِنَّ ٱلَّذِينَ ٱرْتَدُّوا۟ عَلَىٰٓ أَدْبَٰرِهِم مِّنۢ بَعْدِ مَا تَبَيَّنَ لَهُمُ ٱلْهُدَى ٱلشَّيْطَٰنُ سَوَّلَ لَهُمْ وَأَمْلَىٰ لَهُمْ (٢٥) ذَٰلِكَ بِأَنَّهُمْ قَالُوا۟ لِلَّذِينَ كَرِهُوا۟ مَا نَزَّلَ ٱللَّهُ سَنُطِيعُكُمْ فِى بَعْضِ ٱلْأَمْرِ ۖ وَٱللَّهُ يَعْلَمُ إِسْرَارَهُمْ (٢٦) فَكَيْفَ إِذَا تَوَفَّتْهُمُ ٱلْمَلَٰٓئِكَةُ يَضْرِبُونَ وُجُوهَهُمْ وَأَدْبَٰرَهُمْ (٢٧) ذَٰلِكَ بِأَنَّهُمُ ٱتَّبَعُوا۟ مَآ أَسْخَطَ ٱللَّهَ وَكَرِهُوا۟ رِضْوَٰنَهُۥ فَأَحْبَطَ أَعْمَٰلَهُمْ (٢٨) أَمْ حَسِبَ ٱلَّذِينَ فِى قُلُوبِهِم مَّرَضٌ أَن لَّن يُخْرِجَ ٱللَّهُ أَضْغَٰنَهُمْ (٢٩) وَلَوْ نَشَآءُ لَأَرَيْنَٰكَهُمْ فَلَعَرَفْتَهُم بِسِيمَٰهُمْ ۚ وَلَتَعْرِفَنَّهُمْ فِى لَحْنِ ٱلْقَوْلِ ۚ وَٱللَّهُ يَعْلَمُ أَعْمَٰلَكُمْ (٣٠) وَلَنَبْلُوَنَّكُمْ حَتَّىٰ نَعْلَمَ ٱلْمُجَٰهِدِينَ مِنكُمْ وَٱلصَّٰبِرِينَ وَنَبْلُوَا۟ أَخْبَارَكُمْ (٣١) إِنَّ ٱلَّذِينَ كَفَرُوا۟ وَصَدُّوا۟ عَن سَبِيلِ ٱللَّهِ وَشَآقُّوا۟ ٱلرَّسُولَ مِنۢ بَعْدِ مَا تَبَيَّنَ لَهُمُ ٱلْهُدَىٰ لَن يَضُرُّوا۟ ٱللَّهَ شَيْـًٔا وَسَيُحْبِطُ أَعْمَٰلَهُمْ (٣٢) يَٰٓأَيُّهَا ٱلَّذِينَ ءَامَنُوٓا۟ أَطِيعُوا۟ ٱللَّهَ وَأَطِيعُوا۟ ٱلرَّسُولَ وَلَا تُبْطِلُوٓا۟ أَعْمَٰلَكُمْ (٣٣) إِنَّ ٱلَّذِينَ كَفَرُوا۟ وَصَدُّوا۟ عَن سَبِيلِ ٱللَّهِ ثُمَّ مَاتُوا۟ وَهُمْ كُفَّارٌ فَلَن يَغْفِرَ ٱللَّهُ لَهُمْ (٣٤)

Would you then, if you were given the authority, do mischief in the land, and sever your ties of kinship? (22) Such are they whom Allâh has cursed, so that He has made them deaf and blinded their sight. (23) Do they not then think deeply in the Qur'ân, or are their hearts locked up (from understanding it)? (24) Verily, those who have turned back (have apostatise) as disbelievers after the guidance has been manifested to them — Shaitân (Satan) has beautified for them (their false hopes), and (Allâh) prolonged their term (age). (25) This is because they said to those who hate what Allâh has sent down: "We will obey you in part of the matter," but Allâh knows their secrets. (26) Then how (will it be) when the angels will take their souls at death, smiting their faces and their backs? (27) That is because they followed that which angered Allâh, and hated that which pleased Him. So He made their deeds fruitless. (28) Or do those in whose hearts is a disease (of hypocrisy), think that Allâh will not bring to light all their hidden ill-wills? (29) Had We willed, We could have shown them to you, and you should have known them by their marks; but surely, you will know them by the tone of their speech! And Allâh knows (all) your deeds. (30) And surely, We shall try you till We test those who strive hard (for the Cause of Allâh) and As-Sabirun (the patient ones), and We shall test your facts (i.e. the one who is a liar, and the one who is truthful). (31) Verily, those who disbelieve, and hinder (men) from the Path of Allâh (i.e. Islâm), and oppose the Messenger (by standing against him and hurting him), after the guidance has been clearly shown to them, they will not hurt Allâh in the least, but He will make their deeds fruitless, (32) O you who believe! Obey Allâh, and obey the Messenger (Muhammad) and render not vain your deeds. (33) Verily, those who disbelieve, and hinder (men) from the Path of Allâh (i.e. Islâm); then die while they are disbelievers, - Allâh will not forgive them. (34)

Quran 48:6

وَيُعَذِّبَ ٱلْمُنَٰفِقِينَ وَٱلْمُنَٰفِقَٰتِ وَٱلْمُشْرِكِينَ وَٱلْمُشْرِكَٰتِ ٱلظَّآنِّينَ بِٱللَّهِ ظَنَّ ٱلسَّوْءِ ۚ عَلَيْهِمْ دَآئِرَةُ ٱلسَّوْءِ ۖ وَغَضِبَ ٱللَّهُ عَلَيْهِمْ وَلَعَنَهُمْ وَأَعَدَّ لَهُمْ جَهَنَّمَ ۖ وَسَآءَتْ مَصِيرًا

And that He may punish the Munâfiqûn (hypocrites), men and women, and also the Mushrikûn (polytheists) men and women, who think evil thoughts about Allâh, for them is a disgraceful torment, And the Anger of Allâh is upon them, and He has cursed them and prepared Hell for them — and worst indeed is that destination. (6)

Quran 48:13

وَمَن لَّمْ يُؤْمِنۢ بِٱللَّهِ وَرَسُولِهِۦ فَإِنَّآ أَعْتَدْنَا لِلْكَٰفِرِينَ سَعِيرًا

And whosoever does not believe in Allâh and His Messenger (Muhammad), then verily, We have prepared for the disbelievers a blazing Fire. (13)

Quran 48:22-25

وَلَوْ قَٰتَلَكُمُ ٱلَّذِينَ كَفَرُواْ لَوَلَّوُاْ ٱلْأَدْبَٰرَ ثُمَّ لَا يَجِدُونَ وَلِيًّا وَلَا نَصِيرًا (٢٢) سُنَّةَ ٱللَّهِ ٱلَّتِى قَدْ خَلَتْ مِن قَبْلُ ۖ وَلَن تَجِدَ لِسُنَّةِ ٱللَّهِ تَبْدِيلًا (٢٣) وَهُوَ ٱلَّذِى كَفَّ أَيْدِيَهُمْ عَنكُمْ وَأَيْدِيَكُمْ عَنْهُم بِبَطْنِ مَكَّةَ مِنۢ بَعْدِ أَنْ أَظْفَرَكُمْ عَلَيْهِمْ ۚ وَكَانَ ٱللَّهُ بِمَا تَعْمَلُونَ بَصِيرًا (٢٤) هُمُ ٱلَّذِينَ كَفَرُواْ وَصَدُّوكُمْ عَنِ ٱلْمَسْجِدِ ٱلْحَرَامِ وَٱلْهَدْىَ مَعْكُوفًا أَن يَبْلُغَ مَحِلَّهُۥ ۚ وَلَوْلَا رِجَالٌ مُّؤْمِنُونَ وَنِسَآءٌ مُّؤْمِنَٰتٌ لَّمْ تَعْلَمُوهُمْ أَن تَطَـُٔوهُمْ فَتُصِيبَكُم مِّنْهُم مَّعَرَّةٌۢ بِغَيْرِ عِلْمٍ ۖ لِّيُدْخِلَ ٱللَّهُ فِى رَحْمَتِهِۦ مَن يَشَآءُ ۚ لَوْ تَزَيَّلُواْ لَعَذَّبْنَا ٱلَّذِينَ كَفَرُواْ مِنْهُمْ عَذَابًا أَلِيمًا (٢٥)

And if those who disbelieve fight against you, they certainly would have turned their backs, then they would have found neither a Walî (protector, guardian) nor a helper. (22) That has been the Way of Allâh already with those who passed away before. And you will not find any change in the Way of Allâh. (23) And He it is Who has withheld their hands from you and your hands from them in the midst of Makkah, after He had made you victors over them. And Allâh is Ever the All-Seer of what you do. (24) They are the ones who disbelieved (in the Oneness of Allâh — Islâmic Monotheism), and hindered you from Al¬Masjid¬al¬Harâm (at Makkah) and detained the sacrificial animals, from reaching their place of sacrifice. Had there not been believing men and believing women whom you did not know, that you may kill them, and on whose account a sin would have been committed by you without (your) knowledge, that Allâh might bring into His Mercy whom He wills, if they (the believers and the disbelievers) had been apart, We verily would have punished those of them who disbelieved, with painful torment. (25)

Quran 50:2-3

بَلْ عَجِبُوٓا۟ أَن جَآءَهُم مُّنذِرٌ مِّنْهُمْ فَقَالَ ٱلْكَٰفِرُونَ هَٰذَا شَىْءٌ عَجِيبٌ (٢) أَءِذَا مِتْنَا وَكُنَّا تُرَابًا ذَٰلِكَ رَجْعٌۢ بَعِيدٌ (٣)

Nay, they wonder that there has come to them a warner from among themselves. So the disbelievers say: "This is a strange thing! (2) "When we are dead and have become dust (shall we be resurrected?) That is a far return." (3)

Quran 51:8-14

إِنَّكُمْ لَفِى قَوْلٍ مُّخْتَلِفٍ (٨) يُؤْفَكُ عَنْهُ مَنْ أُفِكَ (٩) قُتِلَ ٱلْخَرَّاصُونَ (١٠) ٱلَّذِينَ هُمْ فِى غَمْرَةٍ سَاهُونَ (١١) يَسْـَٔلُونَ أَيَّانَ يَوْمُ ٱلدِّينِ (١٢) يَوْمَ هُمْ عَلَى ٱلنَّارِ يُفْتَنُونَ (١٣) ذُوقُوا۟ فِتْنَتَكُمْ هَـٰذَا ٱلَّذِى كُنتُم بِهِۦ تَسْتَعْجِلُونَ (١٤)

Certainly, you have different ideas (about Muhammad and the Qur'ân). (8) Turned aside therefrom (i.e. from Muhammad and the Qur'ân) is he who is turned aside (by the Decree and Preordainment of Allâh). (9) Cursed be the liars, (10) Who are under a cover of heedlessness (think not about the gravity of the Hereafter), (11) They ask "When will be the Day of Recompense?" (12) (It will be) a Day when they will be tried (punished i.e. burnt) over the Fire! (13) "Taste you your trial (punishment i.e. burning)! This is what you used to ask to be hastened!" (14)

Quran 52:11-16

فَوَيْلٌ يَوْمَئِذٍ لِّلْمُكَذِّبِينَ (١١) ٱلَّذِينَ هُمْ فِى خَوْضٍ يَلْعَبُونَ (١٢) يَوْمَ يُدَعُّونَ إِلَىٰ نَارِ جَهَنَّمَ دَعًّا (١٣) هَـٰذِهِ ٱلنَّارُ ٱلَّتِى كُنتُم بِهَا تُكَذِّبُونَ (١٤) أَفَسِحْرٌ هَـٰذَآ أَمْ أَنتُمْ لَا تُبْصِرُونَ (١٥) ٱصْلَوْهَا فَٱصْبِرُوٓا۟ أَوْ لَا تَصْبِرُوا۟ سَوَآءٌ عَلَيْكُمْ إِنَّمَا تُجْزَوْنَ مَا كُنتُمْ تَعْمَلُونَ (١٦)

Then woe that Day to the beliers; (11) Who are playing in falsehood. (12) The Day when they will be pushed down by force to the Fire of Hell, with a horrible, forceful pushing. (13) This is the Fire which you used to belie. (14) Is this magic, or do you not see? (15) Taste you therein its heat, and whether you are patient of it or impatient of it, it is all the same. You are only being requited for what you used to do. (16)

Quran 52:30-47

أَمْ يَقُولُونَ شَاعِرٌ نَتَرَبَّصُ بِهِ رَيْبَ ٱلْمَنُونِ (٣٠) قُلْ تَرَبَّصُواْ فَإِنِّى مَعَكُم مِّنَ ٱلْمُتَرَبِّصِينَ (٣١) أَمْ تَأْمُرُهُمْ أَحْلَٰمُهُم بِهَٰذَآ أَمْ هُمْ قَوْمٌ طَاغُونَ (٣٢) أَمْ يَقُولُونَ تَقَوَّلَهُۥ بَل لَّا يُؤْمِنُونَ (٣٣) فَلْيَأْتُواْ بِحَدِيثٍ مِّثْلِهِۦٓ إِن كَانُواْ صَٰدِقِينَ (٣٤) أَمْ خُلِقُواْ مِنْ غَيْرِ شَىْءٍ أَمْ هُمُ ٱلْخَٰلِقُونَ (٣٥) أَمْ خَلَقُواْ ٱلسَّمَٰوَٰتِ وَٱلْأَرْضَ بَل لَّا يُوقِنُونَ (٣٦) أَمْ عِندَهُمْ خَزَآئِنُ رَبِّكَ أَمْ هُمُ ٱلْمُصَيْطِرُونَ (٣٧) أَمْ لَهُمْ سُلَّمٌ يَسْتَمِعُونَ فِيهِ فَلْيَأْتِ مُسْتَمِعُهُم بِسُلْطَٰنٍ مُّبِينٍ (٣٨) أَمْ لَهُ ٱلْبَنَٰتُ وَلَكُمُ ٱلْبَنُونَ (٣٩) أَمْ تَسْـَٔلُهُمْ أَجْرًا فَهُم مِّن مَّغْرَمٍ مُّثْقَلُونَ (٤٠) أَمْ عِندَهُمُ ٱلْغَيْبُ فَهُمْ يَكْتُبُونَ (٤١) أَمْ يُرِيدُونَ كَيْدًا فَٱلَّذِينَ كَفَرُواْ هُمُ ٱلْمَكِيدُونَ (٤٢) أَمْ لَهُمْ إِلَٰهٌ غَيْرُ ٱللَّهِ سُبْحَٰنَ ٱللَّهِ عَمَّا يُشْرِكُونَ (٤٣) وَإِن يَرَوْاْ كِسْفًا مِّنَ ٱلسَّمَآءِ سَاقِطًا يَقُولُواْ سَحَابٌ مَّرْكُومٌ (٤٤) فَذَرْهُمْ حَتَّىٰ يُلَٰقُواْ يَوْمَهُمُ ٱلَّذِى فِيهِ يُصْعَقُونَ (٤٥) يَوْمَ لَا يُغْنِى عَنْهُمْ كَيْدُهُمْ شَيْـًٔا وَلَا هُمْ يُنصَرُونَ (٤٦) وَإِنَّ لِلَّذِينَ ظَلَمُواْ عَذَابًا دُونَ ذَٰلِكَ وَلَٰكِنَّ أَكْثَرَهُمْ لَا يَعْلَمُونَ (٤٧)

Or do they say: "(Muhammad is) a poet! We await for him some calamity by time.!" (30) Say (O Muhammad to them): "Wait! I am with you, among the waiters!" (31) Do their minds command them this [i.e. to tell a lie against you (Muhammad)] or are they people transgressing all the bounds? (32) Or do they say: "He (Muhammad) has forged it (this Qur'ân)?" Nay! They believe not! (33) Let them then produce a recital like unto it (the Qur'ân) if they are truthful. (34) Were they created by nothing? or were they themselves the creators? (35) Or did they create the heavens and the earth? Nay, but they have no firm Belief. (36) Or are with them the treasures of your Lord?

Or are they the tyrants with the authority to do as they like? (37) Or have they a stairway (to heaven), by means of which they listen (to the talks of the angels)? Then let their listener produce some manifest proof. (38) Or has He (Allâh) only daughters and you have sons? (39) Or is it that you (O Muhammad) ask a wage from them (for your preaching of Islâmic Monotheism) so that they are burdened with a load of debt? (40) Or that the Ghaib (unseen) is with them, and they write it down? (41) Or do they intend a plot (against you O Muhammad)? But those who disbelieve (in the Oneness of Allâh — Islâmic Monotheism) are themselves plotted against! (42) Or have they an ilâh (a god) other than Allâh? Glorified is Allâh from all that they ascribe as partners (to Him) (43) And if they were to see a piece of the heaven falling down, they would say: "Clouds gathered in heaps!" (44) So leave them alone till they meet their Day, in which they will sink into a fainting (with horror). (45) The Day when their plotting shall not avail them at all nor will they be helped (i.e. they will receive their torment in Hell). (46) And verily, for those who do wrong, there is another punishment (i.e. the torment in this world and in their graves) before this, but most of them know not. (47)

Quran 53:27-28

إِنَّ ٱلَّذِينَ لَا يُؤْمِنُونَ بِٱلْآخِرَةِ لَيُسَمُّونَ ٱلْمَلَٰٓئِكَةَ تَسْمِيَةَ ٱلْأُنثَىٰ (٢٧) وَمَا لَهُم بِهِۦ مِنْ عِلْمٍۖ إِن يَتَّبِعُونَ إِلَّا ٱلظَّنَّۖ وَإِنَّ ٱلظَّنَّ لَا يُغْنِى مِنَ ٱلْحَقِّ شَيْـًٔا (٢٨)

Verily, those who believe not in the Hereafter, name the angels with female names. (27) But they have no knowledge thereof. They follow but a guess, and verily, guess is no substitute for the truth. (28)

Quran 54:2-8

وَإِن يَرَوْا۟ ءَايَةً يُعْرِضُوا۟ وَيَقُولُوا۟ سِحْرٌ مُّسْتَمِرٌّ (٢) وَكَذَّبُوا۟ وَٱتَّبَعُوٓا۟ أَهْوَآءَهُمْ ۚ وَكُلُّ أَمْرٍ مُّسْتَقِرٌّ (٣) وَلَقَدْ جَآءَهُم مِّنَ ٱلْأَنۢبَآءِ مَا فِيهِ مُزْدَجَرٌ (٤) حِكْمَةٌۢ بَـٰلِغَةٌ ۖ فَمَا تُغْنِ ٱلنُّذُرُ (٥) فَتَوَلَّ عَنْهُمْ ۘ يَوْمَ يَدْعُ ٱلدَّاعِ إِلَىٰ شَىْءٍ نُّكُرٍ (٦) خُشَّعًا أَبْصَـٰرُهُمْ يَخْرُجُونَ مِنَ ٱلْأَجْدَاثِ كَأَنَّهُمْ جَرَادٌ مُّنتَشِرٌ (٧) مُّهْطِعِينَ إِلَى ٱلدَّاعِ ۖ يَقُولُ ٱلْكَـٰفِرُونَ هَـٰذَا يَوْمٌ عَسِرٌ (٨)

And if they see a sign, they turn away, and say: "This is continuous magic." (2) They belied (the Verses of Allâh, this Qur'ân), and followed their own lusts. And every matter will be settled [according to the kind of deeds (good deeds will take their doers to Paradise, and similarly evil deeds will take their doers to Hell)]. (3) And indeed there has come to them news (in this Qur'ân) wherein there is (enough warning) to check (them from evil), (4) Perfect wisdom (this Qur'ân), but (the preaching of) warners benefit them not, (5) So withdraw from them. The Day that the caller will call (them) to a terrible thing. (6) They will come forth, with humbled eyes from (their) graves as if they were locusts spread abroad, (7) Hastening towards The caller, the disbelievers will say: "This is a hard Day." (8)

Quran 56:41-57

وَأَصْحَـٰبُ ٱلشِّمَالِ مَآ أَصْحَـٰبُ ٱلشِّمَالِ (٤١) فِى سَمُومٍ وَحَمِيمٍ (٤٢) وَظِلٍّ مِّن يَحْمُومٍ (٤٣) لَّا بَارِدٍ وَلَا كَرِيمٍ (٤٤) إِنَّهُمْ كَانُوا۟ قَبْلَ ذَٰلِكَ مُتْرَفِينَ (٤٥) وَكَانُوا۟ يُصِرُّونَ عَلَى ٱلْحِنثِ ٱلْعَظِيمِ (٤٦) وَكَانُوا۟ يَقُولُونَ أَئِذَا مِتْنَا

وَكُنَّا تُرَابًا وَعِظَـٰمًا أَءِنَّا لَمَبْعُوثُونَ (٤٧) أَوَءَابَآؤُنَا ٱلْأَوَّلُونَ (٤٨) قُلْ إِنَّ ٱلْأَوَّلِينَ وَٱلْءَاخِرِينَ (٤٩) لَمَجْمُوعُونَ إِلَىٰ مِيقَـٰتِ يَوْمٍ مَّعْلُومٍ (٥٠) ثُمَّ إِنَّكُمْ أَيُّهَا ٱلضَّآلُّونَ ٱلْمُكَذِّبُونَ (٥١) لَءَاكِلُونَ مِن شَجَرٍ مِّن زَقُّومٍ (٥٢) فَمَالِـُٔونَ مِنْهَا ٱلْبُطُونَ (٥٣) فَشَـٰرِبُونَ عَلَيْهِ مِنَ ٱلْحَمِيمِ (٥٤) فَشَـٰرِبُونَ شُرْبَ ٱلْهِيمِ (٥٥) هَـٰذَا نُزُلُهُمْ يَوْمَ ٱلدِّينِ (٥٦) نَحْنُ خَلَقْنَـٰكُمْ فَلَوْلَا تُصَدِّقُونَ (٥٧)

And those on the Left Hand how (unfortunate) will be those on the Left Hand? (41) In fierce hot wind and boiling water. (42) And shadow of black smoke. (43) (That shadow) neither cool, nor (even) pleasant, (44) Verily, before that, they indulged in luxury, (45) And were persisting in great sin (joining partners in worship along with Allâh, committing murder and other crimes). (46) And they used to say: "When we die and become dust and bones, shall we then indeed be resurrected? (47) "And also our forefathers?" (48) Say (O Muhammad): "(Yes) verily, those of old, and those of later times. (49) "All will surely be gathered together for appointed Meeting of a known Day. (50) "Then moreover, verily, you the erring-ones, the deniers (of Resurrection)! (51) "You verily will eat of the trees of Zaqqûm. (52) "Then you will fill your bellies therewith, (53) "And drink boiling water on top of it. (54) "And you will drink (that) like thirsty camels!" (55) That will be their entertainment on the Day of Recompense! (56) We created you, then why do you believe not? (57)

Quran 57:12-15

يَوْمَ تَرَى ٱلْمُؤْمِنِينَ وَٱلْمُؤْمِنَٰتِ يَسْعَىٰ نُورُهُم بَيْنَ أَيْدِيهِمْ وَبِأَيْمَٰنِهِم بُشْرَىٰكُمُ ٱلْيَوْمَ جَنَّٰتٌ تَجْرِى مِن تَحْتِهَا ٱلْأَنْهَٰرُ خَٰلِدِينَ فِيهَا ۚ ذَٰلِكَ هُوَ ٱلْفَوْزُ ٱلْعَظِيمُ (١٢) يَوْمَ يَقُولُ ٱلْمُنَٰفِقُونَ وَٱلْمُنَٰفِقَٰتُ لِلَّذِينَ ءَامَنُوا۟ ٱنظُرُونَا نَقْتَبِسْ مِن نُّورِكُمْ قِيلَ ٱرْجِعُوا۟ وَرَآءَكُمْ فَٱلْتَمِسُوا۟ نُورًا فَضُرِبَ بَيْنَهُم بِسُورٍ لَّهُۥ بَابٌۢ بَاطِنُهُۥ فِيهِ ٱلرَّحْمَةُ وَظَٰهِرُهُۥ مِن قِبَلِهِ ٱلْعَذَابُ (١٣) يُنَادُونَهُمْ أَلَمْ نَكُن مَّعَكُمْ ۖ قَالُوا۟ بَلَىٰ وَلَٰكِنَّكُمْ فَتَنتُمْ أَنفُسَكُمْ وَتَرَبَّصْتُمْ وَٱرْتَبْتُمْ وَغَرَّتْكُمُ ٱلْأَمَانِىُّ حَتَّىٰ جَآءَ أَمْرُ ٱللَّهِ وَغَرَّكُم بِٱللَّهِ ٱلْغَرُورُ (١٤) فَٱلْيَوْمَ لَا يُؤْخَذُ مِنكُمْ فِدْيَةٌ وَلَا مِنَ ٱلَّذِينَ كَفَرُوا۟ ۚ مَأْوَىٰكُمُ ٱلنَّارُ ۖ هِىَ مَوْلَىٰكُمْ ۖ وَبِئْسَ ٱلْمَصِيرُ (١٥)

On the Day you shall see the believing men and the believing women their light running forward before them and by their right hands. Glad tidings for you this Day! Gardens under which rivers flow (Paradise), to dwell therein forever! Truly, this is the great success! (12) On the Day when the hypocrites men and women will say to the believers: "Wait for us! Let us get something from your light!" It will be said: "Go back to your rear! Then seek a light!" So a wall will be put up between them, with a gate therein. Inside it will be mercy, and outside it will be torment." (13) (The hypocrites) will call the believers: "Were we not with you?" The believers will reply: "Yes! But you led yourselves into temptations, you looked forward for our destruction; you doubted (in Faith); and you were deceived by false desires, till the Command of Allâh came to pass. And the chief deceiver (Satan) deceived you in respect of Allâh." (14) So this Day no ransom shall be taken from you (hypocrites), nor of those who disbelieved, (in the Oneness of Allâh Islâmic Monotheism). Your abode is the Fire, That is your maula (friend — proper place), and worst indeed is that destination. (15)

Quran 58:5

إِنَّ ٱلَّذِينَ يُحَآدُّونَ ٱللَّهَ وَرَسُولَهُۥ كُبِتُوا۟ كَمَا كُبِتَ ٱلَّذِينَ مِن قَبْلِهِمْ ۚ وَقَدْ أَنزَلْنَآ ءَايَٰتٍۭ بَيِّنَٰتٍ ۚ وَلِلْكَٰفِرِينَ عَذَابٌ مُّهِينٌ (٥)

Verily, those who oppose Allâh and His Messenger (Muhammad) will be disgraced, as those before them (among the past nation), were disgraced. And We have sent down clear Ayât (proofs, evidences, verses, lessons, signs, revelations, etc.). And for the disbelievers is a disgracing torment. (5)

Quran 58:14-20

أَلَمْ تَرَ إِلَى ٱلَّذِينَ تَوَلَّوْا۟ قَوْمًا غَضِبَ ٱللَّهُ عَلَيْهِم مَّا هُم مِّنكُمْ وَلَا مِنْهُمْ وَيَحْلِفُونَ عَلَى ٱلْكَذِبِ وَهُمْ يَعْلَمُونَ (١٤) أَعَدَّ ٱللَّهُ لَهُمْ عَذَابًا شَدِيدًا ۖ إِنَّهُمْ سَآءَ مَا كَانُوا۟ يَعْمَلُونَ (١٥) ٱتَّخَذُوٓا۟ أَيْمَٰنَهُمْ جُنَّةً فَصَدُّوا۟ عَن سَبِيلِ ٱللَّهِ فَلَهُمْ عَذَابٌ مُّهِينٌ (١٦) لَّن تُغْنِىَ عَنْهُمْ أَمْوَٰلُهُمْ وَلَآ أَوْلَٰدُهُم مِّنَ ٱللَّهِ شَيْـًٔا ۚ أُو۟لَٰٓئِكَ أَصْحَٰبُ ٱلنَّارِ ۖ هُمْ فِيهَا خَٰلِدُونَ (١٧) يَوْمَ يَبْعَثُهُمُ ٱللَّهُ جَمِيعًا فَيَحْلِفُونَ لَهُۥ كَمَا يَحْلِفُونَ لَكُمْ ۖ وَيَحْسَبُونَ أَنَّهُمْ عَلَىٰ شَىْءٍ ۚ أَلَآ إِنَّهُمْ هُمُ ٱلْكَٰذِبُونَ (١٨) ٱسْتَحْوَذَ عَلَيْهِمُ ٱلشَّيْطَٰنُ فَأَنسَىٰهُمْ ذِكْرَ ٱللَّهِ ۚ أُو۟لَٰٓئِكَ حِزْبُ ٱلشَّيْطَٰنِ ۚ أَلَآ إِنَّ حِزْبَ ٱلشَّيْطَٰنِ هُمُ ٱلْخَٰسِرُونَ (١٩) إِنَّ ٱلَّذِينَ يُحَآدُّونَ ٱللَّهَ وَرَسُولَهُۥٓ أُو۟لَٰٓئِكَ فِى ٱلْأَذَلِّينَ (٢٠)

Have you (O Muhammad) not seen those (hypocrites) who take as friends a people upon whom is the Wrath of Allâh? They are neither of you (Muslims) nor of them, and they swear to a lie while they know. (14) Allâh has prepared for them a severe torment. Evil indeed is that which they used to do. (15) They have made their oaths a screen (for their evil actions). Thus they hinder (men) from the Path of Allâh, so they shall have a humiliating torment. (16) Their children and their wealth will avail them nothing against Allâh. They will be the dwellers of the Fire, to dwell therein forever. (17) On the Day when Allâh will resurrect them all together (for their account), then they will swear to Him as they swear to you (O Muslims). And they think that they have something (to stand upon). Verily, they are liars! (18) Shaitân (Satan) has overpowered them. So he has made them forget the remembrance of Allâh. They are the party of Shaitân (Satan). Verily, it is the party of Shaitân (Satan) that will be the losers! (19) Those who oppose Allâh and His Messenger (Muhammad), they will be among the lowest (most humiliated). (20)

Quran 59:11-17

﴿ أَلَمْ تَرَ إِلَى ٱلَّذِينَ نَافَقُوا۟ يَقُولُونَ لِإِخْوَٰنِهِمُ ٱلَّذِينَ كَفَرُوا۟ مِنْ أَهْلِ ٱلْكِتَٰبِ لَئِنْ أُخْرِجْتُمْ لَنَخْرُجَنَّ مَعَكُمْ وَلَا نُطِيعُ فِيكُمْ أَحَدًا أَبَدًا وَإِن قُوتِلْتُمْ لَنَنصُرَنَّكُمْ وَٱللَّهُ يَشْهَدُ إِنَّهُمْ لَكَٰذِبُونَ (١١) لَئِنْ أُخْرِجُوا۟ لَا يَخْرُجُونَ مَعَهُمْ وَلَئِن قُوتِلُوا۟ لَا يَنصُرُونَهُمْ وَلَئِن نَّصَرُوهُمْ لَيُوَلُّنَّ ٱلْأَدْبَٰرَ ثُمَّ لَا يُنصَرُونَ (١٢) لَأَنتُمْ أَشَدُّ رَهْبَةً فِى صُدُورِهِم مِّنَ ٱللَّهِ ذَٰلِكَ بِأَنَّهُمْ قَوْمٌ لَّا يَفْقَهُونَ (١٣) لَا يُقَٰتِلُونَكُمْ جَمِيعًا إِلَّا فِى قُرًى مُّحَصَّنَةٍ أَوْ مِن وَرَآءِ جُدُرٍۭ بَأْسُهُم بَيْنَهُمْ شَدِيدٌ تَحْسَبُهُمْ جَمِيعًا وَقُلُوبُهُمْ شَتَّىٰ ذَٰلِكَ بِأَنَّهُمْ قَوْمٌ لَّا يَعْقِلُونَ (١٤) كَمَثَلِ ٱلَّذِينَ مِن قَبْلِهِمْ قَرِيبًا ذَاقُوا۟ وَبَالَ أَمْرِهِمْ وَلَهُمْ عَذَابٌ أَلِيمٌ (١٥) كَمَثَلِ ٱلشَّيْطَٰنِ إِذْ قَالَ لِلْإِنسَٰنِ ٱكْفُرْ فَلَمَّا كَفَرَ قَالَ إِنِّى بَرِىٓءٌ مِّنكَ إِنِّىٓ أَخَافُ ٱللَّهَ رَبَّ ٱلْعَٰلَمِينَ (١٦) فَكَانَ عَٰقِبَتَهُمَآ أَنَّهُمَا فِى ٱلنَّارِ خَٰلِدَيْنِ فِيهَا وَذَٰلِكَ جَزَٰٓؤُا۟ ٱلظَّٰلِمِينَ (١٧)

Have you not observed the hypocrites who say to their friends among the people of the Scripture who disbelieve: "(By Allâh) If you are expelled, we (too) indeed will go out with you, and we shall never obey any one against you, and if you are attacked (in fight), we shall indeed help you." But Allâh is Witness, that they verily, are liars. (11) Surely, if they are expelled, never will they (hypocrites) go out with them, and if they are attacked, they will never help them. And (even) if they do help them, they (hypocrites) will turn their backs, and they will not be victorious. (12) Verily, you (believers in the Oneness of Allâh — Islâmic Monotheism) are more fearful in their breasts than Allâh. That is because they are a people who comprehend not (the Majesty and Power of Allâh). (13) They fight not against you even together, except in fortified townships, or from behind walls. Their enmity among themselves is very great. You would think they were united, but their hearts are divided, That is because they are a people who understand not. (14) They are like their immediate predecessors, they tasted the evil result of their conduct, and (in the Hereafter, there is) for them a painful torment. (15) (Their allies deceived them) like Shaitân (Satan), when he says to man: "Disbelieve in Allâh." But when (man) disbelieves in Allâh, Shaitân (Satan) says: "I am free of you, I fear Allâh, the Lord of the 'Alamîn (mankind, jinn and all that exists)!" (16) So the end of both will be that they will be in the Fire, abiding therein. Such is the recompense of the Zâlimûn (i.e.

polytheists, wrong-doers, disbelievers in Allâh and in His Oneness). (17)

Quran 61:7-9

وَمَنْ أَظْلَمُ مِمَّنِ افْتَرَىٰ عَلَى ٱللَّهِ ٱلْكَذِبَ وَهُوَ يُدْعَىٰ إِلَى ٱلْإِسْلَٰمِ وَٱللَّهُ لَا يَهْدِى ٱلْقَوْمَ ٱلظَّٰلِمِينَ (٧) يُرِيدُونَ لِيُطْفِـُٔوا نُورَ ٱللَّهِ بِأَفْوَٰهِهِمْ وَٱللَّهُ مُتِمُّ نُورِهِۦ وَلَوْ كَرِهَ ٱلْكَٰفِرُونَ (٨) هُوَ ٱلَّذِىٓ أَرْسَلَ رَسُولَهُۥ بِٱلْهُدَىٰ وَدِينِ ٱلْحَقِّ لِيُظْهِرَهُۥ عَلَى ٱلدِّينِ كُلِّهِۦ وَلَوْ كَرِهَ ٱلْمُشْرِكُونَ (٩)

And who does more wrong than the one who invents a lie against Allâh, while he is being invited to Islâm? And Allâh guides not the people who are Zâlimûn (polytheists, wrong-doers and disbelievers) folk. (7) They intend to put out the Light of Allâh (i.e. the Religion of Islâm, this Qur'ân, and the Prophet Muhammad) with their mouths. But Allâh will bring His Light to perfection even though the disbelievers hate (it). (8) He it is Who has sent His Messenger (Muhammad) with guidance and the religion of truth (Islâmic Monotheism) to make it victorious over all (other) religions even though the Mushrikûn (polytheists, pagans, idolaters, and disbelievers) hate (it). (9)

Quran 63:1-8

إِذَا جَآءَكَ ٱلْمُنَٰفِقُونَ قَالُواْ نَشْهَدُ إِنَّكَ لَرَسُولُ ٱللَّهِ وَٱللَّهُ يَعْلَمُ إِنَّكَ لَرَسُولُهُۥ وَٱللَّهُ يَشْهَدُ إِنَّ ٱلْمُنَٰفِقِينَ لَكَٰذِبُونَ (١) ٱتَّخَذُوٓاْ أَيْمَٰنَهُمْ جُنَّةً فَصَدُّواْ عَن سَبِيلِ ٱللَّهِ إِنَّهُمْ سَآءَ مَا كَانُواْ يَعْمَلُونَ (٢) ذَٰلِكَ بِأَنَّهُمْ ءَامَنُواْ ثُمَّ كَفَرُواْ فَطُبِعَ عَلَىٰ قُلُوبِهِمْ فَهُمْ لَا يَفْقَهُونَ (٣) وَإِذَا رَأَيْتَهُمْ تُعْجِبُكَ أَجْسَامُهُمْ وَإِن يَقُولُواْ تَسْمَعْ لِقَوْلِهِمْ كَأَنَّهُمْ خُشُبٌ مُّسَنَّدَةٌ يَحْسَبُونَ كُلَّ صَيْحَةٍ عَلَيْهِمْ هُمُ ٱلْعَدُوُّ

فَاحْذَرْهُمْ قَتَلَهُمُ ٱللَّهُ أَنَّىٰ يُؤْفَكُونَ (٤) وَإِذَا قِيلَ لَهُمْ تَعَالَوْاْ يَسْتَغْفِرْ لَكُمْ رَسُولُ ٱللَّهِ لَوَّوْاْ رُءُوسَهُمْ وَرَأَيْتَهُمْ يَصُدُّونَ وَهُم مُّسْتَكْبِرُونَ (٥) سَوَآءٌ عَلَيْهِمْ أَسْتَغْفَرْتَ لَهُمْ أَمْ لَمْ تَسْتَغْفِرْ لَهُمْ لَن يَغْفِرَ ٱللَّهُ لَهُمْ إِنَّ ٱللَّهَ لَا يَهْدِى ٱلْقَوْمَ ٱلْفَٰسِقِينَ (٦) هُمُ ٱلَّذِينَ يَقُولُونَ لَا تُنفِقُواْ عَلَىٰ مَنْ عِندَ رَسُولِ ٱللَّهِ حَتَّىٰ يَنفَضُّواْ وَلِلَّهِ خَزَآئِنُ ٱلسَّمَٰوَٰتِ وَٱلْأَرْضِ وَلَٰكِنَّ ٱلْمُنَٰفِقِينَ لَا يَفْقَهُونَ (٧) يَقُولُونَ لَئِن رَّجَعْنَآ إِلَى ٱلْمَدِينَةِ لَيُخْرِجَنَّ ٱلْأَعَزُّ مِنْهَا ٱلْأَذَلَّ وَلِلَّهِ ٱلْعِزَّةُ وَلِرَسُولِهِۦ وَلِلْمُؤْمِنِينَ وَلَٰكِنَّ ٱلْمُنَٰفِقِينَ لَا يَعْلَمُونَ (٨)

When the hypocrites come to you (O Muhammad), they say: "We bear witness that you are indeed the Messenger of Allâh." Allâh knows that you are indeed His Messenger and Allâh bears witness that the hypocrites are liars indeed. (1) They have made their oaths a screen (for their hypocrisy). Thus they hinder (men) from the Path of Allâh. Verily, evil is what they used to do. (2) That is because they believed, then disbelieved, therefore their hearts are sealed, so they understand not. (3) And when you look at them, their bodies please you; and when they speak, you listen to their words. They are as blocks of wood propped up. They think that every cry is against them. They are the enemies, so beware of them. May Allâh curse them! How are they denying (or deviating from) the Right Path? (4) And when it is said to them: "Come, so that the Messenger of Allâh may ask forgiveness from Allâh for you", they twist their heads, and you would see them turning away their faces in pride. (5) It is equal to them whether you (Muhammad) ask forgiveness or ask not forgiveness for them. Verily, Allâh guides not the people who are the Fâsiqîn (the rebellious, the disobedient to Allâh) (6) They are the ones who say: "Spend not on those who are with Allâh's Messenger, until they desert him." And to Allâh belong the treasures of the heavens and the earth, but the hypocrites comprehend not. (7) They (hyprocrites) say: "If we return to Al-Madinah, indeed the more honourable will expel therefrom the meaner." But honour, power and glory belong to Allâh, and to His Messenger (Muhammad), and to the believers, but the hypocrites know not. (8)

Quran 64:5-10

أَلَمْ يَأْتِكُمْ نَبَؤُاْ ٱلَّذِينَ كَفَرُواْ مِن قَبْلُ فَذَاقُواْ وَبَالَ أَمْرِهِمْ وَلَهُمْ عَذَابٌ أَلِيمٌ (٥) ذَٰلِكَ بِأَنَّهُۥ كَانَت تَّأْتِيهِمْ رُسُلُهُم بِٱلْبَيِّنَٰتِ فَقَالُوٓاْ أَبَشَرٌ يَهْدُونَنَا فَكَفَرُواْ وَتَوَلَّواْۚ وَّٱسْتَغْنَى ٱللَّهُۚ وَٱللَّهُ غَنِىٌّ حَمِيدٌ (٦) زَعَمَ ٱلَّذِينَ كَفَرُوٓاْ أَن لَّن يُبْعَثُواْۚ قُلْ بَلَىٰ وَرَبِّى لَتُبْعَثُنَّ ثُمَّ لَتُنَبَّؤُنَّ بِمَا عَمِلْتُمْۚ وَذَٰلِكَ عَلَى ٱللَّهِ يَسِيرٌ (٧) فَـَٔامِنُواْ بِٱللَّهِ وَرَسُولِهِۦ وَٱلنُّورِ ٱلَّذِىٓ أَنزَلْنَاۚ وَٱللَّهُ بِمَا تَعْمَلُونَ خَبِيرٌ (٨) يَوْمَ يَجْمَعُكُمْ لِيَوْمِ ٱلْجَمْعِۖ ذَٰلِكَ يَوْمُ ٱلتَّغَابُنِۗ وَمَن يُؤْمِنۢ بِٱللَّهِ وَيَعْمَلْ صَٰلِحًا يُكَفِّرْ عَنْهُ سَيِّـَٔاتِهِۦ وَيُدْخِلْهُ جَنَّٰتٍ تَجْرِى مِن تَحْتِهَا ٱلْأَنْهَٰرُ خَٰلِدِينَ فِيهَآ أَبَدًاۚ ذَٰلِكَ ٱلْفَوْزُ ٱلْعَظِيمُ (٩) وَٱلَّذِينَ كَفَرُواْ وَكَذَّبُواْ بِـَٔايَٰتِنَآ أُوْلَٰٓئِكَ أَصْحَٰبُ ٱلنَّارِ خَٰلِدِينَ فِيهَاۖ وَبِئْسَ ٱلْمَصِيرُ (١٠)

Has not the news reached you of those who disbelieved aforetime? And so they tasted the evil result of their disbelief, and theirs will be a painful torment. (5) That was because there came to them their Messengers with clear proofs (signs), but they said: "Shall mere men guide us?" So they disbelieved and turned away (from the truth), But Allâh was not in need (of them). And Allâh is

Rich (Free of all needs), Worthy of all praise. (6) The disbelievers pretend that they will never be resurrected (for the Account). Say (O Muhammad): "Yes! By my Lord, you will certainly be resurrected, then you will be informed of (and recompensed for) what you did, and that is easy for Allâh. (7) Therefore, believe in Allâh and His Messenger (Muhammad), and in the Light (this Qur'ân) which We have sent down. And Allâh is All-Aware of what you do. (8) (And remember) the Day when He will gather you (all) on the Day of Gathering, that will be the Day of mutual loss and gain (i.e. loss for the disbelievers as they will enter the Hell-fire and gain for the believers as they will enter Paradise). And whosoever believes in Allâh and performs righteous good deeds, He will expiate from him his sins, and will admit him to Gardens under which rivers flow (Paradise) to dwell therein forever, that will be the great success. (9) But those who disbelieved (in the Oneness of Allâh - Islâmic Monotheism) and denied Our Ayât (proofs, evidences, verses, lessons, signs, revelations, etc.), they will be the dwellers of the Fire, to dwell therein forever. And worst indeed is that destination (10)

Quran 67:6-11

وَلِلَّذِينَ كَفَرُواْ بِرَبِّهِمْ عَذَابُ جَهَنَّمَ وَبِئْسَ ٱلْمَصِيرُ (٦) إِذَآ أُلْقُواْ فِيهَا سَمِعُواْ لَهَا شَهِيقًا وَهِيَ تَفُورُ (٧) تَكَادُ تَمَيَّزُ مِنَ ٱلْغَيْظِ كُلَّمَآ أُلْقِىَ فِيهَا فَوْجٌ سَأَلَهُمْ خَزَنَتُهَآ أَلَمْ يَأْتِكُمْ نَذِيرٌ (٨) قَالُواْ بَلَىٰ قَدْ جَآءَنَا نَذِيرٌ فَكَذَّبْنَا وَقُلْنَا مَا نَزَّلَ ٱللَّهُ مِن شَىْءٍ إِنْ أَنتُمْ إِلَّا فِى ضَلَٰلٍ كَبِيرٍ (٩) وَقَالُواْ لَوْ كُنَّا نَسْمَعُ أَوْ نَعْقِلُ مَا

كُنَّا فِىٓ أَصْحَٰبِ ٱلسَّعِيرِ (١٠) فَٱعْتَرَفُوا۟ بِذَنۢبِهِمْ فَسُحْقًا لِّأَصْحَٰبِ ٱلسَّعِيرِ (١١)

And for those who disbelieve in their Lord (Allâh) is the torment of Hell, and worst indeed is that destination (6) When they are cast therein, they will hear the (terrible) drawing in of its breath as it blazes forth (7) It almost bursts up with fury. Every time a group is cast therein, its keeper will ask: "Did no warner come to you?" (8) They will say: "Yes indeed a warner did come to us, but we belied him and said: 'Allâh never sent down anything (of revelation), you are only in great error.'" (9) And they will say: "Had we but listened or used our intelligence, we would not have been among the dwellers of the blazing Fire!" (10) Then they will confess their sin. So, away with the dwellers of the blazing Fire (11)

Quran 67:25-27

وَيَقُولُونَ مَتَىٰ هَٰذَا ٱلْوَعْدُ إِن كُنتُمْ صَٰدِقِينَ (٢٥) قُلْ إِنَّمَا ٱلْعِلْمُ عِندَ ٱللَّهِ وَإِنَّمَآ أَنَا۠ نَذِيرٌ مُّبِينٌ (٢٦) فَلَمَّا رَأَوْهُ زُلْفَةً سِيٓـَٔتْ وُجُوهُ ٱلَّذِينَ كَفَرُوا۟ وَقِيلَ هَٰذَا ٱلَّذِى كُنتُم بِهِۦ تَدَّعُونَ (٢٧)

They say: "When will this promise (i.e. the Day of Resurrection) come to pass if you are telling the truth?" (25) Say: "The knowledge (of its exact time) is with Allâh only, and I am only a plain warner." (26) But when they will see it (the torment on the Day of Resurrection) approaching, the faces of those who disbelieve will change and turn black with sadness and in grief and it will be said (to them): "This is (the promise) which you were calling for!" (27)

Quran 68:51

وَإِن يَكَادُ ٱلَّذِينَ كَفَرُوا۟ لَيُزْلِقُونَكَ بِأَبْصَٰرِهِمْ لَمَّا سَمِعُوا۟ ٱلذِّكْرَ وَيَقُولُونَ إِنَّهُۥ لَمَجْنُونٌ

And verily, those who disbelieve would almost make you slip with their eyes (through hatred) when they hear the Reminder (the Qur'ân), and they say: "Verily, he (Muhammad) is a madman!" (51)

Quran 69:49-51

وَإِنَّا لَنَعْلَمُ أَنَّ مِنكُم مُّكَذِّبِينَ (٤٩) وَإِنَّهُۥ لَحَسْرَةٌ عَلَى ٱلْكَٰفِرِينَ (٥٠) وَإِنَّهُۥ لَحَقُّ ٱلْيَقِينِ (٥١)

And verily, We know that there are some among you that belie (this Qur'ân). (49) And indeed it (this Qur'ân) will be an anguish for the disbelievers (on the Day of Resurrection). (50) And Verily, it (this Qur'ân) is an absolute truth with certainty (51)

Quran 70:36-42

فَمَالِ ٱلَّذِينَ كَفَرُوا۟ قِبَلَكَ مُهْطِعِينَ (٣٦) عَنِ ٱلْيَمِينِ وَعَنِ ٱلشِّمَالِ عِزِينَ (٣٧) أَيَطْمَعُ كُلُّ ٱمْرِئٍ مِّنْهُمْ أَن يُدْخَلَ جَنَّةَ نَعِيمٍ (٣٨) كَلَّا إِنَّا خَلَقْنَٰهُم مِّمَّا يَعْلَمُونَ (٣٩) فَلَا أُقْسِمُ بِرَبِّ ٱلْمَشَٰرِقِ وَٱلْمَغَٰرِبِ إِنَّا لَقَٰدِرُونَ (٤٠) عَلَىٰ أَن نُّبَدِّلَ خَيْرًا مِّنْهُمْ وَمَا نَحْنُ بِمَسْبُوقِينَ (٤١) فَذَرْهُمْ يَخُوضُوا۟ وَيَلْعَبُوا۟ حَتَّىٰ يُلَٰقُوا۟ يَوْمَهُمُ ٱلَّذِى يُوعَدُونَ (٤٢)

So what is the matter with those who disbelieve that they hasten to listen from you (O Muhammad), in order to belie you and to mock at you, and at Allâh's Book (this Qur'ân). (36) (Sitting) in groups on the right and on the left (of you, O Muhammad)? (37) Does every man of them hope to enter the Paradise of Delight? (38) No, that is not like that! Verily, We have created them out of that which they know! (39) So I swear by the Lord of all points of sunrise and sunset in the east and the west that surely We are Able — (40) To replace them by (others) better than them; and We are not to be outrun. (41) So leave them to plunge in vain talk and play about, until they meet their Day which they are promised (42)

Quran 74:31

وَمَا جَعَلْنَا أَصْحَابَ ٱلنَّارِ إِلَّا مَلَٰٓئِكَةً ۖ وَمَا جَعَلْنَا عِدَّتَهُمْ إِلَّا فِتْنَةً لِّلَّذِينَ كَفَرُوا۟ لِيَسْتَيْقِنَ ٱلَّذِينَ أُوتُوا۟ ٱلْكِتَٰبَ وَيَزْدَادَ ٱلَّذِينَ ءَامَنُوٓا۟ إِيمَٰنًا ۙ وَلَا يَرْتَابَ ٱلَّذِينَ أُوتُوا۟ ٱلْكِتَٰبَ وَٱلْمُؤْمِنُونَ ۙ وَلِيَقُولَ ٱلَّذِينَ فِى قُلُوبِهِم مَّرَضٌ وَٱلْكَٰفِرُونَ مَاذَآ أَرَادَ ٱللَّهُ بِهَٰذَا مَثَلًا ۚ كَذَٰلِكَ يُضِلُّ ٱللَّهُ مَن يَشَآءُ وَيَهْدِى مَن يَشَآءُ ۚ وَمَا يَعْلَمُ جُنُودَ رَبِّكَ إِلَّا هُوَ ۚ وَمَا هِىَ إِلَّا ذِكْرَىٰ لِلْبَشَرِ

And We have set none but angels as guardians of the Fire, and We have fixed number (19) only as a trial for the disbelievers, in order that the people of the Scripture (Jews and Christians) may arrive at a certainty [that this Qur'ân is the truth as it agrees with their Books regarding their number (19) which is written in the Taurât (Torah) and the Injeel] and that the believers may increase in Faith (as this Qur'ân is the truth) and that no doubt may be left for the people of the Scripture and the believers, and that those in whose hearts is a disease (of hypocrisy) and the disbelievers may say: "What Allâh intends by this (curious) example ?" Thus Allâh leads astray whom He wills and guides whom He wills. And none can know the hosts of your Lord but He. And this (Hell) is nothing else than a (warning) reminder to mankind. (31)

Quran 74:40-53

فِى جَنَّـٰتٍ يَتَسَآءَلُونَ (٤٠) عَنِ ٱلْمُجْرِمِينَ (٤١) مَا سَلَكَكُمْ فِى سَقَرَ (٤٢) قَالُوا۟ لَمْ نَكُ مِنَ ٱلْمُصَلِّينَ (٤٣) وَلَمْ نَكُ نُطْعِمُ ٱلْمِسْكِينَ (٤٤) وَكُنَّا نَخُوضُ مَعَ ٱلْخَآئِضِينَ (٤٥) وَكُنَّا نُكَذِّبُ بِيَوْمِ ٱلدِّينِ (٤٦) حَتَّىٰ أَتَىٰنَا ٱلْيَقِينُ (٤٧) فَمَا تَنفَعُهُمْ شَفَـٰعَةُ ٱلشَّـٰفِعِينَ (٤٨) فَمَا لَهُمْ عَنِ ٱلتَّذْكِرَةِ مُعْرِضِينَ (٤٩) كَأَنَّهُمْ حُمُرٌ مُّسْتَنفِرَةٌ (٥٠) فَرَّتْ مِن قَسْوَرَةٍ (٥١) بَلْ يُرِيدُ كُلُّ ٱمْرِئٍ مِّنْهُمْ أَن يُؤْتَىٰ صُحُفًا مُّنَشَّرَةً (٥٢) كَلَّا ۖ بَل لَّا يَخَافُونَ ٱلْأَخِرَةَ (٥٣)

In Gardens (Paradise) they will ask one another, (40) About Al-Mujrimûn (polytheists, criminals, disbelievers), (And they will say to them): (41) "What has caused you to enter Hell?" (42) They will say: "We were not of those who used to offer the Salât (prayers) (43) "Nor we used to feed Al-Miskin (the poor); (44) "And we used to talk falsehood (all that which Allâh hated) with vain talkers (45) "And we used to belie the Day of Recompense (46) "Until there came to us (the death) that is certain." (47) So no intercession of intercessors will be of any use to them (48) Then what is wrong with them (i.e. the polythesists the disbelievers) that they turn away from (receiving) admonition? (49) As if they were (frightened) wild donkeys. (50) Fleeing from a hunter, or a lion, or a beast of prey. (51) Nay, everyone of them desires that he should be given pages spread out (coming from Allâh with a writing that Islâm is the right religion, and Muhammad has come with the truth from Allâh the Lord of the heavens and earth). (52) Nay! But they fear not the Hereafter (from Allâh's punishment). (53)

Quran 75:31-35

فَلَا صَدَّقَ وَلَا صَلَّىٰ (٣١) وَلَـٰكِن كَذَّبَ وَتَوَلَّىٰ (٣٢) ثُمَّ ذَهَبَ إِلَىٰ أَهْلِهِ يَتَمَطَّىٰ (٣٣) أَوْلَىٰ لَكَ فَأَوْلَىٰ (٣٤) ثُمَّ أَوْلَىٰ لَكَ فَأَوْلَىٰ (٣٥)

So he (the disbeliever) neither believed (in this Qur'ân, and in the Message of Muhammad) nor prayed! (31) But on the contrary, he belied (this Qur'ân and the Message of Muhammad) and turned away! (32) Then he walked in conceit (full pride) to his family admiring himself! (33) Woe to you [(disbeliever)]! And then (again) woe to you! (34) Again, woe to you [(disbeliever)]! And then (again) woe to you! (35)

Quran 77:14-50

وَمَآ أَدْرَىٰكَ مَا يَوْمُ ٱلْفَصْلِ (١٤) وَيْلٌ يَوْمَئِذٍ لِّلْمُكَذِّبِينَ (١٥) أَلَمْ نُهْلِكِ ٱلْأَوَّلِينَ (١٦) ثُمَّ نُتْبِعُهُمُ ٱلْآخِرِينَ (١٧) كَذَٰلِكَ نَفْعَلُ بِٱلْمُجْرِمِينَ (١٨) وَيْلٌ يَوْمَئِذٍ لِّلْمُكَذِّبِينَ (١٩) أَلَمْ نَخْلُقكُّم مِّن مَّآءٍ مَّهِينٍ (٢٠) فَجَعَلْنَاهُ فِى قَرَارٍ مَّكِينٍ (٢١) إِلَىٰ قَدَرٍ مَّعْلُومٍ (٢٢) فَقَدَرْنَا فَنِعْمَ ٱلْقَادِرُونَ (٢٣) وَيْلٌ يَوْمَئِذٍ لِّلْمُكَذِّبِينَ (٢٤) أَلَمْ نَجْعَلِ ٱلْأَرْضَ كِفَاتًا (٢٥) أَحْيَآءً وَأَمْوَاتًا (٢٦) وَجَعَلْنَا فِيهَا رَوَاسِىَ شَـٰمِخَـٰتٍ وَأَسْقَيْنَـٰكُم مَّآءً فُرَاتًا (٢٧) وَيْلٌ يَوْمَئِذٍ لِّلْمُكَذِّبِينَ (٢٨) ٱنطَلِقُوٓاْ إِلَىٰ مَا كُنتُم بِهِۦ تُكَذِّبُونَ (٢٩) ٱنطَلِقُوٓاْ إِلَىٰ ظِلٍّ ذِى ثَلَـٰثِ شُعَبٍ (٣٠) لَّا ظَلِيلٍ وَلَا يُغْنِى مِنَ ٱللَّهَبِ (٣١) إِنَّهَا تَرْمِى بِشَرَرٍ كَٱلْقَصْرِ (٣٢) كَأَنَّهُۥ جِمَـٰلَتٌ صُفْرٌ (٣٣) وَيْلٌ يَوْمَئِذٍ لِّلْمُكَذِّبِينَ (٣٤) هَـٰذَا يَوْمُ لَا يَنطِقُونَ (٣٥) وَلَا يُؤْذَنُ لَهُمْ فَيَعْتَذِرُونَ (٣٦) وَيْلٌ يَوْمَئِذٍ لِّلْمُكَذِّبِينَ (٣٧) هَـٰذَا يَوْمُ ٱلْفَصْلِ جَمَعْنَـٰكُمْ وَٱلْأَوَّلِينَ (٣٨) فَإِن كَانَ لَكُمْ كَيْدٌ فَكِيدُونِ

(٣٩) وَيْلٌ يَوْمَئِذٍ لِّلْمُكَذِّبِينَ (٤٠) إِنَّ ٱلْمُتَّقِينَ فِى ظِلَٰلٍ وَعُيُونٍ (٤١) وَفَوَاكِهَ مِمَّا يَشْتَهُونَ (٤٢) كُلُواْ وَٱشْرَبُواْ هَنِيئًۢا بِمَا كُنتُمْ تَعْمَلُونَ (٤٣) إِنَّا كَذَٰلِكَ نَجْزِى ٱلْمُحْسِنِينَ (٤٤) وَيْلٌ يَوْمَئِذٍ لِّلْمُكَذِّبِينَ (٤٥) كُلُواْ وَتَمَتَّعُواْ قَلِيلاً إِنَّكُم مُّجْرِمُونَ (٤٦) وَيْلٌ يَوْمَئِذٍ لِّلْمُكَذِّبِينَ (٤٧) وَإِذَا قِيلَ لَهُمُ ٱرْكَعُواْ لَا يَرْكَعُونَ (٤٨) وَيْلٌ يَوْمَئِذٍ لِّلْمُكَذِّبِينَ (٤٩) فَبِأَىِّ حَدِيثٍۭ بَعْدَهُۥ يُؤْمِنُونَ (٥٠)

And what will explain to you what is the Day of sorting out? (14) Woe that Day to the deniers (of the Day of Resurrection)! (15) Did We not destroy the ancients? (16) So shall We make later generations to follow them. (17) Thus do We deal with the Mujrimûn (polytheists, disbelievers, sinners, criminals)! (18) Woe that Day to the deniers (of the Day of Resurrection)! (19) Did We not create you from a despised water (semen)? (20) Then We placed it in a place of safety (womb), (21) For a known period (determined by gestation)? (22) So We did measure, and We are the Best to measure (the things). (23) Woe that Day to the deniers (of the Day of Resurrection)! (24) Have We not made the earth a receptacle? (25) For the living and the dead? (26) And have placed therein firm, and tall mountains; and have given you to drink sweet water? (27) Woe that Day to the deniers (of the Day of Resurrection)! (28) (It will be said to the disbelievers): "Depart you to that which you used to deny! (29) "Depart you to a shadow (of Hell-fire smoke ascending) in three columns, (30) "Neither shady, nor of any use against the fierce flame of the Fire." (31) Verily, It (Hell) throws sparks (huge) as Al-Qasr [a fort or a (huge log of wood)],

(32) As if they were yellow camels or bundles of ropes. (33) Woe that Day to the deniers (of the Day of Resurrection)! (34) That will be a Day when they shall not speak (during some part of it), (35) And they will not be permitted to put forth any excuse. (36) Woe that Day to the deniers (of the Day of Resurrection)! (37) That will be a Day of Decision! We have brought you and the men of old together! (38) So if you have a plot, use it against Me (Allâh)! (39) Woe that Day to the deniers (of the Day of Resurrection)! (40) Verily, the Muttaqûn (pious) shall be amidst shades and springs. (41) And fruits, such as they desire. (42) "Eat and drink comfortably for that which you used to do. (43) Verily, thus We reward the Muhsinûn (good-doers) (44) Woe that Day to the deniers (of the Day of Resurrection)! (45) (O you disbelievers)! Eat and enjoy yourselves (in this worldly life) for a little while. Verily, you are the Mujrimûn (polytheists, disbelievers, sinners, criminals). (46) Woe that Day to the deniers (of the Day of Resurrection)! (47) And when it is said to them: "Bow down yourself (in prayer)!" They bow not down (offer not their prayers). (48) Woe that Day to the deniers (of the Day of Resurrection)! (49) Then in what statement after this (the Qur'ân) will they believe? (50)

Quran 78:21-30

إِنَّ جَهَنَّمَ كَانَتْ مِرْصَادًا (٢١) لِّلطَّٰغِينَ مَـَٔابًا (٢٢) لَّـٰبِثِينَ فِيهَآ أَحْقَابًا (٢٣) لَّا يَذُوقُونَ فِيهَا بَرْدًا وَلَا شَرَابًا (٢٤) إِلَّا حَمِيمًا وَغَسَّاقًا (٢٥) جَزَآءً وِفَاقًا (٢٦) إِنَّهُمْ كَانُوا۟ لَا يَرْجُونَ حِسَابًا (٢٧) وَكَذَّبُوا۟ بِـَٔايَـٰتِنَا كِذَّابًا

(٢٨) وَكُلَّ شَيْءٍ أَحْصَيْنَـٰهُ كِتَـٰبًا (٢٩) فَذُوقُواْ فَلَن نَّزِيدَكُمْ إِلَّا عَذَابًا (٣٠)

Truly, Hell is a place of ambush — (21) A dwelling place for the Tâghûn (those who transgress the boundry limits set by Allâh like polytheists, disbelievers in the Oneness of Allâh, hyprocrites, sinners, criminals), (22) They will abide therein for ages, (23) Nothing cool shall they taste therein, nor any drink. (24) Except boiling water, and dirty wound discharges — (25) An exact recompense (according to their evil crimes) (26) For verily, they used not to look for a reckoning. (27) But they belied Our Ayât (proofs, evidences, verses, lessons, signs, revelations, and that which Our Prophet brought) completely. (28) And all things We have recorded in a Book. (29) So taste you (the results of your evil actions); No increase shall We give you, except in torment. (30)

Quran 83:7-17

كَلَّا إِنَّ كِتَـٰبَ ٱلْفُجَّارِ لَفِى سِجِّينٍ (٧) وَمَآ أَدْرَىٰكَ مَا سِجِّينٌ (٨) كِتَـٰبٌ مَّرْقُومٌ (٩) وَيْلٌ يَوْمَئِذٍ لِّلْمُكَذِّبِينَ (١٠) ٱلَّذِينَ يُكَذِّبُونَ بِيَوْمِ ٱلدِّينِ (١١) وَمَا يُكَذِّبُ بِهِ إِلَّا كُلُّ مُعْتَدٍ أَثِيمٍ (١٢) إِذَا تُتْلَىٰ عَلَيْهِ ءَايَـٰتُنَا قَالَ أَسَـٰطِيرُ ٱلْأَوَّلِينَ (١٣) كَلَّا بَلْ رَانَ عَلَىٰ قُلُوبِهِم مَّا كَانُواْ يَكْسِبُونَ (١٤) كَلَّا إِنَّهُمْ عَن رَّبِّهِمْ يَوْمَئِذٍ لَّمَحْجُوبُونَ (١٥) ثُمَّ إِنَّهُمْ لَصَالُواْ ٱلْجَحِيمِ (١٦) ثُمَّ يُقَالُ هَـٰذَا ٱلَّذِى كُنتُم بِهِ تُكَذِّبُونَ (١٧)

Nay! Truly, the Record (writing of the deeds) of the Fujjâr (disbelievers, polytheists sinners, evil-doers and wicked) is (preserved) in Sijjîn. (7) And what will make you know what Sijjîn is? (8) A Register inscribed. (9) Woe, that Day, to those who deny. (10) Those who deny the Day of Recompense. (11) And none can deny it except every transgressor beyond bounds, (in disbelief, oppression and disobedience to Allâh), the sinner! (12) When Our Verses (of the Qur'ân) are recited to him he says: "Tales of the ancients!" (13) Nay! But on their hearts is the Rân (covering of sins and evil deeds) which they used to earn (14) Nay! Surely, they (evil-doers) will be veiled from seeing their Lord that Day. (15) Then, verily they will indeed enter (and taste) the burning flame of Hell. (16) Then, it will be said to them: "This is what you used to deny!" (17)

Quran 83:29-36

إِنَّ ٱلَّذِينَ أَجْرَمُواْ كَانُواْ مِنَ ٱلَّذِينَ ءَامَنُواْ يَضْحَكُونَ (٢٩) وَإِذَا مَرُّواْ بِهِمْ يَتَغَامَزُونَ (٣٠) وَإِذَا ٱنقَلَبُوٓاْ إِلَىٰٓ أَهْلِهِمُ ٱنقَلَبُواْ فَكِهِينَ (٣١) وَإِذَا رَأَوْهُمْ قَالُوٓاْ إِنَّ هَٰٓؤُلَآءِ لَضَآلُّونَ (٣٢) وَمَآ أُرْسِلُواْ عَلَيْهِمْ حَٰفِظِينَ (٣٣) فَٱلْيَوْمَ ٱلَّذِينَ ءَامَنُواْ مِنَ ٱلْكُفَّارِ يَضْحَكُونَ (٣٤) عَلَى ٱلْأَرَآئِكِ يَنظُرُونَ (٣٥) هَلْ ثُوِّبَ ٱلْكُفَّارُ مَا كَانُواْ يَفْعَلُونَ (٣٦)

Verily, (during the worldly life) those who committed crimes used to laugh at those who believed. (29) And whenever they passed by them, used to wink one to another (in mockery); (30) And when they returned to their own people, they would return jesting; (31) And when they saw them, they said: "Verily, these have indeed gone astray!" (32) But they (disbelievers, sinners) had not been sent as watchers over them (the believers). (33) But this Day (the Day of Resurrection) those who believe will laugh at the disbelievers (34) On (high) thrones, looking (at all things). (35) Are not the disbelievers paid (fully) for what they used to do? (36)

Quran 84:10-24

وَأَمَّا مَنْ أُوتِىَ كِتَبَهُۥ وَرَآءَ ظَهْرِهِۦ (١٠) فَسَوْفَ يَدْعُواْ ثُبُورًا (١١) وَيَصْلَىٰ سَعِيرًا (١٢) إِنَّهُۥ كَانَ فِىٓ أَهْلِهِۦ مَسْرُورًا (١٣) إِنَّهُۥ ظَنَّ أَن لَّن يَحُورَ (١٤) بَلَىٰٓ إِنَّ رَبَّهُۥ كَانَ بِهِۦ بَصِيرًا (١٥) فَلَآ أُقْسِمُ بِٱلشَّفَقِ (١٦) وَٱلَّيْلِ وَمَا وَسَقَ (١٧) وَٱلْقَمَرِ إِذَا ٱتَّسَقَ (١٨) لَتَرْكَبُنَّ طَبَقًا عَن طَبَقٍ (١٩) فَمَا لَهُمْ لَا يُؤْمِنُونَ (٢٠) وَإِذَا قُرِئَ عَلَيْهِمُ ٱلْقُرْءَانُ لَا يَسْجُدُونَ ۩ (٢١) بَلِ ٱلَّذِينَ كَفَرُواْ يُكَذِّبُونَ (٢٢) وَٱللَّهُ أَعْلَمُ بِمَا يُوعُونَ (٢٣) فَبَشِّرْهُم بِعَذَابٍ أَلِيمٍ (٢٤)

But whosoever is given his Record behind his back, (10) He will invoke (for his) destruction, (11) And he shall enter a blazing Fire, and be made to taste its burning. (12) Verily, he was among his people in joy! (13) Verily, he thought that he would never come back (to Us)! (14) Yes! Verily, his Lord has been ever beholding him! (15) So I swear by the afterglow of sunset; (16) And by the night and whatever it gathers in its darkness; (17) And by the moon when it is at the full, (18) You shall certainly travel from stage to stage (in this life and in the Hereafter). (19) What is the matter with them, that they believe not? (20) And when the Qur'ân is recited to them, they fall not prostrate, (21) Nay, those who disbelieve, belie. (22) And Allâh knows best what they gather (of good and bad deeds), (23) So announce to them a painful torment. (24)

Quran 86:15-17

إِنَّهُمْ يَكِيدُونَ كَيْدًا (١٥) وَأَكِيدُ كَيْدًا (١٦) فَمَهِّلِ ٱلْكَافِرِينَ أَمْهِلْهُمْ رُوَيْدًا (١٧)

Verily, they are but plotting a plot (against you O Muhammad). (15) And I (too) am planning a plan. (16) So give a respite to the disbelievers; deal gently with them for a while. (17)

Quran 90:19-20

وَٱلَّذِينَ كَفَرُوا۟ بِـَٔايَـٰتِنَا هُمْ أَصْحَـٰبُ ٱلْمَشْـَٔمَةِ (١٩) عَلَيْهِمْ نَارٌ مُّؤْصَدَةٌ (٢٠)

But those who disbelieved in Our Ayât (proofs, evidences, verses, lessons, signs, revelations, etc.), they are those on the Left Hand (the dwellers of Hell) (19) The Fire will be shut over them (20)

Quran 96:6-18

كَلَّا إِنَّ ٱلْإِنسَـٰنَ لَيَطْغَىٰٓ (٦) أَن رَّءَاهُ ٱسْتَغْنَىٰٓ (٧) إِنَّ إِلَىٰ رَبِّكَ ٱلرُّجْعَىٰٓ (٨) أَرَءَيْتَ ٱلَّذِى يَنْهَىٰ (٩) عَبْدًا إِذَا صَلَّىٰٓ (١٠) أَرَءَيْتَ إِن كَانَ عَلَى ٱلْهُدَىٰٓ (١١) أَوْ أَمَرَ بِٱلتَّقْوَىٰٓ (١٢) أَرَءَيْتَ إِن كَذَّبَ وَتَوَلَّىٰٓ (١٣) أَلَمْ يَعْلَم بِأَنَّ ٱللَّهَ يَرَىٰ (١٤) كَلَّا لَئِن لَّمْ يَنتَهِ لَنَسْفَعًۢا بِٱلنَّاصِيَةِ (١٥) نَاصِيَةٍ كَـٰذِبَةٍ خَاطِئَةٍ (١٦) فَلْيَدْعُ نَادِيَهُ (١٧) سَنَدْعُ ٱلزَّبَانِيَةَ (١٨)

Nay! Verily, man does transgress (in disbelief and evil deed). (6) Because he considers himself self-sufficient. (7) Surely! unto your Lord is the return. (8) Have you seen him who prevents, (9) A slave when he prays? (10) Tell me, if he is on the guidance (of Allâh) (11) Or enjoins piety! (12) Tell me if he denies (the truth, i.e. this Qur'ân), and turns away? (13) Knows he not that Allâh does see (what he does)? (14) Nay! If he ceases not, We will catch him by the forelock — (15) A lying, sinful forelock! (16) Then, let him call upon his council (of helpers), (17) We will call the guards of Hell (to deal with him)! (18)

Quran 98:1-6

لَمْ يَكُنِ ٱلَّذِينَ كَفَرُواْ مِنْ أَهْلِ ٱلْكِتَٰبِ وَٱلْمُشْرِكِينَ مُنفَكِّينَ حَتَّىٰ تَأْتِيَهُمُ ٱلْبَيِّنَةُ (١) رَسُولٌ مِّنَ ٱللَّهِ يَتْلُواْ صُحُفًا مُّطَهَّرَةً (٢) فِيهَا كُتُبٌ قَيِّمَةٌ (٣) وَمَا تَفَرَّقَ ٱلَّذِينَ أُوتُواْ ٱلْكِتَٰبَ إِلَّا مِنْ بَعْدِ مَا جَآءَتْهُمُ ٱلْبَيِّنَةُ (٤) وَمَآ أُمِرُوٓاْ إِلَّا لِيَعْبُدُواْ ٱللَّهَ مُخْلِصِينَ لَهُ ٱلدِّينَ حُنَفَآءَ وَيُقِيمُواْ ٱلصَّلَوٰةَ وَيُؤْتُواْ ٱلزَّكَوٰةَ وَذَٰلِكَ دِينُ ٱلْقَيِّمَةِ (٥) إِنَّ ٱلَّذِينَ كَفَرُواْ مِنْ أَهْلِ ٱلْكِتَٰبِ وَٱلْمُشْرِكِينَ فِى نَارِ جَهَنَّمَ خَٰلِدِينَ فِيهَآ أُوْلَٰٓئِكَ هُمْ شَرُّ ٱلْبَرِيَّةِ (٦)

Those who disbelieve from among the people of the Scripture (Jews and Christians) and Al-Mushrikûn, were not going to leave (their disbelief) until there came to them clear evidence (1) A Messenger (Muhammad) from Allâh, reciting (the Qur'ân) purified pages (2) Wherein are correct and straight laws from Allâh. (3) And the people of the Scripture (Jews and Christians) differed not until after there came to them clear evidence. (4) And they were commanded not, but that they should worship Allâh, and worship none but Him Alone (abstaining from ascribing partners to Him), and perform As-Salât (Iqâmat-as-Salât) and give Zakât: and that is the right religion. (5) Verily, those who disbelieve from among the people of the Scripture (Jews and Christians) and Al-Mushrikûn will abide in the Fire of Hell. They are the worst of creatures. (6)

Quran 104:1-4

وَيْلٌ لِّكُلِّ هُمَزَةٍ لُّمَزَةٍ (١) ٱلَّذِى جَمَعَ مَالاً وَعَدَّدَهُ (٢) يَحْسَبُ أَنَّ مَالَهُ أَخْلَدَهُ (٣) كَلَّا لَيُنۢبَذَنَّ فِى ٱلْحُطَمَةِ (٤)

Woe to every slanderer and backbiter. (1) Who has gathered wealth and counted it, (2) He thinks that his wealth will make him last forever! (3) Nay! Verily, he will be thrown into the crushing Fire (4)

Quran 107:1-7

أَرَءَيْتَ ٱلَّذِى يُكَذِّبُ بِٱلدِّينِ (١) فَذَٰلِكَ ٱلَّذِى يَدُعُّ ٱلْيَتِيمَ (٢) وَلَا يَحُضُّ عَلَىٰ طَعَامِ ٱلْمِسْكِينِ (٣) فَوَيْلٌ لِّلْمُصَلِّينَ (٤) ٱلَّذِينَ هُمْ عَن صَلَاتِهِمْ سَاهُونَ (٥) ٱلَّذِينَ هُمْ يُرَاءُونَ (٦) وَيَمْنَعُونَ ٱلْمَاعُونَ (٧)

Have you seen him who denies the Recompense? (1) That is he who repulses the orphan (harshly), (2) And urges not on the feeding of AlMiskîn (the poor), (3) So woe unto those performers of Salât (prayers) (hypocrites), (4) Those who delay their Salât (prayer from their stated fixed times), (5) Those who do good deeds only to be seen (of men), (6) And prevent Al-Mâ'ûn (small kindnesses). (7)

Quran 109:1-6

قُلْ يَـٰٓأَيُّهَا ٱلْكَـٰفِرُونَ (١) لَا أَعْبُدُ مَا تَعْبُدُونَ (٢) وَلَا أَنتُمْ عَـٰبِدُونَ مَا أَعْبُدُ (٣) وَلَا أَنَا۠ عَابِدٌ مَّا عَبَدتُّمْ (٤) وَلَا أَنتُمْ عَـٰبِدُونَ مَا أَعْبُدُ (٥) لَكُمْ دِينُكُمْ وَلِىَ دِينِ (٦)

Say (O Muhammad): "O Al-Kâfirûn (disbelievers in Allâh, in His Oneness, in His Angels, in His Books, in His Messengers, in the Day of Resurrection, and in Al-Qadar)! (1) "I worship not that which you worship, (2) "Nor will you worship that which I worship. (3) "And I shall not worship that which you are worshipping. (4) "Nor will you worship that which I worship. (5) "To you be your religion, and to me my religion (Islâmic Monotheism)." (6)

Quran 111:1-5

تَبَّتْ يَدَآ أَبِى لَهَبٍ وَتَبَّ (١) مَآ أَغْنَىٰ عَنْهُ مَالُهُۥ وَمَا كَسَبَ (٢) سَيَصْلَىٰ نَارًا ذَاتَ لَهَبٍ (٣) وَٱمْرَأَتُهُۥ حَمَّالَةَ ٱلْحَطَبِ (٤) فِى جِيدِهَا حَبْلٌ مِّن مَّسَدٍۭ (٥)

Perish the two hands of Abû Lahab (an uncle of the Prophet), and perish he! (1) His wealth and his children will not benefit him! (2) He will be burnt in a Fire of blazing flames! (3) And his wife too, who carries wood (thorns of Sadan which she used to put on the way of the Prophet, or use to slander him). (4) In her neck is a twisted rope of Masad (palm fibre). (5)

Narrated Usama bin Zaid:

the Prophet (ﷺ) said, "A Muslim cannot be the heir of a disbeliever, nor can a disbeliever be the heir of a Muslim."

Source: Sahih al-Bukhari 6764

It was narrated that Jabir bin 'Abdullah said:

"The Messenger of Allah (ﷺ) said: 'Between a person and Kufr (disbelief) is abandoning the prayer.'"

Source: Sunan Ibn Majah 1078 Graded: Sahih

Anas bin Malik narrated the Messenger of Allah said:

"Before the Hour there shall be Fitan like a portion of the dark night. Morning will come upon a man as a believer, who will be a disbeliever in the evening, and evening will come upon a believer, who will be a disbeliever in the morning, people will sell their religion for goods of the world."

Source: Jami` at-Tirmidhi 2197 Graded: Hasan

Narrated 'Amr bin Shu'aib:

from his father, from his grandfather that the Messenger of Allah (ﷺ) said: "The Muslim is not killed for disbeliever." And with this chain, it has been narrated that the Prophet (ﷺ) said: "The blood-money paid for disbeliever is half of the blood-money paid for a believer."

Source: Jami` at-Tirmidhi 1413 Grade: Sahih

Abdullah bin 'Amr bin Al-'As said:

The Prophet (ﷺ) saw me dressed in two saffron-coloured garments and asked, "Has your mother commanded you to wear these?" I asked him, "Shall I wash them out?" He replied, "You had better set them to fire."

Another narration is: "These are garments of the disbelievers. So do not wear them."

Source: Riyad as-Salihin 1799 and Sahih Muslim

Ibn 'Abbas said:

"Aishah said: Rather the Messenger of Allah said: 'Allah, the Mighty and Sublime increases the punishment of the disbeliever due to some of his family's weeping for him.'"

Source: Sunan an-Nasa'i 1857 Graded: Sahih

It was narrated that Abu Hurairah said:

"The Messenger of Allah said: 'Whoever has intercourse with a menstruating woman, or with a woman in her rear, or who goes to a fortuneteller and believes what he says, he has disbelieved in that which was revealed to Muhammad.'"

Source: Sunan Ibn Majah 639 Graded: Hasan

Narrated Abu Dhar:

The Prophet (ﷺ) said, "If somebody claims to be the son of any other than his real father knowingly, he but disbelieves in Allah, and if somebody claims to belong to some folk to whom he does not belong, let such a person take his place in the (Hell) Fire."

Source: Sahih al-Bukhari 3508

Umar bin Al-Khattab said:

"The Messenger of Allah (ﷺ) stoned, Abu Bakr stoned, and I stoned. If I didn't dislike that I add to the Book of Allah. I would have written it in the Mushaf, for I fear that there will come a people and they will not find it in the Book of Allah, so they will disbelieve in it."

Source: Jami` at-Tirmidhi 1431 Graded: Sahih

Hudhaifah reported:

The Prophet (ﷺ) prohibited us from wearing brocade or silk and drinking out of gold or silver vessels and said, "These are meant for them (disbelievers) in this world and for you in the Hereafter."

Source: Bukhari and Muslim

Narrated Abu Huraira:

Allah's Messenger (ﷺ) said, "The example of a believer is that of a fresh green plant the leaves of which move in whatever direction the wind forces them to move and when the wind becomes still, it stand straight. Such is the similitude of the believer: He is disturbed by calamities (but is like the fresh plant he regains his normal state soon). And the example of a disbeliever is that of a pine tree (which remains) hard and straight till Allah cuts it down when He will."

Source: Sahih al-Bukhari 7466

Anas bin Malik said:

The Messenger of Allah (ﷺ) said, "There will be no land which will not be trampled by Dajjal (the Antichrist) but Makkah and Al-Madinah; and there will be no passage leading to them which will not be guarded by the angels, arranged in rows. Dajjal will appear in a barren place adjacent to Al- Madinah and the city will be shaken three times. Allah will expel from it every disbeliever and hypocrite."

Source: Riyad as-Salihin 1811 Graded: Sahih

Asma' said:

My mother came to me seeking some act of kindness from me during the treaty of the Quraish (at Hudaibiyyah). While she hated Islam and she was a polytheist. I said Messenger of Allah (ﷺ), my mother has come to me while she hates Islam and she is a disbeliever. May I do an act of kindness to her? He replied Yes, do an act of kindness to her.

Source: Sunan Abi Dawud 1668 Graded: Sahih

Abu Ghalib narrated that Abu Umamah said:

"(The Khawarij) are the worst of the slain who are killed under heaven, and the best of the slain are those who were killed by them. Those (Khawarij) are the dogs of Hell. Those people were Muslims but they became disbelievers." I said: "O Abu Umamah, is that your opinion?" He said: "Rather I heard it from the Messenger of Allah."

Source: Sunan Ibn Majah 176 Graded: Hasan

Narrated Abu Hurairah:

said: "When the Messenger of Allah (ﷺ) died and Abu Bakr became the Khalifah after him, whoever disbelieved from the Arabs disbelieved, so Umar bin Al-Khattab said to Abu Bakr: 'How will you fight the people while the Messenger of Allah has said: 'I have been ordered to fight the people until they say La Ilaha Illallah, and if they say that, then their blood and wealth will be protected from me, except what it makes obligatory upon them, and their reckoning is with Allah?' So Abu Bakr said: 'By Allah I will fight whoever differentiates between Salat and Zakat. For indeed, Zakat is the right due upon wealth. And by Allah! If they withhold even (camel) tethers which they used to give to the Messenger of Allah (ﷺ) I will fight them for withholding it.' So Umar bin Al-Khattab said: 'By Allah! I saw that Allah had opened Abu Bakr's chest to fighting, so I knew that it was correct.'"

Source: Jami` at-Tirmidhi 2607 Graded: Sahih

It was narrated from Abu 'Ubaidah that the Messenger of Allah (ﷺ) said:

"When the Children of Israel became deficient in religious commitment, a man would see his brother committing sin and would tell him not to do it, but the next day, what he had seen him do did not prevent him from eating or drinking with him, or mixing with him. So Allah made the hearts of those who did not commit sin like the hearts of those who did, and He revealed Qur'an concerning them and said: "Those among the Children of Israel who disbelieved were cursed by the tongue of David and 'Eisa, son of Maryam" until he reached: "And had they believed in Allah, and in the Prophet and in what has been revealed to him, never would they have taken them (the disbelievers) as their friends; but many of them are disobedient (to Allah)."[5:78-81] The Messenger of Allah (ﷺ) sat up and said: "No, not until they take the hand of the wrongdoer (i.e. restrain him] and force him to follow the right way."

Source: Sunan Ibn Majah 4006

Graded: Daif by Darussalam

Narrated Sahl bin Abi Hatamah:

Yahya (one of the narrators) said: And I think it was from Rafi' bin Khadij - that 'Abdullah bin Sahl bin Zaid and Muhaiysah bin Mas'ud bin Zaid went out and when they reached Khaibar they separated while there. Then Muhayyisah found 'Abdullah bin Sahl murdered [so he buried him]. Then he went to the Messenger of Allah (ﷺ) along with Huwayyisah bin Mas'ud and Abdur-Rahman bin Sahl. The youngest of the people, Abdur-Rahman, went to speak ahead of his companions. The Messenger of Allah (ﷺ) said to him: "Let the eldest of you speak." So he was silent and two companions spoke. So he conversed with them and they mentioned to the Messenger of Allah (ﷺ) about the murder of 'Abdullah bin Sahl. He said to them: "If fifty of you can swear an oath then you will have the right against the murderer." They said: "How can we take an oath when we did not witness it?" He said: "Then fifty of Jews can swear to clear the charge with you?" They said: "How could we accept the oaths of a disbelieving people?" So when he saw that, the Messenger of Allah (ﷺ) paid the blood-money."

Source: Jami` at-Tirmidhi 1422 Graded: Sahih

Abdullah ibn Mas'ud reported that the Prophet, said:

"Paying attention to the bad omen (tayyara) is association (shirk). It has nothing to do with us. Allah will remove it by reliance on Him."

Source: Al-Adab Al-Mufrad 909 Graded: Sahih by Albani

Ibn Umar said:

The Messenger of Allah said: Act against the polytheists, trim closely the moustache and grow beard.

Source: Sahih Muslim 259c

It was narrated from Bahz bin Hakim, from his father, from his grandfather that the Messenger of Allah (ﷺ) said:

"Allah will not accept any good deed from a polytheist who committed polytheism after having become Muslim, until he leaves the polytheists and joins the Muslims."

Source: Sunan Ibn Majah 2536 Graded: Sahih

Narrated Samurah ibn Jundub:

To proceed, the Messenger of Allah (ﷺ) said: Anyone who associates with a polytheist and lives with him is like him.

Source: Sunan Abi Dawud 2787 Graded: Sahih

Sa'id ibn Ubaydah said:

Ibn Umar heard a man swearing: No, I swear by the Ka'bah. Ibn Umar said to him: I heard the Messenger of Allah (ﷺ) say: He who swears by anyone but Allah is polytheist.

Source: Sunan Abi Dawud 3251 Graded: Sahih

Narrated 'Abdullah bin 'Amr:

The Prophet (ﷺ) said, "Whoever has the following four (characteristics) will be a pure hypocrite and whoever has one of the following four characteristics will have one characteristic of hypocrisy unless and until he gives it up.

1. Whenever he is entrusted, he betrays.

2. Whenever he speaks, he tells a lie.

3. Whenever he makes a covenant, he proves treacherous.

4. Whenever he quarrels, he behaves in a very imprudent, evil and insulting manner."

Source: Sahih Bukhari 34

Narrated Abu Huraira:

Allah's Messenger (ﷺ) said, "Allah the Most Superior said, "The son of Adam slights Me, and he should not slight Me, and he disbelieves in Me, and he ought not to do so. As for his slighting Me, it is that he says that I have a son; and his disbelief in Me is his statement that I shall not recreate him as I have created (him) before."

Source: Sahih al-Bukhari 3193

Narrated Anas bin Malik:

Allah's Prophet used to say, "A disbeliever will be brought on the Day of Resurrection and will be asked.

"Suppose you had as much gold as to fill the earth, would you offer it to ransom yourself?" He will reply, "Yes." Then it will be said to him, "You were asked for something easier than that (to join none in worship with Allah (i.e. to accept Islam, but you refused).

Source: Sahih al-Bukhari 6538

www.ingramcontent.com/pod-product-compliance
Lightning Source LLC
Chambersburg PA
CBHW050248010526
44107CB00003B/239